Management and Cost Accounting

NINTH EDITION

Student Manual

COLIN DRURY

Management and Cost Accounting

NINTH EDITION

Student Manual

Australia • Brazil • Japan • Korea • Mexico • Singapore • Spain • United Kingdom • United States

Student Manual for Management and Cost Accounting, 9th Edition

Colin Drury

Publisher: Andrew Ashwin

Development Editor: Ana Sanches de Arede

Content Project Manager: Sue Povey

Manufacturing Buyer: Elaine Willis

Marketing Manager: Amanda Cheung

Typesetter: MPS Limited

Cover design: Adam Renvoize

Text design: Design Deluxe

For product information and technology assistance, contact
emea.info@cengage.com
For permission to use material from this text or product, and for permission queries, email
emea.permissions@cengage.com

British Library Cataloguing-in-Publication Data
A catalogue record for this book is available from the British Library.

ISBN: 978-1-4080-9394-8

Cengage Learning EMEA
Cheriton House, North Way, Andover, Hampshire, SP10 5BE
United Kingdom

Cengage Learning products are represented in Canada by Nelson Education Ltd.

For your lifelong learning solutions, visit **www.cengage.co.uk**

Purchase your next print book, e-book or e-chapter at
www.cengagebrain.com

Printed in China by RR Donnelley
Print Number: 01   Print Year: 2015

Contents

Preface

This manual is complementary to the main text, *Management and Cost Accounting*. Throughout the main text the illustrations have been kept simple to enable the reader to understand the principles involved in designing and evaluating management and cost accounting systems. It is essential that students work through a wide range of problems to gain experience on the application of principles but there is insufficient classroom time for tutorial guidance to meet this requirement. The Students' Manual provides this guidance by enabling students to work independently on a wide range of problems and compare their answers with the suggested solutions.

The solutions given in this manual are my own and not the approved solutions of the professional body setting the question. Where an essay question is asked and a full answer requires undue repetition of the book, either references are made to the appropriate sections of the main book, or an answer guide or outline is provided. You should note that there will be no 'ideal' answer to questions which are not strictly numerical. Answers are provided which, it is felt, would be generally acceptable in most contexts.

Where possible the questions are arranged in ascending order of difficulty. The reader should select questions which are appropriate to the course which is being pursued. As a general rule questions titled 'Intermediate' are appropriate for a first year course. These questions are mainly concerned with cost accounting which is covered in Part two of the main text. Questions titled 'Advanced' are appropriate for a second year course.

Finally I would like to thank, once again, the Association of Accounting Technicians, the Institute of Chartered Accountants in England and Wales, the Chartered Association of Certified Accountants and the Chartered Institute of Management Accountants for permission to reproduce questions which have appeared in past examinations.

Part I

Questions

An introduction to cost terms and concepts

Questions to Chapter 2

Question 2.1

Intermediate

If actual output is lower than budgeted output, which of the following costs would you expect to be lower than the original budget?

(A) total variable costs

(B) total fixed costs

(C) variable costs per unit

(D) fixed costs per unit

ACCA Foundation Paper 3

Question 2.2

Intermediate

Which of the following would be classed as indirect labour?

(A) assembly workers in a company manufacturing televisions

(B) a stores assistant in a factory store

(C) plasterers in a construction company

(D) an audit clerk in a firm of auditors

CIMA Stage 1 Cost Accounting

Question 2.3

Intermediate

Fixed costs are conventionally deemed to be:

(A) constant per unit of output

(B) constant in total when production volume changes

(C) outside the control of management

(D) those unaffected by inflation

Question 2.4

Advanced

(i) Costs may be classified in a number of ways including classification by behaviour, by function, by expense type, by controllability and by relevance.

(ii) Management accounting should assist in EACH of the planning, control and decision-making processes in an organization.

Discuss the ways in which relationships between statements (i) and (ii) are relevant in the design of an effective management accounting system.

(15 marks)
ACCA Paper 9 Information for Control and Decision Making

Question 2.5

Intermediate

(a) 'Discretionary costs are troublesome because managers usually find it difficult to separate and quantify the results of their use in the business, as compared with variable and other fixed costs.'

You are required to discuss the above statement and include in your answer the meaning of discretionary costs, variable costs and fixed costs; give two illustrations of each of these three named costs.

(12 marks)

(b) A drug company has initiated a research project which is intended to develop a new product. Expenditures to date on this particular research total £500 000 but it is now estimated that a further £200 000 will need to be spent before the product can be marketed. Over the estimated life of the product the profit potential has a net present value of £350 000.

You are required to advise management whether they should continue or abandon the project. Support your conclusion with a numerate statement and state what kind of cost is the £500 000.

(5 marks)

(c) Opportunity costs and notional costs are not recognized by financial accounting systems but need to be considered in many decisions taken by management.

You are required to explain briefly the meanings of opportunity costs and notional costs; give two examples of each to illustrate the meanings you have attached to them.

(8 marks)
(Total 25 marks)
CIMA Stage 2 Cost Accounting

Question 2.6

Intermediate: Relevant costs and cost behaviour

(a) Distinguish between 'opportunity cost' and 'out of pocket cost' giving a numerical example of each using your own figures to support your answer.

(6 marks)

(b) Jason travels to work by train to his five-day-a-week job. Instead of buying daily tickets he finds it cheaper to buy a quarterly season ticket which costs £188 for 13 weeks.

Debbie, an acquaintance, who also makes the same journey, suggests that they both travel in Jason's car and offers to give him £120 each quarter towards his car expenses. Except for weekend travelling and using it for local college attendance near his home on three evenings each week to study for his CIMA Stage 2, the car remains in Jason's garage.

Jason estimates that using his car for work would involve him, each quarter, in the following expenses:

	(£)
Depreciation (proportion of annual figure)	200
Petrol and oil	128
Tyres and miscellaneous	52

You are required to state whether Jason should accept Debbie's offer and to draft a statement to show clearly the monetary effect of your conclusion.

(5 marks)

(c) A company with a financial year 1 September to 31 August prepared a sales budget which resulted in the following cost structure:

		% of sales
Direct materials		32
Direct wages		18
Production overhead:	variable	6
	fixed	24
Administrative and selling costs:	variable	3
	fixed	7
Profit		10

After ten weeks, however, it became obvious that the sales budget was too optimistic and it has now been estimated that because of a reduction in sales volume, for the full year, sales will total £2 560 000 which is only 80 per cent of the previously budgeted figure.

You are required to present a statement for management showing the amended sales and cost structure in pounds and percentages, in a marginal costing format.

(4 marks)
(Total 15 marks)
CIMA Stage 2 Cost Accounting

Cost assignment

Questions to Chapter 3

Question 3.1

Intermediate

A company absorbs overheads on machine hours which were budgeted to be 11 250 with overheads of £258 750. Actual results were 10 980 hours with overheads of £254 692.

Overheads were:

(A) under-absorbed by £2152

(B) over-absorbed by £4058

(C) under-absorbed by £4058

(D) over-absorbed by £2152

CIMA Stage 1

Question 3.2

Intermediate

ABC absorbs fixed production overheads in one of its departments on the basis of machine hours. There were 100 000 budgeted machine hours for the forthcoming period. The fixed production overhead absorption rate was £2.50 per machine hour.

During the period, the following actual results were recorded:

Standard machine hours	110 000
Fixed production overheads	$300 000

Which ONE of the following statements is correct?

(A) Overhead was $25 000 over-absorbed.

(B) Overhead was $25 000 under-absorbed.

(C) Overhead was $50 000 over-absorbed.

(D) No under- or over-absorption occurred.

CIMA Fundamentals of Management Accounting

Question 3.3

Intermediate

A company uses an overhead absorption rate of $3.50 per machine hour, based on 32 000 budgeted machine hours for the period. During the same period the actual total overhead expenditure amounted to $108 875 and 30 000 machine hours were recorded on actual production.

By how much was the total overhead under- or over-absorbed for the period?

(A) under-absorbed by $3875

(B) under-absorbed by $7000

(C) over-absorbed by $3875

(D) over-absorbed by $7000

ACCA F2 Management Accounting

Question 3.4

Intermediate

J Ltd uses standard absorption costing and absorbs production overheads on the basis of standard machine hours. The following budgeted and actual information applied in its last accounting period:

	Budget	**Actual**
Production overhead	$180 000	$178 080
Machine hours	50 000	48 260
Units produced	40 000	38 760

At the end of the period, production overhead will be reported as:

(A) under-absorbed by $4344

(B) under-absorbed by $3660

(C) over-absorbed by $4344

(D) over-absorbed by $3660

CIMA Management Accounting Fundamentals

Question 3.5

Intermediate

The management accountant of Gympie Limited has already allocated and apportioned the fixed overheads for the period although she has yet to reapportion the service centre costs. Information for the period is as follows:

	Production departments		**Service departments**		
	1	**2**	**Stores**	**Maintenance**	**Total**
Allocated and apportioned	£17 500	£32 750	£6 300	£8 450	£65 000
Work done by:					
Stores	60%	30%	—	10%	
Maintenance	75%	20%	5%	—	

What are the total overheads included in production department 1 if the reciprocal method is used to reapportion service centre costs?

(A) £27 618

(B) £28 171

(C) £28 398

(D) £28 453

ACCA Paper 1.2 – Financial Information for Management

Question 3.6

Intermediate: Overhead analysis, calculation of overhead rates and a product cost

Knowing that you are studying for the CIMA qualification, a friend who manages a small business has sought your advice about how to produce quotations in response to the enquiries which their business receives. Their business is sheet metal fabrication – supplying ducting for dust extraction and air conditioning installations. They believe that they have lost orders recently through the use of a job cost estimating system which was introduced, on the advice of their auditors, seven years ago. You are invited to review this system.

Upon investigation, you find that plant-wide, 125 per cent is added to prime costs in order to arrive at a selling price. The percentage added is intended to cover all overheads for the three production departments (Departments P, Q and R), all the selling, distribution and administration costs, and the profit.

You also discover that the selling, distribution and administration costs equate to roughly 20 per cent of total production costs, and that to achieve the desired return on capital employed, a margin of 20 per cent of sales value is necessary.

Any quantity of the compound can be sold for £1.60 per kg. Alternatively, it can be transferred to process II for further processing and packing to be sold as Starcomp for £2.00 per kg. Further materials are added in process II such that for every kilogram of compound used, 2kg of Starcomp result.

Of the 160 000kg per month of work completed in process I, 40 000kg are sold as compound and 120 000kg are passed through process II for sale as Starcomp. Process II has facilities to handle up to 160 000kg of compound per month if required. The monthly costs incurred in process II (other than the cost of the compound) are:

	120 000kg of compound input	160 000kg of compound input
Materials (£)	120 000	160 000
Processing costs (£)	120 000	140 000

Required:

(a) Determine, using the average method, the cost per kilogram of compound in process I, and the value of both work completed and closing work in process for the month just ended.

(11 marks)

(b) Demonstrate that it is worthwhile further processing 120 000kg of compound.

(5 marks)

(c) Calculate the minimum acceptable selling price per kilogram, if a potential buyer could be found for the additional output of Starcomp that could be produced with the remaining compound.

(6 marks)
(Total 22 marks)
ACCA Level 1 Costing

Question 6.7

Intermediate: Preparation of profit statements and decision on further processing

(a) Polimur Ltd operates a process that produces three joint products, all in an unrefined condition. The operating results of the process for October are shown below.

Output from process:

Product A	100 tonnes
Product B	80 tonnes
Product C	80 tonnes

The month's operating costs were £1 300 000. The closing stocks were 20 tonnes of A, 15 tonnes of B and 5 tonnes of C. The value of the closing stock is calculated by apportioning costs according to weight of output. There were no opening stocks and the balance of the output was sold to a refining company at the following prices:

Product A	£5 per kg
Product B	£4 per kg
Product C	£9 per kg

Required:
Prepare an operating statement showing the relevant trading results for October.

(6 marks)

(b) The management of Polimur Ltd have been considering a proposal to establish their own refining operations.

The current market prices of the refined products are:

Product A	£17 per kg
Product B	£14 per kg
Product C	£20.50 per kg

The estimated unit costs of the refining operation are:

	Product A (£ per kg)	Product B (£ per kg)	Product C (£ per kg)
Direct materials	0.50	0.75	2.50
Direct labour	2.00	3.00	4.00
Variable overheads	1.50	2.25	5.50

Prime costs would be variable. Fixed overheads, which would be £700 000 monthly, would be direct to the refining operation. Special equipment is required for refining product B and this would be rented at a cost, not included in the above figures, of £360 000 per month.

It may be assumed that there would be no weight loss in the refining process and that the quantity refined each month would be similar to October's output shown in (a) above.

Required:

Prepare a statement that will assist management to evaluate the proposal to commence refining operations. Include any further comments or observations you consider relevant.

(16 marks)
ACCA Foundation Costing

Question 6.8

Intermediate: Profitability analysis and a decision on further processing

C Ltd operates a process which produces three joint products. In the period just ended costs of production totalled £509 640. Output from the process during the period was:

Product W	276 000 kilos
Product X	334 000 kilos
Product Y	134 000 kilos

There were no opening stocks of the three products. Products W and X are sold in this state. Product Y is subjected to further processing. Sales of Products W and X during the period were:

Product W	255 000 kilos at £0.945 per kilo
Product X	312 000 killos at £0.890 per kilo

128 000 kilos of Product Y were further processed during the period. The balance of the period production of the three products W, X and Y remained in stock at the end of the period. The value of closing stock of individual products is calculated by apportioning costs according to weight of output.

The additional costs in the period of further processing Product Y, which is converted into Product Z, were:

Direct labour	£10 850
Production overhead	£7 070

96 000 kilos of Product Z were produced from the 128 000 kilos of Product Y. A byproduct, BP, is also produced which can be sold for £0.12 per kilo. 8000 kilos of BP were produced and sold in the period.

Sales of Product Z during the period were 94 000 kilos, with a total revenue of £100 110. Opening stock of Product Z was 8000 kilos, valued at £8640. The FIFO method is used for pricing transfers of Product Z to cost of sales.

Selling and administration costs are charged to all main products when sold, at 10 per cent of revenue.

Required:

(a) Prepare a profit and loss account for the period, identifying separately the profitability of each of the three main products.

(14 marks)

(b) C Ltd has now received an offer from another company to purchase the total output of Product Y (i.e. before further processing) for £0.62 per kilo. Calculate the viability of this alternative.

(5 marks)

(c) Discuss briefly the methods of, and rationale for, joint cost apportionment.

(6 marks)
(Total 25 marks)
ACCA Level 1 Cost and Management Accounting 1

Question 7.9

Advanced: Explanation of absorption costing changes in profits and preparation of variable costing profit statements

The Miozip Company operates an absorption costing system which incorporates a factory-wide overhead absorption rate per direct labour hour. For 2014 and 2015 this rate was £2.10 per hour. The fixed factory overhead for 2015 was £600 000 and this would have been fully absorbed if the company had operated at full capacity, which is estimated at 400 000 direct labour hours. Unfortunately, only 200 000 hours were worked in that year so that the overhead was seriously under-absorbed. Fixed factory overheads are expected to be unchanged in 2016 and 2017.

The outcome for 2015 was a loss of £70 000 and the management believed that a major cause of this loss was the low overhead absorption rate which had led the company to quote selling prices which were uneconomic.

For 2016 the overhead absorption rate was increased to £3.60 per direct labour hour and selling prices were raised in line with the established pricing procedures which involve adding a profit mark-up of 50 per cent onto the full factory cost of the company's products. The new selling prices were also charged on the stock of finished goods held at the beginning of 2016.

In December 2016 the company's accountant prepares an estimated Profit and Loss Account for 2016 and a budgeted Profit and Loss Account for 2017. Although sales were considered to be depressed in 2015, they were even lower in 2016 but, nevertheless, it seems that the company will make a profit for that year. A worrying feature of the estimated accounts is the high level of finished goods stock held and the 2017 budget provides for a reduction in the stock level at 31 December 2017 to the (physical) level existing in January 2015. Budgeted sales for 2017 are set at the 2016 sales level.

The summarized profit statements for the three years to 31 December 2017 are as follows:

		Actual 2015		estimated 2016		Budgeted 2017	
		(£)	(£)	(£)	(£)	(£)	(£)
Sales revenue			1 350 000		1 316 250		1 316 250
Opening stock of finished goods		100 000		200 000		357 500	
Factory cost of production		1 000 000		975 000		650 000	
		1 100 000		1 175 000		1 007 500	
Less: Closing stock of finished goods		200 000		357 500		130 000	
Factory cost of goods sold			900 000		817 500		877 500
			450 000		498 750		438 750
Less: Factory overhead under-absorbed			300 000		150 000		300 000
			150 000		348 750		138 750
Administrative and financial costs			220 000		220 000		220 000
	Loss		(£70 000)		£128 750	Loss	(£81 250)

Summarized profit and loss accounts

(a) You are required to write a short report to the board of Miozip explaining why the budgeted outcome for 2017 is so different from that of 2016 when the sales revenue is the same for both years.

(6 marks)

(b) Restate the profit and loss account for 2015, the estimated profit and loss account for 2016 and the budgeted profit and loss account for 2017 using marginal factory cost for stock valuation purposes.

(8 marks)

(c) Comment on the problems which *may* follow from a decision to increase the overhead absorption rate in conditions when cost plus pricing is used and overhead is currently under-absorbed.

(3 marks)

(d) Explain why the majority of businesses use full costing systems whilst most management accounting theorists favour marginal costing.

(5 marks)

NB: Assume in your answers to this question that the value of the pound and the efficiency of the company have been constant over the period under review.

(Total 22 marks)
ACCA Level 2 Management Accounting

Question 7.10

Advanced: Explanation of absorption costing changes in profits and preparation of variable costing profit statements

Mahler Products has two manufacturing departments each producing a single standardized product. The data for unit cost and selling price of these products are as follows:

		Department A (£)		Department B (£)
Direct material cost		4		6
Direct labour cost		2		4
Variable manufacturing overheads		2		4
Fixed manufacturing overheads		12		16
Factory cost		20		30
Profit mark-up	50%	10	25%	7.50
Selling price		30		37.50

The factory cost figures are used in the departmental accounts for the valuation of finished goods stock.

The departmental profit and loss accounts have been prepared for the year to 30 June. These are given below separately for the two halves of the year.

	Departmental profit and loss accounts – year to 30 June			
	1 July–31 December		1 January–30 June	
	Department A (£000)	Department B (000)	Department A (£000)	Department B (£000)
Sales revenue	300	750	375	675
Manufacturing costs:				
Direct material	52	114	30	132
Direct labour	26	76	15	88
Variable overheads	26	76	15	88
Fixed overheads	132	304	132	304
Factory cost of production	236	570	192	612
Add opening stock of finished goods	60	210	120	180
	296	780	312	792
Less closing stock of finished goods	120	180	20	300
Factory cost of goods sold	176	600	292	492
Administrative and selling costs	30	100	30	100
	206	700	322	592
Net profit	94	50	53	83

The total sales revenue was the same in each six-monthly period but in the second half of the year the company increased the sales of Department A (which has the higher profit mark-up) and reduced the sales of Department B (which has the lower profit mark-up). An increase in company profits for the second six months was anticipated but the profit achieved was £8000 lower for the second half of the year than for the first half. The profit for Department A fell by £41 000 while the profit for Department B rose by £33 000. There has been no change in prices of inputs or outputs. You are required:

(a) to explain the situation described in the last paragraph – illustrate your answer with appropriate supporting calculations;

(14 marks)

(b) to redraft the departmental profit and loss accounts using marginal cost to value unsold stock.

(8 marks)
(Total 22 marks)
ACCA Level 2 Management Accounting

Cost–volume–profit analysis

Questions to Chapter 8

Question 8.1

Intermediate

A company manufactures a single product which it sells for £15 per unit. The product has a contribution to sales ratio of 40 per cent. The company's weekly break-even point is sales of £18 000.

What would be the profit in a week when 1500 units are sold?

(A) £900

(B) £1800

(C) £2700

(D) £4500

ACCA Financial Information for Managers

Question 8.2

Intermediate

An organization manufactures a single product which has a variable cost of £36 per unit. The organization's total weekly fixed costs are £81 000 and it has a contribution to sales ratio of 40 per cent. This week it plans to manufacture and sell 5000 units.

What is the organization's margin of safety this week (in units)?

(A) 1625

(B) 2750

(C) 3375

(D) 3500

ACCA Financial Information for Managers

Question 8.3

Intermediate

An organization manufactures and sells a single product which has a variable cost of £24 per unit and a contribution to sales ratio of 40 per cent. Total monthly fixed costs are £720 000.

What is the monthly break-even point (in units)?

(A) 18 000

(B) 20 000

(C) 30 000

(D) 45 000

ACCA Financial Information for Managers

Question 8.4

Intermediate

A company has established a budgeted sales revenue for the forthcoming period of £500 000 with an associated contribution of £275 000. Fixed production costs are £137 500 and fixed selling costs are £27 500.

What is the break-even sales revenue?

(A) £75 625

(B) £90 750

(C) £250 000

(D) £300 000

ACCA Paper 1.2 – Financial Information for Management

Question 8.5

Intermediate: Break-even, contribution and profit–volume graph

(a) From the following information you are required to construct:

    (i)   a break-even chart, showing the break-even point and the margin of safety

    (ii) a chart displaying the contribution level and the profit level

    (iii) a profit–volume chart

Sales	6000 units at
	£12 per unit = £72 000
Variable costs	6000 units at
	£7 per unit = £42 000
Fixed costs	= £20 000

(9 marks)

(b) State the purposes of each of the three charts in (a) above.

(6 marks)

(c) Outline the limitations of break-even analysis.

(5 marks)

(d) What are the advantages of graphical presentation of financial data to executives?

(2 marks)
(Total 22 marks)
AAT

Question 8.6

Intermediate: Profit–volume graph and changes in sales mix

A company produces and sells two products with the following costs:

	Product X	Product Y
Variable costs (per £ of sales)	£0.45	£0.6
Fixed costs	£1 212 000	£1 212 000
	per period	

Total sales revenue is currently generated by the two products in the following proportions:

Product X	70%
Product Y	30%

Required:

(a) Calculate the break-even sales revenue per period, based on the sales mix assumed above.

(6 marks)

(b) Prepare a profit–volume chart of the above situation for sales revenue up to £4 000 000. Show on the same chart the effect of a change in the sales mix to product X 50 per cent, product Y 50 per cent. Clearly indicate on the chart the break-even point for each situation.

(11 marks)

(c) Of the fixed costs £455 000 are attributable to product X. Calculate the sales revenue required on product X in order to recover the attributable fixed costs and provide a net contribution of £700 000 towards general fixed costs and profit.

(5 marks)
(Total 22 marks)
ACCA Level 1 Costing

Question 8.7

Intermediate: Break-even chart with an increase in fixed costs and incorporating expected values

A manufacturer is considering a new product which could be produced in one of two qualities: Standard or De Luxe. The following estimates have been made:

	Standard (£)	De Luxe (£)
Unit labour cost	2.00	2.50
Unit material cost	1.50	2.00
Unit Packaging cost	1.00	2.00
Proposed selling price per unit	7.00	10.00
Budgeted fixed costs per period:		
0–99 999 units	200 000	250 000
100 000 and above	350 000	400 000

At the proposed selling prices, market research indicates the following demand:

Standard

Quantity	Probability
172 000	0.1
160 000	0.7
148 000	0.2

De Luxe

Quantity	Probability
195 500	0.3
156 500	0.5
109 500	0.2

You are required:

(a) to draw separate break-even charts for *each* quality, showing the break-even points;

(7 marks)

(b) to comment on the position shown by the charts and what guidance they provide for management;

(3 marks)

(c) to calculate, for *each* quality, the expected unit sales, expected profits and the margin of safety;

(3 marks)

(d) using an appropriate measure of risk, to advise management which quality should be launched.

(9 marks)
(Total 22 marks)
CIMA Stage 3 Management Accounting Techniques

Question 8.8

Intermediate

Changes In sales mix. XYZ Ltd produces two products and the following budget applies:

	Product X (£)	Product Y (£)
Selling price	6	12
Veriable costs	2	4
Contribution margin	4	8
Fixed costs apportioned	100 000	200 000
Units sold	70 000	30 000

You are required to calculate the break-even points for each product and the company as a whole and comment on your findings

Question 8.9

Intermediate: Calculation of break-even points based on different sales mix assumptions and a product abandonment decision

M Ltd manufactures three products which have the following revenue and costs (£ per unit).

Product	1	2	3
Selling price	2.92	1.35	2.83
Variable costs	1.61	0.72	0.96
Fixed costs:			
Product specific	0.49	0.35	0.62
Product specific	0.46	0.46	0.46
General			

Unit fixed costs are based upon the following annual sales and production volumes (thousand units):

Product 1	2	3
98.2	42.1	111.8

Required:

(a) Calculate:

  (i) the break-even point sales (to the nearest £ hundred) of M Ltd based on the current product mix;

  (9 marks)

  (ii) the number of units of Product 2 (to the nearest hundred) at the break-even point determined in (i) above.

  (3 marks)

(b) Comment upon the viability of Product 2.

  (8 marks)
  (Total 20 marks)
  ACCA Cost and Management Accounting 1

Question 8.10

Intermediate: Calculation of break-even points and limiting factor decision-making

You are employed as an accounting technician by Smith, Williams and Jones, a small firm of accountants and registered auditors. One of your clients is Winter plc, a large department store. Judith Howarth, the purchasing director for Winter plc, has gained considerable knowledge about bedding and soft furnishings and is considering acquiring her own business.

She has recently written to you requesting a meeting to discuss the possible purchase of Brita Beds Ltd. Brita Beds has one outlet in Mytown, a small town 100 miles from where Judith works. Enclosed with her letter was Brita Beds' latest profit and loss account.

This is reproduced below.

Brita Beds Ltd

Profit and loss account – year to 31 May

Sales	(units)	(£)
Model A	1 620	336 960
Model B	2 160	758 160
Model C	1 620	1 010 880
Turnover		2 106 000
Expenses	(£)	
Cost of beds	1 620 000	
Commission	210 600	
Transport	216 000	
Rates and insurance	8 450	
Light heat and power	10 000	
Assistants' salaries	40 000	
Manager's salary	40 000	2 145 050
Loss for year		39 050

Also included in the letter was the following information:

(1) Brita Beds sells three types of bed, models A to C inclusive.

(2) Selling prices are determined by adding 30 per cent to the cost of beds.

(3) Sales assistants receive a commission of 10 per cent of the selling price for each bed sold.

(4) The beds are delivered in consignments of 10 beds at a cost of £400 per delivery. This expense is shown as 'Transport' in the profit and loss account.

(5) All other expenses are annual amounts.

(6) The mix of models sold is likely to remain constant irrespective of overall sales volume.

Task 1

In preparation for your meeting with Judith Howarth, you are asked to calculate:

(a) the minimum number of beds to be sold if Brita Beds is to avoid making a loss;

(b) the minimum turnover required if Brita Beds is to avoid making a loss.

At the meeting, Judith Howarth provides you with further information:

(1) The purchase price of the business is £300 000.

(2) Judith has savings of £300 000 currently earning 5 per cent interest per annum, which she can use to acquire Beta Beds.

(3) Her current salary is £36 550.

To reduce costs, Judith suggests that she should take over the role of manager as the current one is about to retire. However, she does not want to take a reduction in income. Judith also tells you that she has been carrying out some market research. The results of this are as follows:

(1) The number of households in Mytown is currently 44 880.

(2) Brita Beds Ltd is the only outlet selling beds in Mytown.

(3) According to a recent survey, 10 per cent of households change their beds every 9 years, 60 per cent every 10 years and 30 per cent every 11 years.

(4) The survey also suggested that there is an average of 2.1 beds per household.

Task 2

Write a letter to Judith Howarth. Your letter should:

(a) identify the profit required to compensate for the loss of salary and interest;

(b) show the number of beds to be sold to achieve that profit;

(c) calculate the likely maximum number of beds that Brita Beds would sell in a year;

(d) use your answers in (a) to (c) to justify whether or not Judith Howarth should purchase the company and become its manager;

(e) give *two* possible reasons why your estimate of the maximum annual sales volume may prove inaccurate.

On receiving your letter, Judith Howarth decides she would prefer to remain as the purchasing director for Winter plc rather than acquire Brita Beds Ltd. Shortly afterwards, you receive a telephone call from her. Judith explains that Winter plc is redeveloping its premises and that she is concerned about the appropriate sales policy for Winter's bed department while the redevelopment takes place. Although she has a statement of unit profitability, this had been prepared before the start of the redevelopment and had assumed that there would be in excess of 800 square metres of storage space available to the bed department. Storage space is critical as customers demand immediate delivery and are not prepared to wait until the new stock arrives.

The next day, Judith Howarth sends you a letter containing a copy of the original statement of profitability. This is reproduced below:

Model	A	B	C
Monthly demand	35	45	20
(beds)	(£)	(£)	(£)
Unit selling price	240.00	448.00	672.00
Unit cost per bed	130.00	310.00	550.00
Carriage inwards	20.00	20.00	20.00
Staff costs	21.60	40.32	60.48
Department fixed overheads	20.00	20.00	20.00
General fixed overheads	25.20	25.20	25.20
Unit profit	23.20	32.48	(3.68)
Storage required per bed (square metres)	3	4	5

In her letter she asks for your help in preparing a marketing plan which will maximize the profitability of Winter's bed department while the redevelopment takes place. To help you, she has provided you with the following additional information:

(1) Currently storage space available totals 300 square metres.

(2) Staff costs represent the salaries of the sales staff in the bed department. Their total cost of £3780 per month is apportioned to units on the basis of planned turnover.

(3) Departmental fixed overhead of £2000 per month is directly attributable to the department and is apportioned on the number of beds planned to be sold.

(4) General fixed overheads of £2520 are also apportioned on the number of beds planned to be sold. The directors of Winter plc believe this to be a fair apportionment of the store's central fixed overheads.

(5) The cost of carriage inwards and the cost of beds vary directly with the number of beds purchased.

Task 3

(a) Prepare a recommended monthly sales schedule in units which will maximize the profitability of Winter plc's bed department.

(b) Calculate the profit that will be reported per month if your recommendation is implemented.

AAT Technician's Stage

Question 8.11

Intermediate: Decision-making and non-graphical CVP analysis

Fosterjohn Press Ltd is considering launching a new monthly magazine at a selling price of £1 per copy. Sales of the magazine are expected to be 500 000 copies per month, but it is possible that the actual sales could differ quite significantly from this estimate.

Two different methods of producing the magazine are being considered and neither would involve any additional capital expenditure. The estimated production costs for each of the two methods of manufacture, together with the additional marketing and distribution costs of selling the new magazine, are summarized below:

	Method A	Method B
Variable costs	0.55 per copy	0.50 per copy
Specific fixed costs	£80 000 per month	£120 000 per month
Semi-variable costs:		
The following estimates have been obtained:		
350 000 copies	£55 000 per month	£47 500 per month
450 000 copies	£65 000 per month	£52 500 per month
650 000 copies	£85 000 per month	£62 500 per month

It may be assumed that the fixed cost content of the semi-variable costs will remain constant throughout the range of activity shown.

The company currently sells a magazine covering related topics to those that will be included in the new publication and consequently it is anticipated that sales of this existing magazine will be adversely affected. It is estimated that for every ten copies sold of the new publication, sales of the existing magazine will be reduced by one copy.

Sales and cost data of the existing magazine are shown below:

Sales	220 000 copies per month
Selling price	0.85 per copy
Variable costs	0.35 per copy
Specific fixed costs	£80 000 per month

Required:

(a) Calculate, for each production method, the net increase in company profits which will result from the introduction of the new magazine, at each of the following levels of activity:

500 000 copies per month
400 000 copies per month
600 000 copies per month

(12 marks)

(b) Calculate, for each production method, the amount by which sales volume of the new magazine could decline from the anticipated 500 000 copies per month, before the company makes no additional profit from the introduction of the new publication.

(6 marks)

(c) Briefly identify any conclusions which may be drawn from your calculations.

(4 marks)
(Total 22 marks)
ACCA Foundation Costing

Question 8.12

Intermediate: Decision-making and non-graphical CVP analysis

Mr Belle has recently developed a new improved video cassette and shown below is a summary of a report by a firm of management consultants on the sales potential and production costs of the new cassette.

Sales potential: The sales volume is difficult to predict and will vary with the price, but it is reasonable to assume that at a selling price of £10 per cassette, sales would be between 7500 and 10 000 units per month. Alternatively, if the selling price was reduced to £9 per cassette, sales would be between 12 000 and 18 000 units per month.

Production costs: If production is maintained at or below 10 000 units per month, then variable manufacturing costs would be approximately £8.25 per cassette and fixed costs £12 125 per month. However, if production is planned to exceed 10 000 units per month, then variable costs would be reduced to £7.75 per cassette, but the fixed costs would increase to £16 125 per month.

Mr Belle has been charged £2000 for the report by the management consultants and, in addition, he has incurred £3000 development costs on the new cassette.

If Mr Belle decides to produce and sell the new cassette it will be necessary for him to use factory premises which he owns, but are leased to a colleague for a rental of £400 per month. Also he will resign from his part-time current part-time post in an electronics firm where he is earning a salary of £1000 per month.

Required:

(a) Identify in the question an example of

(i) an opportunity cost

(ii) a sunk cost

(3 marks)

(b) Making whatever calculations you consider appropriate, analyze the report from the consultants and advise Mr Belle of the potential profitability of the alternatives shown in the report.

Any assumptions considered necessary or matters which may require further investigation or comment should be clearly stated.

(19 marks)
(Total 22 marks)
ACCA Level 1 Costing

Question 8.13

Advanced: Decision-making and CVP analysis

Bruno Ltd is considering proposals for design changes in one of a range of soft toys. The proposals are as follows:

(a) Eliminate some of the decorative stitching from the toy.

(b) Use plastic eyes instead of glass eyes in the toys (two eyes per toy).

(c) Change the filling material used. It is proposed that scrap fabric left over from the body manufacture be used instead of the synthetic material which is currently used.

The design change proposals have been considered by the management team and the following information has been gathered:

(i) Plastic eyes will cost £15 per hundred whereas the existing glass eyes cost £20 per hundred. The plastic eyes will be more liable to damage on insertion into the toy. It is estimated that scrap plastic eyes will be 10 per cent of the quantity issued from stores as compared to 5 per cent of issues of glass eyes at present.

(ii) The synthetic filling material costs £80 per tonne. One tonne of filling is sufficient for 2000 soft toys.

(iii) Scrap fabric to be used as filling material will need to be cut into smaller pieces before use and this will cost £0.05 per soft toy.

There is sufficient scrap fabric for the purpose.

(iv) The elimination of the decorative stitching is expected to reduce the appeal of the product, with an estimated fall in sales by 10 per cent from the current level. It is not felt that the change in eyes or filling material will adversely affect sales volume. The elimination of the stitching will reduce production costs by £0.60 per soft toy.

(v) The current sales level of the soft toy is 300 000 units per annum. Apportioned fixed costs per annum are £450 000. The net profit per soft toy at the current sales level is £3.

Required:

(a) Using the information given in the question, prepare an analysis which shows the estimated effect on annual profit if all three proposals are implemented, and which enables management to check whether each proposal will achieve an annual target profit increase of £25 000. The proposals for plastic eyes and the use of scrap fabric should be evaluated after the stitching elimination proposal has been evaluated.

(12 marks)

(b) Calculate the percentage reduction in sales due to the stitching elimination at which the implementation of all three design change proposals would result in the same total profit from the toy as that earned before the implementation of the changes in design.

(8 marks)

(c) Prepare a report which indicates additional information which should be obtained before a final decision is taken with regard to the implementation of the proposals.

(10 marks)
(Total 30 marks)
ACCA Level 2 Cost and Management Accounting II

Question 8.14

Advanced: Cost–volume–profit analysis in a hospital

A private hospital is organized into separate medical units which offer specialized nursing care (e.g. maternity unit, paediatric unit). Figures for the paediatric unit for the year to 31 May have just become available. For the year in question the paediatric unit charged patients £200 per patient day for nursing care and £4.4m in revenue was earned.

Costs of running the unit consist of variable costs, direct staffing costs and allocated fixed costs. The charges for variable costs such as catering and laundry are based on the number of patient days spent in hospital. Staffing costs are established from the personnel requirements applicable to particular levels of patient days. Charges for fixed costs such as security, administration etc. are based on bed capacity, currently 80 beds.

The number of beds available to be occupied is regarded as bed capacity and this is agreed and held constant for the whole year. There was an agreement that a bed capacity of 80 beds would apply to the paediatric unit for the 365 days of the year to 31 May.

The tables below show the variable, staffing and fixed costs applicable to the paediatric unit for the year to 31 May.

Variable costs (based on patient days)	£
Catering	450 000
Laundry	150 000
Pharmacy	500 000
	1 100 000

Staffing costs

Each speciality recruits its own nurses, supervisors and assistants. The staffing requirements for the paediatric unit are based on the actual patient days, see the following table:

Patient days per annum	Supervisors	Nurses	Assistants
Up to 20 500	4	10	20
20 500 to 23 000	4	13	24
Over 23 000	4	15	28

The annual costs of employment are: supervisors £22 000 each, nurses £16 000 each and assistants £12 000 each.

Fixed costs (based on bed capacity)	£
Administration	850 000
Security	80 000
Rent and property	720 000
	1 650 000

During the year to 31 May the paediatric unit operated a 100 per cent occupancy (i.e. all 80 beds occupied) for 100 days of the year. In fact, the demand on these days was for at least 20 beds more.

As a consequence of this, in the budget for the next year, an increase in the bed capacity has been agreed. Twenty extra beds will be contracted for the whole of the year. It is assumed that the 100 beds will be fully occupied for 100 days, rather than being restricted to 80 beds on those days. An increase of 10 per cent in employment costs for the next year, due to wage rate rises, will occur for all personnel. The revenue per patient day, all other cost factors and the remaining occupancy will be the same as the previous year.

Required:

(a) Determine, for the current year to 31 May, the actual number of patient days, the bed occupancy percentage, the net profit/loss and the break-even number(s) of patient days for the paediatric unit.

(6 marks)

(b) Determine the budget for the next year to 31 May showing the revised number of patient days, the bed occupancy percentage, the net profit/loss and the number of patient-days required to achieve the same profit/loss as computed in (a) above.

(5 marks)

(c) Comment on your findings from (a) and (b) offering advice to the management of the unit.

(6 marks)

(d) A business or operating unit can have both financial and social objectives and at times these can be in conflict. Briefly explain and give an example.

(3 marks)
(20 marks)
ACCA Paper 8 Managerial Finance

Question 8.15

Advanced: CVP analysis and decision-making including a graphical presentation

In the last quarter it is estimated that YNQ will have produced and sold 20 000 units of their main product by the end of the year. At this level of activity it is estimated that the average unit cost will be:

	£
Direct material	30
Direct labour	10
Overhead: Fixed	10
Variable	10
	60

This is in line with the standards set at the start of the year. The management accountant of YNQ is now preparing the budget for the next year. He has incorporated into his preliminary calculations the following expected cost increases:

Raw material:	price increase of 20%
Direct labour:	wage rate increase of 5%
Variable overhead:	increase of 5%
Fixed overhead:	increase of 25%

The production manager believes that if a cheaper grade of raw material were to be used, this would enable the direct material cost per unit to be kept to £31.25 for the next year. The cheaper material would, however, lead to a reject rate estimated at 5 per cent of the completed output and it would be necessary to introduce an inspection stage at the end of the manufacturing process to identify the faulty items. The cost of this inspection process would be £40 000 per year (including £10 000 allocation of existing factory overhead).

Established practice has been to reconsider the product's selling price at the time the budget is being prepared. The selling price is normally determined by adding a markup of 50 per cent to unit cost. On this basis the product's selling price for last year has been £90 but the sales manager is worried about the implications of continuing the cost-plus 50 per cent rule for next year. He estimates that demand for the product varies with price as follows:

Price:	£80	£84	£88	£90	£92	£96	£100
Demand (000)	25	23	21	20	19	17	15

(a) You are required to decide whether YNQ should use the regular or the cheaper grade of material and to calculate the best price for the product, the optimal level of production and the profit that this should yield. Comment briefly on the sensitivity of the solution to possible errors in the estimates.

(14 marks)

(b) Indicate how one might obtain the answer to part (a) from an appropriately designed cost–volume–profit graph. You should design such a graph as part of your answer but the graph need not be drawn to scale providing that it demonstrates the main features of the approach that you would use.

(8 marks)
(Total 22 marks)
ACCA Level 2 Management Accounting

Question 8.16

Advanced: CVP analysis and changes in product mix

Dingbat Ltd is considering renting additional factory space to make two products, Thingone and Thingtwo. You are the company's management accountant and have prepared the following monthly budget:

Sales (units)	Thingone 4 000 (£)	Thingtwo 2 000 (£)	Total 6 000 (£)
Sales revenue	80 000	100 000	180 000
Variable material and labour costs	(60 000)	(62 000)	(122 000)
Fixed production overheads (allocated on direct labour hours)	(9 900)	(18 000)	(27 900)
Fixed administration overheads (allocated on sales value)	(1 600)	(2 000)	(3 600)
Profit	8 500	18 000	26 500

The fixed overheads in the budget can only be avoided if neither product is manufactured. Facilities are fully interchangeable between products.

As an alternative to the manual production process assumed in the budget, Dingbat Ltd has the option of adopting a computer-aided process. This process would cut variable costs of production by 15 per cent and increase fixed costs by £12 000 per month.

The management of Dingbat Ltd is confident about the cost forecasts, but there is considerable uncertainty over demand for the new products.

The management believes the company will have to depart from its usual cash sales policy in order to sell Thingtwo. An average of three months' credit would be given and bad debts and administration costs would probably amount to four per cent of sales revenue for this product.

Both products will be sold at the prices assumed in the budget. Dingbat Ltd has a cost of capital of two per cent per month. No stocks will be held.

Requirements:

(a) Calculate the sales revenues at which operations will break-even for each process (manual and computer-aided) and calculate the sales revenues at which Dingbat Ltd will be indifferent between the two processes:

(i) if Thingone alone is sold;

(4 marks)

(ii) if Thingone and Thingtwo units are sold in the ratio 4:1, with Thingtwo being sold on credit.

(6 marks)

(b) Explain the implications of your results with regard to the financial viability of Thingone and Thingtwo.

(5 marks)

(c) Discuss the major factors to be considered in the pricing and sales forecasting for new productions.

(10 marks)
(Total 25 marks)
ICAEW P2 Management Accounting

Measuring relevant costs and revenues for decision-making

Questions to Chapter 9

Question 9.1

Intermediate

A company requires 600kg of raw material Z for a contract it is evaluating. It has 400kg of material Z in stock which were purchased last month. Since then the purchase price of material Z has risen by 8 per cent to £27 per kg. Raw material Z is used regularly by the company in normal production.

What is the total relevant cost of raw material Z to the contract?

(A) £15 336

(B) £15 400

(C) £16 200

(D) £17 496

ACCA – Financial Information for Management

Question 9.2

Intermediate

Equipment owned by a company has a net book value of £1800 and has been idle for some months. It could not be used on a six-month contract which is being considered. If not used on this contract, the equipment would be sold now for a net amount of £2000. After use on the contract, the equipment would have no saleable value and would be dismantled. The cost of dismantling and disposing of it would be £800.

What is the total relevant cost of the equipment to the contract?

(A) £1200

(B) £1800

(C) £2000

(D) £2800

ACCA – Financial Information for Management

Question 9.3

Intermediate

JJ Ltd manufactures three products: W, X and Y. The products, use a series of different machines but there is a common machine that is a bottleneck.

The standard selling price and standard cost per unit for each product for the forthcoming period are as follows:

	W £	X £	Y £
Selling price	200	150	150
Cost			
Direct material	41	20	30
Labour	30	20	36
Overheads	60	40	50
Profit	69	70	34
Bottleneck machine – minutes per unit	9	10	7

40 per cent of the overhead cost is classified as variable.

Using a throughput accounting approach, what would be the ranking of the products for best use of the bottleneck?

(3 marks)
CIMA P1 Management Accounting: Performance Evaluation

Question 9.4

Intermediate: Decision on which of two mutually exclusive contracts to accept

A company in the civil engineering industry with headquarters located 22 miles from London undertakes contracts anywhere in the United Kingdom.

The company has had its tender for a job in north east England accepted at £288 000 and work is due to begin in March. However, the company has also been asked to undertake a contract on the south coast of England. The price offered for this contract is £352 000. Both of the contracts cannot be taken simultaneously because of constraints on staff site management personnel and on plant available. An escape clause enables the company to withdraw from the contract in the north-east, provided notice is given before the end of November and an agreed penalty of £28 000 is paid.

The following estimates have been submitted by the company's quantity surveyor:

Cost estimates	North-east (£)	South-coast (£)
Materials:		
In stock at original cost, Material X	21 600	
In stock at original cost, Material Y		24 800
Firm orders placed at original cost, Material X	30 400	
Not yet ordered – current cost, Material X	60 000	
Not yet ordered – current cost, Material Z		71 200
Labour – hired locally	86 000	110 000
Site management	34 000	34 000
Staff accommodation and travel for site management	6 800	5 600
Plant on site – depreciation	9 600	12 800
Interest on capital, 8%	5 120	6 400
Total local contract costs	253 520	264 800
Headquarters costs allocated at rate of 5% on total contract costs	12 676	13 240
	266 196	278 040
Contract price	288 000	352 000
Estimated profit	21 804	73 960

Notes:

(1) X, Y and Z are three building materials. Material X is not in common use and would not realize much money if re-sold; however, it could be used on other contracts but only as a substitute for another material currently quoted at 10 per cent less than the original cost of X. The price of Y, a material in common use, has doubled since it was purchased; its net realizable value if re-sold would be its new price less 15 per cent to cover disposal costs. Alternatively it could be kept for use on other contracts in the following financial year.

(2) With the construction industry not yet recovered from the recent recession, the company is confident that manual labour, both skilled and unskilled, could be hired locally on a subcontracting basis to meet the needs of each of the contracts.

(3) The plant which would be needed for the south coast contract has been owned for some years and £12 800 is the year's depreciation on a straight-line basis. If the north-east contract is undertaken, less plant will be required but the surplus plant will be hired out for the period of the contract at a rental of £6000.

(4) It is the company's policy to charge all contracts with notional interest at 8 per cent on estimated working capital involved in contracts. Progress payments would be receivable from the contractee.

(5) Salaries and general costs of operating the small headquarters amount to about £108 000 each year. There are usually ten contracts being supervised at the same time.

(6) Each of the two contracts is expected to last form March to February which, coincidentally, is the company's financial year.

(7) Site management is treated as a fixed cost.

You are required, as the management accountant to the company:

(a) to present comparative statements to show the net benefit to the company of undertaking the more advantageous of the two contracts;

(12 marks)

(b) to explain the reasoning behind the inclusion in (or omission from) your comparative financial statements, of each item given in the cost estimates and the notes relating thereto.

(13 marks)
(Total 25 marks)
CIMA Stage 2 Cost Accounting

Question 9.5

Advanced: Relevant costs for bidding for a contract

M is the holding company of a number of companies, within the engineering sector. One of these subsidiaries is PQR which specialises in building machines for manufacturing companies. PQR uses absorption costing as the basis of its routine accounting system for profit reporting.

PQR is currently operating at 90% of its available capacity, and has been invited by an external manufacturing company, to tender for the manufacture of a bespoke machine. It PQR's tender is accepted by the manufacturing company then it is likely that another company within the M group will be able to obtain work in the future servicing the machine. As a result, the Board of Directors of M are keen to win the tender for the machine and are prepared to accept a price from the manufacturing company that is based on the relevant costs of building the machine.

An engineer from PQR has already met with the manufacturing company to determine the specification of the machine and he has worked with a non-qualified accountant from PQR to determine the following cost estimate for the machine.

	Note	$
Engineering specification	1	1 500
Direct material A	2	61 000
Direct Material B	3	2 500
Components	4	6 000
Direct Labour	5	12 500
Supervision	6	350
Machine hire	7	2 500
Overhead costs	8	5 500
Total		91 850

Notes:

(1) The engineer that would be in charge of the project to build the machine has already met with the manufacturing company, and subsequently prepared the specification for the machine. This has taken three days of his time and his salary and related costs are $500 per day. The meeting with the manufacturing company only took place because of this potential work; no other matters were discussed at the meeting.

(2) The machine would require l0 000 square metres of Material A. This material is regularly used by PQR. There is currently 15 000 square metres in inventory, 10 000 square metres were bought for $6 per square metre and the remainder were bought for $6.30 per square metre. PQR uses the weighted average basis to value its inventory. The current market price of Material A is $7 per square metre, and the inventory could be sold for $6.50 per square metre.

(3) The machine would also require 250 metre lengths of Material B. This is not a material that is regularly used by PQR and it would have to be purchased specifically for this work. The current market price is $10 per metre length, but the sole supplier of this material has a minimum order size of 300 metre lengths. PQR does not fore see any future use of any unused lengths of Material B, and expects that the net revenue from its sale would be negligible.

(4) The machine would require 500 components. The components could be produced by HK, another company within the M group. The direct costs to HK of producing each component is $8, and normal transfer pricing policy within the M group is to add a 50% mark up to the direct cost to determine the transfer price. HK has unused capacity which would allow them to produce 350 components, but thereafter any more components could only be produced by reducing the volume of other components that are currently sold to the external market. These other components, although different, require the same machine time per unit as those required by PQR, have a direct cost of $6 per component and currently are sold for $9 each.

Alternatively PQR can buy the components from the external market tor $14 each.

(5) The machine will require 1000 hours of skilled labour. The current market rate for engineers with the appropriate skills is $15 per hour. PQR currently employs engineers that have the necessary skills at a cost of $12.50 per hour, but they do not have any spare capacity. They could be transferred from their existing duties if temporary replacements were to be engaged at a cost of $14 per hour.

(6) The project would be supervised by a senior engineer who currently works 150 hours per month and is paid an annual salary of $42 000. The project is expected to take a total of one month to complete, and if it goes ahead is likely to take up 10% of the supervisor's time during that month. If necessary the supervisor will work overtime which is unpaid.

(7) It will be necessary to hire a specialist machine for part of the project. In total the project will require the machine for 5 days but it is difficult to predict exactly for which five days the machine will be required within the overall project time of one month. One option is to hire the machine for the entire month at a cost of $5000 and then sub-hire the machine for $150 per day when it is not required by PQR. PQR expects that it would be able to sub-hire the machine for 20 days. Alternatively PQR could hire the machine on the days it requires and its availability would be guaranteed at a cost of $500 per day.

(8) PQR's fixed production overhead cost budget for the year totals $200 000 and is absorbed into its project costs using a skilled direct labour hour absorption rate, based on normal operating capacity of 80 per cent PQR's capacity budget for the year is a total of 50 000 skilled direct labour hours. PQR's latest annual forecast is for overhead costs to total $220 000, and for capacity to be as originally budgeted.

Required:

(a) You are employed as assistant Management Accountant of the M group. For each of the resource items identified you are to:

(i) discuss the basis of the valuation provided for each item;

(ii) discuss whether or not you agree with the valuation provided in the context of the proposed tender;

(iii) prepare a revised schedule of relevant costs for the tender document on behalf of the M group.

(15 marks)

(b) Assume that PQR successfully wins the bid to build the machine for a selling price of $100 000 and that the costs incurred are as expected. Discuss the conflict that will arise between the profit expected from the project by the Board of M on a relevant cost basis and the project profit that will be reported to them by PQR using its routine accounting practices. Use at least two specific examples from the bid to explain the conflict that you discuss.

(5 marks)

(c) Discuss two non-financial matters that you consider relevant to this decision.

(5 marks)
(Total 25 marks)
CIMA P2 Performance Management

Question 9.6

Advanced: Relevant costs for bidding for a contract

CDF is a manufacturing company within the DF group. CDF has been asked to provide a quotation for a contract for a new customer and is aware that this could lead to farther orders. As a consequence, CDF will produce the quotation by using relevant costing instead of its usual method of full cost plus pricing.

The following information has been obtained in relation to the contract:

Material D

40 tonnes of material D would be required. This material is in regular use by CDF and has a current purchase price of $38 per tonne. Currently, there are 5 tonnes in inventory which cost $35 per tonne. The resale value of the material in inventory is $24 per tonne.

Components

4000 components would be required. These could be bought externally for $15 each or alternatively they could be supplied by RDF, another company within the DF manufacturing group. The variable cost of the component if it were manufactured by RDF would be $8 per unit, and RDF adds 30% to its variable cost to contribute to its fixed costs plus a further 20% to this total cost in order to set its internal transfer price. RDF has sufficient capacity to produce 2500 components without affecting its ability to satisfy its own external customers. However in order to make the extra 1500 components required by CDF, RDF would have to forgo other external sales of $50 000 which have a contribution to sales ratio of 40%.

Labour hours

850 direct labour hours would be required. All direct labour within CDF is paid on an hourly basis with no guaranteed wage agreement. The grade of labour required is currently paid $10 per hour, but department W is already working at 100 per cent capacity. Possible ways of overcoming this problem are:

• Use workers in department Z, because it has sufficient capacity. These workers are paid $15 per hour.
• Arrange for sub-contract workers to undertake some of the other work that is performed in department W. The sub-contract workers would cost $13 per hour.

Specialist machine

The contract would require a specialist machine. The machine could be hired for $15 000 or it could be bought for $50 000. At the end of the contract if the machine were bought, it could be sold for $30 000. Alternatively it could be modified at a cost of $5000 and then used on other contracts instead of buying another essential machine that would cost $45 000.

The operating costs of the machine are payable by CDF whether it hires or buys the machine. These costs would total $12 000 in respect of the new contract.

Supervisor

The contract would be supervised by an existing manager who is paid an annual salary of $50 000 and has sufficient capacity to carry out this supervision. The manager would receive a bonus of $500 for the additional work.

Development time

15 hours of development time at a cost of $3 000 have already been worked in determining the resource requirements of the contract.

Fixed overhead absorption rate

CDF uses an absorption rate of $20 per direct labour hour to recover its general fixed overhead costs. This includes $5 per hour for depreciation.

Required:

(a) Calculate the relevant cost of the contract to CDF. You must present your answer in a schedule that clearly shows the relevant cost value for each of the items identified above. You should also explain each relevant cost value you have included in your schedule and why any values you have excluded are not relevant.

Ignore taxation and the time value of money.

(19 marks)

(b) Discuss TWO problems that can arise as a result of setting prices using relevant costing.

(6 marks)
(Total 25 marks)
CIMA P2 Performance Management

Question 9.7

Advanced: Relevant costs of building a new engine

RFT, an engineering company, has been asked to provide a quotation for a contract to build a new engine. The potential customer is not a current customer of RFT, but the directors of RFT are keen to try and win the contract as they believe that this may lead to more contracts in the future. As a result they intend pricing the contract using relevant costs.

The following information has been obtained from a two-hour meeting that the Production Director of RFT had with the potential customer. The Production Director is paid an annual salary equivalent to $1200 per 8-hour day.

110 square metres of material A will be required. This is a material that is regularly used by RFT and there are 200 square metres currently in inventory. These were bought at a cost of $12 per square metre. They have a resale value of $10.50 per square metre and their current replacement cost is $12.50 per square metre.

30 litres of material B will be required. This material will have to be purchased for the contract because it is not otherwise used by RFT. The minimum order quantity from the supplier is 40 litres at a cost of $9 per litre. RFT does not expect to have any use for any of this material that remains after this contract is completed.

60 components will be required. These will be purchased from HY. The purchase price is $50 per component.

A total of 235 direct labour hours will be required. The current wage rate for the appropriate grade of direct labour is $11 per hour. Currently RFT has 75 direct labour hours of spare capacity at this grade that is being paid under a guaranteed wage agreement. The additional hours would need to be obtained by either (i) overtime at a total cost of $14 per hour; or (ii) recruiting temporary staff at a cost of $12 per hour. However, if temporary staff are used they will not be as experienced as RFT's existing workers and will require 10 hours supervision by an existing supervisor who would be paid overtime at a cost of $18 per hour for this work.

25 machine hours will be required. The machine to be used is already leased for a weekly leasing cost of $600. It has a capacity of 40 hours per week. The machine has sufficient available capacity for the contract to be completed. The variable running cost of the machine is $7 per hour.

The company absorbs its fixed overhead costs using an absorption rate of $20 per direct labour hour.

Required:

(a) Calculate the relevant cost of building the new engine.

You should present your answer in a schedule that clearly shows the relevant cost value for each of the items identified above. You should also explain each relevant cost value you have included in your schedule and why the values you have excluded are not relevant.

(13 marks)

(b) HY, the company that is to supply RFT with the components that are required for this contract, is another company in the same group as RFT. Each component is being transferred to RFT taking account of HY's opportunity cost of the component. The variable cost that will be incurred by HY is $28 per component.

Discuss the factors that would be considered by HY to determine die opportunity cost of the component.

(5 marks)
(Total 18 marks)
CIMA P2 Performance Management

Question 9.8

Intermediate: Impact of a product abandonment decision and CVP analysis

(a) Budgeted information for A Ltd for the following period, analyzed by product, is shown below:

	Product I	Product II	Product III
Sales units (000s)	225	376	190
Selling price (£ per unit)	11.00	10.50	8.00
Variable costs (£ per unit)	5.80	6.00	5.20
Attributable fixed costs (£000s)	275	337	296

General fixed costs, which are apportioned to products as a percentage of sales, are budgeted at £1 668 000.

Required:

(i) Calculate the budgeted profit of A Ltd, and of each of its products.

(5 marks)

(ii) Recalculate the budgeted profit of A Ltd on the assumption that Product III is discontinued, with no effect on sales of the other two products. State and justify other assumptions made.

(5 marks)

(iii) Additional advertising, to that included in the budget for Product I, is being considered.

Calculate the minimum extra sales units required of Product I to cover additional advertising expenditure of £80 000. Assume that all other existing fixed costs would remain unchanged.

(3 marks)

(iv) Calculate the increase in sales volume of Product II that is necessary in order to compensate for the effect on profit of a 10 per cent reduction in the selling price of the product. State clearly any assumptions made.

(5 marks)

(b) Discuss the factors which influence cost behaviour in response to changes in activity.

(7 marks)
(Total 25 marks)
ACCA Cost and Management Accounting 1

Question 9.9

Advanced: Outsourcing decision based on relevant costs

WZ is a manufacturing company with two factories. The company's West factory currently produces a number of products. Four of these products use differing quantities of the same resources. Details of these four products and their resource requirements are as follows:

Product	J $/unit	K $/unit	L $/unit	M $/unit
Selling price	56	40	78	96
Direct labour ($8 per hour)	20	16	24	20
Direct material A ($3 per litre)	6	3	0	9
Direct material B ($5 per kg)	10	0	15	20
Variable overhead (see note 1)				
Labour related	1.25	1	1.50	1.25
Machine related	1.25	2	0.75	1
Total variable cost	38.50	22	41.25	51.25
Other data:				
Machine hours per unit	5	8	3	4
Maximum demand per week	1 000	3 500	2 800	4 500

Notes:

(1) An analysis of the variable overhead shows that some of it is caused by the number of labour hours and the remainder is caused by the number of machine hours.

(2) Currently WZ purchases a component P from a external supplier for $35 per component. A single unit of this component is used in producing N the company's only other product. Product N is produced in WZ's other factory and does not use any of the resources identified above. Product N currently yields a positive contribution. WZ could manufacture the component in its West factory, but to do so would require: 1 hour of direct labour, 0.5 machine hours, and 2kgs of direct material B. WZ purchases 500 components per week. WZ could not produce the component in its other factory.

(3) The purchasing director has recently advised you that the availability of direct materials A and B is to be restricted to 21 000 litres and 24 000kgs per week respectively. This restriction is unlikely to change for at least 10 weeks. No restrictions aree expected on any other resources.

(4) WZ does not hold inventory of either finished goods or raw materials.

(5) WZ has already signed a contract, which must be fulfilled, to deliver the following units of its products each week for the next 10 weeks:

Product	Contract units
J	100
K	200
L	150
M	250

These quantities are in addition to the maximum demand identified above.

Required:

(a) Calculate whether WZ should continue to purchase the component P or whether it should manufacture it internally during the next 10 weeks.

(11 marks)

(b) Prepare a statement to show the optimum weekly usage of the West factory's available resources.

Note: You are NOT required to use linear programming.

(3 marks)

(c) (i) Assuming no other changes, calculate the purchase price of the component P at which your advice in part (a) above would change.

(4 marks)

(ii) Explain TWO non-financial factors that should be considered before deciding whether or not to manufacture the component internally.

(4 marks)

(d) If you were to solve part (*b*) above using linear programming state the following:

- the objective function
- the inequality for the material A constraint
- the inequality for the material B constraint

(3 marks)
(Total 25 marks)
CIMA P2 Performance Management

Question 9.10

Advanced: Alternative uses of obsolete materials

Brown Ltd is a company that has in stock some materials of type XY that cost £75 000 but that are now obsolete and have a scrap value of only £21 000. Other than selling the material for scrap, there are only two alternative uses for them.

Alternative 1: Converting the obsolete materials into a specialized product, which would require the following additional work and materials:

Material A	600 units
Material B	1 000 units
Direct labour:	
5 000 hours unskilled youth labour	
5 000 hours semi-skilled	
5 000 hours highly skilled	15 000 hours
Extra selling and delivery expenses	£27 000
Extra advertising	£18 000

The conversion would produce 900 units of saleable product, and these could be sold for £400 per unit.

Material A is already in stock and is widely used within the firm. Although present stocks together with orders already planned will be sufficient to facilitate normal activity, any extra material used by adopting this alternative will necessitate such materials being replaced immediately. Material B is also in stock, but it is unlikely that any additional supplies can be obtained for some considerable time because of an industrial dispute. At the present time material B is normally used in the production of product Z, which sells at £390 per unit and incurs total variable cost (excluding material B) of £210 per unit. Each unit of product Z uses four units of material B.

The details of materials A and B are as follows:

	Material A (£)	Material B (£)
Acquisition cost at time of purchase	100 per unit	10 per unit
Net realizable value	85 per unit	18 per unit
Replacement cost	90 per unit	—

Alternative 2: Adapting the obsolete materials for use as a substitute for a sub-assembly that is regularly used within the firm. Details of the extra work and materials required are as follows:

Material C 1000 units
Direct labour:
4000 hours unskilled youth labour
1000 hours semi-skilled
4000 hours highly skilled.

1200 units of the sub-assembly are regularly used per quarter, at a cost of £900 per unit. The adaptation of material XY would reduce the quantity of the sub-assembly purchased from outside the firm to 900 units for the next quarter only. However, since the volume purchased would be reduced, some discount would be lost, and the price of those purchased from outside would increase to £950 per unit for that quarter.

Material C is not available externally, but is manufactured by Brown Ltd. The 1000 units required would be available from stocks, but would be produced as extra production. The standard cost per unit of material C would be as follows:

	(£)
Direct labour, 6 hours unskilled youth labour	36
Raw materials	13
Variable overhead, 6 hours at £1	6
Fixed overhead, 6 hours at £3	18
	73

The wage rates and overhead recovery rates for Brown Ltd are:

Variable overhead	£1 per direct labour hour
Fixed overhead	£3 per direct labour hour
Unskilled youth labour	£6 per direct labour hour
Semi-skilled labour	£8 per direct labour hour
Highly skilled labour	£10 per direct labour hour

The unskilled youth labour youth is employed on a casual basis and sufficient labour can be acquired to exactly meet the production requirements. Semi-skilled labour is part of the permanent labour force, but the company has temporary excess supply of this type of labour at the present time. Highly skilled labour is in short supply and cannot be increased significantly in the short term; this labour is presently engaged in meeting the demand for product L, which requires four hours of highly skilled labour. The contribution (sales less direct labour and material costs and variable overheads) from the sale of one unit of product L is £24.

Given this information, you are required to present cost information advising whether the stocks of material XY should be sold, converted into a specialized product (alternative 1) or adapted for use as a substitute for a sub-assembly (alternative 2).

Question 9.11

Advanced: Limiting factors and optimal production programme

A market gardener is planning his production for next season, and has asked you as a cost accoutant, to recommended the optimal mix of vegetable production for the coming year. He has given you the following data relating to the current year.

	Potatoes	Turnips	Parsnips	Carrots
Area occupied (acres)	25	20	30	25
Yield per acre (tonnes)	10	8	9	12
Selling price per tonne (£)	100	125	150	135
Variable cost per acre (£)				
Fertilizers	30	25	45	40
Seeds	15	20	30	25
Pesticides	25	15	20	25
Direct wages	400	450	500	570

Fixed overhead per annum £54 000

The land that is being used for the production of carrots and parsnips can be used for either crop, but not for potatoes or turnips. The land being used for potatoes and turnips can be used for either crop, but not for carrots or parsnips. In order to provide an adequate market service, the gardener must produce each year at least 40 tonnes each of potatoes and turnips and 36 tonnes each of parsnips and carrots.

(a) You are required to present a statement to show:

  (i) the profit for the current year;

  (ii) the profit for the production mix that you would recommend.

(b) Assuming that the land could be cultivated in such a way that any of the above crops could be produced and there was no market commitment, you are required to:

  (i) advise the market gardener on which crop he should concentrate his production;

  (ii) calculate the profit if he were to do so;

  (iii) calculate in sterling the breakeven point of sales.

(25 marks)
CIMA Cost Accounting 2

Question 9.12

Advanced: Limiting factors and optimal product mix for a single constraint and multiple constraints

WRX manufactures three products using different quantities of the same resources. Details of these products are as follows:

Product	W $/unit	R $/unit	X $/unit
Market selling price	90	126	150
Direct labour ($7/hour)	14	28	35
Material A ($3/kg)	15	12	21
Material B ($6/kg)	24	36	30
Variable overhead ($4/hour)	8	16	20
Fixed overhead	12	7	12
	73	99	118
Profit	17	27	32

The management of WRX has predicted the demand for these products for July as follows:

Product W	500 units
Product R	800 units
Product X	1 600 units

These demand estimates do NOT include an order from a major customer to supply 400 units per month of each of the three products, at a discount of $10 per unit from the market selling price.

During July the management of WRX anticipate that there will be a shortage of material B, and that only 17 500kgs will be available.

It is not possible for WRX to hold inventory of any raw materials, work in progress or finished products.

Required:

(a) Prepare calculations to show the optimum product mix to maximise WRX's profit for July, assuming that the order with the major customer is supplied in full.

(7 marks)

WRX has now realised that the contract with the major customer does not have to be met in full for any of the three products. The customer will accept whatever WRX is prepared to supply at the contracted prices but they will charge a financial penalty if WRX does not supply them in full in July.

(b) Calculate the lowest value of the financial penalty that the major customer would need to insert in the contract to ensure that WRX meets its order in full in July.

(8 marks)

(c) Now that you have presented your answers to (a) and (b) above to the management team of WRX, the production manager has advised that, due to holidays, the number of direct labour hours available will be reduced to a total of 9800 hours in July.

A decision has been made that WRX will fullfil its order with the major customer in full in July, and it has been agreed that a linear programming model will be used to determine the optimum usage of the resources that will be available after setting aside those required for the major customer's order.

Required:

(i) Identify the objective function and the constraints to be used in the linear programming model to determine the optimum usage of the remaining resources to maximise the company's profits for July.

(6 marks)

(ii) The optimal solution has been determined as:

W	500 units
R	0 units
X	880 units

Explain which of the constraints you stated in (c)(i) are binding on the solution. (You are not required to draw a graph.)

(4 marks)
(Total 25 marks)
CIMA P2 Performance Management

Question 9.13

Throughput accounting

Yam Co is involved in the processing of sheet metal into products A, B and C using three processes, pressing, stretching and rolling. Like marry businesses Yam faces tough price competition in what is a mature world market.

The factory has 50 production lines each of which contain the three processes: raw material for the sheet metal is first pressed then stretched and finally rolled. The processing capacity varies for each process and the factory manager has provided the following data:

Processing time per metre in hours

	Product A	Product B	Product C
Pressing	0.50	0.50	0.40
Stretching	0.25	0.40	0.25
Rolling	0.40	0.25	0.25

The factory operates for 18 hours each day for five days per week. It is closed for only two weeks of the year for holidays when maintenance is carried out. On average one hour of labour is needed for each of the 225 000 hours of factory time. Labour is paid $10 per hour.

The raw materials cost per metre is $3.00 for product A, $2.50 for product B and $1.80 for product C. Other factory costs (excluding labour and raw materials) are $18 000 000 per year. Selling prices per metre are $70 for product A, $60 for product B and $27 for product C.

Yam carries very little inventory.

Required:

(a) Identity the bottleneck process and briefly explain why this process is described as a 'bottleneck'.

(3 marks)

(b) Calculate the throughput accounting ratio (TPAR) for each product assuming that the bottleneck process is fully utilized.

(8 marks)

(c) Assuming that the TPAR of product C is less than 1:
  (i) Explain how Yam could improve the TPAR of product C.

(4 marks)

  (ii) Briefly discuss whether this supports the suggestion to cease the production of product C and briefly outline three other factors that Yam should consider before a cessation decision is taken.

(5 marks)
(20 marks)
ACCA: F5 Performance Management

Question 9.14

Advanced: Throughput accounting

Ride Ltd is engaged in the manufacturing and marketing of bicycles. Two bicycles are produced. These are the 'Roadster' which is designed for use on roads and the 'Everest' which is a bicycle designed for use in mountainous areas. The following information relates to the year ending 31 December.

(1) Unit selling price and cost data are as follows:

	Roadster £	Everest £
Selling price	200	280
Material cost	80	100
Variable production conversion costs	20	60

(2) Fixed production overheads attributable to the manufacture of the bicycles will amount to £4 050 000.

(3) Expected demand is as follows:

Roadster	150 000 units
Everest	70 000 units

(4) Each bicycle is completed in the finishing department. The number of each type of bicycle that can be completed in one hour in the finishing department is as follows:

Roadster	6.25
Everest	5.00

There are a total of 30 000 hours available within the finishing department.

(5) Ride Ltd operates a just in time (JIT) manufacturing system with regard to the manufacture of bicycles and aims to hold very little work in progress and no finished goods stocks whatsoever.

Required:

(a) Using marginal costing principles, calculate the mix (units) of each type of bicycle which will maximize net profit and state the value of that profit.

(6 marks)

(b) Calculate the throughput accounting ratio for each type of bicycle and briefly discuss when it is worth producing a product where throughput accounting principles are in operation. Your answer should assume that the variable overhead cost amounting to £4 800 000 incurred as a result of the chosen product mix in part (a) is fixed in the short-term.

(5 marks)

(c) Using throughput accounting principles, advise management of the quantities of each type of bicycle that should be manufactured which will maximize net profit and prepare a projection of the net profit that would be earned by Ride Ltd in the year ending 31 December.

(5 marks)

(d) Explain two aspects in which the concept of 'contribution' in throughput accounting differs from its use in marginal costing.

(4 marks)
ACCA 3.3: Performance Management

Pricing decisions and profitability analysis

Questions to Chapter 10

Question 10.1

Intermediate

The following information relates to questions (i) and (ii):

In the following price, revenue and cost functions, which have been established by an organization for one of its products, Q, represent the number of units produced and sold per week:

Price (£ per unit) = 50 − 0.025Q

Marginal revenue (£ per unit) = 50 − 0.05Q

Total weekly cost = 1000 + 15Q

(i) What price per unit should be set in order to maximize weekly profit?

    (A) £15.00

    (B) £17.50

    (C) £25.00

    (D) £32.50

(ii) What would the weekly total contribution be if the price of the product was set at £20 per unit?

    (A) £2000

    (B) £3000

    (C) £5000

    (D) £6000

ACCA – Financial Information for Management

Question 10.2

Advanced: Calculation of cost-plus selling price and an evaluation of pricing decisions

A firm manufactures two products EXE and WYE in departments dedicated exclusively to them. There are also three service departments: stores, maintenance and administration. No stocks are held as the products deteriorate rapidly. Direct costs of the products, which are variable in the context of the whole business, are identified to each department. The step-wise apportionment of service department costs to the manufacturing departments is based on estimates of the usage of the service provided. These are expressed as percentages and assumed to be reliable over the current capacity range. The general factory overheads of £3.6m, which are fixed, are apportioned on the basis of floor space occupied. The company establishes product costs based on budgeted volume and marks up these costs by 25 per cent in order to set target selling prices.

Extracts from the budgets for the forthcoming year are provided below:

	Annual volume (units)	
	EXE	**WYE**
Max capacity	200 000	100 000
Budget	150 000	70 000

	EXE	**WYE**	**Stores**	**Maintenance**	**Admin**
Costs (£m)					
Material	1.8	0.7	0.1	0.1	
Other variable	0.8	0.5	0.1	0.2	0.2

	EXE	WYE	Stores	Maintenance	Admin
Departmental usage (%)					
Maintenance	50	25	25		
Administration	40	30	20	10	
Stores	60	40			
Floor space (sq m)	640	480	240	80	160

Required:

Workings may be £000 with unit prices to the nearest penny.

(a) Calculate the budgeted selling price of one unit of EXE and WYE based on the usual mark up.

(5 marks)

(b) Discuss how the company may respond to each of the following independent events, which represent additional business opportunities.

(i) an enquiry from an overseas customer for 3000 units only of WYE where a price of £35 per unit is offered;

(ii) an enquiry for 50000 units of WYE to be supplied in full at regular intervals during the forthcoming year at a price which is equivalent to full cost plus 10 per cent.

In both cases support your discussion with calculations and comment on any assumptions or matters on which you would seek clarification.

(11 marks)

(c) Explain the implications of preparing product full costs based on maximum capacity rather than annual budget volume.

(4 marks)
(Total 20 marks)
ACCA Paper 8 Managerial Finance

Question 10.3

Advanced: Preparation of full cost and marginal cost information

A small company is engaged in the production of plastic tools for the garden. Sub-totals on the spreadsheet of budgeted overheads for a year reveal:

	Moulding department	Finishing department	General factory overhead
Variable overhead (£000)	1600	500	1050
Fixed overhead (£000)	2500	850	1750
Budgeted activity			
Machine hours (000)	800	600	
Practical capacity			
Machine hours (000)	1200	800	

For the purposes of reallocation of general factory overhead it is agreed that the variable overheads accrue in line with the machine hours worked in each department. General factory fixed overhead is to be reallocated on the basis of the practical machine hour capacity of the two departments.

It has been a long-standing company practice to establish selling prices by applying a mark-up on full manufacturing cost of between 25 per cent and 35 per cent.

A possible price is sought for one new product which is in a final development stage. The total market for this product is estimated at 200000 units per annum. Market research indicates that the company could expect to obtain and hold about 10 per cent of the market. It is hoped the product will offer some improvement over competitors' products, which are currently marketed at between £125 and £135 each.

The product development department have determined that the direct material content is £9 per unit. Each unit of the product will take two labour hours (four machine hours) in the moulding department and three labour hours (three machine hours) in finishing. Hourly labour rates are £10.00 and £11.00 respectively.

Management estimate that the annual fixed costs which would be specifically incurred in relation to the product are: supervision £20000, depreciation of a recently acquired machine £120000 and advertising £27000. It may be assumed that these costs are included in the budget given above. Given the state state of development of this new product, management do not consider it necessary to make revisions, to the budgeted activity levels given above, for any possible extra machine hours involved in its manufacture.

Required:

(a) Briefly explain the role of costs in pricing.

(6 marks)

(b) Prepare full cost and marginal cost information which may help with the pricing decision.

(9 marks)

(c) Comment on the cost information and suggest a price range which should be considered.

(5 marks)
(Total 20 marks)
ACCA Paper 8 Managerial Finance

Question 10.4

Advanced: Pricing decision based on price/demand relationships and impact of product life cycle stages

A manufacturer of electrical appliances is continually reviewing its product range and enhancing its existing products by developing new models to satisfy the demands of its customers. The company intends to always have products at each stage of the product life cycle to ensure the company's continued presence in the market.

Currently the company is reviewing three products:

Product K was introduced to the market some time ago and is now about to enter the maturity stage of its life cycle. The maturity stage is expected to last for ten weeks. Each unit has a variable cost of $38 and takes 1 standard hour to produce. The Managing Director is unsure which of four possible prices the company should charge during the next ten weeks. The following table shows the results of some market research into the level of weekly demand at alternative prices:

Selling price per unit	$100	$85	$80	$75
Weekly demand (Units)	600	800	1 200	1 400

Product L was introduced to the market two months ago using a penetration pricing policy and is now about to enter its growth stage. This stage is expected to last for 20 weeks. Each unit has a variable cost of $45 and takes 1.25 standard hours to produce. Market research has indicated that there is a linear relationship between its selling price and the number of units demanded, of the form $P = a - bx$. At a selling price of $100 per unit demand is expected to be 1000 units per week. For every $10 increase in selling price the weekly demand will reduce by 200 units and for every $10 decrease in selling price the weekly demand will increase by 200 units.

Product M is currently being tested and is to be launched in ten weeks' time. This is an innovative product which the company believes will change the entire market. The company has decided to use a market skimming approach to pricing this product during its introduction stage.

The company currently has a production facility which has a capacity of 2000 standard hours per week. This facility is being expanded but the extra capacity will not be available for ten weeks.

Required:

(a) (i) Calculate which of the four selling prices should be charged for product K. in order to maximise its contribution during its maturity stage.

(3 marks)

As a result, in order to utilise all of the spare capacity from your answer to (i) above:

(ii) Calculate the selling price of product L during its growth stage.

(6 marks)
(Total for requirement (a) − 9 marks)

(b) Compare and contrast penetration and skimming pricing strategies during the introduction stage, using product M to illustrate your answer.

(6 marks)

(c) Explain with reasons, for each of the remaining stages of M's product life cycle, the changes that would be expected in the

   (i)   average unit production cost

   (ii) unit selling price

(10 marks)
(Total 25 marks)
CIMA P2 Performance management

Question 10.5

Advanced: Limiting factor resource allocation and comparison of marginal revenue to determine optimum output and price

(a) A manufacturer has three products, A, B, and C. Currently sales, cost and selling price details and processing time requirements are as follows:

	Product A	Product B	Product C
Annual sales (units)	6 000	6 000	750
Selling price (£)	20.00	31.00	39.00
Unit cost (£)	18.00	24.00	30.00
Processing time required per unit (hours)	1	1	2

The firm is working at full capacity (13 500 processing hours per year). Fixed manufacturing overheads are absorbed into unit costs by a charge of 200 per cent of variable cost. This procedure fully absorbs the fixed manufacturing overhead. Assuming that:

(i) processing time can be switched from one product line to another;

(ii) the demand at current selling prices is:

Product A	Product B	Product C
11 000	8 000	2 000

and

(iii) the selling prices are not to be altered. You are required to calculate the best production programme for the next operating period and to indicate the increase in net profit that this should yield. In addition identify the shadow price of a processing hour.

(11 marks)

(b) A review of the selling prices is in progress and it has been estimated that, for each product, an increase in the selling price would result in a fall in demand at the rate of 2000 units for an increase of £1 and similarly, that a decrease of £1 would increase demand by 2000 units. Specifically the following price/demand relationships would apply:

Product A		Product B		Product C	
Selling price (£)	Estimated demand	Selling price (£)	Estimated demand	Selling price (£)	Estimated demand
24.50	2 000	34.00	2 000	39.00	2 000
23.50	4 000	33.00	4 000	38.00	4 000
22.50	6 000	32.00	6 000	37.00	6 000
21.50	8 000	31.00	8 000	36.00	8 000
20.50	10 000	30.00	10 000	35.00	10 000
19.50	12 000	29.00	12 000	34.00	12 000
18.50	14 000	28.00	14 000	33.00	14 000

From this information you are required to calculate the best selling prices, the revised best production plan and the net profit that this plan should produce.

(11 marks)
(Total 22 marks)
ACCA Level 2 Management Accounting

Question 10.6

Advanced: Calculation of optimal selling price and profit using differential calculus

HZ is reviewing the selling price of one of its products. The current selling price of the product is $45 per unit and annual demand is forecast to be 130 000 units at this price. Market research shows that the level of demand would be affected by any change in the selling price Detailed analysis of this research shows that for every $1 increase in selling price, annual demand would reduce by 10 000 units and that for every $1 decrease in selling price, annual demand would increase by 10 000 units.

A forecast of the costs that would be incurred by HZ in respect of this product at differing activity levels is as follows:

Annual production and sales (units)	100 000	160 000	200 000
	$000	$000	$000
Direct materials	280	448	560
Direct labour	780	1 248	1 560
Variable overhead	815	1 304	1 630
Fixed overhead	360	360	360

The company seeks your help in determining the optimum selling price to maximise its profits

Required:

(a) Calculate the optimum forecast annual profit from the product.

(6 marks)

(b) Explain the effect on the optimal price and quantity sold of independent changes to:

(i) the direct material cost per unit

(2 marks)

(ii) the annual fixed overhead cost

(2 marks)
(Total 10 marks)

Note: If Price (P) = a − bx then Marginal Revenue = a − 2bx

CIMA P2 Performance Management

Question 10.7

Advanced: Calculation of optimum selling prices using differential calculus

Alvis Taylor has budgeted that output and sales of his single product, flonal, will be 100 000 for the forthcoming year. At this level of activity his unit variable costs are budgeted to be £50 and his unit fixed costs £25. His sales manager estimates that the demand for flonal would increase by 1000 units for every decrease of £1 in unit selling price (and vice-versa), and that at a unit selling price of £200 demand would be nil.

Information about two price increases has just been received from suppliers. One is for materials (which are included in Alvis Taylor's variable costs), and one is for fuel (which is included in his fixed costs). Their effect will be to increase both the variable costs and the fixed costs by 20 per cent in total over the budgeted figures.

Alvis Taylor aims to maximize profits from his business.

You are required, in respect of Alvis Taylor's business:

(a) to calculate, *before the cost increases:*

(i) the budgeted contribution and profit at the budgeted level of sales of 100 000 units, and

(ii) the level of sales at which profits would be maximized, and the amount of those maximum profits;

(7 marks)

(b) to show whether and by how much Alvis Taylor should adjust his selling price, in respect of the increases in, respectively:

(i) fuel costs

(ii) materials costs;

(6 marks)

(c) to show whether and by how much it is worthwhile for Alvis Taylor, following the increases in costs, to spend £1 000 000 on a TV advertising campaign if this were confidently expected to have the effect during the next year (but not beyond then) that demand would still fall by 1000 units for every increase of £1 in unit selling price (and vice-versa), but that it would not fall to nil until the unit selling price was £210;

(5 marks)

(d) to comment on the results which you have obtained in (a)–(c) above and on the assumptions underlying them.

(7 marks)
(Total 25 marks)
ICAEW Management Accounting

Question 10.8

Advanced

PT manufactures and sells a number of products. All of its products have a life cycle of six months or less. PT uses a four stage life cycle model (Introduction; Growth; Maturity; and Decline) and measures the profits from its products at each stage of their life cycle.

PT has recently developed an innovative product. Since the product is unique it was decided that it would be launched with a market skimming pricing policy. However PT expects that other companies will try to enter the market very soon.

This product is generating significant unit profits during the Introduction stage of its life cycle. However there are concerns that the unit profits will reduce during the other stages of the product's life cycle.

Required:

For each of the

(i) growth and

(ii) maturity stages of the new product's life cycle

explain the likely changes that will occur in the unit selling prices AND in the unit production costs, compared to the preceding stage.

(10 marks)
CIMA P2 Performance Management

Question 10.9

Advanced

Discuss the extent to which cost data are useful in the determination of pricing policy. Explain the advantages and disadvantages of presenting cost data for possible utilization in pricing policy determination using an absorption, rather than a direct, costing basis.

(14 marks)
ACCA P2 Management Accounting

Question 10.10

Advanced

'In providing information to the product manager, the accountant must recognize that decision-making is essentially a process of choosing between competing alternatives, each with its own combination of income and costs; and that the relevant concepts to employ are future incremental costs and revenues and opportunity cost, not full cost which includes past or sunk costs.' (Sizer)

Descriptive studies of pricing decisions taken in practice have, on the other hand, suggested that the inclusion of overhead and joint cost allocations in unit product costs is widespread in connection with the provision of information for this class of decision. Furthermore, these costs are essentially historic costs.

You are required to:

(a) explain the reasoning underlying the above quotation;

(10 marks)

(b) suggest reasons why overhead and joint cost allocation is nevertheless widely used in practice in connection with information for pricing decisions;

(10 marks)

(c) set out your own views as to the balance of these arguments.

(5 marks)
(Total 25 marks)
ICAEW Management Accounting

Question 10.11

Advanced

At one of its regular monthly meetings the board of Giant Steps Ltd was discussing its pricing and output policies. Giant Steps Ltd is a multi-product firm, operating in several distinct but related competitive markets. It aims to maximize profits.

You are required to comment critically and concisely on any four of the following six statements which were included in the taped record of the meeting:

(a) Profit is maximized by charging the highest possible price.

(b) The product manager's pricing policy should be to set a price which will maximize demand, by ensuring that contribution per unit is maximized.

(c) Allocation of overheads and joint costs enables management to compare performance between products, projects or divisions.

(d) Allocation of overheads and joint costs is a way of accountants grabbing power and influence from marketing and production people.

(e) Our management accounts must be consistent with our published external accounts, so we must follow SSAP 9 on overhead allocation.

(f) Expenditure on Research and Development would be a past or sunk cost, and no matter what decision about output or price was eventually made it would have no bearing on the recovery of that expenditure.

(12 marks)
ICAEW Management Accounting

Activity-based costing

Questions to Chapter 11

Question 11.1

Intermediate

DRP Limited has recently introduced an activity-based costing system. It manufactures three products, details of which are set out below:

	Product D	Product R	Product P
Budgeted annual production (units)	100 000	100 000	50 000
Batch size (units)	100	50	25
Machine set-ups per batch	3	4	6
Purchase orders per batch	2	1	1
Processing time per unit (minutes)	2	3	3

Three cost pools have been identified. Their budgeted costs for the year ending 30 June are as follows:

Machine set-up costs	£150 000
Purchasing of materials	£70 000
Processing	£80 000

The budgeted machine set-up cost per unit of product R is nearest to

(A) £0.52

(B) £0.60

(C) £6.52

(D) £26.09

(3 marks)
CIMA Management Accounting – Performance Management

Question 11.2

Intermediate: Comparison of traditional product costing with ABC

Having attended a CIMA course on activity-based costing (ABC) you decide to experiment by applying the principles of ABC to the four products currently made and sold by your company. Details of the four products and relevant information are given below for one period:

Product	A	B	C	D
Output in units	120	100	80	120
Costs per unit:	(£)	(£)	(£)	(£)
Direct material	40	50	30	60
Direct labour	28	21	14	21
Machine hours (per unit)	4	3	2	3

The four products are similar and are usually produced in production runs of 20 units and sold in batches of 10 units.

The production overhead is currently absorbed by using a machine hour rate, and the total of the production overhead for the period has been analyzed as follows:

	(£)
Machine department costs (rent, business rates, depreciation and supervision)	10 430
Set-up costs	5 250
Stores receiving	3 600
Inspection/Quality control	2 100
Materials handling and dispatch	4 620

You have ascertained that the 'cost drivers' to be used are as listed below for the overhead costs shown:

Cost	Cost driver
Set up costs	Number of production runs
Stores receiving	Requisitions raised
Inspection/Quality control	Number of production runs
Materials handling and despatch	Orders executed

The number of requisitions raised on the stores was 20 for each product and the number of orders executed was 42, each order being for a batch of 10 of a product.

You are required:

(a) to calculate the total costs for each product if all overhead costs are absorbed on a machine hour basis;

(4 marks)

(b) to calculate the total costs for each product, using activity-based costing;

(7 marks)

(c) to calculate and list the unit product costs from your figures in (a) and (b) above, to show the differences and to comment briefly on any conclusions which may be drawn which could have pricing and profit implications.

(4 marks)
(Total 15 marks)
CIMA Stage 2 Cost Accounting

Question 11.3

Advanced: ABC overhead calculation

W is a manufacturing company that produces three products: X, Y and Z. Each uses the same resources, but in different quantities as shown in the table of budgeted data below:

Product	X	Y	Z
Budgeted production	1 500	2 500	4 000
Direct labour hours per unit	2	4	3
Machine hours per unit	3	2	3
Batch size	50	100	500
Machine setups per batch	2	3	1
Purchase orders per batch	4	4	6
Material movements per batch	10	5	4

W's budgeted production overhead costs are $400 000 and current practice is to absorb these costs into product costs using an absorption rate based on direct labour hours. As a result the production overhead cost attributed to each product unit is:

Product X $32   Product Y $64   Product Z $48

The management of S are considering changing to an activity based method of attributing overhead costs to products and as a result have identified the following cost drivers and related cost pools:

Cost pool	$	Cost driver
Machine maintenance	100 000	machine hours
Machine setups	70 000	machine setups
Purchasing	90 000	purchase orders
Material handling	60 000	material movements

The remaining $80 000 of overhead costs are caused by a number of different factors and activities that are mainly labour related and are to be attributed to products on the basis of labour hours.

Required:

(a) Calculate the production overhead cost attributed to each product unit using an activity based approach.

(7 marks)

(b) Explain how W has applied Pareto Analysis when determining its cost drivers and how it may continue to use Pareto Analysis to control its production costs.

(3 marks)
(Total 10 marks)
CIMA P2 Performance Management

Question 11.4

Advanced: Computation of ABC product costs

XY provides accountancy services and has three different categories of client: limited companies, self employed individuals, and employed individuals requiring taxation advice. XY currently charges its clients a fee by adding a 20 per cent mark-up to total costs. Currently the costs are attributed to each client based on the hours spent on preparing accounts and providing advice.

XY is considering charging to an activity based costing system. The annual costs and the causes of these costs have been analyzed as follows:

	$
Accounts preparation and advice	580 000
Requesting missing information	30 000
Issuing fee payment reminders	15 000
Holding client meetings	60 000
Travelling to clients	40 000

The following details relate to three of XY's clients and to XY as a whole:

	Client			
	A	B	C	XY
Hours spent on preparing accounts and providing advice	1 000	250	340	18 000
Requests for missing information	4	10	6	250
Payment reminders sent	2	8	10	400
Client meetings held	4	1	2	250
Miles travelled to meet clients	150	600	0	10 000

Required:

Prepare calculations to show the effect on fees charged to each of these three clients of changing to the new costing system.

(10 marks)
CIMA P2 Performance Management

Question 11.5

Advanced: ABC profitability analysis

A healthcare company specializes in hip, knee and shoulder replacement operations, known as surgical procedures. As well as providing these surgical procedures the company offers pre operation and post operation in-patient care, in a fully equipped hospital, for those patients who will be undergoing the surgical procedures.

Surgeons are paid a fixed fee for each surgical procedure they perform and an additional amount for any follow-up consultations. Post procedure follow up consultations are only undertaken if there are any complications in relation to the surgical procedure. There is no additional fee charged to patients for any follow up consultations. All other staff are paid annual salaries.

The company's existing costing system uses a single overhead rate, based on revenue, to charge the costs of support activities to the procedures. Concern has been raised about the inaccuracy of procedure costs and the company's accountant has initiated a project to implement an activity-based costing (ABC) system.

The project team has collected the following data on each of the procedures.

Procedure information	Hip	Knee	Shoulder
Fee charged to patients per procedure	$8 000	$10 000	$6 000
Number of procedures per annum	600	800	400
Average time per procedure	2.0 hours	1.2 hours	1.5 hours
Number of procedures per theatre session	2	1	4
In-patient days per procedure	3	2	1
Surgeon's fee per procedure	$1 200	$1 800	$1 500
% of procedures with complications	8%	5%	10%
Surgeon's fee per follow up consultation	$300	$300	$300
Cost of medical supplies per procedure	$400	$200	$300

The project team has obtained the following information about the support activities.

Activity	Cost driver	Overheads $000
Theatre preparation for each session	Number of theatre preparations	864
Operating theatre usage	Procedure time	1 449
Nursing and ancillary services	In-patient days	5 428
Administration	Sales revenue	1 216
Other overheads	Number of procedures	923

Required:

(a) Calculate the profit per procedure for each of the three procedures, using the current basis for charging the costs of support activities to procedures.

(5 marks)

(b) Calculate the profit per procedure for each of the three procedures using activity-based costing.

(13 marks)

(c) Discuss the ways in which the information obtained by the project team may be of benefit to the management of the company.

(7 marks)
(Total 25 marks)
CIMA P1 Performance Operations

Question 11.6

Advanced: ABC profitability analysis

GH produces three models of speedboat for sale to the retail market. GH currently operates a standard absorption costing system. Budgeting information for next year is given below:

Model of speedboat	Superior $000	Deluxe $000	Ultra $000	Total $000
Sales	54 000	86 400	102 000	242 400
Direct material	17 600	27 400	40 200	85 200
Direct labour	10 700	13 400	16 600	40 700
Production overhead				69 600
Gross profit				46 900

	Superior	Deluxe	Ultra
Production/sales (number of boats)	1 000	1 200	800
Machine hours per boat	100	200	300

The production overhead cost is absorbed using a machine hour rate.

GH is considering changing to an activity based costing system. The main activities and their associated cost drivers and overhead cost have been identified as follows:

		Production overhead cost
Activity	Cost Driver	$000
------------	-------------------------------------	---------
Machining	Machine hours	13 920
Set up	Number of set ups	23 920
Quality inspection	Number of quality inspections	14 140
Stores receiving	Number of component deliveries	6 840
Stores issue	Number of issues from stones	10 780
		69 600

The analysis also revealed the following information:

	Superior	Deluxe	Ultra
Budgeted production (number of boats)	1 000	1 200	800
Boats per production run	5	4	2
Quality inspections per production run	10	20	30
Number of component deliveries	510	600	800
Number of issues from stores	4 000	5 000	7 000

The machines are set up for each production run of each model.

Required:

(a) Calculate the total gross profit for each model of speedboat:

(i) using the current absorption costing system;

(4 marks)

(ii) using the proposed activity based costing system.

(12 marks)

(b) Explain why an activity based costing system may produce more accurate product costs than a traditional absorption costing system.

(3 marks)

(c) Explain the possible other benefits to the company of introducing an activity based costing system. You should use the figures calculated in part (a) to illustrate your answer.

(6 marks)
(Total 25 marks)
CIMA P1 Performance Operations

Question 11.7

Advanced: ABC profitability analysis

A company sells and services photocopying machines. Its sales department sells the machines and consumables, including ink and paper, and its service department provides an after sales service to its customers. The after sales service includes planned maintenance of the machine and repairs in the event of a machine breakdown. Service department customers are charged an amount per copy that differs depending on the size of the machine.

The company's existing costing system uses a single overhead rate, based on total sales revenue from copy charges, to charge the cost of the Service Department's support activities to each size of machine. The Service Manager has suggested that the copy charge should more accurately reflect the costs involved. The company's accountant has decided to implement an activity-based costing system and has obtained the following information about the support activities of the service department:

Activity	Cost Driver	Overheads per annum $000
Customer account handling	Number of customers	126
Planned maintenance scheduling	Number of planned maintenance visits	480
Unplanned maintenance scheduling	Number of unplanned maintenance visits	147
Spare part procurement	Number of purchase orders	243
Other overheads	Number of machines	600
Total overheads		1596

The following data have also been collected for each machine size:

	Small photocopiers	Medium photocopiers	Large photocopiers
Charge per copy	$0.03	$0.04	$0.05
Average number of copies per year per machine	60000	120000	180000
Number of machines	300	800	500
Planned maintenance visits per machine per year	4	6	12
Unplanned maintenance visits per machine per year	1	1	2
Total number of purchase orders per year	500	1200	1000
Cost of parts per maintenance visit	$100	$300	$400
Labour cost per maintenance visit	$60	$80	$100

Each customer has a service contract lor two machines on average.

Required:

(a) Calculate the annual profit per machine for each of the three sizes of machine, using the current basis for charging the costs of support activities to machines.

(4 marks)

(b) Calculate the annual profit per machine for each of the three sizes of machine using activity-based costing.

(14 marks)

(c) Explain the potential benefits to the company of using an activity-based costing system.

(7 marks)
(Total 25 marks)
CIMA P1 Performance Operations

Question 11.8

Advanced: Pricing quotation using ABC and traditional costing

Brick by Brick (BBB) is a building business that provides a range of building services to the public. Recently they have been asked to quote for garage conversions (GC) and extensions to properties (EX) and have found that they are winning fewer GC contracts than expected.

BBB has a policy to price all jobs at budgeted total cost plus 50 per cent. Overheads are currently absorbed on a labour hour basis. BBB thinks that a switch to activity based costing (ABC) to absorb overheads would reduce the cost associated to GC and hence make them more competitive.

You are provided with the following data:

Overhead category	Annual overheads $	Activity driver	Total number of activities per year
Supervisors	90000	Site visits	500
Planners	70000	Planning documents	250
Property related	240000	Labour hours	40000
Total	400000		

A typical GC costs $3500 in materials and takes 300 labour hours to complete. A GC requires only one site visit by a supervisor and needs only one planning document to be raised. The typical EX costs $8000 in materials and takes 500 hours to complete. An EX requires six site visits and five planning documents. In all cases labour is paid $15 per hour.

Required:

(a) Calculate the cost and quoted price of a GC and of an EX using labour hours to absorb the overheads.

(5 marks)

(b) Calculate the cost and the quoted price of a GC and of an EX using ABC to absorb the overheads.

(5 marks)

(c) Assuming that the cost of a GC falls by nearly 7 per cent and the price of an EX rises by about 2 per cent as a result of the change to ABC, suggest possible pricing strategies for the two products that BBB sells and suggest two reasons other than high prices for the current poor sales of the GC.

(6 marks)

(d) One BBB manager has suggested that only marginal cost should be included in budget cost calculations as this would avoid the need for arbitrary overhead allocations to products. Briefly discuss this point of view and comment on the implication for the amount of mark-up that would be applied to budget costs when producing quotes for jobs.

(4 marks)
(Total 20 marks)
ACCA F5 Performance Management

Decision-making under conditions of risk and uncertainty

Questions to Chapter 12

Question 12.1

Advanced: Regret matrix

The manager of a retail store that sells electronic goods is deciding which of three credit agreements to offer to its customers. Past experience has shown that there are three possible reactions to each of the agreements. The profit will depend on customers' reaction to the agreement on offer.

The profit for each of the possible outcomes is as follows:

Customer reaction	Agreement A $	Agreement B $	Agreement C $
Strong	52 600	44 800	64 700
Moderate	43 700	36 200	41 600
Weak	38 200	34 500	33 100

Required:

(i) Prepare a regret matrix and use it to identify the agreement that the manager would select if the minimax regret criterion was used to make the decision.

(3 marks)

(ii) Describe the attitude to risk of a manager that is risk averse.

(2 marks)
(Total 5 marks)
CIMA P1 Performance Operations

Question 12.2

Intermediate: Expected value requiring a decision tree

Firlands Limited, a retail outlet, is faced with a decision regarding whether or not to expand and build small or large premises at a prime location. Small premises would cost £300 000 to build and large premises would cost £550 000.

Regardless of the type of premises built, if high demand exists then the net income is expected to be £1 500 000. Alternatively, if low demand exists, then net income is expected to be £600 000.

If large premises are built then the probability of high demand is 0.75. If the smaller premises are built then the probability of high demand falls to 0.6. Firlands has the option of undertaking a survey costing £50 000. The survey predicts whether there is likely to be a good or bad response to the size of the premises. The likelihood of there being a good response, from previous surveys, has been estimated at 0.8.

If the survey indicates a good response then the company will build the large premises. If the survey does give a good result then the probability that there will be high demand from the large premises increases to 0.95.

If the survey indicates a bad response then the company will abandon all expansion plans.

Required:

Using decision tree analysis, establish the best course of action for Firlands Limited.

(10 marks)
ACCA Paper 1.2 – Financial Information for Management

Question 12.3

Advanced: Value of perfect information

FP can choose from three mutually exclusive projects. The net cash flows from the projects will depend on market demand. All of the projects will last for only one year. The forecast net cash flows and their associated probabilities are given below:

Market demand	Weak	Average	Good
Probability	0.30	0.50	0.20
	$000	$000	$000
Project A	400	500	600
Project B	300	350	400
Project C	500	450	650

Required:

(i) Calculate the expected value of the net cash flows from each of the THREE projects.

(ii) Calculate the value of perfect information regarding market demand.

(4 marks)
CIMA P1 Performance Operations

Question 12.4

Advanced: Joint probabilities and expected values

A company is planning to launch a new product. The price at which it can sell the product will be determined by the number of other entrants into the market. The possible selling prices and variable costs and their respective associated probabilities are as follows:

Selling price per unit		Variable cost per unit	
$	Probability	$	Probability
80	0.25	40	0.20
100	0.30	60	0.55
120	0.45	80	0.25

Selling price and variable cost per unit are independent of each other.

Required:

(i) Calculate the probability of the contribution being greater than $39 per unit.

(3 marks)

(ii) Calculate the expected value of the contribution per unit.

(2 marks)
(Total 5 marks)
CIMA P1 Performance Operations

Question 12.5

Advanced: Value of perfect information

A company has to decide which of three mutually exclusive projects to invest in during the next year. The directors believe that the success of the projects will vary depending on consumer demand. There is a 20 per cent chance that consumer demand will be above average; a 45 per cent chance that consumer demand will be average and a 35 per cent chance that consumer demand will be below average.

The net present value for each of the possible outcomes is as follows:

Consumer demand	Project A $000s	Project B $000s	Project C $000s
Above average	400	300	800
Average	500	400	600
Below average	700	600	300

A market research company believes it can provide perfect information on potential consumer demand in this market.

Required:

Calculate, on the basis of expected value, the maximum amount that should be paid for the information from the market research company.

(5 marks)
CIMA P1 Performance Operations

DECISION-MAKING UNDER CONDITIONS OF RISK AND UNCERTAINTY

Question 12.6

Advanced: Value of information

A company has to decide which of three mutually exclusive projects to undertake. The directors believe that success of the projects will depend on consumer reaction. There is a 25 per cent chance that consumer reaction will be strong, a 40 per cent chance that consumer reaction will be good and a 35 per ecnt chance that consumer reaction will be weak. The company uses expected value to make this type of decision.

The net present value for each of the possible outcomes is as follows:

Consumer demand	Project A $000s	Project B $000s	Project C $000s
Strong	1 000	1 600	1 200
Good	250	300	375
Weak	200	140	100

A market research company believes it can provide perfect information on consumer reaction.

Required:

Calculate the maximum amount that should be paid for the information from the market research company.

(5 marks)
CIMA P1 Performance Operations

Question 12.7

Advanced: Calculation of expected value and the presentation of a probability distribution

The Dunburgh Bus Company operated during the year ended 31 May 2015 with the following results:

(i)   Average variable costs were £0.75 per bus mile.

(ii) Total fixed costs were £1 750 000.

(iii) The fare structure per journey was as follows:

Adults 0 to 3 miles	£0.20
4 to 5 miles	£0.30
over 5 miles	£0.50
Juveniles (any distance)	£0.15
Senior citizens (any distance)	£0.10

(iv) Total passenger journeys paid for were 24 000 000 which represented 60 per cent capacity utilization. The capacity utilized comprised 60 per cent adult, 20 per cent juvenile and 20 per cent senior citizen journeys. The adult journeys were broken down into 0–3 miles: 50 per cent, 4–5 miles: 30 per cent, over 5 miles: 20 per cent.

(v) Twenty routes were operated with four buses per route, each bus covering 150 miles per day for 330 days of the year. The remaining days were taken up with maintenance work on the buses.

(vi) Advertising revenue from displays inside and outside the buses totalled £250 000 for the year. This is a fixed sum from contracts which will apply to each year up to 31 May 2017.

It is anticipated that all costs will increase by 10 per cent due to inflation during the year to 31 May 2016 and that fares will be increased by 5 per cent during the year. Whilst the fare increase of 5 per cent has already been agreed and cannot be altered, it is possible that inflation might differ from the 10 per cent rate anticipated.

Required:

(a) Prepare a statement showing the calculation of the net profit or loss for the year ended 31 May 2015.

(5 marks)

(b) Calculate the average percentage capacity utilization at which the company will break even during the forthcoming year to 31 May 2016 if all fares are increased by 5 per cent, cost inflation is 10 per cent as anticipated and the passenger mix and bus operating activity are the same as for the year to 31 May 2015.

(5 marks)

(c) Now assume that management have some doubts about the level of capacity utilization and rate of cost inflation which will apply in the year to 31 May 2016. Other factors are as previously forecast. Revised estimates of the likely levels of capacity utilization and inflation are as follows:

Capacity utilization	Probability	Inflation	Probability
70%	0.1	8%	0.3
60%	0.5	10%	0.6
50%	0.4	12%	0.1

(Capacity utilization rates and inflation rates are independent of each other.)

   (i) Calculate the expected value of net profit or loss for the year to 31 May 2016 and show the range of profits or losses which may occur.

(9 marks)

   (ii) Draw up a table of the possible profits and losses and their probabilities as calculated in (i) for the year ended 31 May 2016 in a way which brings to the attention of management the risks and opportunities which are implied and comment briefly on the figures.

(5 marks)

(d) Comment on factors which have not been incorporated into the model used in (c) above which may affect its usefulness to management in profit forecasting.

(6 marks)
(Total 30 marks)
ACCA Level 2 Cost Accounting II

Question 12.8

Advanced: Pricing decisions under conditions of uncertainty

(a) Allegro Finishes Ltd is about to launch an improved version of its major product – a pocket size chess computer – onto the market. Sales of the original model (at £65 per unit) have been at the rate of 50 000 per annum but it is now planned to withdraw this model and the company is now deciding on its production plans and pricing policy.

The standard variable cost of the new model will be £50 which is the same as that of the old, but the company intends to increase the selling price to recover the research and development expenditure that has been incurred. The research and development costs of the improved model are estimated at £750 000 and the intention is that these should be written off over 3 years. Additionally there are annual fixed overheads of approximately £800 000 allocated to this product line.

The sales director has estimated the maximum annual demand figures that would obtain at three alternative selling prices. These are as follows:

Selling price (£)	Estimated maximum annual demand (physical units)
70	75 000
80	60 000
90	40 000

You are required to prepare a cost–volume–profit chart that would assist the management to choose a selling price and the level of output at which to operate. Identify the best price and the best level of output. Outline briefly any reservations that you have with this approach.

(5 marks)

(b) With the facts as stated for part (a), now assume the sales director is considering a more sophisticated approach to the problem. He has estimated, for each selling price, an optimistic, a pessimistic and a most likely demand figure and associated probabilities for each of these. For the £90 price the estimates are:

	Annual demand	Probability of demand
Pessimistic	20 000	0.2
Most likely	35 000	0.7
Optimistic	40 000	0.1
		1.0

On the cost side, it is clear that the standard unit variable cost of £50 is an 'ideal' which has rarely been achieved in practice. An analysis of the past 20 months shows that the following pattern of variable cost variances (per unit of output) has arisen:

An adverse variance of around £10 arose on four occasions, an adverse variance of around £5 arose on 14 occasions and a variance of around 0 arose on two occasions.

There is no reason to think that the pattern for the improved model will differ significantly from this or that these variances are dependent upon the actual demand level.

From the above, calculate the expected annual profit for a selling price of £90.

(6 marks)

(c) A tabular summary of the result of an analysis of the data for the other two selling prices (£70 and £80) is as follows:

	£70	£80
Probability of a loss of £500 000 or more	0.02	0.00
Probability of a loss of £300 000 or more	0.07	0.05
Probability of a loss of £100 000 or more	0.61	0.08
Probability of break-even or worse	0.61	0.10
Probability of break-even or better	0.39	0.91
Probability of a profit of £100 000 or more	0.33	0.52
Probability of a profit of £300 000 or more	0.03	0.04
Probability of a profit of £500 000 or more	0.00	0.01
Expected value of profit (loss)	55 750	68 500

You are required to compare your calculations in part (b) with the above figures and to write a short memo to the sales director outlining your advice and commenting on the use of subjective discrete probability distributions in problems of this type.

(9 marks)

(d) Assume that there is a 10 per cent increase in the fixed overheads allocated to this product line and a decision to write off the research and development costs in one year instead of over three years. Indicate the general effect that this would have on your analysis of the problem.

(2 marks)
(Total 22 marks)
ACCA Level 2 Management Accounting

Question 12.9

Advanced: Pricing decision based on competitor's response

In the market for one of its products, MD and its two major competitors (CN and KL) together account for 95 per cent of total sales.

The quality of MD's products is viewed by customers as being somewhat better than that of its competitors and therefore at similar prices it has an advantage. During the past year, however, when MD raised its price to £1.2 per litre, competitors kept their prices at £1.0 per litre and MD's sales declined even though the total market grew in volume.

MD is now considering whether to retain or reduce its price for the coming year. Its expectations about its likely volume at various prices charged by itself and its competitors are as follows:

Prices per litre			
MD (£)	CN (£)	KL (£)	MD's expected sales million litres
1.2	1.2	1.2	2.7
1.2	1.2	1.1	2.3
1.2	1.2	1.0	2.2
1.2	1.1	1.1	2.4
1.2	1.1	1.0	2.2
1.2	1.1	1.0	2.1
1.1	1.1	1.1	2.8
1.1	1.0	1.0	2.4
1.1	1.0	1.0	2.3
1.0	1.0	1.0	2.9

Experience has shown that CN tends to react to MD's price level and KL tends to react to CN's price level. MD therefore assesses the following probabilities:

If MD's price per litre is (£)	There is a probability of	That CN's price per litre will be (£)
1.2	0.2	1.2
	0.4	1.1
	0.4	1.0
	1.0	
1.1	0.3	1.1
	0.7	1.0
	1.0	
1.0	1.0	1.0 ·

If CN's price per litre is (£)	There is a probability of	That KL's per litre will be (£)
1.2	0.1	1.2
	0.6	1.1
	0.3	1.0
	1.0	
1.1	0.3	1.1
	0.7	1.0
	1.0	
1.0	1.0	1.0

Costs per litre of the product are as follows:

Direct wages	£0.24
Direct materials	£0.12
Departmental expenses:	
Indirect wages, maintenance and supplies	16⅔% of direct wages
Supervision and depreciation	£540 000 per annum
General works expenses (allocated)	16⅔% of prime cost
Selling and administration expenses (allocated)	50% of manufacturing cost

You are required to state whether, on the basis of the data given above, it would be most advantageous for MD to fix its price per litre for the coming year at £1.2, £1.1 or £1.0.

Support your answer with relevant calculations.

(20 marks)
CIMA P3 Management Accounting

Question 12.10

Advanced: Expected value, maximin and regret criterion

Stow Health Centre specializes in the provision of sports/exercise and medical/dietary advice to clients. The service is provided on a residential basis and clients stay for whatever number of days suits their needs.

Budgeted estimates for the next year ending 30 June are as follows:

(i) The maximum capacity of the centre is 50 clients per day for 350 days in the year.

(ii) Clients will be invoiced at a fee per day. The budgeted occupancy level will vary with the client fee level per day and is estimated at different percentages of maximum capacity as follows:

Client fee per day	Occupancy level	Occupancy as percentage of maximum capacity
£180	High	90%
£200	Most likely	75%
£220	Low	60%

(iii) Variable costs are also estimated at one of three levels per client day. The high, most likely and low levels per client day are £95, £85 and £70 respectively. The range of cost levels reflect only the possible effect of the purchase prices of goods and services.

Required:

(a) Prepare a summary which shows the budgeted contribution earned by Stow Health Centre for the year ended 30 June for each of nine possible outcomes.

(6 marks)

(b) State the client fee strategy for the next year to 30 June which will result from the use of each of the following decision rules:

(i) *maximax;* (ii) *maximin;* (iii) *minimax* regret.

Your answer should explain the basis of operation of each rule. Use the information from your answer to (a) as relevant and show any additional working calculations as necessary.

(9 marks)

(c) The probabilities of variable cost levels occurring at the high, most likely and low levels provided in the question are estimated as 0.1, 0.6 and 0.3 respectively. Using the information available, determine the client fee strategy which will be chosen where maximization of expected value of contribution is used as the decision basis.

(5 marks)

(d) The calculations in (a) to (c) concern contribution levels which may occur given the existing budget.

Stow Health Centre has also budgeted for fixed costs of £1 200 000 for the next year to 30 June.

Discuss ways in which Stow Health Centre may instigate changes, in ways other than through the client fee rate, which may influence client demand, cost levels and profit.

Your answer should include comment on the existing budget and should incorporate illustrations which relate to each of four additional performance measurement areas appropriate to the changes you discuss.

(15 marks)
(Total 35 marks)
ACCA Paper 9 Information for Control and Decision Making

Question 12.11

Advanced: Explanation of risk and uncertainty

The owner, Z, of a business has been attending a course on scenario planning and decision making. As a result of that advice the owner has produced, by using cost volume and profit, analysis 12 scenarios for a new product that the business will launch in the near future. There are four possible marketing packages that could be used (A, B, C or D) and there are three possible market conditions (poor, average or good) that could be encountered. The Net Present Value of the cash flows resulting from each of the scenarios is shown in the table below.

Market conditions	Marketing package			
	A $000	B $000	C $000	D $000
Poor	180	230	220	190
Average	190	200	210	275
Good	550	260	210	500

Unfortunately Z missed the session on how to deal with risk and uncertainty. He has sent the above table to the tutor for the course and has asked for help. The tutor replied 'I will send you some notes. Based on your table you will need the methods in the section on "Uncertainty". If you can estimate the probability of each type of market condition occurring you need "Risk based methods". However, whichever method you use, your decision will be influenced by your attitude.'

Required:

Note: calculations are NOT required.

Explain FOUR methods that could help Z to decide which marketing package to choose. Your answer should include THREE methods to deal with uncertainty. ONE methods to deal with risk, and an explanation of the 'attitude' that would be associated with the decision maker using each of the four methods.

(10 marks)
CIMA P2 Performance Management

Capital investment decisions: appraisal methods

Questions to Chapter 13

Question 13.1

Intermediate

Using an interest rate of 10 per cent per year the net present value (NPV) of a project has been correctly calculated as $50. If the interest rate is increased by 1 per cent the NPV of the project falls by $20.

What is the internal rate of return (IRR) of the project?

(A) 7.5%

(B) 11.7%

(C) 12.5%

(D) 20.0%

ACCA F2 Management Accounting

Question 13.2

Intermediate

Mr Manaton has recently won a competition where he has the choice between receiving $5000 now or an annual amount forever starting now (i.e. a level perpetuity starting immediately). The interest rate is 8 per cent per annum.

What would be the value of the annual perpetuity to the nearest $?

(A) $370

(B) $500

(C) $400

(D) $620

ACCA F2 Management Accounting

Question 13.3

Intermediate

An investor has the choice between two investments. Investment Exe offers interest of 4 per cent per year compounded semi-annually for a period of three years. Investment Wye offers one interest payment of 20 per cent at the end of its four-year life.

What is the annual effective interest rate offered by the two investments?

	Investment Exe	Investment Wye
(A)	4.00%	4.66%
(B)	4.00%	5.00%
(C)	4.04%	4.66%
(D)	4.04%	5.00%

CIMA P1 Performance Operations

Question 13.4

Intermediate

A $100 bond has a yield to maturity of 6 per cent per annum and is due to mature in three years' time. The next interest payment is due in one year's time. Today's market value of the bond is $108.06.

Required:

Calculate the coupon rate on the bond.

(4 marks)
CIMA P1 Performance Operations

Question 13.5

Intermediate

PJ is considering building a warehouse on a piece of land which will be leased at an annual cost of $4000 in perpetuity. The lease payments will be made annually in advance.

PJ has a cost of capital of 12 per cent per annum.

Required:

Calculate the present value of the lease payments.

(3 marks)
CIMA P1 Performance Operations

Question 13.6

Intermediate

A bond has a coupon rate of 6 per cent and will repay its nominal value of $100 when it matures after four years.

The bond will be purchased today for $103 ex-interest and held until maturity.

Required:

Calculate, to 0.01 per cent, the yield to maturity for the bond based on today's purchase price.

(5 marks)
CIMA P1 Performance Operations

Question 13.7

Intermediate

A bond has a coupon rate of 6 per cent per annum and will repay its face value of $100 on its maturity in four years' time. The yield to maturity on similar bonds is 4 per cent per annum. The annual interest has just been paid for the current year.

Required:

Calculate the expected market value of the bond at today's date.

(3 marks)

Question 13.8

Intermediate

A company is considering an investment project that has a life of four years and requires an initial investment of $800 000. Net cash inflows are estimated to be $281 000 per year. The project has a positive net present value of $53 397 when discounted at 12 per cent per annum. Ignore tax and inflation.

Required:

Calculate, to the nearest 1 per cent, the maximum discount rate at which the project will be financially viable.

(3 marks)
CIMA P1 Performance Operations

Question 13.9

Intermediate

An investment project has the following expected cash flows over its economic life of three years:

	(£)
Year 0	(142 700)
1	51 000
2	62 000
3	73 000

Required:

(a) Calculate the net present value (NPV) of the project at discount rates of 0, 10 and 20 per cent respectively.

(b) Draw a graph of the project NPVs calculated in (b) and use the graph to estimate, and clearly indicate, the project internal rate of return (IRR) to the nearest integer percentage.

(8 marks)
ACCA Foundation Stage Paper 3

Question 13.10

Advanced: Comparison of NPV and IRR and relationship between profits and NPV

Khan Ltd is an importer of novelty products. The directors are considering whether to introduce a new product, expected to have a very short economic life. Two alternative methods of promoting the new product are available, details of which are as follows:

Alternative 1 would involve heavy initial advertising and the employment of a large number of agents. The directors expect that an immediate cash outflow of £100 000 would be required (the cost of advertising) which would produce a net cash inflow after one year of £255 000. Agents' commission, amounting to £157 500, would have to be paid at the end of two years.

Alternative 2 would involve a lower outlay on advertising (£50 000, payable immediately), and no use of agents. It would produce net cash inflows of zero after one year and £42 000 at the end of each of the subsequent two years.

Mr Court, a director of Khan Ltd, comments, 'I generally favour the payback method for choosing between investment alternatives such as these. However, I am worried that the advertising expenditure under the second alternative will reduce our reported profit next year by an amount not compensated by any net revenues from sale of the product in that year. For that reason I do not think we should even consider the second alternative.'

The cost of capital of Khan Ltd is 20 per cent per annum. The directors do not expect capital or any other resource to be in short supply during the next three years. You are required to:

(a) calculate the net present values and estimate the internal rates of return of the two methods of promoting the new product;

(10 marks)

(b) advise the directors of Khan Ltd which, if either, method of promotion they should adopt, explaining the reasons for your advice and noting any additional information you think would be helpful in making the decision;

(8 marks)

(c) comment on the views expressed by Mr Court.

(7 marks)

Ignore taxation.

(Total 25 marks)
ICAEW Financial Management

Question 13.11

Advanced: NPV Evaluation of alternative options and profitability index

A bus operator has been experiencing a fall in passenger numbers over the past few years as a result of intense competition from other transport providers. The company directors are concerned to improve profit and are considering two possible alternatives.

Passenger volume last year was 20 000 passengers per day. The average fare was $2 per passenger per day and variable costs per passenger per day were $0.50. If no investment is made the current passenger volume, average fares and variable costs will remain the same on current routes for the next five years. The company operates a full service for 365 days of the year.

Project 1

The company hired a management consultant, at a cost of $50 000, to review the company's fare structure. The consultant recommended that the company reduce fares by 10 per cent which will result in a 20 per cent increase in passenger volume in the first year. In order to maintain this level of passenger numbers, fares will remain at the reduced rate for years 2 to 5.

The increase in passenger numbers will result in the need for four new buses costing $250 000 each. The new buses will be depreciated on a straight line basis over their useful life of five years. They will have no residual value at the end of their useful life. Other annual fixed costs, including advertising costs, will increase by $100 000 in the first year and will remain at that level for the life of the project. Variable costs will remain at $0.50 per passenger per day for the life of the project.

Project 2

Increase the number of buses to enable new routes to be opened. The new buses are expected to cost $5 000 000 in total and have a useful life of five years with no residual value. Fixed costs, including straight line depreciation, are expected to increase by \$3 500 000 in the first year, as a result of opening the new routes. Fixed costs will remain at the higher level for the life of the project. Additional working capital of \$1 000 000 will also be required.

The passenger numbers for year 1 on the new routes are predicted as follows:

Passenger numbers per day	Probability
6 000	50%
9 000	30%
12 000	20%

It is expected that passenger numbers will increase by 3 per cent per annum for the following four years. The average fare per passenger for year 1 will be \$2 and will remain at that level for the life of the project. Variable costs will remain at \$0.50 per passenger per day for the life of the project.

Additional Information

Taxation and inflation should be ignored.

The company uses a cost of capital of 8 per cent per annum.

Required:

(a) (i) Advise the management of the company which project should be undertaken based on a financial appraisal of the projects.

You should use net present value (NPV) to appraise the projects.

(13 marks)

(ii) Explain TWO other major factors that should be considered before a final decision is made.

(4 marks)

(b) Calculate the sensitivity of the choice between Project 1 and Project 2 to a change in passenger numbers for Project 2.

(4 marks)
(Total 21 marks)
CIMA P1 Performance Operations

Question 13.12

Advanced: NPV evaluation of alternative options

All of the 100 accountants employed by X Ltd are offered the opportunity to attend six training courses per year. Each course lasts for several days and requires the delegates to travel to a specially selected hotel for the training. The current costs incurred for each course are:

Delegate costs:

	£ per delegate per course
Travel	200
Accommodation, food and drink	670
	870

It is expected that the current delegate costs will increase by 5 per cent per annum.

Course costs:

	£ per course
Room hire	1 500
Trainers	6 000
Course material	2 000
Equipment hire	1 500
Course administration	750
	11 750

It is expected that the current course costs will increase by 2.5 per cent per annum. The Human Resources Director of X Ltd is concerned at the level of costs that these courses incur and has recently read an article about the use of the internet for the delivery of training courses (e-learning). She decided to hire an external consultant at a cost of £5000 to advise the company on how to implement an e-learning solution. The consultant prepared a report which detailed the costs of implementing and running an e-learning solution:

	Notes	£
Computer hardware	(1)	1 500 000
Software licences	(2)	35 000 per annum
Technical manager	(3)	30 000 per annum
Camera and sound crew	(4)	4 000 per course
Trainers and course material	(5)	2 000 per course
Broadband connection	(6)	300 per delegate per annum

Notes:

(1) The computer hardware will be depreciated on a straight-line basis over five years. The scrap value at the end of the five years is expected to be £50 000.

(2) The company would sign a software licence agreement which fixes the annual software licence fee for five years. This fee is payable in advance.

(3) An employee working in the IT Department currently earning £20 000 per annum will be promoted to technical manager for this project. This employee's position will be replaced. The salary of the technical manager is expected to increase by 6 per cent per annum.

(4) The company supplying the camera and sound crew for recording the courses for internet delivery has agreed to hold its current level of pricing for the first two years but then it will increase costs by 6 per cent per annum. All courses will be recorded in the first quarter of the year of delivery.

(5) The trainers will charge a fixed fee of £2000 per course for the delivery and course material in the first year and expect to increase this by 6 per cent per annum thereafter. The preparation of the course material and the recording of the trainers delivering the courses will take place in the first quarter of the year of delivery.

(6) All of the accountants utilizing the training courses will be offered £300 towards broadband costs which will allow them to access the courses from home. They will claim this expense annually in arrears. Broadband costs are expected to decrease by 5 per cent per annum after the first year as it becomes more widely used by internet users.

X Ltd uses a 14 per cent cost of capital to appraise projects of this nature.

Ignore taxation.

Required:

As the Management Accountant for X Ltd,

(a) prepare a financial evaluation of the options available to the company and advise the directors on the best course of action to take, from a purely financial point of view (your answer should state any assumptions you have made);

(16 marks)

(b)

(i) using the annual equivalent technique (see Learning Note 14.1 on the accompanying website), calculate the breakeven number of delegates per annum taking each of the six e-learning courses that is required to justify the implementation of the e-learning solution (you should assume that the number of delegates taking the e-learning courses will be the same in each of the five years);

(6 marks)

(ii) comment on the implications of the breakeven number you have calculated in your answer to (b) (i).

(3 marks)
(Total 25 marks)
CIMA Management Accounting – Decision Making

Question 13.13

Advanced: NPV calculations for alternative options

Amber plc operates a daily return high-speed train service between the UK and mainland Europe, via the channel tunnel. In an attempt to reduce overheads, the company is considering using an outside supplier to take over responsibility for all on-train catering services. Amber invited tenders for a five-year contract, and at the same time the senior management accountant drafted a schedule of costs for in-house provision of an equivalent service. This cost schedule, together with the details of the lowest price tender which was received, are given below. (See Table 13.1 and additional information.)

TABLE 13.1 *In-House Provision of Train Catering Services Schedule of Costs, Amber plc*

Variable costs	Pence per £ sales
Direct material	55
Variable overhead	12
Fixed costs (allocated to products)	
Labour (Year 1)	10
Purchase/storage management	3
Depreciation (catering equipment)	4
Insurance	2
Total cost	86

The train service operates 360 days per year and a single restaurant carriage is adequate to service the catering needs of a train carrying up to 600 passengers. The tendered contract (and the in-house schedule of costs) is for the provision of one catering carriage per train. Past sales data indicates that 45 per cent of passengers will use the catering service, spending an average of £4.50 each per single journey, or £9.00 per return journey. This is expected to remain unchanged over the next five years, unless Amber invests in quality improvements.

Statistical forecasts of the level of demand for the train service, under differing average weather conditions and average exchange rates over the next five years are shown in Table 13.2.

TABLE 13.2 *Forecast Passenger Figures (per single journey)*

Exchange rate Euro/£	UK weather conditions		
	Poor	Reasonable	Good
1.52	500	460	420
1.54	550	520	450
1.65	600	580	500

The differing weather conditions are all assumed to be equally likely.

Based upon historical trends, the probability of each different exchange rate occurring is estimated as follows:

Rate €/£	Probability
1.52	0.2
1.54	0.5
1.65	0.3

Additional information

(1) Labour costs are expected to rise at a rate of 5 per cent per year over the next five years.

(2) Variable costs per pound sales are expected to remain unchanged over the next five years.

(3) Some catering equipment will need to be replaced at the end of Year 2 at a cost of £500 000. This would increase the depreciation charge on catering equipment to 5 pence per pound sales. The equipment value at the end of Year 5 is estimated to be £280 000.

(4) The outside supplier (lowest price tender) has agreed to purchase immediately (for cash) the existing catering equipment owned by Amber plc at a price equal to the current book value, i.e. £650 000. The supplier would charge Amber a flat fee of £250 per day for the provision of this catering service, and Amber would receive 5 per cent of gross catering receipts where these exceeded an average of £2200 per day in each 360-day period. The quality of the catering service is expected to be unaffected by the contracting out.

(5) In the event of Amber deciding to contract out the catering, the following fixed costs will be saved:

Depreciation	£35 000 per year
Purchasing/storage costs	£18 000 per year
Insurance	£3 000 per year
Labour costs	£74 844 (Year 1)

(6) The cost of capital for Amber plc is 12 per cent.

Assume that all cash flows occur at the end of each year. Taxation may be ignored in answering this question.

Required:

(a) Calculate the expected number of passengers per single journey for the train service.

(5 marks)

(b) Draft a table of annual cash flows and, using discounted cash flow analysis, determine which of the two alternatives (in-house provision or contracting out) is preferred.

(16 marks)

(c) Calculate and comment upon the financial effect on the decision of a forecast 10 per cent increase in the number of passengers purchasing food and beverages on each train if the in-house catering service were to be improved. Any such improvement would require Amber investing £10 000 per year over five years on staff training.

(7 marks)

(d) Comment on the limitations of using demand forecasts, such as that given in Table 13.2, for the purposes of the decision in question.

(5 marks)

(e) Identify and critically comment upon three non-financial factors which need to be taken into account when a business is considering this type of decision.

(7 marks)
(Total 40 marks)
CIMA Management Accounting – Decision Making

Question 13.14

Advanced: Evaluation of a proposed investment of computer integrated manufacturing equipment and a discussion of NPV and ARR

Abert, the production manager of Blom plc, a manufacturer of precision tools, has recently attended a major international exhibition on Computer Integrated Manufacturing (CIM). He has read of the improvements in product quality and profitability achieved by companies which have switched to this new technology. In particular, his Japanese competitors are believed to use CIM equipment extensively. Abert is sufficiently concerned about his company's future to commission a report from Saint-Foix Ltd, a vendor of CIM equipment, as to the appropriateness of utilizing CIM for all his manufacturing operations.

The report, which has recently been prepared, suggests that the following costs and benefits will accrue to Blom plc as a result of investing in an appropriate CIM system:

(1) *Costs of implementing CIM*

   (i) Capital equipment costs will be £40m. The equipment will have an estimated life of 10 years, after which time its disposal value will be £10m.

   (ii) Proper use of the equipment will require the substantial re-training of current employees. As a result of the necessary changes in the production process, and the time spent on retraining, Blom plc will lose production (and sales) in its first two years of implementation. The lost production (and sales) will cost the company £10m per annum.

   (iii) The annual costs of writing software and maintaining the computer equipment will be £4m.

(2) *Benefits of implementing CIM*

   (i) The use of CIM will enhance the quality of Blom plc's products. This will lead to less reworking of products, and a consequent reduction in warranty costs. The annual cost savings are expected to be £12m per annum.

   (ii) The CIM equipment will use less floor space than the existing machinery. As a result one existing factory will no longer be needed. It is estimated that the factory can be let at an annual rental of £2m.

   (iii) Better planning and flow of work will result in an immediate reduction in the existing levels of working capital from £13m to £8m.

The directors of Blom plc currently require all investments to generate a positive net present value at a cost of capital of 15 per cent and to show an accounting rate of return in the first year of at least 15 per cent. You may assume that all cash flows arise at the end of the year, except for those relating to the equipment and re-training costs, and the reduction in working capital. It is Blom plc's intention to capitalize re-training costs for management accounting purposes.

Requirements:

(a) Determine whether Blom plc should invest in the CIM technology on the basis of its existing investment criteria.

(10 marks)

(b) Discuss possible reasons as to why Blom plc currently requires its long-term investments to meet both the net present value and the accounting rate of return criteria.

(8 marks)

(c) Discuss the additional factors Blom plc should consider when deciding whether to switch to CIM technology.

(7 marks)
(Total 25 marks)
ICAEW P2 Financial Management

Capital investment decisions: the impact of capital rationing, taxation, inflation and risk

Questions to Chapter 14

Question 14.1

Advanced

A five year investment project has a positive net present value of $320 000 when discounted at the cost of capital of 10 per cent per annum. The project includes annual net cash inflows of $100 000 which occur at the end of each of the five years.

The percentage reduction in the annual net cash inflow that would result in the project not being financially viable is:

(A) 31.25%

(B) 118.5%

(C) 84.4%

(D) 18.5%

(2 marks)
CIMA P1 Performance Operations

Question 14.2

Advanced

A company's management is considering investing in a project with an expected life of four years. It has a positive net present value of $180 000 when cash flows are discounted at 8 per cent per annum. The project's cash flows include a cash outflow of $100 000 for each of the four years. No tax is payable on projects of this type.

The percentage increase in the annual cash outflow that would cause the company's management to reject the project from a financial perspective is, to the nearest 0.1 per cent:

(A) 54.3%

(B) 45.0%

(C) 55.6%

(D) 184.0%

(2 marks)
CIMA P1 Performance Operations

Question 14.3

Advanced: Equivalent annual cost to determine optimum replacement cycle (this question incorporates material relating to Learning Note 14.1)

ST needs to replace its fleet of delivery vans and is considering two alternative types of van as the replacement. One of the vans has an estimated life of four years whilst the other has an estimated life of five years. The vans will be required for the foreseeable future.

The estimated cash flows over the life of the van are given below:

Year	Van A $	Van B $
0	(25 000)	(30 000)
1	(2 000)	(3 000)
2	(2 000)	(3 000)
3	(3 000)	(3 000)
4	5 000	(4 000)
5		(6 000)

The company's cost of capital is 8 per cent per annum.

Required:

Demonstrate, by calculation, which of the two vans should be purchased.

(5 marks)
CIMA P1 Performance Operations

Question 14.4

Advanced: Expected NPV and capital rationing

The Independent Film Company plc is a film distribution company which purchases distribution rights on films from small independent producers, and sells the films on to cinema chains for national and international screening. In recent years the company has found it difficult to source sufficient films to maintain profitability. In response to the problem, the Independent Film Company has decided to invest in commissioning and producing films in its own right. In order to gain the expertise for this venture, the Independent Film Company is considering purchasing an existing filmmaking concern, at a cost of £400 000. The main difficulty that is anticipated for the business is the increasing uncertainty as to the potential success/failure rate of independently produced films. Many cinema chains are adopting a policy of only buying films from large international film companies, as they believe that the market for independent films is very limited and specialist in nature. The Independent Film Company is prepared for the fact that they are likely to have more films that fail than that succeed, but believe that the proposed film production business will nonetheless be profitable.

Using data collected from the existing distribution business and discussions with industry experts, they have produced cost and revenue forecasts for the five years of operation of the proposed investment. The company aims to complete the production of three films per year. The after tax cost of capital for the company is estimated to be 14 per cent.

Year 1 sales for the new business are uncertain, but expected to be in the range of £4–10 million. Probability estimates for different forecast values are as follows:

Sales (£ million)	Probability
4	0.2
5	0.4
7	0.3
10	0.1

Sales are expected to grow at an annual rate of 5 per cent. Anticipated costs related to the new business are as follows:

Cost type	£'000
Purchase of film-making company	400
Annual legal and professional costs	20
Annual lease rental (office equipment)	12
Studio and set hire (per film)	180
Camera/specialist equipment hire (per film)	40
Technical staff wages (per film)	520
Screenplay (per film)	50
Actors' salaries (per film)	700
Costumes and wardrobe hire (per film)	60
Set design and painting (per film)	150
Annual non-production staff wages	60

Additional information:

(i)   No capital allowances are available.

(ii) Tax is payable one year in arrears, at a rate of 33 per cent and full use can be made of tax refunds as they fall due.

(iii) Staff wages (technical and non-production staff) and actors' salaries, are expected to rise by 10 per cent per annum.

(iv) Studio hire costs will be subject to an increase of 30 per cent in Year 3.

(v)   Screenplay costs per film are expected to rise by 15 per cent per annum due to a shortage of skilled writers.

(vi) The new business will occupy office accommodation which has to date been let out for an annual rent of £20 000. Demand for such accommodation is buoyant and the company anticipates no problems in finding future tenants at the same annual rent.

(vii) A market research survey into the potential for the film production business cost £25 000.

Required:

(a) Using DCF analysis, calculate the expected net present value of the proposed investment. (Workings should be rounded to the nearest £000.)

(15 marks)

(b) Outline the main limitations of using expected values when making investment decisions.

(6 marks)

(c) In addition to the possible purchase of the film-making business, the company has two other investment opportunities, the details of which are given below:

	Year 0	Year 1	Year 2	Year 3	Year 4	Year 5	Year 6
			Post-tax cash flows, £'000				
Investment X	(200)	200	200	150	100	100	100
Investment Y	(100)	80	80	40	40	40	40

The Independent Film Company has a total of £400 000 available for capital investment in the current year. No project can be invested in more than once.

Required:

(i) Define the term profitability index, and briefly explain how it may be used when a company faces a problem of capital rationing in any single accounting period.

(4 marks)

(ii) Calculate the profitability index for each of the investment projects available to the Independent Film Company, i.e. purchase of the film production company, Investment X and Investment Y, and outline the optimal investment strategy. Assume that all of the projects are indivisible.

(6 marks)

(iii) Explain the limitations of using a profitability index in a situation where there is capital rationing.

(4 marks)

(d) Briefly explain how the tax treatment of capital purchases can affect an investment decision.

(5 marks)
(Total 40 marks)
ACCA Paper 8 – Managerial Finance

Question 14.5

Advanced: Inflation adjustments and sensitivity analysis

Burley plc, a manufacturer of building products, mainly supplies the wholesale trade. It has recently suffered falling demand due to economic recession, and thus has spare capacity. It now perceives an opportunity to produce designer ceramic tiles for the home improvement market. It has already paid £0.5m for development expenditure, market research and a feasibility study. The initial analysis reveals scope for selling 150 000 boxes per annum over a five-year period at a price of £20 per box. Estimated operating costs, largely based on experience, are as follows: Cost per box of tiles (£) (at today's prices):

Material cost	8.00
Direct labour	2.00
Variable overhead	1.50
Fixed overhead (allocated)	1.50
Distribution, etc.	2.00

Production can take place in existing facilities although initial re-design and setup costs would be £2m after allowing for all relevant tax reliefs. Returns from the project would be taxed at 33 per cent.

Burley's shareholders require a nominal return of 14 per cent per annum after tax, which includes allowance for generally expected inflation of 5.5 per cent per annum. It can be assumed that all operating cash flows occur at year ends.

Required:

(a) Assess the financial desirability of this venture in real terms, finding both the net present value and the internal rate of return to the nearest 1 per cent) offered by the project.

Note: Assume no tax delay.

(7 marks)

(b) Briefly explain the purpose of sensitivity analysis in relation to project appraisal, indicating the drawbacks with this procedure.

(6 marks)

(c) Determine the values of

    (i)   price

    (ii) volume

at which the project's NPV becomes zero.

Discuss your results, suggesting appropriate management action.

(7 marks)
(Total 20 marks)
ACCA Paper 8 Managerial Finance

Question 14.6

Advanced: NPV, IRR, payback, inflation and taxation

EF operates tourist attractions in major capital cities. The company is considering opening a new attraction in Eastern Europe.

The initial capital investment will be $120 million. EF plans to operate the attraction for five years after which it will be sold to another operator at an estimated price $50 million at Year 5 prices.

A market research survey has estimated the following visitor numbers and associated probabilities, revenue and operating costs:

Revenue and variable costs

Number of visitors per year	Probability
1.2 million	30%
0.8 million	50%
0.6 million	20%

It is expected that the number of visitors per year will remain constant for the life of the project.

The entrance fee for the attraction will be $40. Each visitor is expected to spend an average of $15 on souvenirs and $5 on refreshments.

The variable costs are estimated to be $25 per visitor. This includes the variable cost of operating the attraction and the cost of souvenirs and refreshments.

Fixed operating costs

The company will lease the land on which the attraction is to be situated at a cost of $500 000 per annum. The lease cost will remain the same throughout the life of the project.

Maintenance costs are estimated to be $200 000 per annum.

Inflation

All of the values above, other than the amount payable by the purchaser at the end of the five year period, have been expressed in terms of current prices. The lease cost of $500 000 per annum will apply throughout the life of the project and is not subject to inflation.

A general rate of inflation of 4 per cent per annum is expected to apply to all revenues and costs, excluding the lease cost throughout the life of the project, starting in Year 1.

Other information

The company uses net present value based on the expected values of cash flow when evaluating projects of this type.

The company has a money cost of capital of 12 per cent per annum.

The company's Financial Director has provided the following taxation information:

- The initial investment will qualify for tax depreciation at 25 per cent of the reducing balance per annum with a balancing adjustment in the year of disposal.
- The first claim for tax deprecation will be made against the profits from Year 1.
- Taxation rate: 30 per cent of taxable profits. Half of the tax is payable in the year in which it arises, the balance is payable in the following year.

All cash flows apart from the initial investment of $120 million should be assumed to occur at the end of the year.

Required:

(a) Evaluate the project from a financial perspective. You should use net present value as the basis of you revaluation and show your workings in $000.

(14 marks)

(b) (i) Calculate the internal rate of return (IRR) of the project.

(4 marks)

(ii) Calculate the payback period for the project. You should assume for this purpose that all cash flows occur evenly throughout the year.

(3 marks)

(c) Explain the difference between the real cost of capital and the money cost of capital. You should include a numerical example to illustrate your answer.

(4 marks)
(Total 25 marks)
CIMA P1 Performance Operations

Question 14.7

Advanced: NPV, payback and taxation

JK is a profitable international pharmaceutical company that develops, produces and markets drugs that are licensed as medication. The pharmaceutical industry has grown rapidly and faces challenges in preventing and controlling environmental pollution. Over the past few years there has been growing pressure on the industry from government, shareholders and other stakeholders to improve its environmental management performance. JK has taken a proactive approach to environmental management and has invested significant resources introducing pollution prevention and clean manufacturing practices into its operation in order to reduce waste and minimize negative environmental impacts. The company has used marketing and advertising campaigns to develop an image as a company that is at the cutting edge of 'green' technology.

As part of its environmental management programme, JK is considering investing in a new system that will significantly reduce hazardous emissions and waste.

The estimates for the proposed investment are as follows:

Initial investment	$60 million
Useful life	6 years
Residual value	$12 million
Annual income from sale of recycled waste	$5 million
Annual savings in waste disposal costs	$5.5 million
Annual fixed maintenance costs per annum	$1.5 million
Other annual fixed operating costs per annum (including depreciation)	$10.6 million

JK has experienced a number of external environmental failures over the past few years which have resulted in total costs to JK, including government fines, of $20 million per annum. The environmental officer has estimated that, as a direct result of this investment, future external environmental failure costs that will be borne by JK and their associated probabilities are as follows:

Annual external environmental failure costs	Probability
$18 million	30%
$12 million	25%
$10 million	35%
$5 million	10%

The company uses expected value for this type of analysis.

Depreciation of the initial investment will be calculated using the straight line method and has been included in other fixed operating costs.

The company's financial director has provided the following taxation information:

• Tax depreciation: 25 per cent per annum of the reducing balance, with a balancing adjustment in the year of disposal.
• Taxation rate: 30 per cent of taxable profits. Half of the tax is payable in the year in which it arises, the balance is paid in the following year.

The company uses a cost of capital of 12 per cent per annum to evaluate projects of this type. Ignore inflation.

Required:

(a) Evaluate the investment in the proposed system using net present value as the basis of your evaluation. Your workings should be shown in $m to one decimal place.

(13 marks)

(b) (i) Calculate the payback period for the investment.

(3 marks)

(ii) Discuss the advantages and disadvantages of payback as a method of investment appraisal.

(5 marks)

(c) Explain TWO factors related to JK's approach to environmental issues that should be considered before making a final decision about the project.

(4 marks)
(Total 25 marks)
CIMA P1 Performance Operations

Question 14.8

Advanced: NPV, taxation and equivalent annual cost to determine optimum replacement cycle (this question incorporates material relating to Learning Note 14.1)

A car rental company is considering setting up a division to provide chauffeur driven limousines for weddings and other events. The proposed investment will include the purchase of a fleet of 20 limousines at a cost of $200 000 each. It is estimated that the limousines will have a useful life of five years and a resale value of $30 000 each at the end of their useful life. The company uses the straight line method of depreciation.

Revenue and variable costs

Each limousine will be hired to customers for $800 per day. The variable costs, including fuel, cleaning and the chauffeur's wages, will be $300 per day. The limousines will be available for hire 350 days of the year. A market specialist was hired at a cost of $20 000 to estimate the demand for the limousines in Year 1. The market specialist estimated that each limousine will be hired for 260 days in Year 1 and that the number of days' hire will increase by ten days each year for the remaining life of the project.

Fixed costs

Each limousine will incur fixed costs, including maintenance and depreciation, of $45 000 a year. The administration of the division is expected to cost $300 000 each year. The garaging of the limousines will not require any additional investment but will utilize existing facilities for which there is no other use. The head office will charge the division an annual fee of 10 per cent of sales revenue for the use of these facilities.

Taxation

The company's financial director has provided the following taxation information:

• Tax depreciation: 25 per cent per annum of the reducing balance, with a balancing adjustment in the year of disposal. The limousines will be eligible for tax depreciation.
• Taxation rate: 30 per cent of taxable profits. Half of the tax is payable in the year in which it arises, the balance is paid in the following year.

Other information

Ignore inflation.

The company uses a cost of capital of 12 per cent per annum to evaluate projects of this type.

Required:

(a) Evaluate whether the company should go ahead with the project. You should use net present value as the basis of your evaluation.

(14 marks)

The company is also carrying out a review of its existing car rental business. The company is deciding whether it should replace the cars that it uses after one, two or three years. The cars will not be kept longer than three years due to the higher risk of breakdowns.

The estimated relevant cash flows for the three possible options for each car can be obtained from the following information:

Year	Cash outflows $	Residual Value $
0	(30 000)	
1	(1 500)	21 000
2	(2 700)	15 000
3	(3 600)	9 000

The company uses a cost of capital of 12 per cent for decisions of this type.

Required:

(b) Calculate, using the annualized equivalent method, whether the cars should be replaced after one, two or three years. You should ignore taxation and inflation.

(7 marks)

(c) Explain the limitations of the annualized equivalent method for making decisions to replace non-current assets.

(4 marks)
(Total 25 marks)
CIMA P1 Performance Operations

Question 14.9

Advanced: NPV calculation, choice of discount rate and sensitivity analysis

The managing director of Tigwood Ltd believes that a market exists for 'microbooks'. He has proposed that the company should market 100 best-selling books on microfiche which can be read using a special microfiche reader that is connected to a television screen. A microfiche containing an entire book can be purchased from a photographic company at 40 per cent of the average production cost of best-selling paperback books.

It is estimated that the average cost of producing paperback books is £1.50, and the average selling price of paperbacks is £3.95 each. Copyright fees of 20 per cent of the average selling price of the paperback books would be payable to the publishers of the paperbacks plus an initial lump sum which is still being negotiated, but is expected to be £1.5 million. No tax allowances are available on this lump sum payment. An agreement with the publishers would be signed for a period of six years. Additional variable costs of staffing, handling and marketing are 20 pence per microfiche, and fixed costs are negligible.

Tigwood Ltd has spent £100 000 on market research, and expects sales to be 1 500 000 units per year at an initial unit price of £2.

The microfiche reader would be produced and marketed by another company.

Tigwood would finance the venture with a bank loan at an interest rate of 16 per cent per year. The company's money (nominal) cost of equity and real cost of equity are estimated to be 23 per cent per year and 12.6 per cent per year respectively. Tigwood's money weighted average cost of capital and real weighted average cost of capital are 18 per cent per year and 8 per cent per year respectively. The risk free rate of interest is 11 per cent per year and the market return is 17 per cent per year.

Corporate tax is at the rate of 35 per cent, payable in the year the profit occurs. All cash flows may be assumed to be at the year end, unless otherwise stated.

Required:

(a) Calculate the expected net present value of the microbooks project.

(5 marks)

(b) Explain the reasons for your choice of discount rate in your answer to part (a). Discuss whether this rate is likely to be the most appropriate rate to use in the analysis of the proposed project.

(5 marks)

(c) (i) Using sensitivity analysis, estimate by what percentage each of the following would have to change before the project was no longer expected to be viable:

initial outlay

annual contribution

the life of the agreement

the discount rate.

(ii) What are the limitations of this sensitivity analysis?

(10 marks)

(d) What further information would be useful to help the company decide whether to undertake the microbook project?

(5 marks)
(Total 25 marks)
ACCA Level 3 Financial Management

The budgeting process

Questions to Chapter 15

Question 15.1

Intermediate

A company has the following budget for the next month:

Finished product	
Sales	7 000 units
Production units	7 200 units

Materials	
Usage per unit	3kg
Opening stock	400kg
Closing stock	500kg

What is the material purchases budget for the month?

(A) 20 900kg

(B) 21 100kg

(C) 21 500kg

(D) 21 700kg.

ACCA – Financial Information for Management

Question 15.2

Intermediate

H has a budgeted production for the next budget year of 12 000 units spread evenly over the year. It expects the same production level to continue for the next two years. Each unit uses 4kg of material.

The estimated opening raw material inventory at the start of the next budget year is 3000kg. H's future policy will be to hold sufficient raw material inventory at the end of each month to cover 110 per cent of the following month's production.

The budgeted material cost is $8 per kg for purchases up to 49 000kg. The excess of purchases over 49 000kg in a year will be at cost of $7.50 per kg.

Calculate the material purchases budget for the year in $.

(3 marks)
CIMA P1 Performance Operations

Question 15.3

Advanced

You have recently been appointed as an assistant management accountant in a large company, PC Co. When you meet the production manager, you overhear him speaking to one of his staff, saying:

'Budgeting is a waste of time. I don't see the point of it. It tells us what we can't afford but it doesn't keep us from buying it. It simply makes us invent new ways of manipulating figures. If all levels of management aren't involved in the setting of the budget, they might as well not bother preparing one.'

Required:

(a) Identify and explain SIX objectives of a budgetary control system.

(9 marks)

(b) Discuss the concept of a participative style of budgeting in terms of the six objectives identified in part (a).

(11 marks)
(Total 20 marks)
ACCAF5 Performance Management

Question 15.4

Advanced

'Public sector organizations are often judged by their economy, efficiency and effectiveness. Consequently they should use an approach to budgeting other than incremental budgeting.'

Required:

Explain ONE advantage and TWO disadvantages of public sector organizations using incremental budgeting.

(5 marks)
CIMA P1 Performance Operations

Question 15.5

Intermediate

PP is a telecoms provider. It has been operating for five years and has experienced good results; profits have increased by an average of 15 per cent each year. It is accepted within the company that this success has been the result of the continuous stream of new and varied 'cutting edge' products that PP offers. The Research and Development Division has enjoyed the freedom of working with the directive of 'Be creative'.

The Director of the Research and Development Division of PP is not happy. At a recent board meeting she said:

'The Research and Development Division is finding it extremely difficult to maintain its current levels of achievement. The Division is suffering from a lack of funds as a result of PP's budgeting system. We receive an uplift of 5 per cent each year from the previous year's budget. This does not provide the necessary funds or freedom to be able to keep the company ahead of the competition. I would like to see incremental budgeting replaced by zero based budgeting in my division'.

Required:

Discuss the potential disadvantages of implementing zero based budgeting for the allocation of funds to the Research and Development Division from the perspective of the Director of Research and Development.

(10 marks)
CIMA P2 Performance Management

Question 15.6

Advanced

Traditional budgeting systems are incremental in nature and tend to focus on cost centres. Activity based budgeting links strategic planning to overall performance measurement aiming at continuous improvement.

(a) Explain the weaknesses of an incremental budgeting system.

(5 marks)

(b) Describe the main features of an activity based budgeting system and comment on the advantages claimed for its use.

(10 marks)
(Total 15 marks)
ACCA Paper 9 Information for Control and Decision Making

Question 15.7

Advanced

Budgeting has been criticized as

- a cumbersome process which occupies considerable management time;
- concentrating unduly on short-term financial control;
- having undesirable effects on the motivation of managers;
- emphasizing formal organization structure.

Requirements:

(a) Explain these criticisms.

(8 marks)

(b) Explain what changes can be made in response to these criticisms to improve the budgeting process.

(12 marks)
(Total 20 marks)
CIMA Stage 4 Management Accounting

Question 15.8

Advanced

For a number of years, the research division of Z plc has produced its annual budget (for new and continuing projects) using incremental budgeting techniques. The company is now under new management and the annual budget for the next year is to be prepared using zero based budgeting techniques.

Required:

(a) Explain the differences between incremental and zero based budgeting techniques.

(5 marks)

(b) Explain how Z plc could operate a zero based budgeting system for its research projects.

(8 marks)

The operating divisions of Z plc have in the past always used a traditional approach to analyzing costs into their fixed and variable components. A single measure of activity was used, which, for simplicity, was the number of units produced. The new management does not accept that such a simplistic approach is appropriate for budgeting in the modern environment and has requested that the managers adopt an activity-based approach to their budgets.

Required:

(c)

(i) Briefly explain activity-based budgeting (ABB).

(3 marks)

(ii) Explain how activity-based budgeting would be implemented by the operating divisions of Z plc.

(9 marks)
(Total 25 marks)
CIMA Management Accounting – Performance Management

Question 15.9

Intermediate: Budget preparation and flexible budgets

X Plc manufactures specialist insulating products that are used in both residential and commercial buildings. One of the products, Product W, is made using two different raw materials and two types of labour. The company operates a standard absorption costing system and is now preparing its budgets for the next four quarters. The following information has been identified for Product W:

Sales	
Selling price	£220 per unit
Sales demand	
Quarter 1	2 250 units
Quarter 2	2 050 units
Quarter 3	1 650 units
Quarter 4	2 050 units
Quarter 5	1 250 units
Quarter 6	2 050 units

Costs	
Materials	
A	5kg per unit @ £4 per kg
B	3kg per unit @ £7 per kg
Labour	
Skilled	4 hours per unit @ £15 per hour
Semi-skilled	6 hours per unit @ £9 per hour
Annual overheads	£280 000

40 per cent of these overheads are fixed and the remainder varies with total labour hours. Fixed overheads are absorbed on a unit basis.

Inventory holiday policy	
Closing inventory of finished goods	30 per cent of the following quarter's sales demand
Closing inventory of materials	45 per cent of the following quarter's materials usage

The management team are concerned that X Plc has recently faced increasing competition in the market place for Product W. As a consequence there have been issues concerning the availability and costs of the specialized materials and employees needed to manufacture Product W, and there is concern that these might cause problems in the current budget setting process.

(a) Prepare the following budgets for each quarter for X Plc:

  (i) production budget in units;

  (ii) raw material purchases budget in kgs and value for Material B.

(5 marks)

(b) X Plc has just been informed that Material A may be in short supply during the year for which it is preparing budgets. Discuss the impact this will have on budget preparation and other areas of X Plc.

(5 marks)

(c) Assuming that the budgeted production of Product W was 7700 units and that the following actual results were incurred for labour and overheads in the year:

Actual production	7 250 units
Actual overheads	
Variable	£185 000
Fixed	£105 000
Actual labour costs	
Skilled – £16.25 per hour	£568 750
Semi-skilled – £8 per hour	£332 400

Prepare a flexible budget statement for X Plc showing the total variances that have occurred for the above four costs only.

(5 marks)

(d) X Plc currently uses incremental budgeting. Explain how zero based budgeting could overcome the problems that might be faced as a result of the continued use of the current system.

(5 marks)

(e) Explain how rolling budgets are used and why they would be suitable for X Plc.

(5 marks)
(Total 25 marks)
CIMA P1 Management Accounting: Performance Evaluation

Question 15.10

Intermediate: Preparation of functional budgets and budgeted profit statement

A division of Bud plc is engaged in the manual assembly of finished products F1 and F2 from bought-in components. These products are sold to external customers. The budgeted sales volumes and prices for month 9 are as follows:

Product	Units	Price
F1	34 000	£50.00
F2	58 000	£30.00

Finished goods stockholding budgeted for the end of month 9, is 1000 units of F1 and 2000 units of F2, with no stock at the beginning of that month. The purchased components C3 and C4 are used in the finished products in the quantities shown below. The unit price is for just-in-time delivery of the components; the company holds no component stocks.

	Component	
Product	C3	C4
F1 (per unit)	8 units	4 units
F2 (per unit)	4 units	3 units
Price (each)	£1.25	£1.80

The standard direct labour times and labour rates and the budgeted monthly manufacturing overhead costs for the assembly and finishing departments for month 9 are given below:

Product	Assembly	Finishing
F1 (per unit)	30 minutes	12 minutes
F2 (per unit)	15 minutes	10 minutes
Labour rate (per hour)	£10.00	£12.00
Manufacturing overhead cost for the month	£617 500	£204 000

Every month a predetermined direct labour hour recovery rate is computed in each department for manufacturing overhead and applied to items produced in that month.

The selling overhead of £344 000 per month is applied to products based on a predetermined percentage of the budgeted sales value in each month.

Required:

(a) Prepare summaries of the following budgets for month 9:

 (i) component purchase and usage (units and value);

 (ii) direct labour (hours and value);

 (iii) departmental manufacturing overhead recovery rates;

 (iv) selling overhead recovery rate;

 (v) stock value at the month-end.

(8 marks)

(b) Tabulate the standard unit cost and profit of each of F1 and F2 in month 9.

(3 marks)

(c) Prepare a budgeted profit and loss account for month 9 which clearly incorporates the budget values obtained in (a) above.

(3 marks)

(d) Explain clearly the implications of the company's treatment of manufacturing overheads, i.e. computing a monthly overhead rate, compared to a predetermined overhead rate prepared annually.

(6 marks)
(Total 20 marks)
ACCA Paper 8 Managerial Finance

Question 15.11

Intermediate: Preparation of functional budgets, cash budget and master budget

The budgeted balance sheet data of Kwan Tong Umbago Ltd is as follows:

1 March

	Cost (£)	Depreciation to date (£)	Net (£)
Fixed assets			
Land and buildings	500 000	—	500 000
Machinery and equipment	124 000	84 500	39 500
Motor vehicles	42 000	16 400	25 600
	666 000	100 900	565 100
Working capital: Current assets			
Stock of raw materials (100 units)		4 320	
Stock of finished goods (110 units)[a]		10 450	
Debtors (January £7 680 February £10 400)		18 080	
Cash and bank		6 790	
Less current liabilities		39 640	
Creditors		3 900	35 740
(raw materials)			600 840

Represented by:

Ordinary share capital (fully paid) £1 shares	500 000
Share premium	60 000
Profit and loss account	40 840
	600 840

*ᵃThe stock of finished goods was valued at marginal cost

The estimates for the next four-month period are as follows:

	March	April	May	June
Sales (units)	80	84	96	94
Production (units)	70	75	90	90
Purchases of raw materials (units)	80	80	85	85
Wages and variable overheads at £65 per unit	£4 550	£4 875	£5 850	£5 850
Fixed overheads	£1 200	£1 200	£1 200	£1 200

The company intends to sell each unit for £219 and has estimated that it will have to pay £45 per unit for raw materials. One unit of raw material is needed for each unit of finished product.

All sales and purchases of raw materials are on credit. Debtors are allowed two months' credit and suppliers of raw materials are paid after one month's credit. The wages, variable overheads and fixed overheads are paid in the month in which they are incurred.

Cash from a loan secured on the land and buildings of £120 000 at an interest rate of 7.5 per cent is due to be received on 1 May. Machinery costing £112 000 will be received in May and paid for in June.

The loan interest is payable half yearly from September onwards. An interim dividend to 31 March of £12 500 will be paid in June. Depreciation for the four months, including that on the new machinery is:

Machinery and equipment	£15 733
Motor vehicles	£3 500

The company uses the FIFO method of stock valuation. Ignore taxation.

Required:

(a) Calculate and present the raw materials budget and finished goods budget in terms of units, for each month from March to June inclusive.

(5 marks)

(b) Calculate the corresponding sales budgets, the production cost budgets and the budgeted closing debtors, creditors and stocks in terms of value.

(5 marks)

(c) Prepare and present a cash budget for each of the four months.

(6 marks)

(d) Prepare a master budget, i.e. a budgeted trading and profit and loss account, for the four months to 30 June, and budgeted balance sheet as at 30 June.

(10 marks)

(e) Advise the company about possible ways in which it can improve its cash management.

(9 marks)
(Total 35 marks)
ACCA Paper 8 Managerial Finance

Question 15.12

Intermediate: Preparation of cash budgets

The management of Beck plc have been informed that the union representing the direct production workers at one of their factories, where a standard product is produced, intends to call a strike. The accountant has been asked to advise the management of the effect the strike will have on cash flow. The following data have been made available:

	Week 1	Week 2	Week 3
Budgeted sales	400 units	500 units	400 units
Budgeted production	600 units	400 units	nil

The strike will commence at the beginning of week 3 and it should be assumed that it will continue for at least four weeks. Sales at 400 units per week will continue to be made during the period of the strike until stocks of finished goods are exhausted. Production will stop at the end of week 2. The current stock level of finished goods is 600 units. Stocks of work in progress are not carried.

The selling price of the product is £60 and the budgeted manufacturing cost is made up as follows:

	(£)
Direct materials	15
Direct wages	7
Variable overheads	8
Fixed overheads	18
Total	£48

Direct wages are regarded as a variable cost. The company operates a full absorption costing system and the fixed overhead absorption rate is based upon a budgeted fixed overhead of £9000 per week. Included in the total fixed overheads is £700 per week for depreciation of equipment. During the period of the strike direct wages and variable overheads would not be incurred and the cash expended on fixed overheads would be reduced by £1500 per week.

The current stock of raw materials are worth £7500; it is intended that these stocks should increase to £11 000 by the end of week 1 and then remain at this level during the period of the strike. *All direct materials are paid for one week after they have been received. Direct wages are paid one week in arrears. It should be assumed that all relevant overheads are paid for immediately the expense is incurred.* All sales are on credit, 70 per cent of the sales value is received in cash from the debtors at the end of the first week after the sales have been made and the balance at the end of the second week.

The current amount outstanding to material suppliers is £8000 and direct wage accruals amount to £3200. Both of these will be paid in week 1. The current balance owing from debtors is £31 200, of which £24 000 will be received during week 1 and the remainder during week 2. The current balance of cash at bank and in hand is £1000.

Required:

(a)

(i) Prepare a cash budget for weeks 1 to 6 showing the balance of cash at the end of each week together with a suitable analysis of the receipts and payments during each week.

(13 marks)

(ii) Comment upon any matters arising from the cash budget which you consider should be brought to management's attention.

(4 marks)

(b) Explain why the reported profit figure for a period does not normally represent the amount of cash generated in that period.

(5 marks)
(Total 22 marks)
ACCA Level 1 Costing

Question 15.13

Intermediate: Budget preparation and comments on sales forecasting methods

You have recently been appointed as the management accountant to Alderley Ltd, a small company manufacturing two products, the Elgar and the Holst. Both products use the same type of material and labour but in different proportions. In the past, the company has had poor control over its working capital. To remedy this, you have recommended to the directors that a budgetary control system be introduced. This proposal has now been agreed.

Because Alderley Ltd's production and sales are spread evenly over the year, it was agreed that the annual budget should be broken down into four periods, each of 13 weeks, and commencing with the 13 weeks ending 4 April. To help you in this task, the sales and production directors have provided you with the following information:

(1) Marketing and production data

	Elgar	Holst
Budgeted sales for 13 weeks (units)	845	1235
Material content per unit (kilograms)	7	8
Labour per unit (standard hours)	8	5

(2) Production labour

The 24 production employees work a 37-hour, five-day week and are paid £8 per hour. Any hours in excess of this involve Alderley in paying an overtime premium of 25 per cent. Because of technical problems, which will continue over the next 13 weeks, employees are only able to work at 95 per cent efficiency compared to standard.

(3) Purchasing and opening stocks

The production director believes that raw material will cost £12 per kilogram over the budget period. He also plans to revise the amount of stock being kept. He estimates that the stock levels at the commencement of the budget period will be as follows:

Raw materials	Elgar	Holst
2328 kilograms	163 units	361 units

(4) Closing stocks

At the end of the 13-week period closing stocks are planned to change. On the assumption that production and sales volumes for the second budget period will be similar to those in the first period:

- raw material stocks should be sufficient for 13 days' production;
- finished stocks of the Elgar should be equivalent to 6 days' sales volume;
- finished stocks of the Holst should be equivalent to 14 days' sales volume.

Task 1

Prepare in the form of a statement the following information for the 13-week period to 4 April:

(a) the production budget in units for the Elgar and Holst;

(b) the purchasing budget for Alderley Ltd in units;

(c) the cost of purchases for the period;

(d) the production labour budget for Alderley Ltd in hours;

(e) the cost of production labour for the period.

Note: Assume a five-day week for both sales and production.

The managing director of Alderley Ltd, Alan Dunn, has also only recently been appointed. He is keen to develop the company and has already agreed to two new products being developed. These will be launched in 18 months' time. While talking to you about the budget, he mentions that the quality of sales forecasting will need to improve if the company is to grow rapidly. Currently, the budgeted sales figure is found by initially adding 5 per cent to the previous year's sales volume and then revising the figure following discussions with the marketing director. He believes this approach is increasingly inadequate and now requires a more systematic approach.

A few days later, Alan Dunn sends you a memo. In that memo, he identifies three possible strategies for increasing sales volume. They are:

- more sales to existing customers;
- the development of new markets;
- the development of new products.

He asks for your help in forecasting likely sales volumes from these sources.

Task 2

Write a brief memo to Alan Dunn. Your memo should:

(a) identify *four* ways of forecasting future sales volume;

(b) show how each of your four ways of forecasting can be applied to *one* of the sales strategies identified by Alan Dunn and justify your choice;

(c) give *two* reasons why forecasting methods might not prove to be accurate.

AAT Technicians Stage

Question 15.14

Advanced: Comments on budget preparation and zero-based budgeting

A public sector organization is extending its budgetary control and responsibility accounting system to all departments. One such department concerned with public health and welfare is called 'Homecare'. The department consists of staff who visit elderly 'clients' in their homes to support them with their basic medical and welfare needs.

A monthly cost control report is to be sent to the department manager, a copy of which is also passed to a director who controls a number of departments. In the system, which is still being refined, the budget was set by the director and the manager had not been consulted over the budget or the use of the monthly control report.

Shown below is the first month's cost control report for the Homecare department.

Cost Control Report – Homecare Department Month ending May

	Budget	Actual	(Overspend)/ Underspend
Visits	10 000 £000s	12 000 £000s	(2 000) £000s
Department expenses:			
Supervisory salary	2 000	2 125	(125)
Wages (permanent staff)	2 700	2 400	300
Wages (casual staff)	1 500	2 500	(1 000)
Office equipment depreciation	500	750	(250)
Repairs to equipment	200	20	180
Travel expenses	1 500	1 800	(300)
Consumables	4 000	6 000	(2 000)
Administration and telephone	1 000	1 200	(200)
Allocated administrative costs	2 000	3 000	(1 000)
	15 400	19 795	(4 395)

In addition to the manager and permanent members of staff, appropriately qualified casual staff are appointed on a week to week basis to cope with fluctuations in demand. Staff use their own transport and travel expenses are reimbursed. There is a central administration overhead charge over all departments. Consumables consist of materials which are used by staff to care for clients. Administration and telephone are costs of keeping in touch with the staff who often operate from their own homes. As a result of the report, the director sent a memo to the manager of the Homecare department pointing out that the department must spend within its funding allocation and that any spending more than 5 per cent above budget on any item would not be tolerated. The director requested an immediate explanation for the serious overspend.

You work as the assistant to the directorate management accountant. On seeing the way the budget system was developing, he made a note of points he would wish to discuss and develop further, but was called away before these could be completed.

Required:

(a) Develop and explain the issues concerning the budgetary control and responsibility accounting system which are likely to be raised by the management accountant. You should refer to the way the budget was prepared, the implications of a 20 per cent increase in the number of visits, the extent of controllability of costs, the implications of the funding allocation, social aspects and any other points you think appropriate. You may include numerical illustrations and comment on specific costs, but you are not required to reproduce the cost control report.

(14 marks)

(b) Briefly explain zero-based budgeting (ZBB), describe how (in a situation such as that above) it might be implemented, and how as a result it could improve the budget setting procedure.

(6 marks)
(Total 20 marks)
ACCA Paper 8 Managerial Finance

Question 15.15

Advanced: Preparation of activity-based and flexible budgets

AHW plc is a food processing company that produces high-quality, part-cooked meals for the retail market. The five different types of meal that the company produces (Products A to E) are made by subjecting ingredients to a series of processing activities. The meals are different, and therefore need differing amounts of processing activities.

Budget and actual information for October is shown below:

Budgeted data

	Product A	Product B	Product C	Product D	Product E
Number of batches	20	30	15	40	25
Processing activities per batch:					
Processing activity W	4	5	2	3	1
Processing activity X	3	2	5	1	4
Processing activity Y	3	3	2	4	2
Processing activity Z	4	6	8	2	3

Budgeted costs of processing activities:

	£000
Processing activity W	160
Processing activity X	130
Processing activity Y	80
Processing activity Z	200

All costs are expected to be variable in relation to the number of processing activities.

Actual data

Actual output during October was as follows:

	Product A	Product B	Product C	Product D	Product E
Number of batches	18	33	16	35	28

Actual processing costs incurred during October were:

	£000
Processing activity W	158
Processing activity X	139
Processing activity Y	73
Processing activity Z	206

Required:

(a) Prepare a budgetary control statement (to the nearest £000) that shows the original budget costs, flexible budget costs, the actual costs, and the total variances of each processing activity for October.

(15 marks)

Your control statement has been issued to the managers responsible for each processing activity and the finance director has asked each of them to explain the reasons for the variances shown in your statement. The managers are not happy about this as they were not involved in setting the budgets and think that they should not be held responsible for achieving targets that were imposed upon them.

Required:

(b) Explain briefly the reasons why it might be preferable for managers not to be involved in setting their own budgets.

(5 marks)

(c)

(i) Explain the difference between fixed and flexible budgets and how each may be used to control production costs and non-production costs (such as marketing costs) within AHW plc.

(4 marks)

(ii) Give two examples of costs that are more appropriately controlled using a fixed budget, and explain why a flexible budget is less appropriate for the control of these costs.

(3 marks)

Many organizations use linear regression analysis to predict costs at different activity levels. By analyzing past data, a formula such as

$$y = ax + b$$

is derived and used to predict future cost levels.

Required:

(d) Explain the meaning of the terms y, a, x and b in the above equation.

(3 marks)
(Total 30 marks)
CIMA Management Accounting – Performance Management

Management control systems

Questions to Chapter 16

Question 16.1

Intermediate

(a) Identify and explain the essential elements of an effective cost control system.

(13 marks)

(b) Outline possible problems which may be encountered as a result of the introduction of a system of cost control into an organization.

(4 marks)
(Total 17 marks)

Question 16.2

Advanced

You are required, within the context of budgetary control, to:

(a) explain the specific roles of planning, motivation and evaluation;

(7 marks)

(b) describe how these roles may conflict with each other;

(7 marks)

(c) give three examples of ways by which the management accountant may resolve the conflict described in (b).

(6 marks)
(Total 20 marks)
CIMA P3 Management Accounting

Question 16.3

Advanced

(a) Explain the ways in which the attitudes and behaviour of managers in a company are liable to pose more threat to the success of its budgetary control system than are minor technical inadequacies that may be in the system.

(15 marks)

(b) Explain briefly what the management accountant can do to minimize the disruptive effects of such attitudes and behaviour.

(5 marks)
(Total 20 marks)
CIMA P3 Management Accounting

Question 16.4

Advanced

What are the behavioural aspects which should be borne in mind by those who are designing and operating standard costing and budgetary control systems?

(20 marks)
CIMA Cost Accounting 2

Question 16.5

Advanced

One purpose of management accounting is to influence managers' behaviour so that their resulting actions will yield a maximum benefit to the employing organization. In the context of this objective, you are required to discuss:

(a) how budgets can cause behavioural conflict;

(b) how this behavioural conflict may be overcome;

(c) the importance of the feedback of information; and

(d) the purpose of goal congruence.

(20 marks)
CIMA P3 Management Accounting

Question 16.6

Advanced

KL is a transport company that has recently won a five-year government contract to provide rail transport services. The company appointed a new Director to take responsibility for the government contract. She has worked in various positions in other rail transport companies for a number of years. She has put together a team of managers by recruiting some of her former colleagues and some of KL's current managers.

The contract stipulates that the company should prepare detailed budgets for its first year of operations to show how it intends to meet the various operating targets that are stated in the contract. The new Director is undecided about whether she should prepare the budgets herself or whether she should involve her management team, including the newly recruited managers, in the process.

Required:

Produce a report, addressed to the new Director, that discusses participative budgeting.

Note: your report must

- explain TWO potential benefits and TWO potential disadvantages of involving the new and existing managers in the budget setting process;
- provide a recommendation to the new Director.

(10 marks)
CIMA P2 Performance Management

Question 16.7

Advanced

The level of efficiency assumed in the setting of standards has important motivational implications. Discuss.

(8 marks)
ACCA Level 2 Management Accounting

Question 16.8

Advanced

In discussing the standard setting process for use within budgetary control and/or standard costing systems, the following has been written: 'The level of standards appears to play a role in achievement motivation…'

Required:

(a) Briefly distinguish between the motivational and managerial reporting objectives of both budgetary control and standard costing. Describe the extent to which these two objectives place conflicting demands on the standard of performance utilized in such systems.

(6 marks)

(b) Describe three levels of efficiency which may be incorporated in the standards used in budgetary control and/or standard costing systems. Outline the main advantages and disadvantages of each of the three levels described.

(6 marks)

(c) Discuss the advantages and disadvantages of involving employees in the standard setting process.

(8 marks)
(Total 20 marks)
ACCA P2 Management Accounting

Question 16.9

Advanced

The typical budgetary control system in practice does not encourage *goal congruence*, contains *budgetary slack*, ignores the *aspiration levels* of participants and attempts to control operations by *feedback*, when *feedforward* is likely to be more effective; in summary the typical budgetary control system is likely to have dysfunctional effects.

You are required to

(a) explain briefly *each* of the terms in italics;

(6 marks)

(b) describe how the major dysfunctional effects of budgeting could be avoided.

(11 marks)
(Total 17 marks)
CIMA Stage 3 Management Accounting Techniques

Question 16.10

Advanced

Accounting information plays a major part in the planning and control activities of any organization. Often these planning and control activities, in which budgets feature prominently, are undertaken within a structure known as responsibility accounting.

Required:

(a) Briefly explain responsibility accounting and describe three potential difficulties with operating a system of responsibility accounting.

(6 marks)

(b) Explain 'feedback' and 'feed-forward' in the context of budgetary control. Present a simple diagram to illustrate each.

(7 marks)

(c) Typical purposes of budgets are:
   (i)   resource allocation
   (ii) authorization
   (iii) control.

Explain each of these giving an example from the setting of a non-profit organization.

(7 marks)
(Total 20 marks)
ACCA Paper 8 Managerial Finance

Question 16.11

Advanced

One of the major practical difficulties of applying a financial reporting and control system based on flexible budgeting to a service or overhead department is in identifying and measuring an appropriate unit of activity with which to 'flex' the budget.

Required:

(a) Describe and comment on the desirable attributes of such a measure in the context of a valid application of flexible budgeting to a service centre or to a cost centre where standard costing is not applicable.

(c. 8 marks)

(b) Explain the difficulties in obtaining such a measure.

(c. 6 marks)

(c) List three suitable measures of activity, indicating the circumstances in which each would be suitable and the circumstances in which each of them would be misleading or unsuitable.

(c. 6 marks)
(Total 20 marks)
ACCA P2 Management Accounting

Question 16.12

Advanced

Several assumptions are commonly made by accountants when preparing or interpreting budgetary information.

You are required to explain why each of the following five assumptions might be made by accountants when designing a system of budgeting, and to set out in each case also any arguments which, in your view, raise legitimate doubts about their validity:

(a) budgeted performance should be reasonably attainable but not too loose;

(5 marks)

(b) participation by managers in the budget-setting process leads to better performance;

(5 marks)

(c) management by exception is the most effective system of routine reporting;

(5 marks)

(d) a manager's budget reports should exclude all matters which are not completely under his or her control;

(5 marks)

(e) budget statements should include only matters which can be easily and accurately measured in monetary terms.

(5 marks)
(Total 25 marks)
ICAEW Management Accounting

Question 16.13

Intermediate: Preparation of a flexible budget performance report

The Viking Smelting Company established a division, called the reclamation division, two years ago, to extract silver from jewellers' waste materials. The waste materials are processed in a furnace, enabling silver to be recovered. The silver is then further processed into finished products by three other divisions within the company. A performance report is prepared each month for the reclamation division which is then discussed by the management team. Sharon Houghton, the newly appointed financial controller of the reclamation division, has recently prepared her first report for the four weeks to 31 May. This is shown below:

Performance Report Reclamation Division
4 weeks to 31 May

	Actual	Budget	Variance	Comments
Production (tonnes)	200	250	50 (F)	
	(£)	(£)	(£)	
Wages and social security costs	46 133	45 586	547 (A)	Overspend
Fuel	15 500	18 750	3 250 (F)	
Consumables	2 100	2 500	400 (F)	
Power	1 590	1 750	160 (F)	
Divisional overheads	21 000	20 000	1 000 (A)	Overspend
Plant maintenance	6 900	5 950	950 (A)	Overspend
Central services	7 300	6 850	450 (A)	Overspend
Total	100 523	101 386	863 (F)	

In preparing the budgeted figures, the following assumptions were made for May:

- the reclamation division was to employ four teams of six production employees;
- each employee was to work a basic 42-hour week and be paid £7.50 per hour for the four weeks of May;
- social security and other employment costs were estimated at 40 per cent of basic wages;
- a bonus, shared amongst the production employees, was payable if production exceeded 150 tonnes. This varied depending on the output achieved –
  (1) if output was between 150 and 199 tonnes, the bonus was £3 per tonne produced;
  (2) if output was between 200 and 249 tonnes, the bonus was £8 per tonne produced;
  (3) if output exceeded 249 tonnes the bonus was £13 per tonne produced;
- the cost of fuel was £75 per tonne;
- consumables were £10 per tonne;

- power comprised a fixed charge of £500 per four weeks plus £5 per tonne for every tonne produced;
- overheads directly attributable to the division were £20 000;
- plant maintenance was to be apportioned to divisions on the basis of the capital values of each division;
- the cost of Viking's central services was to be shared equally by all four divisions.

You are the deputy financial controller of the reclamation division. After attending her first monthly meeting with the board of the reclamation division, Sharon Houghton arranges a meeting with you. She is concerned about a number of issues, one of them being that the current report does not clearly identify those expenses and variances which are the direct responsibility of the reclamation division.

Task 1

Sharon Houghton asks you to prepare a flexible budget report for the reclamation division for May in a form consistent with responsibility accounting. On receiving your revised report. Sharon tells you about the other questions raised at the management meeting when the original report was presented. These are summarized below:

(i) Why are the budget figures based on 2-year-old data taken from the proposal recommending the establishment of the reclamation division?

(ii) Should the budget data be based on what we were proposing to do or what we actually did do?

(iii) Is it true that the less we produce the more favourable our variances will be?

(iv) Why is there so much maintenance in a new division with modern equipment and why should we be charged with the actual costs of the maintenance department even when they overspend?

(v) Could the comments explaining the variances be improved?

(vi) Should all the variances be investigated?

(vii) Does showing the cost of central services on the divisional performance report help control these costs and motivate the divisional managers?

Task 2

Prepare a memo for the management of the reclamation division. Your memo should:

(a) answer their queries and justify your comments;

(b) highlight the main objective of your revised performance report developed in Task 1 and give two advantages of it over the original report.

AAT Technicians Stage

Question 16.14

Advanced: Flexible budgets

A newly formed engineering company has just completed its first three months of trading. The company manufactures only one type of product. The external accountant for the company has produced the following statement to present at a meeting to review performance for the first quarter.

Performance report for the quarter ending 31 October

	Budget		Actual		Variance
Sales units		12 000		13 000	1 000
Production units		14 000		13 500	(500)
	$000	$000	$000	$000	$000
Sales		360		385	25
Direct materials	70		69		1
Direct labour	140		132		8
Variable production overhead	42		43		(1)
Fixed production overhead	84		85		(1)
Inventory adjustment	(48)		(12)		(36)
Cost of sales		288		317	(29)
Gross profit		72		68	(4)

The external accountant has stated that he values inventory at the budgeted total production cost per unit.

Required:

(a) Produce an amended statement for the quarter ending 31 October that is based on a flexed budget.

(6 marks)

(b) Explain ONE benefit and ONE limitation of the statement you have produced.

(4 marks)
(Total 10 marks)
CIMA P2 Performance Management

Question 16.15

Intermediate: Preparation of flexible budgets

Data

Rivermede Ltd makes a single product called the Fasta. Last year, Steven Jones, the managing director of Rivermede Ltd, attended a course on budgetary control. As a result, he agreed to revise the way budgets were prepared in the company. Rather than imposing targets for managers, he encouraged participation by senior managers in the preparation of budgets.

An initial budget was prepared but Mike Fisher, the sales director, felt that the budgeted sales volume was set too high. He explained that setting too high a budgeted sales volume would mean his sales staff would be de-motivated because they would not be able to achieve that sales volume. Steven Jones agreed to use the revised sales volume suggested by Mike Fisher.

Both the initial and revised budgets are reproduced below complete with the actual results for the year ended 31 May.

Rivermede Ltd – budgeted and actual costs for the year ended 31 May

Fast production and sales (units)	Original budget 24 000 (£)	Revised budget 20 000 (£)	Actual results 22 000 (£)	Variances from revised budget (£)	(F)
Variable costs					
Material	216 000	180 000	206 800	26 800	(A)
Labour	288 000	240 000	255 200	15 200	(A)
Semi-variable costs					
Heat, light and power	31 000	27 000	33 400	6 400	(A)
Fixed costs					
Rent, rates and depreciation	40 000	40 000	38 000	2 000	(F)
	575 000	487 000	533 400	46 400	(A)

Assumptions in the two budgets:

(1) No change in input prices

(2) No change in the quantity of variable inputs per Fasta.

As the management accountant at Rivermede Ltd, one of your tasks is to check that invoices have been properly coded. On checking the actual invoices for heat, light and power for the year to 31 May, you find that one invoice for £7520 had been incorrectly coded. The invoice should have been coded to materials.

Task 1

(a) Using the information in the original and revised budgets, identify:

- the variable cost of material and labour per Fasta;
- the fixed and unit variable cost within heat, light and power.

(b) Prepare a flexible budget, including variances, for Rivermede Ltd after correcting for the miscoding of the invoice.

Data

On receiving your flexible budget statement, Steven Jones states that the total adverse variance is much less than the £46 400 shown in the original statement. He also draws your attention to the actual sales volume being greater than in the revised budget. He believes these results show that a participative approach to budgeting is better for the company and wants to discuss this belief at the next board meeting. Before doing so, Steven Jones asked for your comments.

Task 2

Write a memo to Steven Jones. Your memo should:

(a) *briefly* explain why the flexible budgeting variances differ from those in the original statement given in the data to task 1;

(b) give *two* reasons why a favourable cost variance may have arisen other than through the introduction of participative budgeting;

(c) give *two* reasons why the actual sales volume compared with the revised budget's sales volume may not be a measure of improved motivation following the introduction of participative budgeting.

AAT Technicians Stage

Question 16.16

Intermediate: Demand forecasts and preparation of flexible budgets

Data

Happy Holidays Ltd sells holidays to Xanadu through newspaper advertisements. Tourists are flown each week of the holiday season to Xanadu, where they take a 10-day touring holiday. In the current financial year, Happy Holidays began to use the least-squares regression formula to help forecast the demand for its holidays. You are employed by Happy Holidays as an accounting technician in the financial controller's department. A colleague of yours has recently used the least-squares regression formula on a spreadsheet to estimate the demand for holidays per year. The resulting formula was:

$$y = 640 + 40x$$

where y is the annual demand and x is the year. The data started with the number of holidays sold seven years ago and was identified in the formula as year 1. In each subsequent year the value of x increases by 1 so, for example, the current financial year was year 8. To obtain the *weekly* demand the result is divided by 25, the number of weeks Happy Holidays operates in Xanadu.

Task 1

(a) Use the least-squares regression formula developed by your colleague to estimate the weekly demand for holidays in Xanadu for the next year.

(b) In preparation for a budget meeting with the financial controller, draft a brief note. Your note should identify three weaknesses of the least-squares regression formula in forecasting the weekly demand for holidays in Xanadu.

Data

The budget and actual costs for holidays to Xanadu for the 10 days ended 27 November of the current financial year is reproduced below.

**Happy Holidays Ltd Cost Statement 10 days ended
27 November**

	Fixed budget (£)	Actual (£)	Variances (£)
Aircraft seats	18 000	18 600	600 A
Coach hire	5 000	4 700	300 F
Hotel rooms	14 000	14 200	200 A
Meals	4 800	4 600	200 F
Tour guide	1 800	1 700	100 F
Advertising	2 000	1 800	200 F
Total costs	45 600	45 600	0

Key: A = adverse, F = favourable

The financial controller gives you the following additional information:

Cost and volume information:

- each holiday lasts 10 days;
- meals and hotel rooms are provided for each of the 10 days;
- the airline charges £450 per return flight per passenger for each holiday but the airline will only sell seats at this reduced price if Happy Holidays purchases seats in blocks of 20;

- the costs of coach hire, the tour guide and advertising are fixed costs;
- the cost of meals was budgeted at £12 per tourist per day;
- the cost of a single room was budgeted at £60 per day;
- the cost of a double room was budgeted at £70 per day;
- 38 tourists travelled on the holiday requiring 17 double rooms and 4 single rooms.

Sales information

- the price of a holiday is £250 more if using a single room.

Task 2

Write a memo to the financial controller. Your memo should:

(a) take account of the cost and volume information to prepare a revised cost statement using flexible budgeting and identifying any variances;

(b) state and justify which of the two cost statements is more useful for management control of costs;

(c) identify *three* factors to be taken into account in deciding whether or not to investigate individual variances.

AAT Technicians Stage

Standard costing and variance analysis 1

Questions to Chapter 17

Question 17.1

Intermediate

A company uses a standard absorption costing system. The following figures are available for the last accounting period in which actual profit was $108 000.

	$
Sales volume profit variance	6 000 adverse
Sales price variance	5 000 favourable
Total variable cost variance	7 000 adverse
Fixed cost expenditure variance	3 000 favourable
Fixed cost volume variance	2 000 adverse

What was the standard profit for actual sales in the last accounting period?

(A) $101 000

(B) $107 000

(C) $109 000

(D) $115 000

Question 17.2

Intermediate

A company uses standard marginal costing. Last month the standard contribution on actual sales was $40 000 and the following variances arose:

Sales price variance $1000 Favourable

Sales volume contribution variance $3500 Adverse

Fixed overhead expenditure variance $2000 Adverse

There were no variable cost variances last month.

What was the actual contribution for last month?

(A) $35 500

(B) $37 500

(C) $39 000

(D) $41 000

Question 17.3

Intermediate

A company operates a standard absorption costing system. Details of budgeted and actual figures for February are given below:

	Budget	Actual
Production (units)	29 000	26 000
Direct labour hours per unit	3.0	2.8
Direct labour cost per hour	$10.00	$10.40

(a) The labour rate variance for the period was:

   (A) $34 800   A
   (B) $34 800   F
   (C) $29 120   A
   (D) $31 200   A

(2 marks)

(b) The labour efficiency variance for the period was:

   (A) $58 000   F
   (B) $60 320   F
   (C) $52 000   F
   (D) $54 080   F

(2 marks)
(Total 4 marks)

Question 17.4

Intermediate

G Ltd repairs electronic calculators. The wages budget for the last period was based on a standard repair time of 24 minutes per calculator and a standard wage rate of $10.60 per hour.

After the end of the budget period, the following was reported:

Number of repairs	31 000
Labour rate variance	$3 100 (A)
Labour efficiency variance	Nil

Based on the above information, the actual wage rate during the period was

(A) $10.35 per hour
(B) $10.60 per hour
(C) $10.85 per hour
(D) $11.10 per hour

CIMA – Management Accounting Fundamentals

Question 17.5

Intermediate: Variance analysis and reconciliation of standard with actual cost

SK Limited makes and sells a single product 'Jay' for which the standard cost is as follows:

		£ per unit
Direct materials	4 kilograms at £12.00 per kg	48.00
Direct labour	5 hours at £7.00 per hour	35.00
Variable production overhead	5 hours at £2.00 per hour	10.00
Fixed production overhead	5 hours at £10.00 per hour	50.00
		143.00

The variable production overhead is deemed to vary with the hours worked. Overhead is absorbed into production on the basis of standard hours of production and the normal volume of production for the period just ended was 20 000 units (100 000 standard hours of production).

For the period under consideration, the actual results were:

	18 000 units
Production of 'Jay'	**(£)**
Direct material used – 76 000kg at a cost of	836 000
Direct labour cost incurred – for 84 000 hours worked	604 800
Variable production overhead incurred	172 000
Fixed production overhead incurred	1 030 000

You are required:

(a) to calculate and show, by element of cost, the standard cost for the output for the period;

(2 marks)

(b) to calculate and list the relevant variances in a way which reconciles the standard cost with the actual cost (*Note:* Fixed production overhead sub-variances of capacity and volume efficiency (productivity) are *not* required).

(9 marks)

(c) to comment briefly on the usefulness to management of statements such as that given in your answer to (b) above.

(4 marks)
(Total 15 marks)
CIMA Stage 2 Cost Accounting

Question 17.6

Advanced: Reconciliation of budget and actual profit for a standard absorption costing system

KHL manufactures a single product and operates a budgetary control system that reports performance using variances on a monthly basis. The company has an agreement with a local suppler and calls off raw materials as and when required. Consequently there is no inventory of raw materials.

The following details have been extracted from the budget working papers for the year:

	Annual	Activity	(units)
	50 000	70 000	90 000
	$000	$000	$000
Sales revenue	3 200	4 480	5 760
Direct materials (3kgs per unit)	600	840	1 080
Direct labour (two hours per unit)	1 000	1 400	1 800
Variable overhead (two hours per unit)	400	560	720
Fixed overhead (two hours per unit)*	600	600	600

*The fixed overhead absorption rate of $5 per hour was based on an annual budget of 60 000 units of the product being produced at a constant monthly rate throughout the year, with the fixed overhead cost being incurred in equal monthly amounts.

The following actual performance relates to February:

	$	$
Sales revenue (5 700 units)		330 600
Direct materials (18 600kgs)	70 680	
Direct labour (11 500 hours)	128 800	
Variable overhead (11 500 hours)	47 150	
Fixed overhead absorbed	60 000	
	306 630	
Finished goods inventory adjustment	15 000	291 630
Gross profit		38 970
Fixed overhead over-absorption		3 000
Profit		41 970

For February budgeted sales were 6000 units, the selling price variance was $34 200 Adverse and the sales volume profit variance was $4 200 Adverse. The actual fixed overhead incurred was $57 000.

Budgeted profit for February was $84 000.

Required:

Prepare a statement for February that reconciles the budgeted profit of $84 000 with the actual profit of $41 970.

You should show the variances in as much detail as possible given the data provided.

(10 marks)
CIMA P2 Performance Management

Question 17.7

Advanced: Variance analysis reconciling budgeted variable cost with actual variable cost

XXX uses a standard marginal costing system. Data relating to Y, the only product that it manufactures are as follows:

	Standard cost per unit of Y	$
Materials	6kg @ 10 per kg	60
Labour	five hours @ $9 per hour	45
Variable overhead	six machine hours @ $5 per machine hour	30
Total variable production cost		135

Based on the above standard cost data the following out-turn performance report was produced for February:

	Budget	Actual
Output (units)	1 100	1 100
	$	$
Materials	66 000	69 240
Labour	49 500	57 820
Variable overheads	33 000	35 000
Total variable costs	148 500	162 060

The Production Director has criticised the above report because 'It does not give me the information I need to be able to make informed decisions. It tells me that the costs were higher but I need to be able to identify areas of responsibility'.

You have been asked to provide a statement that is better suited to the needs of the Production Director. You have obtained the following information:

Materials: 5770kg were purchased and used.

Labour: The standard rate of $9 per hour had not been updated to incorporate a 5 per cent pay rise. The 5900 hours that were paid included 460 hours of idle time.

Variable overhead: 6400 machine hours were used.

Required:

Prepare a statement that reconciles the budget variable production cost with the actual variable production cost. Your statement should show the variances in as much detail as possible.

(10 marks)

Question 17.8

Intermediate: Calculation of labour variances and actual material inputs working backwards from variances

A company manufactures two components in one of its factories. Material A is one of several materials used in the manufacture of both components.

The standard direct labour hours per unit of production and budgeted production quantities for a 13-week period were:

	Standard direct labour hours	Budgeted production quantities
Component X	0.40 hours	36 000 units
Component Y	0.56 hours	22 000 units

The standard wage rate for all direct workers was £14.00 per hour. Throughout the 13-week period 53 direct workers were employed, working a standard 40-hour week.

The following actual information for the 13-week period is available:

Production:

Component X, 35 000 units

Component Y, 25 000 units

Direct wages paid, £386 540

Material A purchases, 47 000 kilos costing £85 110

Material A price variance, £430 F

Material A usage (component X), 33 426 kilos

Material A usage variance (component X), £320.32 A

Required:

(a) Calculate the direct labour variances for the period.

(5 marks)

(b) Calculate the standard purchase price for material A for the period and the standard usage of material A per unit of production of component X.

(8 marks)

(c) Describe the steps, and information, required to establish the material purchase quantity budget for material A for a period.

(7 marks)
(Total 20 marks)
ACCA Cost and Management Accounting 1

Question 17.9

Intermediate: Calculation of actual input data working back from variances

The following data relate to actual output, costs and variances for the four-weekly accounting period number 4 of a company that makes only one product. Opening and closing work in progress figures were the same.

	(£000)
Actual production of product XY	18 000 units
Actual costs incurred:	
Direct materials purchased and used (150 000kg)	210
Direct wages for 32 000 hours	328
Variable production overhead	38

	(£000)
Variances:	
Direct materials price	15 F
Direct materials usage	9 A
Direct labour rate	8 A
Direct labour efficiency	40 F
Variable production overhead expenditure	6 A
Variable production overhead efficiency	4 F
Variable production overhead varies with labour hours worked.	
A standard marginal costing system is operated.	

You are required to present a standard product cost sheet for one unit of product XY.

(16 marks)
CIMA Cost Accounting Stage 2

Question 17.10

Intermediate: Comparison of absorption and marginal costing variances

You have been provided with the following data for S plc for September:

Accounting method: Variances:	Absorption (£)	Marginal (£)
Selling price	1 900 (A)	1 900 (A)
Sales volume	4 500 (A)	7 500 (A)
Fixed overhead expenditure	2 500 (F)	2 500 (F)
Fixed overhead volume	1 800 (A)	n/a

During September production and sales volumes were as follows:

	Sales	Production
Budget	10 000	10 000
Actual	9 500	9 700

Required:

(a) Calculate:

(i) the standard contribution per unit;

(ii) the standard profit per unit;

(iii) the actual fixed overhead cost total.

(9 marks)

(b) Using the information presented above, explain why different variances are calculated depending upon the choice of marginal or absorption costing.

(8 marks)

(c) Explain the meaning of the fixed overhead volume variance and its usefulness to management.

(5 marks)

(d) Fixed overhead absorption rates are often calculated using a single measure of activity. It is suggested that fixed overhead costs should be attributed to cost units using multiple measures of activity (activity-based costing).

Explain 'activity-based costing' and how it may provide useful information to managers.

(Your answer should refer to both the setting of cost driver rates and subsequent overhead cost control.)

(8 marks)
(Total 30 marks)
CIMA Operational Cost Accounting Stage 2

Standard costing and variance analysis 2: further aspects

Questions to Chapter 18

Questions 18.1

Intermediate: Calculation of labour, material and overhead variances plus appropriate accounting entries

JC Limited produces and sells one product only, Product J, the standard cost for which is as follows for one unit.

	(£)
Direct material X – 10 kilograms at £20	200
Direct material Y – 5 litres at £6	30
Direct wages – 5 hours at £14	70
Fixed production overhead	50
Total standard cost	350
Standard gross profit	90
Standard selling price	440

The fixed production overhead is based on an expected annual output of 10 800 units produced at an even flow throughout the year; assume each calendar month is equal. Fixed production overhead is absorbed on direct labour hours. During April, the first month of the financial year, the following were the actual results for an actual production of 800 units.

		(£)
Sales on credit:		352 000
800 units at £440		
Direct materials:		
X 7 800 kilograms	159 900	
Y 4 300 litres	23 650	
Direct wages: 4 200 hours	57 750	
Fixed production overhead	47 000	
		288 300
Gross profit		63 700

The material price variance is extracted at the time of receipt and the raw materials stores control is maintained at standard prices.

The purchases, bought on credit, during the month of April were:

  X 9000 kilograms at £20.50 per kg from K Limited

  Y 5000 litres at £5.50 per litre from C plc.

Assume no opening stocks.

Wages owing for March brought forward were £6000.

Wages paid during April (net) £53 750.

Deductions from wages owing to the Inland Revenue for PAYE and NI were £5000 and the wages accrued for April were £5000. The fixed production overhead of £47 000 was made up of expense creditors of £33 000, none of which was paid in April, and depreciation of £14 000.

The company operates an integrated accounting system. You are required to:

(a) (i) calculate price and usage variances for each material;

    (ii) calculate labour rate and efficiency variances;

    (iii) calculate fixed production overhead expenditure, efficiency and volume variances;

(9 marks)

(b) show all the accounting entries in T accounts for the month of April – the work in progress account should be maintained at standard cost and each balance on the separate variance accounts is to be transferred to a Profit and Loss Account which you are also required to show;

(18 marks)

(c) explain the reason for the difference between the actual gross profit given in the question and the profit shown in your profit and loss account.

(3 marks)
(Total 30 marks)
CIMA Stage 2 Cost Accounting

Question 18.2

Advanced: Reconciliation statement involving sales mix/quantity variances

PQ produces two products, Product B and Product C. The company uses a standard absorption costing system that absorbs overheads on the basis of direct labour hours. The company operates a just-in-time purchasing and production system and no inventory of raw materials or finished goods is held.

Standard selling prices are determined by adding a 100 per cent mark-up to total production costs per unit.

The following budget and actual data relate to August.

Budget data:

	Product B	Product C
Production and sales	2 200 units	1 800 units
Standard production costs per unit:	$	$
Direct material ($5 per kg)	25.00	35.00
Direct labour (57 per hour)	14.00	10.50
Variable overhead	3.00	2.25
Fixed overhead	8.00	6:00

Actual data:

	Product B	Product C
Production and sales	3 000 units	1 500 units
Selling price per unit	$110	$105

Production costs:	
Direct material	$124 800 (25 600kg)
Direct labour	$ 67 980 (9 140 hours)
Variable overheads	$14 300
Fixed overheads	$ 27 000

The company produces a monthly variance analysis report which has previously included the calculation of the sales volume profit variance. The new management accountant has decided to extend this analysis and replace the sales volume profit variance with the sales mix profit margin variance and the sales quantity profit variance.

Required:

(a) Prepare a statement that reconciles the budgeted gross profit and actual gross profit for August. The variances should be shown in as much detail as possible including the individual sales mix profit margin variances and the individual sales quantity profit variances.

(17 marks)

(b) Explain the benefits to the company of separating the sales volume profit variance into the sales mix profit margin variance and the sales quantity profit variance. You should use the figures calculated in part (a) to illustrate your answer.

(4 marks)

(c) Explain TWO reasons why a standard costing system may not be considered appropriate in a modern manufacturing environment.

(4 marks)
(Total 25 marks)
CIMA P1 Performance Operations

Question 18.3

Advanced: Material mix and yield variances and planning and operating variances

HR is a paint manufacturer that produces a range of paints which it sells to trade and retail outlets.
The standard material cost for 100 litres of white paint is given below:

Raw Material	Volume (litres)	Standard cost per litre $	Standard cost $
A	28	1.40	39.20
B	27	1.20	32.40
C	8	3.65	29.20
D	42	2.60	109.20
	105		210.00

During February, HR produced 7 800 litres of white paint using the following raw materials:

Raw Material	Volume (litres)	Actual cost per litre $
A	2 800	1.50
B	2 700	1.30
C	1 000	4.00
D	1 900	2.50
	8 400	

There was no opening or closing inventory of raw materials.

Required:

(a) Prepare a statement that reconciles the standard material cost to the actual material cost for February. Your statement should include the individual material price variances, the individual material mix variances and the total material yield variance.

(10 marks)

(b) State THREE factors that a company would need to consider before deciding whether to investigate a variance.

(3 marks)

(c) HR uses skilled staff to operate the machinery that converts me raw materials for the paint into the finished product. The standard direct labour hours for each 100 litres of white paint produced are as follows:

   Eight direct labour hours at $24 per hour

During February, 640 direct labour hours were worked at a total cost of $16 500. It has now been realised that a new wage rate of $26 per hour had been agreed with the workers.

Required:

(i) Calculate the labour rate planning variance for February.

(2 marks)

(ii) Calculate the operational labour rate variance and the operational labour efficiency variance for February.

(4 marks)

(iii) Explain the importance of separating variances into their planning and operational components.
   You should use the figures calculated in part (c) to illustrate your answer.

(6 marks)
(Total 25 marks)
CIMA P1 Performance Operations

Question 18.4

Advanced: Sales and planning and mix variances

Carad Co is an electronics company which makes two types of televisions – plasma screen TVs and LCD TVs. It operates within a highly competitive market and is constantly under pressure to reduce prices. Carad Co operates a standard costing system and performs a detailed variance analysis of both products on a monthly basis. Extracts from the management information for the month of November are shown below:

		Note
Total number of units made and sold	1 400	1
Material price variance	$28 000 A	2
Total labour variance	$6 050 A	3

Notes:

(1) The budgeted total sales volume for TVs was 1 180 units, consisting of an equal mix of plasma screen TVs and LCD screen TVs. Actual sales volume was 750 plasma TVs and 650 LCD TVs. Standard sales prices are $350 per unit for the plasma TVs and $300 per unit for the LCD TVs. The actual sales prices achieved during November were $330 per unit for plasma TVs and $290 per unit for LCD TVs. The standard contributions for plasma TVs and LCD TVs are $190 and $180 per unit respectively.

(2) The sole reason for this variance was an increase in the purchase price of one of its key components, X. Each plasma TV made and each LCD TV made requires one unit of component X, for which Carad Co's standard cost is $60 per unit. Due to a shortage of components in the market place, the market price for November went up to $85 per unit for X. Carad Co actually paid $80 per unit for it.

(3) Each plasma TV uses two standard hours of labour and each LCD TV uses one-and-a-half standard hours of labour. The standard cost for labour is $14 per hour and this also reflects the actual cost per labour hour for the company's permanent staff in November. However, because of the increase in sales and production volumes in November, the company also had to use additional temporary labour at the higher cost of $18 per hour. The total capacity of Carad's permanent workforce is 2200 hours production per month, assuming full efficiency. In the month of November, the permanent workforce were wholly efficient, taking exactly two hours to complete each plasma TV and exactly one-and-a-half hours to produce each LCD TV. The total labour variance therefore relates solely to the temporary workers, who took twice as long as the permanent workers to complete their production.

Required:

(a) Calculate the following for the month of November, showing all workings clearly:

(i) the sales price variance and sales volume contribution variance;

(6 marks)

(ii) the material price planning variance and material price operational variance;

(2 marks)

(iii) the labour rate variance and the labour efficiency variance.

(7 marks)

(b) Explain the reasons why Carad Co would be interested in the material price planning variance and the material price operational variance.

(5 marks)
(Total 20 marks)
ACCA F5 Performance Management

Question 18.5

Advanced: Reconciliation statement involving planning and control variances plus relevance of standard costing to total quality management

Lock Co makes a single product – a lock – and uses marginal costing. The standard cost card for one unit is as follows:

Standard cost card	$
Selling price	80
Direct materials (4kg at $3 per kg)	12
Direct labour (two hours at $10 per hour)	20
Variable overhead (two hours at $2 per hour)	4
Marginal cost	36

A junior member of the accounts team produced the following variance statement for the month of May.

	Budget (1 000 units) $	Actual (960 units) $	Variances $
Sales	80 000	76 800	3 200 Adv
Less: Marginal cost			
Direct materials	(12 000)	(11 126)	874 Fav
Direct labour	(20 000)	(18 240)	1 760 Fav
Variable overheads	(4 000)	(3 283)	717 Fav
Contribution	44 000	44 151	151 Fav

Lock Co used 3648kg of materials in the period and the labour force worked – and was paid for – 1824 hours. Until recently, Lock Co has had a market share of 25 per cent. In the month of May, however, the market faced an unexpected 10 per cent decline in the demand for locks.

Required:

(a) Prepare a statement which reconciles budgeted contribution to actual contribution in as much detail as possible. Do not calculate the sales price and the labour rate variances, since both of these have a value of nil. Clearly show all other workings.

(12 marks)

(b) The production director at Lock Co believes that the way to persistently increase market share in the long term is to focus on quality, and is hoping to introduce a Total Quality Management (TQM) approach. The finance director also shares this view and has said, 'standard costing will no longer have a place within the organisation if TQM is introduced.'

Discuss the view that there is no longer a place for standard costing if TQM is introduced at Lock Co.

(8 marks)
(Total 20 marks)
ACCA F5 Performance Management

Question 18.6

Advanced: Direct material and mix variances

GRV is a chemical processing company that produces sprays used by farmers to protect their crops. One of these sprays is made by mixing three chemicals. The standard material cost details for 1 litre of this spray is as follows:

	$
0.4 litres of chemical A @ $ 30 per litre	12.00
0.3 litres of chemical B @ $ 20 per litre	6.00
0.5 litres of chemical C @ $ 15 per litre	7.50
Standard material cost of 1 litre of spray	25.50

During August GRV produced 1000 litres of this spray using the following chemicals:

600 litres of chemical A costing $18 000
250 litres of chemical B costing $8 000
500 litres of chemical C costing $8 500

You are the Management Accountant of GRV and the Production Manager has sent you the following email:

I was advised by our purchasing department that the worldwide price of chemical B had risen by 50 per cent. As a result, I used an increased proportion of chemical A than is prescribed in the standard mix so that our costs were less affected by this price change.

Required:

(a) Calculate the following operational variances:

(i) direct material mix and

(3 marks)

(ii) direct material yield

(2 marks)

(b) Discuss the decision taken by the Production Manager.

(5 marks)
(Total 10 marks)
CIMA P2 Performance Management

STANDARD COSTING AND VARIANCE ANALYSIS 2: FURTHER ASPECTS

Question 18.7

Advanced: Sales mix and market size variances

A company produces and sells DVD players and Blu-ray players.

Extracts from the budget for April are shown in the following table:

	Sales (players)	Selling price (per player)	Standard cost (per player)
DVD	3 000	$75	$50
Blu-ray	1 000	$200	$105

The Managing Director has sent you a copy of an email she received from the Sales Manager. The content of the email was as follows:

> We have had an excellent month. There was on adverse sales price variance on the DVDs of $18 000 but I compensated for that by raising the price of Blu-ray players. Unit sales of DVD players were as expected but sales of the Blu-rays were exceptional and gave a total sales volume profit variance of $19 000. I think I deserve a bonus!

The Managing Director has asked for your opinion on these figures. You obtained the following information:

Actual results for April were:

	Sales (players)	Selling price (per players)
DVD	3 000	$69
Blu-ray	1 200	$215

The total market demand for DVD players was as budgeted but as a result of distributors reducing the price of Blu-ray discs the total market for Blu-ray players grew by 50 per cent in April. The company had sufficient capacity to meet the revised market demand for 1 500 units of its Blu-ray players and therefore maintained its market share.

Required:

(a) Calculate the following operational variances based on the revised market details:

(i) the total sales mix profit margin variance;

(2 marks)

(ii) the total sales volume profit variance.

(2 marks)

(b) Explain, using the above scenario, the importance of calculating planning and operational variances for responsibility centres.

(6 marks)
(Total 10 marks)
CIMA P2 Performance Management

Question 18.8

Advanced: Sales mix and quantity variances and planning and operating variances

Milbao plc make and sell three types of electronic game for which the following budget/standard information and actual information is available for a four-week period:

		Standard unit data		
Model	Budget sales (units)	Selling price (£)	Variable cost (£)	Actual sales (units)
Superb	30 000	100	40	36 000
Excellent	50 000	80	25	42 000
Good	20 000	70	22	18 000

Budgeted fixed costs are £2 500 000 for the four-week period. Budgeted fixed costs should be charged to product units at an overall budgeted average cost unit where it is relevant to do so.

Required:

(a) Calculate the sales volume variance for each model and in total for the four-week period where (i) turnover (ii) contribution and (iii) net profit is used as the variance valuation base.

(9 marks)

(b) Discuss the relative merits of each of the valuation bases of the sales volume variance calculated in (a) above.

(6 marks)

(c) Calculate the *total* sales quantity and sales mix variances for Milbao plc for the four-week period, using contribution as the valuation base. (Individual model variances are not required.)

(4 marks)

(d) Comment on why the individual model variances for sales mix and sales quantity may provide misleading information to management. (No calculations are required.)

(4 marks)

(e) The following additional information is available for the four-week period:

(1) The actual selling price and variable costs of Milbao plc are 10 and 5 per cent lower respectively, than the original budget/standard.

(2) General market prices have fallen by 6 per cent from the original standard. Short-term strategy by Milbao plc accounts for the residual fall in selling price.

(3) Three per cent of the variable cost reduction from the original budget/standard is due to an over-estimation of a wage award, the remainder, i.e. 2 per cent is due to short-term operational improvements.

(i) Prepare a summary for a four-week period for model 'Superb' *only*, which reconciles original budget contribution with actual contribution where planning and operational variances are taken into consideration.

(8 marks)

(ii) Comment on the usefulness to management of planning and operational variance analysis in feedback and feedforward control.

(4 marks)
(Total 35 marks)
ACCA Paper 9 Information for Control and Decision Making

Question 18.9

Advanced: Activity-based standard costing

X Ltd has recently automated its manufacturing plant and has also adopted a Total Quality Management (TQM) philosophy and a Just in Time (JIT) manufacturing system. The company currently uses a standard absorption costing system for the electronic diaries which it manufactures.

The following information for the last quarter has been extracted from the company records.

	Budget	Actual
Fixed production overheads	$100 000	$102 300
Labour hours	10 000	11 000
Output (electronic diaries)	100 000	105 000

Fixed production overheads are absorbed on the basis of direct labour hours.

The following fixed production overhead variances have been reported:

	$
Expenditure variance	2 300 (A)
Capacity variance	10 000 (F)
Efficiency variance	5 000 (A)
Total	2 700 (F)

If the fixed production overheads had been further analyzed and classified under an Activity Based Costing (ABC) system, the above information would then have been presented as follows:

	Budget	Actual
Costs:		
Material handling	$30 000	$30 800
Set up	$70 000	$71 500
Output (electronic diaries)	100 000	105 000
Activity:		
Material handling (orders executed)	5 000	5 500
Set up (production runs)	2 800	2 600

The following variances would have been reported:

	$
Overhead expenditure variance material handling	2 200 (F)
Set ups	6 500 (A)
Overhead efficiency variance material handling	1 500 (A)
Set ups	8 500 (F)
Total	2 700 (F)

Required:

(a) Explain why and how X Ltd may have to adapt its standard costing system now that it has adopted TQM and JIT in its recently automated manufacturing plant.

(9 marks)

(b) Explain the meaning of the fixed overhead variances calculated under the standard absorption costing system and discuss their usefulness to the management of X Ltd for decision-making.

(6 marks)

(c) For the variances calculated under the ABC classification,

   (i) explain how they have been calculated;

   (ii) discuss their usefulness to the management of X Ltd for decision-making.

(10 marks)
(Total 25 marks)
CIMA Management Accounting – Decision Making

Question 18.10

Advanced: Investigation of variances

(a) The Secure Locke Company operates a system of standard costing, which it uses amongst other things as the basis for calculating certain management bonuses. In September the Company's production of 100 000 keys was in accordance with budget. The standard quantity of material used in each key is one unit; the standard price is £0.05 per unit. In September 105 000 units of material were used, at an actual purchase price of £45 per thousand units (which was also the replacement cost).

The materials buyer is given a bonus of 10 per cent of any favourable materials price variance. The production manager is given a bonus of 10 per cent of any favourable materials quantity variance.

You are required:

   (i) to calculate the materials cost variances for September;

(4 marks)

   (ii) to record all relevant bookkeeping entries in journal form;

(2 marks)

   (iii) to evaluate the bonus system from the view-points of the buyer, the production manager, and the company.

(6 marks)

(b) In October there was an adverse materials quantity variance of £500. A decision has to be made as to whether to investigate the key-making process to determine whether it is out of control.

On the basis of past experience the cost of an investigation is estimated at £50. The cost of correcting the process if it is found to be out of control is estimated at £100. The probability that the process is out of control is estimated at 0.50.

You are required:

(i) to calculate the minimum present value of the expected savings that would have to be made in future months in order to justify making an investigation;

(6 marks)

(ii) to suggest why the monthly cost savings arising from a systematic investigation are unlikely to be as great as the adverse materials variance of £500 which was experienced in the month of October;

(3 marks)

(iii) to calculate, if the expected present value of cost savings was *first* £600 and *second* £250, the respective levels of probability that the process was out of control, at which the management would be indifferent about whether to conduct an investigation.

(4 marks)
(Total 25 marks)
ICAEW Management Accounting

Divisional financial performance measures

Questions to Chapter 19

Question 19.1

Intermediate

A company has a capital employed of $200 000. It has a cost of capital of 12 per cent per year. Its residual income is $36 000.

What is the company's return on investment?

(A) 30%

(B) 12%

(C) 18%

(D) 22%

Question 19.2

Advanced

(a) 'Because of the possibility of goal incongruence, an optimal plan can only be achieved if divisional budgets are constructed by a central planning department, but this means that divisional independence is a pseudo-independence.' Discuss the problems of establishing divisional budgets in the light of this quotation.

(9 marks)

(b) 'Head office' will require a division to submit regular reports of its performance.

Describe, discuss and compare three measures of divisional operating performance that might feature in such reports.

(8 marks)
(Total 17 marks)
ACCA Level 2 Management Accounting

Question 19.3

Advanced

A long-established, highly centralized company has grown to the extent that its chief executive, despite having a good supporting team, is finding difficulty in keeping up with the many decisions of importance in the company.

Consideration is therefore being given to re-organizing the company into profit centres. These would be product divisions, headed by a divisional managing director, who would be responsible for all the divisions' activities relating to its products.

You are required to explain, in outline:

(a) the types of decision areas that should be transferred to the new divisional managing directors if such a reorganization is to achieve its objectives;

(b) the types of decision areas that might reasonably be retained at company head office;

(c) the management accounting problems that might be expected to arise in introducing effective profit centre control.

(20 marks)
CIMA P3 Management Accounting

Question 19.4

Advanced

A recently formed group of companies is proposing to use a single return on capital employed (ROCE) rate as an index of the performance of its operating companies which differ considerably from one another in size and type of activities.

It is, however, particularly concerned that the evaluations it makes from the use of this rate should be valid in terms of measurement of performance.

You are required to:

(a) mention *four* considerations in calculating the ROCE rate to which the group will need to attend, to ensure that its intentions are achieved; for each consideration give an example of the type of problem that can arise;

(8 marks)

(b) mention *three* types of circumstance in which a single ROCE rate might not be an adequate measure of performance and, for each, explain what should be done to supplement the interpretation of the results of the single ROCE rate.

(12 marks)
(Total 20 marks)
CIMA P3 Management Accounting

Question 19.5

Advanced

Residual Income and Return on Investment are commonly used measures of performance. However, they are frequently criticized for placing too great an emphasis on the achievement of short-term results, possibly damaging longer-term performance.

You are required to discuss

(a) the issues involved in the long-term: short-term conflict referred to in the above statement;

(11 marks)

(b) suggestions which have been made to reconcile this difference.

(11 marks)
(Total 22 marks)
CIMA Stage 4 Management Accounting – Control and Audit

Question 19.6

Advanced: Appropriate performance measures for different goals

The executive directors and the seven divisional managers of Kant Ltd spent a long weekend at a country house debating the company's goals. They concluded that Kant had multiple goals, and that the performance of senior managers should be assessed in terms of all of them. The goals identified were:

(i) to generate a reasonable financial return for shareholders;

(ii) to maintain a high market share;

(iii) to increase productivity annually;

(iv) to offer an up-to-date product range of high quality and proven reliability;

(v) to be known as responsible employers;

(vi) to acknowledge social responsibilities;

(vii) to grow and survive autonomously.

The finance director was asked to prepare a follow-up paper, setting out some of the implications of these ideas. He has asked you, as his personal assistant, to prepare comments on certain issues for his consideration.

You are required to set out briefly, with reasons:

(a) suitable measures of performance for each of the stated goals for which you consider this to be possible.

(18 marks)

(b) an outline of your view as to whether any of the stated goals can be considered to be sufficiently general to incorporate all of the others.

(7 marks)
(Total 25 marks)
ICAEW Management Accounting

Question 19.7

Advanced: Calculation and comments on residual income and ROI

(a) Brace Co is an electronics company specializing in the manufacture of home audio equipment. Historically, the company has used solely financial performance measures to assess the performance of the company as a whole. The company's Managing Director has recently heard of the 'balanced scorecard approach' and is keen to learn more.

Required:

Describe the balanced scorecard approach to performance measurement.

(10 marks)

(b) Brace Co is split into two divisions, A and B, each with their own cost and revenue streams. Each of the divisions is managed by a divisional manager who has the power to make all investment decisions within the division. The cost of capital for both divisions is 12 per cent. Historically, investment decisions have been made by calculating the return on investment (ROI) of any opportunities and at present, the return on investment of each division is 16 per cent.

A new manager who has recently been appointed in division A has argued that using residual income (RI) to make investment decisions would result in 'better goal congruence' throughout the company.

Each division is currently considering the following separate investments:

	Project for Division A	**Project for Division B**
Capital required for investment	$82.8 million	$40.6 million
Sales generated by investment	$44.6 million	$21.8 million
Net profit margin	28%	33%

The company is seeking to maximize shareholder wealth.

Required:

Calculate both the return on investment and residual income of the new investment for each of the two divisions. Comment on these results, taking into consideration the manager's views about residual income.

(10 marks)
(Total 20 marks)

Question 19.8

Advanced: Discussion of the effect of an investment on ROI

The Northern Hotel manager has investment decision authority. The manager is considering investing $800 000 in the construction of a leisure facility at the hotel. The hotel has permission to build the leisure facility, but will have to accept the terms of an agreement with the local community before beginning its construction. The facility is expected to generate additional annual profit for the hotel over the next five years as follows:

	$000
2015	110
2016	120
2017	155
2018	145
2019	130

At the end of 2019 the facility will have to be sold to the local community for $550 000. If the facility is built, it will be depreciated on a straight line basis over the five year period (i.e. $50 000 per annum).

The investment has a positive net present value of $225 000 when discounted at the group's cost of capital.

The manager of the hotel receives an annual bonus if the hotel's Return on Net Assets is maintained or improved. This was 20 per cent for 2014 based on net assets at the end of the year.

Required:

Discuss the effect of this investment on the future performance of the Northern Hotel and whether, in the light of this, the hotel manager is likely to proceed with the investment.

(7 marks)

Questions 19.9

Advanced: Conflict between NPV and performance measurement

Linamix is the chemicals division of a large industrial corporation. George Elton, the divisional general manager, is about to purchase new plant in order to manufacture a new product. He can buy either the Aromatic or the Zoman plant, each of which have the same capacity and expected four year life, but which differ in their capital costs and expected net cash flows, as shown below:

	Aromatic	**Zoman**
Initial capital investment	£6 400 000	£5 200 000
Net cash flows (before tax)		
2015	£2 400 000	£2 600 000
2016	£2 400 000	£2 200 000
2017	£2 400 000	£1 500 000
2018	£2 400 000	£1 000 000
Net present value	£315 634	£189 615
(@ 16% p.a.)		

In the above calculations it has been assumed that the plant will be installed and paid for by the end of December 2014, and that the net cash flows accrue at the end of each calendar year. Neither plant is expected to have a residual value after decommissioning costs.

Like all other divisional managers in the corporation, Elton is expected to generate a before tax return on his divisional investment in excess of 16 per cent p.a., which he is currently just managing to achieve. Anything less than a 16 per cent return would make him ineligible for a performance bonus and may reduce his pension when he retires in early 2017. In calculating divisional returns, divisional assets are valued at net book values at the beginning of the year. Depreciation is charged on a straight line basis.

Requirements:

(a) Explain, with appropriate calculations, why neither return on investment nor residual income would motivate Elton to invest in the process showing the higher net present value. To what extent can the use of alternative accounting techniques assist in reconciling the conflict between using accounting-based performance measures and discounted cash flow investment appraisal techniques?

(12 marks)

(b) Managers tend to use post-tax cash flows to evaluate investment opportunities, but to evaluate divisional and managerial performance on the basis of pre-tax profits. Explain why this is so and discuss the potential problems that can arise, including suggestions as to how such problems can be overcome.

(8 marks)

(c) Discuss what steps can be taken to avoid dysfunctional behaviour which is motivated by accounting-based performance targets.

(5 marks)
(Total 25 marks)
ICAEW Management Accounting and Financial Management 2

Question 19.10

Advanced: Calculation and comparison of ROI and residual income using straight line and annuity methods of depreciation (This question relates to material covered in Learning Note 19.1)

Alpha division of a retailing group has five years remaining on a lease for premises in which it sells self-assembly furniture. Management are considering the investment of £600 000 on immediate improvements to the interior of the premises in order to stimulate sales by creating a more effective selling environment.

The following information is available:

(i) The expected increased sales revenue following the improvements is £500 000 per annum. The average contribution: sales ratio is expected to be 40 per cent.

(ii) The cost of capital is 16 per cent and the division has a target return on capital employed of 20 per cent, using the net book value of the investment at the beginning of the year in its calculation.

(iii) At the end of the five-year period the premises improvements will have a nil residual value.

Required:

(a) Prepare *two* summary statements for the proposal for years 1 to 5, showing residual income and return on capital employed for each year. Statement 1 should incorporate straight-line depreciation.

Statement 2 should incorporate annuity depreciation at 16 per cent.

(12 marks)

(b) Management staff turnover at Alpha division is high. The division's investment decisions and management performance measurement are currently based on the figures for the first year of a proposal.

(i) Comment on the use of the figures from statements 1 and 2 in (a) above as decision-making and management performance measures.

(ii) Calculate the net present value (NPV) of the premises improvement proposal and comment on its compatibility with residual income as a decision-making measure for the proposal's acceptance or rejection.

(8 marks)

(c) An alternative forecast of the increase in sales revenue per annum from the premises improvement proposal is as follows:

Year:	1	2	3	4	5
Increased sales revenue (£000)	700	500	500	300	200

All other factors remain as stated in the question.

(i) Calculate year 1 values for residual income and return on capital employed where (1) straight-line depreciation and (2) annuity depreciation at 16 per cent are used in the calculations.

(ii) Calculate the net present value of the proposal.

(iii) Comment on management's evaluation of the amended proposal in comparison with the original proposal using the range of measures calculated in (a), (b) and (c).

(10 marks)
(Total 30 marks)
ACCA Level 2 Cost and Management Accounting II

Question 19.11

Advanced: Computation and discussion of economic value added

The managers of Toutplut Inc were surprised at a recent newspaper article which suggested that the company's performance in the last two years had been poor. The CEO commented that turnover had increased by nearly 17 per cent and pre-tax profit by 25 per cent between the last two financial years, and that the company compared well with others in the same industry.

$ million

Profit and loss account extracts for the year

	2014	2015
Turnover	326	380
Pre-tax accounting profit[1]	67	84
Taxation	23	29
Profit after tax	44	55
Dividends	15	18
Retained earnings	29	37

Balance sheet extracts for the year ending

	2014	2015
Fixed assets	120	156
Net current assets	130	160
	250	316
Financed by:		
Shareholders' funds	195	236
Medium- and long-term bank loans	55	80
	250	316

[1] After deduction of the economic depreciation of the company's fixed assets. This is also the depreciation used for tax purposes.

Other information:

(i)   Toutplut had non-capitalized leases valued at $10 million in each year 2013–2015.

(ii) Balance Sheet capital employed at the end of 2013 was $223 million.

(iii) The company's pre-tax cost of debt was estimated to be 9 per cent in 2014, and 10 per cent in 2015.

(iv) The company's cost of equity was estimated to be 15 per cent in 2014 and 17 per cent in 2015.

(v)   The target capital structure is 60 per cent equity, 40 per cent debt.

(vi) The effective tax rate was 35 per cent in both 2014 and 2015.

(vii) Economic depreciation was $30 million in 2014 and $35 million in 2015.

(viii) Other non-cash expenses were $10 million per year in both 2014 and 2015.

(ix) Interest expense was $4 million in 2014 and $6 million in 2015.

Required:

(a) Estimate the economic valued added (EVA) for Toutplut Inc for both 2014 and 2015. State clearly any assumptions that you make. Comment upon the performance of the company.

(7 marks)

(b) Explain the relationship between economic value added and net present value.

(2 marks)

(c) Briefly discuss the advantages and disadvantages of EVA.

(6 marks)
(Total 15 marks)
ACCA Paper 3.7 Strategic Financial Management

Question 19.12

Advanced: Economic valued added approach to divisional performance measurement

The most recent published results for V plc are shown below:

	Published (£m)
Profit before tax for year ending 31 December	13.6
Summary consolidated balance sheet at 31 December	
Fixed assets	35.9
Current assets	137.2
Less: Current liabilities	(95.7)
Net current assets	41.5
Total assets *less* current liabilities	77.4
Borrowings	(15.0)
Deferred tax provisions	(7.6)
Net assets	54.8
Capital and reserves	54.8

An analyst working for a stockbroker has taken these published results, made the adjustments shown below, and has reported his conclusion that 'the management of V pic is destroying value'.

Analyst's adjustments to profit before tax:

	(£m)
Profit before tax	13.6
Adjustments	
Add: Interest paid (net)	1.6
R&D (Research and Development)	2.1
Advertising	2.3
Amortization of goodwill	1.3
Less: Taxation paid	(4.8)
Adjusted profit	16.1

Analyst's adjustments to summary consolidated balance sheet at 31 December

	(£m)	
Capital and reserves	54.8	
Adjustments		
Add: Borrowings	15.0	
Deferred tax provisions	7.6	
R&D	17.4	Last seven years, expenditure
Advertising	10.5	Last five years, expenditure
Goodwill	40.7	Written off against reserves on acquisitions in previous years
Adjusted capital employed	146.0	
Required return	17.5	12% cost of capital
Adjusted profit	16.1	
Value destroyed	1.4	

The chairman of V plc has obtained a copy of the analyst's report.

Requirement:

(a) Explain, as management accountant of V plc, in a report to your Chairman, the principles of the approach taken by the analyst. Comment on the treatment of the specific adjustments to R&D, Advertising, Interest and Borrowings and Goodwill.

(12 marks)

(b) Having read your report, the Chairman wishes to know which division or divisions are 'destroying value', when the current internal statements show satisfactory returns on investment (ROIs). The following summary statement is available:

Divisional performance, year ending 31 December

	Division A (Retail) (£m)	Division B (Manufacturing) (£m)	Division C (Services) (£m)	Head office (£m)	Total (£m)
Turnover	81.7	63.2	231.8	—	376.7
Profit before interest and tax	5.7	5.6	5.8	(1.9)	15.2
Total assets less current liabilities	27.1	23.9	23.2	3.2	77.4
ROI	21.0%	23.4%	25.0%		

Some of the adjustments made by the analyst can be related to specific divisions:

- Advertising relates entirely to Division A (Retail)
- R&D relates entirely to Division B (Manufacturing)
- Goodwill write-offs relate to

> Division B (Manufacturing) £10.3m
> Division C (Services) £30.4m

- The deferred tax relates to

> Division B (Manufacturing) £1.4m
> Division C (Services) £6.2m

- Borrowings and interest, per divisional accounts, are:

	Division A Retail (£m)	Division B (Mfg) (£m)	Division C (Services) (£m)	Head office (£m)	Total (£m)
Borrowings	—	6.6	6.9	1.5	15.0
Interest paid/(received)	(0.4)	0.7	0.9	0.4	1.6

Requirement:

Explain, with appropriate comment, in a report to the Chairman, where 'value is being destroyed'. Your report should include:

- a statement of divisional performance:
- an explanation of any adjustments you make;
- a statement and explanation of the assumptions made; and
- comment on the limitations of the answers reached.

(20 marks)

(c) The use of ROI has often been criticized as emphasizing short-term profit, but many companies continue to use the measure. Explain the role of ROI in managing business performance, and how the potential problems of short-termism may be overcome.

(8 marks)
(Total 40 marks)
CIMA Stage 4 Management Accounting Control Systems

Transfer pricing in divisionalized companies

Questions to Chapter 20

Question 20.1

Impact of cost-plus transfer price on decision making and divisional profits

Enormous Engineering (EE) plc is a large multidivisional engineering company having interests in a wide variety of product markets. The Industrial Products Division (IPD) sells component parts to consumer appliance manufacturers, both inside and outside the company. One such part, a motor unit, it sells solely to external customers, but buys the motor itself internally from the Electric Motor Division. The Electric Motor Division (EMD) makes the motor to IPD specifications and it does not expect to be able to sell it to any other customers.

In preparing the budgets IPD estimated the number of motor units it expects to be able to sell at various prices as follows:

Price (ex works) (£)	Quantity sold (units)
50	1 000
40	2 000
35	3 000
30	4 000
25	6 000
20	8 000

It then sought a quotation from EMD, who offered to supply the motors at £16 each based on the following estimate:

	(£)
Materials and bought-in parts	2
Direct labour costs	4
Factory overhead (150% of direct labour costs)	6
Total factory cost	12
Profit margin (33¹/₃% on factory cost)	4
Quoted price	£16

Factory overhead costs are fixed. All other costs are variable.

Although it considered the price quoted to be on the high side, IPD nevertheless believed that it could still sell the completed unit at a profit because it incurred costs of only £4 (material £1 and direct labour £3) on each unit made. It therefore placed an order for the coming year.

On reviewing the budget the finance director of EE noted that the projected sales of the motor unit were considerably less than those for the previous year, which was disappointing as both divisions concerned were working well below their capacities. On making enquiries he was told by IPD that the price reduction required to sell more units would reduce rather than increase profit and that the main problem was the high price charged by EMD. EMD stated that they required the high price in order to meet their target profit margin for the year, and that any reduction would erode their pricing policy.

You are required to:

(a) develop tabulations for each division, and for the company as a whole, that indicate the anticipated effect of IPD selling the motor unit at each of the prices listed;

(10 marks)

(b) (i) show the selling price which IPD should select in order to maximize its own divisional profit on the motor unit;

(2 marks)

(ii) show the selling price which would be in the best interest of EE as a whole;

(2 marks)

(iii) explain why this latter price is not selected by IPD;

(1 mark)

(c) state:

(i) what changes you would advise making to the transfer pricing system so that it will motivate divisional managers to make better decisions in future;

(5 marks)

(ii) what transfer price will ensure overall optimality in this situation.

(5 marks)
(Total 25 marks)
ICAEW Management Accounting

Question 20.2

Advanced: Determining optimal transfer prices for three different scenarios

Manuco Ltd has been offered supplies of special ingredient Z at a transfer price of £15 per kg by Helpco Ltd which is part of the same group of companies. Helpco Ltd processes and sells special ingredient Z to customers external to the group at £15 per kg. Helpco Ltd bases its transfer price on cost plus 25 per cent profit mark-up. Total cost has been estimated as 75 per cent variable and 25 per cent fixed.

Required:

Discuss the transfer prices at which Helpco Ltd should offer to transfer special ingredient Z to Manuco Ltd in order that group profit maximizing decisions may be taken on financial grounds in each of the following situations:

(a) Helpco Ltd has an external market for all of its production of special ingredient Z at a selling price of £15 per kg. Internal transfers to Manuco Ltd would enable £1.50 per kg of variable packing cost to be avoided.

(b) Conditions are as per (i) but Helpco Ltd has production capacity for 3000kg of special ingredient Z for which no external market is available.

(c) Conditions are as per (ii) but Helpco Ltd has an alternative use for some of its spare production capacity. This alternative use is equivalent to 2000kg of special ingredient Z and would earn a contribution of £6000.

(13 marks)
ACCA Paper 9 Information for Control and Decision Making

Question 20.3

Advanced: Make or buy decision and intercompany trading

Companies RP, RR, RS and RT are members of a group. RP wishes to buy an electronic control system for its factory and, in accordance with group policy, must obtain quotations from companies inside and outside of the group.

From outside of the group the following quotations are received:

Company A quoted £33 200.

Company B quoted £35 000 but would buy a special unit from RS for £13 000. To make this unit, however, RS would need to buy parts from RR at a price of £7500.

The inside quotation was from RS whose price was £48 000. This would require RS buying parts from RR at a price of £8000 and units from RT at a price of £30 000.

However, RT would need to buy parts from RR at a price of £11 000.

Additional data are as follows:

(1) RR is extremely busy with work outside the group and has quoted current market prices for all its products.

(2) RS costs for the RP contract, including purchases from RR and RT, total £42 000. For the Company B contract it expects a profit of 25 per cent on the cost of its own work.

(3) RT prices provide for a 20 per cent profit margin on total costs.

(4) The variable costs of the group companies in respect of the work under consideration are:

RR: 20 per cent of selling price

RS: 70 per cent of own cost (excluding purchases from other group companies)

RT: 65 per cent of own cost (excluding purchases from other group companies).

You are required, from a group point of view, to:

(a) recommend, with appropriate calculations, whether the contract should be placed with RS or Company A or Company B;

(b) state briefly *two* assumptions you have made in arriving at your recommendations.

(30 marks)
CIMA P3 Management Accounting

Question 20.4

Advanced: Return on investment, residual income and transfer pricing

The NAW Group manufactures healthcare products which it markets both under its own brand and in unbranded packs. The group has adopted a divisional structure. Division O, which is based in a country called Homeland, and manufactures three pharmaceutical products for sale in the domestic market. Budgeted information in respect of Division O for the year ending 31 May 2015 is as follows:

Sales information:

Product		'Painfree'	'Digestisalve'	'Awaysafe'
Sales packs (000s)	NAW Brand	5 000	5 000	15 000
	Unbranded	15 000	20 000	—
Selling price per pack (£)	NAW Brand	2.40	4.80	8.00
	Unbranded	1.20	3.60	—

Cost of sales information:

Variable manufacturing costs per pack:	Material and conversion costs	Packaging costs
	£	£
'Painfree'		
NAW Brand	0.85	0.15
Unbranded	0.85	0.05
'Digestisalve'		
NAW Brand	1.85	0.25
Unbranded	1.85	0.15
'Awaysafe'		
NAW Brand	2.80	0.40

Other relevant information is as follows:

(1) Each of the three products is only sold in tablet form in a single pack-size which contains 12 tablets. During the year to 31 May 2015 it is estimated that a maximum of 780 million tablets could be manufactured. All three products are manufactured by the same process therefore management have the flexibility to alter the product mix. Management expect that sales volume will increase by 10 per cent in the year ending 31 May 2016.

(2) Advertising expenditure has been committed to under a fixed term contract with a leading consultancy and is therefore regarded as a fixed cost by management.

Advertising expenditure in respect of the turnover of branded products in the year ending 31 May 2015 is apportioned as follows:

Product:	Advertising expenditure as a % of turnover
Painfree	5
Digestisalve	10
Awaysafe	12

(3) The average capital employed in the year to 31 May 2015 is estimated to be £120 million. The company's cost of capital is 10 per cent.

(4) The management of the NAW Group use both Return on Investment (ROI) and Residual Income (RI) to assess divisional performance.

(5) Budgeted fixed overheads (excluding advertising) for Division O during the year ended 31 May 2015 amount to £81 558 000.

(6) There is no planned change in manufacturing capacity between the years ended 31 May 2015 and 31 May 2016.

(7) Ignore taxation for all calculations other than those in part (c).

Required:

(a) (i) Prepare a statement of budgeted profit in respect of Division O for the year ending 31 May 2015.

Your answer should show the annual budgeted contribution of each branded and unbranded product. Calculate BOTH the residual income (RI) and Return of Investment (ROI) for Division O.

(7 marks)

(ii) Name and comment on THREE factors, other than profit maximization, that the management of the NAW Group ought to consider when deciding upon the product mix strategy for the year ending 31 May 2016.

(3 marks)

(iii) Suggest THREE reasons why the management of the NAW Group may have chosen to use Residual Income (RI) in addition to Return on Investment (ROI) in order to assess divisional performance.

(3 marks)

Division L of the NAW Group is based in Farland. The management of Division L purchases products from various sources, including other divisions of the group, for subsequent resale. The manager of Division L has requested two alternative quotations from Division O in respect of the year ended 31 May 2015:

(1) Quotation 1 – Purchasing five million packs of 'Awaysafe'.

(2) Quotation 2 – Purchasing nine million packs of 'Awaysafe'.

The management of the NAW Group has made a decision that a minimum of 15 million packs of 'Awaysafe' must be reserved for Homeland customers in order to ensure that customer demand can be satisfied and the product's competitive position is further established in the Homeland market.

The management of the NAW Group is willing, if necessary, to reduce the budgeted sales quantities of other products in order to satisfy the requirements of Division L. They wish, however, to minimize the loss of contribution to the group.

The management of Division L is aware of the availability of another product that competes with 'Awaysafe' which could be purchased at a local currency price that is equivalent to £5.50 per pack. The NAW Group's policy is that all divisions are allowed the autonomy to set transfer prices and purchase from whatever sources they choose. The management of Division O intend to use market price less 30 per cent as the basis for each of the quotations.

(b) (i) From the viewpoint of the NAW Group, comment on the appropriateness of the decision by the management of Division O to use an adjusted market price as a basis for the preparation of Quotations 1 and 2, and the implications of the likely decision by the management of Division L.

(3 marks)

(ii) Recommend the prices that should be quoted by Division O for 'Awaysafe', in respect of Quotations 1 and 2, which will ensure that the profitability of the NAW Group as a whole is not adversely affected by the decision of the management of Division L.

(3 marks)

(iii) Discuss the proposition that transfer prices should be based on opportunity costs.

(4 marks)

(c) (i) After much internal discussion concerning Quotation 2 by the management of the NAW Group, Division O is not prepared to supply nine million packs of 'Awaysafe' to Division L at a price lower than market price less 30 per cent. All profits earned in Farland are subject to taxation at a rate of 20 per cent. Division O pays tax in Homeland at a rate of 40 per cent on all profits.

Advise the management of the NAW Group whether the management of Division L should be directed to purchase 'Awaysafe' from Division O, or purchase a similar product from a local supplier. Supporting calculations should be provided.

(6 marks)

(ii) Identify and comment on the major issues that can arise with regard to transfer pricing in a multinational organization.

(5 marks)

(d) Evaluate the extent to which the management of the NAW Group could make use of the product life cycle model in the determination of its product pricing strategy.

(6 marks)
(Total 40 marks)
ACCA Paper 3.3 Performance Management

Question 20.5

Advanced: Impact of transfer price on NPV for a division and the group and impact of transfer price on supplying and receiving divisions

TY comprises two trading divisions. Both divisions use the same accounting policies. The following statement shows the performance of each division for the year ended 31 August:

Division	T $000	Y $000
Sales	3 600 000	3 840 000
Variable Cost	1 440 000	1 536 000
Contribution	2 160 000	2 304 000
Fixed Costs	1 830 000	1 950 000
Operating Profit	330 000	354 000
Capital Employed	3 167 500	5 500 000

Division Y manufactures a single component which it sells to Division T and to external customers. During the year to 31 August Division Y operated at 80 per cent capacity and produced 200 000 components. 25 per cent of the components were sold to Division T at a transfer price of $15 360 per component. Division T manufactures a single product. It uses one of the components that it buys from Division Y in each unit of its finished product, which it sells to an external market.

Investment by Division T

Division T is currently operating at its full capacity of 50 000 units per year and is considering investing in new equipment which would increase its present capacity by 25 per cent. The machine has a useful life of three years. This would enable Division T to expand its business into new markets. However, to achieve this it would have to sell these additional units of its product at a discounted price of $60 000 per unit. The capital cost of the investment is $1.35bn and the equipment can be sold for $400m at the end of three years.

Division T believes that there would be no changes to its cost structure as a result of the expansion and that it would be able to sell all of the products that it could produce from the extra capacity. It is company policy of TY that all divisions use a 10 per cent cost of capital to evaluate investments.

Required:

(a) Prepare an analysis of the sales made by Division Y for the year ended 31 August to show the contribution earned from external sales and from internal sales.

(3 marks)

(b) Assuming that the current transfer pricing policy continues,

(i) Evaluate, using NPV, the investment in the new equipment from the perspective of Division T;

(8 marks)

(ii) Evaluate, using NPV, the investment in the new equipment from the perspective of TY.

Ignore taxation and inflation.

(4 marks)

(c) Discuss the appropriateness of the current transfer pricing policy from the perspective of EACH of the divisional managers AND the company as a whole.

(10 marks)
(Total 25 marks)
CIMA P2 Performance Management

Question 20.6

Advanced: Calculation of divisional profits based on different demand levels and impact on profits from receiving division buying externally

S Division and R Division are two divisions in the SR group of companies. S Division manufactures one type of component which it sells to external customers and also to R Division.

Details of S Division are as follows:

Market price per component	$200
Variable cost per component	$105
Fixed costs	$1 375 000 per period
Demand from R Division	20 000 components per period
Capacity	35 000 components per period

R Division assembles one type of product which it sells to external customers. Each unit of that product requires two of the components that are manufactured by S Division.

Details of R Division are as follows:

Selling price per unit	$800
Variable cost per unit:	
Two components from S	2 @ transfer price
Other variable costs	$250
Fixed costs	$900 000 per period
Demand	10 000 units per period
Capacity	10 000 units per period

Group Transfer Pricing Policy

Transfers must be at opportunity cost

R must buy the components from S.

S must satisfy demand from R before making external sales.

Required:

(a) Calculate the profit for each division if the external demand per period for the components that are made by S Division is:

(i)   15 000 components

(ii) 19 000 components

(iii) 35 000 components

(12 marks)

(b) Calculate the financial impact on the Group if R Division ignored the transfer pricing policy and purchased all of the 20 000 components that it needs from an external supplier for $170 each. Your answer must consider the impact at each of the three levels of demand (15 000, 19 000 and 35 000 components) from external customers for the component manufactured by S Division.

(6 marks)

(c) The Organization for Economic Co-operation and Development (OECD) produced guidelines with the aim of standardizing national approaches to transfer pricing. The guidelines state that where necessary transfer prices should be adjusted using an 'arm's length' price.

Required:

Explain:

(i)   An 'arm's length' price

(ii) The THREE methods that tax authorities can use to determine an 'arm's length' price

(7 marks)
(Total 25 marks)
CIMA P2 Performance Management

Question 20.7

Advanced: Divisional profit, ROI and RI profit computations and impact of a capacity increase on divisional profits

CD is a producer of soft drinks. The company has two divisions: Division C and Division D.

Division C manufactures metal cans that are sold to Division D and also to external customers. Division D produces soft drinks and sells them to external customers in the cans that it obtains from Division C.

CD is a relatively new company. Its objective is to grow internationally and challenge the existing global soft drinks producers. CD aims to build its brand based on the distinct taste of its soft drinks.

Division C annual budget information	$
Market selling price per 1 000 cans	130
Variable costs per can	0.04
Fixed costs	2 400 000
Net assets	4 000 000
Production capacity	40 000 000 cans
External demand for cans	38 000 000 cans
Demand from Division D	20 000 000 cans

Division D annual budget information	$
Selling price per canned soft drink	0.50
Variable costs per canned soft drink (excluding the can)	0.15
Cost of a can (from Division C)	At transfer price
Fixed costs	1 750 000
Net assets	12 650 000
Sales volume	20 000 000 canned soft drinks

Transfer Pricing Policy

Division C is required to satisfy the demand of Division D before selling cans externally. The transfer price for a can is full cost plus 20 per cent.

Performance Management Targets

Divisional performance is assessed on Return on Investment (ROI) and Residual Income (RI). Divisional managers are awarded a bonus if they achieve the annual ROI target of 25 per cent. CD has a cost of capital of 7 per cent.

Required:

(a) Produce a profit statement for each division detailing sales and costs, showing external sales and inter-divisional transfers separately where appropriate.

(6 marks)

(b) Calculate both the ROI and the RI for Division C and Division D.

(4 marks)

The directors of CD are concerned about the future performance of the company and, together with the divisional managers, have now agreed the following:

- A machine that would increase annual production capacity to 50 000 000 cans at Division C will be purchased. The purchase of this machine will increase the net assets of Division C by $500 000. Assume that there is no impact on unit variable costs or fixed costs resulting from this purchase.
- Inter-divisional transfers will be priced at opportunity cost.

Required:

(c) Produce a revised profit statement for each division detailing sales and costs, showing external sales and inter-divisional transfers separately where appropriate.

(6 marks)

It has now been decided that inter-divisional transfers are not required to be priced at opportunity cost.

(d) Calculate the minimum transfer price per can that Division C could charge for the 20 million cans required by Division D in order for Division C to achieve the target ROI.

(5 marks)

(e) Explain TWO non-financial measures that could also be used to monitor the performance of the manager of Division D against the objectives of CD company.

(4 marks)
(Total 25 marks)
CIMA P2 Performance Management

Question 20.8

Advanced: Determination of optimal transfer prices for divisions and the group using differential calculus

Scenario for part (a)

The OB group has two divisions: the Optics Division and the Body Division. The Optics Division produces optical devices, including lenses for cameras. The lenses can be sold directly to external customers or they can be transferred to the Body Division where they are sold with a camera body as a complete camera.

Optics Division

The relationship between the selling price of a lens and the quantity demanded by external customers is such that at a price of $6000 there will be no demand but demand will increase by 600 lenses for every $300 decrease in the price. The variable cost of producing a lens is $1200. The fixed costs of the division are $12 million each year. The Optics Division has the capacity to satisfy the maximum possible demand if required.

Body Division

After the lens has been included with a body to make a complete camera the relationship between selling price and demand is such that at a price of $8000 there will be no demand for the complete camera but demand will increase by 300 complete cameras for every $100 decrease in the price. The Body Division has annual fixed costs of $15 million and has the capacity to satisfy the maximum possible demand if required. The total variable costs of a camera body and packaging it with a lens are $1750 (this does not include the cost of a lens).

Note: If $P = a - bx$ then Marginal Revenue (MR) will be given by $MR = a - 2bx$.

Required:

(a) Calculate the total revenue that would be generated by the complete cameras if:

   (i) the Manager of the Optics Division set the transfer price of a lens equal to the selling price which would be set to maximize profits from the sale of lenses to external customers;

   (ii) the transfer price of a lens was set to maximize the profits of the OB group from the sale of complete cameras.

(10 marks)

Scenario for parts (b) and (c)

The FF group is a divisionalized company that specializes in the production of processed fish. Each division is a profit centre. The Smoke Division (SD) produces smoked fish. The Packaging Division (PD) manufactures boxes for packaging products.

Smoke Division (SD)

The Manager of SD has just won a fixed price contract to supply 500 000 units of smoked fish to a chain of supermarkets. This will fully utilize the capacity of SD for the next year. Budget details for the next year are:

Variable cost per unit	$12.00 (excluding the box)
Fixed costs	$6.0 million
Revenue	$13.5 million
Output	500 000 units of smoked fish

Eacn unit of smoked fish requires one box.

Packaging Division (PD)

The Packaging Division has agreed to supply 500 000 boxes to SD at the same price that it sells boxes to external customers. Budget details for PD (including the order from SD) for the next year are:

Variable production cost	$1.40 per box
Fixed costs	$2.4 million
Output	4.48 million boxes
Capacity	4.50 million boxes

Company Policy

It has been announced today that FF will be introducing a new performance appraisal system. The Divisional Managers will only be paid a bonus if the profit of their division is at least 12 per cent of assets consumed during the next year. The value of the assets consumed is assumed to be the same as the fixed costs.

Required:

(b) Calculate, following the change to the company policy:

   (i) the minimum price per box that PD would be willing to charge;

(3 marks)

   (ii) the maximum price per box that SD would be willing to pay.

(4 marks)
(Total for part (b) = 7 marks)

(c) The Manager of SD is unhappy about paying the same price per box as an external customer and thinks that transfer prices should be set using an opportunity cost-based approach.

Discuss the view that transfer prices should be set using opportunity cost. You should use the data from the FF group to illustrate your answer.

(8 marks)
(Total 25 marks)
CIMA P2 Performance Management

Question 20.9

Advanced: Setting an optimal transfer price when there is an intermediate imperfect market

Memphis plc is a multi-division firm operating in a wide range of activities. One of its divisions, Division A, produces a semi-finished product Alpha, which can be sold in an outside market. It can also be sold to Division B, which can use it in manufacturing its finished product Beta. Assume also that the marginal cost of each division is a rising linear function of output, and that the goal for Memphis plc is to maximize its total profits. Relevant information about both divisions is given below.

Output of Alpha (units)	Total cost of Alpha (£000)	Revenue from outside selling of Alpha (£000)	Net marginal revenue of Beta (£000)
60	112	315	47
70	140	350	45
80	170	380	43
90	203	405	40
100	238	425	36
110	275	440	33
120	315	450	30
130	359	455	25

You are required to calculate the optimal transfer price for Alpha and the optimal activity level for each division.

(10 marks)
ICAEW Management Accounting

Cost management

Questions to Chapter 21

Question 21.1

Advanced

QW is a company that manufactures machine parts from sheet metal to specific customer order for industrial customers. QW is considering diversification into the production of metal ornaments. The ornaments would be produced at a constant rate throughout the year. It there plans to sell these ornaments from inventory through wholesalers and via direct mail to consumers.

Presently, each of the machine parts is specific to a customer's order. Consequently, the company does not hold an inventory of finished items but it does hold the equivalent of one day's production of sheet metal so as to reduce the risk of being unable to produce goods demanded by customers at short notice. There is a one-day lead time for delivery of sheet metal to QW from its main supplier though additional supplies could be obtained at less competitive prices.

Demand for these industrial goods is such that delivery is required almost immediately after the receipt of the customer order. QW is aware that if it is unable to meet an order immediately the industrial customer would seek an alternative supplier, despite QW having a reputation for high quality machine parts.

The management of QW is not aware of the implications of the diversification for its production and inventory policies.

Required:

(a) Compare and contrast QW's present production and inventory policy and practices with a traditional production system that uses constant production levels and holds inventory to meet peaks of demand.

(5 marks)

(b) Discuss the importance of a Total Quality Management (TQM) system in a just-in-time (JIT) environment Use QW to illustrate your discussion.

(5 marks)
(Total 10 marks)
CIMA P2 Performance Management

Question 21.2

Advanced

A traditional view of the environment in which goods are manufactured and sold is where stocks of materials and components are held. Such stocks are then used to manufacture products to agreed standard specifications, aiming at maximizing the use of production capacity. Finished goods are held in stock to satisfy steady demand for the product range at agreed prices.

Required:

(a) Discuss aspects of the operation of the management accounting function which are likely to apply in the above system.

(5 marks)

(b) Describe an alternative sequence from purchasing to the satisfaction of customer demand, which may be more applicable in the current business environment. Your answer should refer to the current 'techniques or philosophies' which are likely to be in use.

(5 marks)

(c) Name specific ways in which changes suggested in (b) will affect the operation of the management accounting function.

(5 marks)
(Total 15 marks)
ACCA Paper 9 Information for Control and Decision Making

Question 21.3

Advanced

Within a diversified group, one division, which operates many similar branches in a service industry, has used internal benchmarking and regards it as very useful. Group central management is now considering the wider use of benchmarking.

Requirements:

(a) Explain the aims, operation, and limitations of internal benchmarking, and explain how external benchmarking differs in these respects.

(10 marks)

(b) A multinational group wishes to internally benchmark the production of identical components made in several plants in different countries. Investments have been made with some plants in installing new Advanced Manufacturing Technology (AMT) and supporting this with manufacturing management systems such as just-in-time (JIT) and Total Quality Management (TQM). Preliminary comparisons suggest that the standard cost in plants using new technology is no lower than that in plants using older technology.

Requirement:

Explain possible reasons for the similar standard costs in plants with differing technology. Recommend appropriate benchmarking measures, recognizing that total standard costs may not provide the most useful measurement of performance.

(10 marks)
(Total 20 marks)
CIMA Stage 4 Management Accounting – Control Systems

Question 21.4

Advanced

MLC, which was established in 2008, manufactures a range of garden sheds and summerhouses using timber purchased from a number of suppliers.

The recently appointed managing director has expressed increasing concern about the falling sales volumes, rising costs and hence declining profits over the last two years.

Required:

Discuss how business process re-engineering could help to improve the profits of MLC.

(10 marks)
CIMA P2 Performance Management

Question 21.5

Advanced

In order to compete globally many companies have adopted Kaizen Costing. Consequently they are changing their performance measurement system and are abandoning standard costing system as they think traditional standard costing and variance analysis is of little use in the modern environment.

Required:

Discuss why Kaizen Costing could tie more useful for performance measurement than standard costing and variance analysis in sued companies.

(10 marks)
CIMA P2 Performance Management

Question 21.6

Advanced

JYT manufactures and sells a range of products. It is not dominant in the market in which it operates and, as a result, it has to accept the market price for each of its products. The company is keen to ensure that it continues to compete and earn satisfactory profit at each stage throughout a product's life cycle.

Required:

Explain how JYT could use Target Costing AND Kaizen Costing to improve its future performance.

Your answer should include an explanation of the differences between Target Costing and Kaizen Costing.

(10 marks)
CIMA P2 Performance Management

Question 21.7

Advanced: Preparation of cost of quality report

SHG realizes that its present performance reporting system does not highlight quality costs. The reports contain the information below, but the directors require this to be reported in an appropriate format.

The following information is available in respect of the year ended 31 May:

(1) Production data:

Units requiring rework	1 500
Units requiring warranty repair service	1 800
Design engineering hours	66 000
Inspection hours (manufacturing)	216 000

(2) Cost data:

	$
Design engineering cost per hour	75
Inspection cost per hour (manufacturing)	40
Rework cost per heating system unit reworked (manufacturing)	3 000
Customer support cost per repaired unit (marketing)	200
Transportation costs per repaired unit (distribution)	240
Warranty repair costs per repaired unit	3 200

(3) Staff training costs amounted to $150 000 and additional product testing costs were $49 000.

(4) The marketing director has estimated that sales of 1400 units were lost as a result o bad publicity in trade journals. The average contribution per heating system unit is estimated at $6000.

Required:

Prepare a cost of quality report for SHG that shows its costs of quality (using appropriate headings) for the year ended 31 May.

(10 marks)
CIMA P2 Performance Management

Question 21.8

Advanced: Preparation of quality cost statement

A company manufactures a single product. The selling price, production cost and contribution per unit for this product for 2013 have been predicted as follows:

		$ per unit
Selling price		90.00
Direct materials (components)	30.00	
Direct labour	35.00	
Variable overhead	10.00	75.00
Contribution		15.00

The company has forecast that demand for the product for the next year will be 24 000 units. However to satisfy this level of demand, production of 35 294 units will be required because:

- 15 per cent of the items delivered to customers (4235 units) will be rejected as faulty and will require free replacement. The cost of delivering the replacement item is $5 per unit;
- 20 per cent of the items manufactured (7059 units) will be discovered to be faulty before they are despatched to customers.

In addition, before production commences, 10 per cent of the components that the company purchases are damaged while in storage.

As a consequence of all of the above, total quality costs for the year amount to $985 885.

The company is now considering the following proposal:

(1) Spending $30 000 per annum on a quality inspector which would reduce the percentage of faulty items delivered to customers to 13 per cent; and

(2) Spending \$500 000 per annum on training courses for the production workers which management believes will reduce and sustain the level of faulty production to 10 per cent.

Required:

(a) Prepare a statement that shows the quality costs that the company would expect to incur if it accepted the above proposal. Your answer should clearly show the costs analyzed using the four recognized quality cost headings.

(7 marks)

(b) Recommend with reasons, whether or not the company should accept the proposal.

(3 marks)
(Total 10 marks)
CIMA P2 Performance Management

Question 21.9

Advanced

You are financial controller of a medium-sized engineering business. This business was family-owned and managed for many years but has recently been acquired by a large group to become its engineering division.

The first meeting of the management board with the newly appointed divisional managing director has not gone well.

He commented on the results of the division:

- sales and profits were well below budget for the month and cumulatively for the year, and the forecast for the rest of the year suggested no improvement;
- working capital was well over budget;
- even if budget were achieved the return on capital employed was well below group standards.

He proposed a total quality management (TQM) programme to change attitudes and improve results.

The initial responses of the managers to these comments were:

- the production director said there was a limit to what was possible with obsolete machines and facilities and only a very short-term order book;
- the sales director commented that it was impossible to get volume business when deliveries and quality were unreliable and designs out of date;
- the technical director said that there was little point in considering product improvements when the factory could not be bothered to update designs and the sales executives were reluctant to discuss new ideas with new potential customers.

You have been asked to prepare reports for the next management board meeting to enable a more constructive discussion.

You are required:

(a) to explain the critical success factors for the implementation of a programme of total quality management. Emphasize the factors that are crucial in changing attitudes from those quoted;

(11 marks)

(b) to explain how you would measure quality cost, and how the establishment of a system of measuring quality costs would contribute to a TQM programme.

(9 marks)
(Total 20 marks)
CIMA Stage 4 Management Accounting

Question 21.10

Advanced: Calculation of cost of quality

CAL manufactures and sells solar panels for garden lights. Components are bought in and assembled into metal frames that are machine manufactured by CAL. There are a number of alternative suppliers of these solar panels. Some of CAL's competitors charge a lower price, but supply lower quality panels; whereas others supply higher quality panels than CAL but for a much higher price.

CAL is preparing its budgets for the coming year and has estimated that the market demand for its type of solar panels will be 100 000 units and that its share will be 20 000 units (i.e. 20 per cent of the available market). The standard cost details of each solar panel are as follows:

		\$ per unit
Selling price		60
Bought-in components (1 set)	15	
Assembly &. machining cost	25	
Delivery cost	5	45
Contribution		15

An analysis of CAL's recent performance revealed that 2 per cent of the solar panels supplied to customers were returned for free replacement, because the customer found that they were faulty. Investigation of these returned items shows that the components had been damaged when they had been assembled into the metal frame. These returned panels cannot be repaired and have no scrap value. If the supply of faulty solar panels to customers could be eliminated then, due to improved customer perception, CAL's market share would increase to 25 per cent.

Required:

(a) Explain, with reference to CAL, quality conformance costs and quality non-conformance costs and the relationship between them.

(4 marks)

(b) Assuming that CAL continues with its present systems and that the percentage of quality failings is as stated above:

(i) Calculate, based on the budgeted figures and sales returns rate, the total relevant costs of quality for the coming year.

(4 marks)

(ii) Calculate the maximum saving that could be made by implementing an inspection process for the solar panels, immediately before the goods are delivered.

(2 marks)
(Total 10 marks)
CIMA P2 Performance Management

Question 21.11

Advanced: Establishing a target cost and target price

The Universal Health System (UHS) provides the entire healthcare service to residents in Illopia. The UHS is funded centrally through revenues from taxpayers. However, the government is not involved in the day-to-day running of the UHS, which is largely managed regionally by a number of self-governing trusts, such as the Sickham UHS Trust.

The Sickham UHS Trust runs one hospital in Sickham and, like other trusts in Illopia, receives 70 per cent of its income largely from the UHS' 'payments by results' scheme, which was established two years ago. Under this scheme, the trust receives a pre-set tariff (fee income) for each service it provides. If the Trust manages to provide any of its services at a lower cost than the pre-set tariff, it is allowed to use the surplus as it wishes. Similarly, it has to bear the cost of any deficits itself. Currently, the Trust knows that a number of its services simply cannot be provided at the tariff paid and accepts that these always lead to a deficit. Similarly, other services always seem to create a surplus. This is partly because different trusts define their services and account for overheads differently. Also, it is partly due to regional differences in costs, which are not taken into account by the scheme, which operates on the basis that 'one tariff fits all'.

The remaining 30 per cent of the Trust's income comes from transplant and heart operations. Since these are not covered by the scheme, the payment the Trust receives is based on the actual costs it incurs, in providing the operations. However, the Trust is not allowed to exceed the total budget provided for these operations in any one year.

Over recent years, the Trust's board of directors has become increasingly dissatisfied with the financial performance of the Trust and has blamed it on poor costing systems, leading to an inability to control costs. As a result, the finance director and his second in command – the financial controller – have now been replaced. The board of directors has taken this decision after complaining that 'the Trust simply cannot sustain the big deficit between income and spending'. The new financial controller comes from a manufacturing background and is a great advocate of target costing, believing that the introduction of a target costing system at the Sickham UHS Trust is the answer to all of its problems. The new financial director is unconvinced, believing target costing to be only really suitable in manufacturing companies.

Required:

(a) Explain the main steps involved in developing a target price and target cost for a product in a typical manufacturing company.

(6 marks)

(b) Explain four key characteristics that distinguish services from manufacturing.

(4 marks)

(c) Describe how the Sickham UHS Trust is likely, in the current circumstances, to try to derive:

(i) a target cost for the services that it provides under the 'payment by results' scheme; and

(2 marks)

(ii) a target cost for transplants and heart operations,

(2 marks)

(d) Discuss THREE of the particular difficulties that the Sickham UHS Trust may find in using target costing in its service provision.

(6 marks)
(Total 20 marks)
ACCA F5 Performance management

Question 21.12

Advanced: Construction of life cycle curves, investment appraisal and sensitivity analysis

(a) Scovet plc uses its production capacity in dedicated product line format to satisfy demand for a rolling range of products. Such products have limited life cycles. A turnover value of £20m is taken as a measure of the annual production capacity of the company. The turnover figures (actual and forecast) are shown below for each of products A, B and C from the beginning of the life cycle of each product up to 2019. These are the only products for which Scovet plc has sales (actual or forecast) for the years 2016 to 2019.

Scovet plc
Sales turnover (£ million) – actual or forecast

Product	2011	2012	2013	2014	2015	2016	2017	2018	2019
	A	A	A	A	A	F	F	F	F
A	2.0	4.0	6.0	7.0	4.5	3.0	2.0	1.5	nil
B	nil	nil	3.0	6.0	8.0	9.0	3.0	1.0	nil
C	nil	nil	nil	4.0	5.0	6.5	7.5	8.0	7.0

Note: A = actual; F = forecast

Other relevant information (forecast) relating to the products for the years 2016 and 2017 is as follows:

(1) Contribution to sales ratios (per cent): product A (70 per cent); product B (75 per cent); product C (60 per cent).

(2) Product specific fixed costs:

	2016 £m	2017 £m
Product A	2.0	1.1
Product B	4.0	1.8
Product C	2.8	3.0

(3) Company fixed costs for year; £2.5m.

Required:

(i) Using the graph paper provided, show the life cycle pattern for EACH of products A, B and C expressed in terms of turnover (£m).

(4 marks)

(ii) Comment on the shape of the life cycle curves in the graphs prepared in (i).

(5 marks)

(iii) Prepare a profit/loss analysis for each of years 2016 and 2017 which shows the analysis by product including product turnover, contribution and profit and also company net profit or loss.

(4 marks)

(iv) Comment briefly on the figures in the analysis which you prepared in (iii) above.

(4 marks)

(b) Scovet plc has identified a market for a new product D for which the following estimated information is available:

(1) Sales turnover for the years 2017, 2018 and 2019 of £6m, £7m and £6m respectively. No further sales are expected after 2019.

(2) Contribution to sales percentage of 60 per cent for each year.

(3) Product specific fixed costs in the years 2017, 2018 and 2019 of £2.5m, £2.2m and £1.8m respectively.

(4) Capital investment of £4.5m on 1 January 2017 with nil residual value at 31 December 2019. The cost of capital from 1 January 2017 is expected to be 10 per cent per annum.

Assume all cash flows (other than the initial investment) take place on 31 December of each year. Ignore taxation.

Required:

(i) Determine whether the new product is viable on financial grounds.

(4 marks)

(ii) Calculate the minimum target contribution to sales ratio (per cent) at which product D will be viable in financial terms where all other factors remain unchanged.

(3 marks)

(iii) Suggest actions which should allow the investigation of variable cost in order that the target contribution to sales ratio (per cent) calculated in (ii) may be achieved.

(3 marks)

(c) Suggest alternative strategies which may be formulated by Scovet plc in order to improve the overall financial position in the period 2017 to 2019 inclusive where only products A, B, C and D are available for incorporation in the calculations. Comment on the extent of the need for such strategies and include an explanation of any cost/benefit information which would be required.

(8 marks)
(Total 35 marks)
ACCA Paper 9 Information of Control and Decision Making

Question 21.13

Advanced: Calculation of costs before and after introduction of a quality management programme

Calton Ltd make and sell a single product. The existing product unit specifications are as follows:

Direct material X:	8 sq. metres at £4 per sq. metre
Machine time:	0.6 running hours
Machine cost per gross hour:	£40
Selling price:	£100

Calton Ltd require to fulfil orders for 5000 product units per period. There are no stocks of product units at the beginning or end of the period under review. The stock level of material X remains unchanged throughout the period.

The following additional information affects the costs and revenues:

(1) Five per cent of incoming material from suppliers is scrapped due to poor receipt and storage organization.

(2) Four per cent of material X input to the machine process is wasted due to processing problems.

(3) Inspection and storage of material X costs £0.10 per sq. metre purchased.

(4) Inspection during the production cycle, calibration checks on inspection equipment, vendor rating and other checks cost £25 000 per period.

(5) Production quantity is increased to allow for the downgrading of 12.5 per cent of product units at the final inspection stage. Downgraded units are sold as 'second quality' units at a discount of 30 per cent on the standard selling price.

(6) Production quantity is increased to allow for returns from customers which are replaced free of charge. Returns are due to specification failure and account for five per cent of units initially delivered to customers. Replacement units incur a delivery cost of £8 per unit. 80 per cent of the returns from customers are rectified using 0.2 hours of machine running time per unit and are re-sold as 'third quality' products at a discount of 50 per cent on the standard selling price. The remaining returned units are sold as scrap for £5 per unit.

(7) Product liability and other claims by customers are estimated at three per cent of sales revenue from standard product sales.

(8) Machine idle time is 20 per cent of gross machine hours used (i.e. running hours = 80 per cent of gross hours).

(9) Sundry costs of administration, selling and distribution total £60 000 per period.

(10) Calton Ltd is aware of the problem of excess costs and currently spends £20 000 per period in efforts to prevent a number of such problems from occurring.

Calton Ltd is planning a quality management programme which will increase its excess cost prevention expenditure from £20 000 to £60 000 per period. It is estimated that this will have the following impact:

(1) A reduction in stores losses of material X to 3 per cent of incoming material.

(2) A reduction in the downgrading of product units at inspection to 7.5 per cent of units inspected.

(3) A reduction in material X losses in process to 2.5 per cent of input to the machine process.

(4) A reduction in returns of products from customers to 2.5 per cent of units delivered.

(5) A reduction in machine idle time to 12.5 per cent of gross hours used.

(6) A reduction in product liability and other claims to 1 per cent of sales revenue from standard product sales.

(7) A reduction in inspection, calibration, vendor rating and other checks by 40 per cent of the existing figure.

(8) A reduction in sundry administration, selling and distribution costs by 10 per cent of the existing figure.

(9) A reduction in machine running time required per product unit to 0.5 hours.

Required:

(a) Prepare summaries showing the calculation of (i) total production units (pre-inspection), (ii) purchases of material X (sq. metres), (iii) gross machine hours. In each case the figures are required for the situation both before and after the implementation of the additional quality management programme, in order that the orders for 5000 product units may be fulfilled.

(10 marks)

(b) Prepare profit and loss accounts for Calton Ltd for the period showing the profit earned both before and after the implementation of the additional quality management programme.

(10 marks)

(c) Comment on the relevance of a quality management programme and explain the meaning of the terms internal failure costs, external failure costs, appraisal costs and prevention costs giving examples for each, taken where possible from the information in the question.

(10 marks)
(Total 30 marks)
ACCA Level 2 Cost and Management Accounting II

Strategic performance management

Questions to Chapter 22

Question 22.1

Advanced

ZY is an airline operator. It is implementing a balanced scorecard to measure the success of its strategy to expand its operations. It has identified two perspectives and two associated objectives. They are:

Perspective	Objective
Growth	Fly to new destinations
Internal capabilities	Reduce time between touch down and take off

(i) For the 'growth perspective' of ZY, recommend a performance measure and briefly justify your choice of the measure by explaining how it will reflect the success of the strategy.

(2 marks)

(ii) (For the 'internal capabilities perspective' of ZY, state data that you would gather and explain how this could be used to ensure the objective is met.

(2 marks)
(Total 4 marks)
CIMA P1 Management Accounting: Performance Evaluation

Question 22.2

Advanced

CM Limited was formed ten years ago to provide business equipment solutions to local businesses. It has separate divisions for research, marketing, product design, technology and communication services, and now manufactures and supplies a wide range of business equipment (copiers, scanners, printers, fax machines and similar items).

To date it has evaluated its performance using monthly financial reports that analyze profitability by type of equipment. The managing director of CM Limited has recently returned from a course on which it had been suggested that the 'balanced Scorecard' could be a useful way of measuring performance.

Required:

(a) Explain the 'balanced scorecard' and how it could be used by CM Limited to measure its performance.

(13 marks)

While on the course, the managing director of CM Limited overheard someone mention how the performance of their company had improved after they introduced 'benchmarking'.

Required:

(b) Explain 'benchmarking' and how it could be used to improve the performance of CM Limited.

(12 marks)
(Total 25 marks)
CIMA Management Accounting – Performance Management

Question 22.3

Advanced

Discuss the advantages which may be claimed for Kaplan and Norton's balanced scorecard as a basis for performance measurement over traditional management accounting views of performance measurement. Your answer should include specific examples of quantitative measures for each aspect of the balanced scorecard.

(15 marks)
CIMA Management Accounting – Performance Management

Question 22.4

Advanced

The Pathology Laboratory service of the County Hospital provides diagnostic services to support the care provided by the County Hospital, local General Practitioners, other hospitals and healthcare providers. The importance of the work done by the Pathology Laboratory was summarized by the Head of the laboratory:

'Over 70 per cent of diagnostic and treatment decisions made by doctors are based on medical laboratory test results. Without our work, doctors would not be able to confirm their diagnosis. Laboratory results give us the ability to identify diseases in their earliest stages so that we have a better chance of treating people effectively. The types of tests performed by our highly-trained staff encompass the entire spectrum of human disease, from routine diagnostic services to clinical laboratories that specialize in bone marrow transplants. The laboratories provide over four million tests each year, providing doctors with the information needed for diagnosis and treatment of all kinds of condition. Our vision is to continually improve the efficiency of the laboratory to ensure the best economic approach to patient care.'

The management team of the County Hospital has decided that the use of the balanced scorecard should be cascaded down to departmental level. Consequently, departmental managers have been given the task of designing a balanced scorecard for their departments.

Required:

Recommend an objective and a suitable performance measure for each of three non-financial perspectives of a balanced scorecard that the Pathology Laboratory could use.

Note: in your answer you should state three perspectives and then recommend an objective and a performance measure for each one of your three perspectives.

(10 marks)

Question 22.5

Advanced

ZJET is an airline company that operates both domestically and internationally using a fleet of 20 aircraft. Passengers book flights using the internet or by telephone and pay for their flights at the time of booking using a debit or credit card.

The airline has also entered into profit sharing arrangements with hotels and local car hire companies that allow rooms and cars to be booked by the airline's passengers through the airline's web site.

ZJET currently measures its performance using financial ratios. The new Managing Director has suggested that other measures are equally important as financial measures and has suggested using the Balanced Scorecard.

Required:

(a) Discuss how the Balanced Scorecard differs from traditional financial performance measurement.

(4 marks)

(b) Explain THREE non-financial performance measures (ONE from EACH of THREE different perspectives of the Balanced Scorecard) that ZJET could use as part of its performance measurement process.

(6 marks)
(Total 10 marks)

Question 22.6

Advanced: Financial and non-financial performance measures

BS Ltd provides consultancy services to small and medium sized businesses. Three types of consultants are employed offering administrative, data processing and marketing advice respectively. The consultants work partly on the client's premises and partly in BS Ltd premises, where chargeable development work in relation to each client contract will be undertaken. Consultants spend some time negotiating with potential clients attempting to secure contracts from them. BS Ltd has recently implemented a policy change which allows for a number of follow-up (remedial) hours at the client's premises after completion of the contract in order to eliminate any problems which have arisen in the initial stages of operation of the system.

Contract negotiation and remedial work hours are not charged directly to each client. BS Ltd carries out consultancy for new systems and also offers advice on existing systems which a client may have introduced before BS Ltd became involved. BS Ltd has a policy of retaining its consultancy staff at a level of 60 consultants on an ongoing basis.

Additional information for the year ended 30 April is as follows:

(i) BS Ltd invoices clients £75 per chargeable consultant hour.

(ii) Consultant salaries are budgeted at an average per consultant of £30 000 per annum. Actual salaries include a bonus for hours in excess of budget paid for at the budgeted average rate per hour.

(iii) Sundry operating costs (other than consultant salaries) were budgeted at £3 500 000. Actual was £4 100 000.

(iv) BS Ltd capital employed (start year) was £6 500 000.

(v) Table 22.1 shows an analysis of sundry budgeted and actual quantitative data.

Required:

(a) (i) Prepare an analysis of actual consultancy hours for the year ended 30 April which shows the increase or decrease from the standard/allowed non-chargeable hours. This increase or decrease should be analyzed to show the extent to which it may be shown to be attributable to a change from standard in:

1. standard chargeable hours; 2. remedial advice hours;

3. contract negotiation hours; 4. other non-chargeable hours.

(13 marks)

(ii) Calculate the total value of each of 1 to 4 in (a) above in terms of chargeable client income per hour.

(4 marks)

(b) BS Ltd measure business performance in a number of ways. For each of the undemoted measures, comment on the performance of BS Ltd using quantitative data from the question and your answer to (a) to assist in illustrating your answer:

(i) Financial performance

(ii) Competitive performance

(iii) Quality of Service

(iv) Flexibility

(v) Resource utilization

(vi) Innovation

(18 marks)
(Total 35 marks)

TABLE 22.1 *BS Ltd Sundry statistics for year ended 30 April*

	Budget	Actual
Number of consultants:	30	23
Administration		
Data processing	12	20
Marketing	18	17
Consultants hours analysis:		
contract negotiation hours	4 800	9 240
remedial advice hours	2 400	7 920
other no-rechargeable hours	12 000	22 440
general development work hours (Chargeable)	12 000	6 600
customer premises contract hours	88 800	85 800
Gross hours	120 000	132 000
Chargeable hours analysis:		
new systems	70%	60%
existing systems advice	30%	40%
Number of clients enquiries received:		
new systems	450	600
existing systems advice	400	360
Number of client contracts worked on:		
new Systems	180	210
existing systems advice	300	283
Number of client complaints	5	20
Contracts requiring remedial advice	48	75

ACCA Information for Control and Decision Making

Question 22.7

Advanced: Financial and non-financial performance measures

Compuaid Ltd provides advisory services to home computer customers. Three types of advisor are employed offering advice by telephone, written/email replies and home visits respectively.

Appendix 1.1 shows sundry statistics for the past 12 month period for Compuaid Ltd and also for two competitor companies A and B.

Additional information relating to Compuaid Ltd for the past 12 month period is as follows:

(i) Home visit travel and remedial work hours are not charged directly to customers.

(ii) All service workers incur some 'idle time' which is not charged directly to customers.

(iii) A number of customers pay a fixed annual fee of £100 for the advisory service. This entitles them to 24 hour priority access to the service and a maximum of five hours of advice without further charge.

Appendix 1.1 shows the total hours of advice (both budget and actual) taken up by customers. Assume that no customer requires more than the five hours allowable.

(iv) All other time for the advisory service and home visits is billed to customers at £20 per hour.

(v) The budgeted wage rate per hour for advisory service staff is £8. This was also the actual rate paid.

(vi) Sundry operating expenses (other than advisor wages) were budgeted at £950 000. Actual operating expenses incurred were £1 000 000.

Actual information for the period under review for competitor companies A and B is as follows:

(i) Similar policies to those used by Compuaid Ltd are operated with regard to idle time, home visit travel and remedial hours.

(ii) Fixed annual fee advisory service schemes, similar to that of Compuaid Ltd, are operated. The annual fee charged per customer by company A and company B is £75 and £100 respectively.

(iii) Other revenue and cost information is as follows:

	Company A £	Company B £
Total revenue (excluding annual fee income):		
Enquiry advice	756 180	1 266 000
Home visits	87 500	810 000
Total wage costs	720 000	1 099 000
Sundry operating expenses	650 000	1 250 000

Required:

(a) (i) Prepare budgeted and actual profit and loss accounts for the 12-month period under review for Compuaid Ltd and also actual profit and loss accounts for companies A and B.

(8 marks)

(ii) Discuss the financial performance of Compuaid Ltd, incorporating details of relative customer billing rates, company service wage rates and annual agreement advice 'level of uptake' in your answer.

(12 marks)

(b) Comment on the performance of Compuaid Ltd, incorporating relevant percentage and ratio statistics in the context of each of the following:

(i) competitiveness;

(ii) quality;

(iii) resource utilization.

(15 marks)
(Total 35 marks)

Appendix 1.1
Sundry Statistics for the previous 12 month period

	Compuaid Budget	Compuaid Actual	Competitor A Actual	Competitor B Actual
Number of service employees:				
Telephone advisor	22	27	25	44
Written/email advisors	15	17	8	10
Home visit staff	12	14	2	21
Service employee hours analysis:				
Home visit travel hours	2 500	4 800	390	4 500
Idle time – home visit staff	2 000	2 600	2 800	6 000
– advisors	4 000	4 800	1 000	7 000
Remedial work for home visits	500	2 000	600	5 200
'Annual agreement' advisor call uptake	14 600	15 300	29 700	35 000
Advisor time billed to customers	58 400	72 100	42 010	63 300
Home visits billed to customers	22 000	23 200	3 500	36 000
Total hours	104 000	124 800	80 000	157 000
Number of home visit enquiries received	15 000	16 000	2 000	24 000
Number of home visits obtained/completed	10 000	8 000	1 400	15 000
Number of home visits requiring remedial work	300	1 200	400	3 400
Number of customer complaints – home visits	100	160	70	225
Number of customer complaints – advisors	73	131	35	196
Number of annual agreement customers	5 840	7 650	6 600	10 000

ACCA Paper 9 Information for Control and Decision Making

Question 22.8

Advanced: Performance measurement focusing on financial and non-financial measures

Ochilpark plc has identified and defined a market in which it wishes to operate. This will provide a 'millennium' focus for an existing product range. Ochilpark plc has identified a number of key competitors and intends to focus on close co-operation with its customers in providing products to meet their specific design and quality requirements. Efforts will be made to improve the effectiveness of all aspects of the cycle from product design to after sales service to customers. This will require inputs from a number of departments in the achievement of the specific goals of the 'millennium' product range. Efforts will be made to improve productivity in conjunction with increased flexibility of methods.

An analysis of financial and non-financial data relating to the 'millennium' proposal is shown in Schedule 3.1.

Required:

(a) (i) Prepare a table (£m) of the total costs for the 'millennium' proposal for each of years 2016, 2017 and 2018 (as shown in Schedule 3.1), detailing target costs, internal and external failure costs, appraisal costs and prevention costs. The following information should be used in the preparation of the analysis:

	2016	2017	2018
Target costs – variable (as % of sales)	40%	40%	40%
– fixed (total)	£2m	£2m	£2.5m
Internal failure costs (% of total target cost)	20%	10%	5%
External failure costs (% of total target cost)	25%	12%	5%
Appraisal costs	£0.5m	£0.5m	£0.5m
Prevention costs	£2m	£1m	£0.5m

(4 marks)

(ii) Explain the meaning of each of the cost classifications in (i) above and comment on their trend and inter-relationship. You should provide examples of each classification.

(8 marks)

(b) Prepare an analysis (both discursive and quantitative) of the 'millennium' proposal for the period 2016 to 2018. The analysis should use the information provided in the question, together with the data in Schedule 3.1. The analysis should contain the following:

(i) A definition of corporate 'vision or mission' and consideration of how the millennium proposal may be seen as identifying and illustrating a specific sub-set of this 'vision or mission'.

(5 marks)

(ii) Discussion and quantification of the proposal in both marketing and financial terms.

(6 marks)

(iii) Discussion of the external effectiveness of the proposal in the context of ways in which (1) Quality and (2) Delivery are expected to affect customer satisfaction and hence the marketing of the product.

(4 marks)

(iv) Discussion of the internal efficiency of the proposal in the context of ways in which the management of (1) Cycle Time and (2) Waste are expected to affect productivity and hence the financial aspects of the proposal.

(4 marks)

(v) Discussion of the links between internal and external aspects of the expected trends in performance.

(4 marks)
(Total 35 marks)
ACCA Paper 9 Information for Control and Decision Making

Schedule 3.1
'Millennium' proposal – estimated statistics

	2016	**2017**	**2018**
Total market size (£m)	120	125	130
Ochilpark plc sales (£m)	15	18	20
Ochilpark plc – total costs (£m)	14.1	12.72	12.55
Ochilpark plc sundry statistics:			
Production achieving design quality standards (%)	95%	97%	98%
Returns from customers as unsuitable (% of deliveries)	3.0%	1.5%	0.5%
Cost of after sales service (£m)	1.5	1.25	1.0
Sales meeting planned delivery dates (%)	90%	95%	99%
Average cycle time (customer enquiry to delivery) (weeks)	6	5.5	5
Components scrapped in production (%)	7.5%	5.0%	2.5%
Idle machine capacity (%)	10%	6%	2%

Cost estimation and cost behaviour

Questions to Chapter 23

Question 23.1

Basic

A hospital's records show that the cost of carrying out health checks in the last five accounting periods has been as follows:

Period	Number of patients seen	Total cost $
1	650	17 125
2	940	17 800
3	1 260	18 650
4	990	17 980
5	1 150	18 360

Using the high–low method and ignoring inflation, the estimated cost of carrying out health checks on 850 patients in period 6 is:

(A) $17 515
(B) $17 570
(C) $17 625
(D) $17 680

CIMA – Management Accounting Fundamentals

Question 23.2

Intermediate

Brisbane Limited has recorded the following sales information for the past six months:

Month	Advertising expenditure £000	Sales revenue £000
1	1.5	30
2	2	27
3	1.75	25
4	3	40
5	2.5	32
6	2.75	38

The following has also been calculated:

Σ(Advertising expenditure) = £13 500

Σ(Sales revenue) = £192 000

Σ(Advertising expenditure $\times$ Sales revenue) = £447 250 000

Σ(Sales revenue^2) = £6 322 000 000

Σ(Advertising expenditure^2) = £32 125 000.

What is the value of b, i.e. the gradient of the regression line (see formulae 23.1 and 23.2)?

(A) 0.070
(B) 0.086
(C) 8.714
(D) 14.286

ACCA – Financial Information for Management

Question 23.3

Intermediate: Linear regression analysis

A company is seeking to establish whether there is a linear relationship between the level of advertising expenditure and the subsequent sales revenue generated.

Figures for the last eight months are as follows:

Month	Advertising expenditure £000	Sales revenue £000
1	2.65	30.0
2	4.25	45.0
3	1.00	17.5
4	5.25	46.0
5	4.75	44.5
6	1.95	25.0
7	3.50	43.0
8	3.00	38.5
Total	26.35	289.5

Further information is available as follows:

Σ(Advertising expenditure $\times$ Sales revenue) = £1055.875

Σ(Advertising expenditure)^2 = £101.2625

Σ(Sales revenue)^2 = £11 283.75

All of the above are given in £ million.

Required:

(a) On a suitable graph plot advertising expenditure against sales revenue or *vice versa* as appropriate. Explain your choice of axes.

(5 marks)

(b) Using regression analysis calculate, using formulae 23.1 and 23.2 in the text, a line of best fit. Plot this on your graph from (a).

(5 marks)
(Total 10 marks)
ACCA – Financial Information for Management

Question 23.4

Advanced: Linear regression analysis with price level adjustments

Savitt Ltd manufactures a variety of products at its industrial site in Ruratania. One of the products, the LT, is produced in a specially equipped factory in which no other production takes place. For technical reasons the company keeps no stocks of either LTs or the raw material used in their manufacture. The costs of producing LTs in the special factory during the past four years have been as follows:

	2013 (£)	2014 (£)	2015 (£)	(2016) (estimated) (£)
Raw materials	70 000	100 000	130 000	132 000
Skilled labour	40 000	71 000	96 000	115 000
Unskilled labour	132 000	173 000	235 000	230 000
Power	25 000	33 000	47 000	44 000
Factory overheads	168 000	206 000	246 000	265 000
Total production costs	£435 000	£583 000	£754 000	£786 000
Output (units)	160 000	190 000	220 000	180 000

The costs of raw materials and skilled and unskilled labour have increased steadily during the past four years at an annual compound rate of 20 per cent, and the costs of factory overheads have increased at an annual compound rate of 15 per cent during the same period. Power prices increased by 10 per cent on 1 January 2014 and by 25 per cent on 1 January of each subsequent year. All costs except power are expected to increase by a further 20 per cent during 2017. Power prices are due to rise by 25 per cent on 1 January 2017.

The directors of Savitt Ltd are now formulating the company's production plan for 2017 and wish to estimate the costs of manufacturing the product LT. The finance director has expressed the view that 'the full relevant cost of producing LTs can be determined only if a fair share of general company overheads is allocated to them'. No such allocation is included in the table of costs above.

You are required to:

(a) use linear regression analysis to estimate the relationship of total production costs to volume for the product LT for 2017 (ignore general company overheads and do *not* undertake a separate regression calculation for each item of cost);

(12 marks)

(b) discuss the advantages and limitations of linear regression analysis for the estimation of cost–volume relationships;

(8 marks)

(c) comment on the view expressed by the finance director.

(5 marks)
(Total 25 marks)

Ignore taxation.

ICAEW Elements of Financial Decisions

Question 23.5

Intermediate: Cost estimation using the linear regression formula

The management accountant at Josephine Ltd is trying to predict the quarterly total maintenance cost for a group of similar machines. She has extracted the following information for the last eight quarters:

Quarter number	1	2	3	4	5	6	7	8
Total maintenance cost (£'000)	265	302	222	240	362	295	404	400
Production units ('000)	20	24	16	18	26	22	32	30

The effects of inflation have been eliminated from the above costs.

The management accountant is using linear regression to establish an equation of the form $y = a + bx$ and has produced the following preliminary calculations:

Σ(total maintenance cost $\times$ production units) = £61 250 million

Σ(total maintenance cost)^2 = £809 598 million

Σ(production units)^2 = 4 640 million

Required:

(a) Establish the equation which will allow the management accountant to predict quarterly total maintenance costs for given level of production. Interpret your answer in terms of fixed and variable maintenance costs.

(7 marks)

(b) Using the equation established in (a), predict the total maintenance cost for the next quarter when planned production is 44 000 units. Suggest a major reservation, other than the effect of inflation. you would have about this prediction.

(3 marks)
(10 marks)
ACCA – Financial Information for Management

Question 23.6

Advanced: Learning curve

A new product has a budgeted total profit of $75 000 from the first 64 units. The time taken to produce the first unit was 225 hours. The labour rate is $40 per hour. A 90 per cent learning curve is expected to apply indefinitely.

Note: The learning index for a 90 per cent learning curve is -0.152

Required:

Calculate the sensitivity of the budgeted total profit from the first 64 units to independent changes in:

(i) The labour rate

(ii) The learning rate.

(10 marks)

Question 23.7

Advanced: Learning curve

PWR is a manufacturing company that is about to launch a new product: Product Z. Details of the variable costs incurred in producing one unit of Product Z are as follows:

Labour	$25 per hour
Materials	$52 per unit
Variable overheads	$5 per labour hour

Learning curve

Product Z is produced in batches of ten units. The first batch of ten units is expected to take 15 labour hours. There will be 95 per cent learning curve that will continue until 64 batches have been produced.

Note: The learning index for a 95 per cent learning curve $= -0.074$

Required:

(a) (i) Calculate the time required to produce the 64th batch of Product Z.

(3 marks)

(ii) Calculate the total variable cost of the 64th batch of Product Z.

(2 marks)

(b) Explain THREE conditions that must exist in the production process of Product Z for the learning curve effect to be realised.

(5 marks)
(Total 10 marks)

Question 23.8

Advanced: Learning curve

A company has developed a new product. Details are as follows:

Selling price and product life cycle

The product will have a life cycle of 10 000 units. It is estimated that the first 9000 units will be sold for $124 each and then the product will enter the 'decline' stage of its life cycle. It is difficult to forecast the selling price for the 1000 units that will be sold during this stage.

Costs

Labour will be paid at $12 per hour. Other variable costs will be $38 per unit. Fixed costs will total $80 000 over the life cycle of the product. The labour rate and both of these costs will not change throughout the product's life cycle.

Learning curve

The first batch of 100 units will take 1500 labour hours to produce. There will be an 85 per cent learning curve that will continue until 6400 units have been produced. Batches after this level will each take the same amount of time as the 64th batch. The batch size will always be 100 units.

Required:

Calculate

(a) the cumulative average time per batch for the first 64 batches

(2 marks)

(b) the time taken for the 64th batch

(3 marks)

(c) the average selling price of the final 1000 units that will allow the company to earn a total profit of $1 00 000 from the product

(5 marks)
(Total 10 marks)

Note: The learning index for an 85 per cent learning curve is -0.2345

Question 23.9

Advanced: Estimation of costs and incremental hours using the learning curve

BL plc has developed a new product, the Webcam IV, to add to its existing range of computer peripherals. Each unit of the Webcam IV will be sold for £60 in a highly competitive market.

The initial estimated unit costs of a Webcam IV are as follows:

	£
Direct materials	28.00
Variable processing cost:	
18 minutes @ £25/hour	7.50
	35.50

There are also annual product specific fixed costs of £240 000. These are to be incurred at a constant rate throughout the year. No units of the Webcam IV have yet been made.

BL plc plans to make and sell 1000 units each month during the year commencing 1 April.

The following adjustments are to be made to the initial estimated costs when determining the standard cost of the product:

(i)   There is an expected material loss equal to 5 per cent of the material used. This loss has no value and its cost is to be borne by the product.

(ii) A 90 per cent learning curve effect is expected to apply.

Note: The formula for a 90 per cent learning curve is $y = ax^{-0.1520}$.

Required:

(a) Calculate the standard variable cost of production of the Webcam IV for April.

(3 marks)

(b) Calculate the standard variable cost of production for September (month 6) given that output in every month will be in accordance with the budgeted output of 1000 units per month and the 90 per cent learning curve effect will continue to apply.

(6 marks)

The actual results for the month of April were as follows:

Sales	900 units @ £62 each unit
Production	1 000 units
Direct materials used cost	£31 870
Variable processing: 2425 minutes costing	£1 070
Fixed costs incurred	£24 840

It has now been recognized that an 80 per cent rate of learning should have been used for the original standard cost (instead of the 90 per cent learning curve that was used).

Note: The formula for an 80 per cent learning curve is $y = ax^{-0.320}$.

Required:

(c) Prepare a statement for April using a contribution approach that reconciles the budgeted profit based on the original standard costs (based on the 90 per cent learning curve) with the actual profit. Your statement should clearly identify the revised budgeted profit, the standard profit, and the planning and operating variances in as much detail as possible. Assume that stock is valued at revised standard cost.

(12 marks)

(d) Explain the importance of recognizing the effects of the learning curve when preparing performance reports.

(4 marks)
(Total 25 marks)
CIMA Management Accounting – Performance Management

Quantitative models for the planning and control of inventories

Questions to Chapter 24

Question 24.1

Intermediate

A domestic appliance retailer with multiple outlets stocks a popular toaster known as the Autocrisp 2000, for which the following information is available:

Average sales	75 per day
Maximum sales	95 per day
Minimum sales	50 per day
Lead time	12–18 days
Re-order quantity	1750

(i) Based on the data above, at what level of stocks would a replenishment order be issued?

(A) 1050

(B) 1330

(C) 1710

(D) 1750

(ii) Based on the data above, what is the maximum level of stocks possible?

(A) 1750

(B) 2860

(C) 3460

(D) 5210

CIMA Stage 1

Question 24.2

Intermediate: Calculation of EOQ

One of the components used by K Ltd is ordered from a specialist supplier. The daily usage for this component and the time between placing and receiving an order (the lead time) can vary as follows:

Maximum usage	750 per day
Average usage	580 per day
Minimum usage	450 per day
Maximum lead time	15 days
Average lead time	12 days
Minimum lead time	8 days.

Calculate the number of units that can be ordered at the re-order level if, as a result of storage problems, the company cannot allow stock to rise above 15 000 units.

(3 marks)
CIMA Management Accounting Fundamentals

Question 24.3

Intermediate

The purchase price of an item of inventory is $25 per unit. In each three month period the usage of the item is 20 000 units. The annual holding costs associated with one unit equate to 6 per cent of its purchase price. The cost of placing an order for the item is $20.

What is the Economic Order Quantity (EOQ) for the inventory item to the nearest whole unit?

(A) 730

(B) 894

(C) 1461

(D) 1633

ACCA F2 Management Accounting

Question 24.4

Intermediate

The following data are given for sub-questions (a) and (b) below

FP is a retailer of office products. For one particular model of calculator there is an annual demand of 26 000 units. Demand is predictable and spread evenly throughout the year. Supplies are received two weeks after placing the order and no buffer inventory is required.

The calculators cost $14 each. Ordering costs are $160 per order. The annual cost of holding one calculator in inventory is estimated to be 10 per cent of the purchase cost.

(a) The economic order quantity (EOQ) for this model of calculator will be:

    (A) 2438 units

    (B) 771 units

    (C) 67 units

    (D) 2060 units

(2 marks)

(b) FP has decided not to use the EOQ and has decided to order 2600 calculators each time an order is placed. The total ordering and holding costs per annum will be:

    (A) $5240

    (B) $19 800

    (C) $208 014

    (D) $3420

(2 marks)
P1 Performance Operations

Question 24.5

Advanced: Impact of JIT on stockholding costs

XY a company that manufactures a range of timber products, is considering changing to a just-in-time (JIT) production system.

Currently XY employs staff who are contracted to work and be paid for a total of 3 937.75 hours per month. Their labour efficiency ratio is 96 per cent and, as a result, they are able to produce 3780 standard hours of output each month in normal working hours.

Overtime working is used to meet additional demand, though the management of XY try to avoid the need for this because it is paid at a 50 per cent premium to the normal hourly rate of $10 per hour. Instead, XY plan production so that in months of lower demand inventory levels increase to enable sales demand to be met in other months. XY has determined that the cost of holding inventory is $6 per month for each standard hour of output that is held in inventory.

XY has forecast the demand for its products for the next six months as follows:

Month	Demand (Standard hours)
1	3 100
2	3 700
3	4 000
4	3 300
5	3 600
6	4 980

You may assume that all production costs (other than labour) are either fixed or are not driven by labour hours worked, and that there is zero inventory at the start of month 1 and at the end of month 6. Assume also that production and sales occur evenly during each month at present, and that the minimum contracted hours will remain the same with the JIT system.

Required:

(a) With the current production system,

   (i) Calculate for each of the six months and the period in total, the total inventory holding costs.

   (ii) Calculate the total production cost savings made by changing to a JIT production system.

(6 marks)

(b) Explain TWO other factors that should be considered by XY before changing to a JIT production system.

(4 marks)
(Total 10 marks)
CIMA P2 Performance Operations

Question 24.6

Advanced: EOQ and JIT management methods

TNG Co expects annual demand for product X to be 255 380 units. Product X has a selling price of £19 per unit and is purchased for £11 per unit from a supplier, MKR Co. TNG places an order for 50 000 units of product X at regular intervals throughout the year. Because the demand for product X is to some degree uncertain, TNG maintains a safety (buffer) stock of product X which is sufficient to meet demand for 28 working days. The cost of placing an order is £25 and the storage cost for Product X is 10 pence per unit per year.

TNG normally pays trade suppliers after 60 days but MKR has offered a discount of 1 per cent for cash settlement within 20 days.

TNG Co has a short-term cost of debt of 8 per cent and uses a working year consisting of 365 days.

Required:

(a) Calculate the annual cost of the current ordering policy. Ignore financing costs in this part of the question.

(4 marks)

(b) Calculate the annual saving if the economic order quantity model is used to determine an optimal ordering policy. Ignore financing costs in this part of the question.

(5 marks)

(c) Determine whether the discount offered by the supplier is financially acceptable to TNG Co.

(4 marks)

(d) Critically discuss the limitations of the economic order quantity model as a way of managing stock.

(4 marks)

(e) Discuss the advantages and disadvantages of using just-in-time stock management methods.

`(8 marks)
(Total 25 marks)
ACCA 2.4: Financial Management and Control

Question 24.7

Advanced: Calculation of EOQ, discussion of the limitations of EOQ and a discussion of JIT

The newly appointed managing director of a division of Bondini plc is concerned about the length of the division's cash operating cycle. Extracts from the latest budget are given below:

Budgeted Profit and Loss Account for the year ending 30 June 2016

	(£000)	(£000)
Sales (43 200 units at £55)		2 376
Opening stock (21 600 units at £30)	648	
Purchases (43 200 units at £30)	1 296	
	1 944	
Closing stock (21 600 units at £30)	648	1 296
Budgeted gross profit		1 080

Budgeted Balance Sheet as at 30 June 2016

	(£000)
Current Assets	
Stock	648
Trade debtors	198
Current Liabilities	
Trade creditors	216

The following information has also been gathered for the managing director:

(1) Sales were made evenly during the 12 months to 30 June 2015.

(2) The amount for trade creditors relates only to purchases of stock.

(3) The division is charged interest at the rate of 15 per cent per annum on the average level of net assets held in a year.

(4) The company rents sufficient space in a warehouse to store the necessary stock at an annual cost of £3.25 per unit.

(5) The costs of ordering items of stock are as follows:

Insurance cost per order	£900
Transport cost per order	£750

(6) There will be no change in debtor and creditor payment periods.

In addition, the division maintains a purchasing department at an annual budgeted cost of £72 000.

The managing director has heard about the economic order quantity (EOQ) model and would prefer this basis to be used to calculate the order quantity. He estimates that the buffer stock level should be equal to one month's sales in order to prevent loss of revenue due to stock-outs.

Requirements:

(a) Calculate the EOQ for the division and, assuming that the division uses this as the basis for ordering goods from 1 July 2015, calculate the cash amounts which would be paid to trade creditors in each of the eight months to 28 February 2016.

(12 marks)

(b) Determine the length of the cash operating cycle at 30 June 2015 and calculate the improvement that will have taken place by 30 June 2016.

(4 marks)

(c) Discuss the practical limitations of using the EOQ approach to determining order quantities.

(5 marks)

(d) Describe the advantages and disadvantages of the just-in-time approach (i.e. when minimal stocks are maintained and suppliers deliver as required).

(4 marks)
(Total 25 marks)
ICAEW P2 Financial Management

Question 24.8

Advanced: Calculation of EOQ and safety stocks assuming uncertainty

The retailing division of Josefa plc sells Hofers and its budget for the coming year is given below:

	(£)	(£)
Sales (4 200 units at £85 each)		357 000
Cost of goods sold:		
Opening stock (200 units at £65 per unit)	13 000	
Purchases (4 200 units at £750 per unit)	294 000	
	307 000	
Closing stock (200 units at £70 per unit)	14 000	293 000
Gross profit		64 000
Purchasing department cost		
Variable (7 orders at £300 per order)	2 100	
Fixed	8 400	
Transportation costs for goods received	5 250	
(7 orders at £750 per order)		
Stock insurance costs based on average	2 000	
stockholding (500 units at £4 per unit)		
Fixed warehouse costs	43 000	
		60 750
Budgeted net profit		3 250

The supplier of Hofers is responsible for their transportation and charges Josefa plc accordingly. Recently the supplier has offered to reduce the cost of transportation from £750 per order to £650 per order if Josefa plc will increase the order size from the present 600 units to a minimum of 1000 units.

The management of Josefa plc is concerned about the retailing division's stock ordering policy. At present, a buffer stock of 200 units is maintained and sales occur evenly throughout the year. Josefa plc has contracted to buy 4200 Hofers and, irrespective of the order quantity, will pay for them in equal monthly instalments throughout the year. Transportation costs are to be paid at the beginning of the year. The cost of capital of Josefa plc is 20 per cent p.a.

Requirements:

(a) Determine the quantity of Hofers which Josefa plc should order, assuming the buffer stock level of 200 units is maintained, and calculate the improvement in net profit that will result.

(11 marks)

(b) Calculate what the buffer stock level should be, assuming that:

(i) Josefa plc changes its ordering frequency to one order (of 700 units) every two months;

(ii) stockout costs are £18 per unit;

(iii) the distribution of sales within each two-month period is not even but the following two-monthly sales pattern can occur:

2-monthly sales	Probability
500 units	0.15
600 units	0.20
700 units	0.30
800 units	0.20
900 units	0.15

(7 marks)

(c) Discuss the problems which might be experienced in attempting to maintain a stock control system based upon economic order quantities and buffer stocks.

Ignore taxation.

(7 marks)

(Total 25 marks)

ICAEW P2 Financial Management

Question 24.9

Advanced: Safety stocks and uncertain demand and quantity discounts

Runswick Ltd is a company that purchases toys from abroad for resale to retail stores. The company is concerned about its stock (inventory) management operations. It is considering adopting a stock management system based upon the economic order quantity (EOQ) model.

The company's estimates of its stock management costs are shown below:

Percentage of purchase price of toys per year

Storage costs	3
Insurance	1
Handling	1
Obsolescence	3
Opportunity costs of funds invested in stock	10

'Fixed' costs associated with placing each order for stock are £311.54.

The purchase price of the toys to Runswick Ltd is £4.50 per unit. There is a two week delay between the time that new stock is ordered from suppliers and the time that it arrives.

The toys are sold by Runswick at a unit price of £6.30. The variable cost to Runswick of selling the toys is £0.30 per unit. Demand from Runswick's customers for the toys averages 10 000 units per week, but recently this has varied from 6000 to 14 000 units per week. On the basis of recent evidence the probability of unit sales in any two week period has been estimated as follows:

Sales (units)	Probability
12 000	0.05
16 000	0.20
20 000	0.50
24 000	0.20
28 000	0.05

If adequate stock is not available when demanded by Runswick's customers in any two-week period, approximately 25 per cent of orders that cannot be satisfied in that period will be lost, and approximately 75 per cent of customers will be willing to wait until new stock arrives.

Required:

(a) Ignoring taxation, calculate the optimum order level of stock over a one year planning period using the economic order quantity model.

(3 marks)

(b) Estimate the level of safety stock that should be carried by Runswick Ltd.

(6 marks)

(c) If Runswick Ltd were to be offered a quantity discount by its suppliers of 1 per cent for orders of 30 000 units or more, evaluate whether it would be beneficial for the company to take advantage of the quantity discount. Assume for this calculation that no safety stock is carried.

(4 marks)

(d) Estimate the expected total annual costs of stock management if the economic order quantity had been (i) 50 per cent higher, (ii) 50 per cent lower than its actual level. Comment upon the sensitivity of total annual costs to changes in the economic order quantity. Assume for this calculation that no safety stock is carried.

(4 marks)

(e) Discuss briefly how the effect of seasonal sales variations might be incorporated within the model.

(3 marks)

(f) Assess the practical value of this model in the management of stock.

(5 marks)
(Total 25 marks)
ACCA Level 3 Financial Management

The application of linear programming to management accounting

Questions to Chapter 25

Question 25.1

Advanced: Optimal output and calculation of shadow prices using graphical approach

Brass Ltd produces two products, the Masso and the Russo. Budgeted data relating to these products on a unit basis for August are as follows:

	Masso (£)	Russo (£)
Selling price	150	100
Materials	80	30
Salesmen's commission	30	20

Each unit of product incurs costs of machining and assembly. The total capacity available in August is budgeted to be 700 hours of machining and 1000 hours of assembly, the cost of this capacity being fixed at £7000 and £10000 respectively for the month, whatever the level of usage made of it. The number of hours required in each of these departments to complete one unit of output is as follows:

	Masso	Russo
Machining	1.0	2.0
Assembly	2.5	2.0

Under the terms of special controls recently introduced by the government in accordance with EEC requirements, selling prices are fixed and the maximum permitted output of either product in August is 400 units (i.e. Brass Ltd may produce a maximum of 800 units of product). At the present controlled selling prices the demand for the products exceeds this considerably.

You are required:

(a) to calculate Brass Ltd's optimal production plan for August, and the profit earned;

(10 marks)

(b) to calculate the value to Brass Ltd of an independent marginal increase in the available capacity for each of machining and assembly, assuming that the capacity of the other department is not altered and the output maxima continue to apply;

(10 marks)

(c) to state the principal assumptions underlying your calculations in (a) above, and to assess their general significance.

(5 marks)
(Total 25 marks)
ICAEW Management Accounting

Question 25.2

Advanced: Optimal output and calculation of shadow prices using graphical approach

Higgins Co (HC) manufactures and sells pool cues and snooker cues. The cues both use the same type of good quality wood (ash) which can be difficult to source in sufficient quantity. The supply of ash is restricted to 5400kg per period. Ash costs $40 per kg.

The cues are made by skilled craftsmen (highly skilled labour) who are well known for their workmanship. The skilled craftsmen take years to train and are difficult to recruit. HC's craftsmen are generally only able to work for 12000 hours in a period. The craftsmen are paid $18 per hour.

HC sells the cues to a large market. Demand for the cues is strong, and in any period, up to 15000 pool cues and 12000 snooker cues could be sold. The selling price for pool cues is $41 and the selling price for snooker cues is $69.

Manufacturing details for the two products are as follows:

	Pool cues	Snooker cues
Craftsmen time per cue	0.5 hours	0.75 hours
Ash per cue	270g	270g
Other variable costs per cue	$1.20	$4.70

HC does not keep inventory.

Required:

(a) Calculate the contribution earned from each cue.

(2 marks)

(b) Determine the optimal production plan for a typical period assuming that HC is seeking to maximize the contribution earned. You should use a linear programming graph (using the graph paper provided), identify the feasible region and the optimal point and accurately calculate the maximum contribution that could be earned using whichever equations you need.

(12 marks)

Some of the craftsmen have offered to work overtime, provided that they are paid double time for the extra hours over the contracted 12 000 hours. HC has estimated that up to 1200 hours per period could be gained in this way.

Required:

(c) Explain the meaning of a shadow price (dual price) and calculate the shadow price of both the labour (craftsmen) and the materials (ash).

(5 marks)

(d) Advise HC whether to accept the craftsmens' initial offer of working overtime, discussing the rate of pay requested, the quantity of hours and one other factor that HC should consider.

(6 marks)
(25 marks)
ACCA Performance Management

Question 25.3

Advanced: Optimal output and calculation of shadow prices using graphical approach

MF plc manufactures and sells two types of product to a number of customers. The company is currently preparing its budget for the year ending 31 December which it divides into 12 equal periods.

The cost and resource details for each of the company's product types are as follows:

	Product type M £	Product type F £
Selling price per unit	200	210
Variable costs per unit		
Direct material P (£2.50 per litre)	20	25
Direct material Q (£4.00 per litre)	40	20
Direct labour (£14.00 per hour)	28	35
Overhead (£4.00 per hour)	16	20
Fixed production cost per unit	40	50
	Units	Units
Maximum sales demand in period 1	1 000	3 000

The fixed production cost per unit is based upon an absorption rate of £20 per direct labour hour and a total annual production activity of 90 000 direct labour hours. One-twelfth of the annual fixed production cost will be incurred in period 1.

In addition to the above costs, non-production overhead costs are expected to be £57 750 in period 1.

During period 1, the availability of material P is expected to be limited to 31 250 litres. Other materials and sufficient direct labour are expected to be available to meet demand.

It is MF plc's policy not to hold stocks of finished goods.

Required:

(a) Calculate the number of units of product types M and F that should be produced and sold in period 1 in order to maximize profit.

(4 marks)

(b) Using your answer to (a) above, prepare a columnar budgeted profit statement for period 1 in a marginal cost format.

(4 marks)

After presenting your statement to the budget management meeting, the production manager has advised you that in period 1 the other resources will also be limited. The maximum resources available will be:

Material P	31 250 litres
Material Q	20 000 litres
Direct labour	8 750 hours

It has been agreed that these factors should be incorporated into a revised plan and that the objective should be to make as much profit as possible from the available resources.

Required:

(c) Use graphical linear programming to determine the revised production plan for period 1. State clearly the number of units of product types M and F that are to be produced.

(10 marks)

(d) Using your answer to part (c) above, calculate the profit that will be earned from the revised plan.

(3 marks)

(e) Calculate and explain the meaning of the shadow price for material Q.

(5 marks)

(f) Discuss the other factors that should be considered by MF plc in relation to the revised production plan.

(4 marks)
(Total 30 marks)
CIMA Management Accounting – Performance Management

Question 25.4

Advanced: Optimal output, shadow prices and decision making using the graphical approach

The instruments department of Max Ltd makes two products: the XL and the YM. Standard revenues and costs per unit for these products are shown below:

	XL		YM	
	(£)	(£)	(£)	(£)
Selling price		200		180
Variable costs:				
Material A (£10 per kg)	(40)		(40)	
Direct labour (£8 per hour)	(32)		(16)	
Plating (£12 per hour)	(12)		(24)	
Other variable costs	(76)		(70)	
		(160)		(150)
Fixed overheads (allocated at £7 per direct labour hour)	(28)		(14)	
Standard profit per unit		12		16

Plating is a separate automated operation and the costs of £12 per hour are for plating materials and electricity.

In any week the maximum availability of inputs is limited to the following:

Material A	120kg
Direct labour	100 hours
Plating time	50 hours

A management meeting recently considered ways of increasing the profit of the instrument department. It was decided that each of the following possible changes to the existing situation should be examined *independently* of each other.

(1) The selling price of product YM could be increased.

(2) Plating time could be sold as a separate service at £16 per hour.

(3) A new product, ZN, could be sold at £240 per unit. Each unit would require the following:

Material A	5kg
Direct labour	5 hours
Plating time	1 hour
Other variable costs	£90

(4) Overtime could be introduced and would be paid at a premium of 50 per cent above normal rates.

Requirements:

(a) Formulate a linear programme to determine the production policy which maximizes the profits of Max Ltd in the present situation (i.e. ignoring the alternative assumptions in 1 to 4 above), solve, and specify the optimal product mix and weekly profit.

(6 marks)

(b) Determine the maximum selling price of YM at which the product mix calculated for requirement (a) would still remain optimal.

(3 marks)

(c) Show how the linear programme might be modified to accommodate the sale of plating time at £16 per hour (i.e. formulate but do not solve).

(3 marks)

(d) Using shadow prices (dual values), calculate whether product ZN would be a profitable addition to the product range.

(4 marks)

(e) Ignoring the possibility of extending the product range, determine whether overtime working would be worthwhile, and if so state how many overtime hours should be worked.

(3 marks)

(f) Discuss the limitations of the linear programming approach to the problems of Max Ltd.

(6 marks)
(Total 25 marks)
ICAEW P2 Management Accounting

Question 25.5

Advanced: Calculation optimal production and shadow prices and impact of a change in demand and cost of resources

Cut and Stitch (CS) make two types of suits using skilled tailors (labour) and a delicate and unique fabric (material). Both the tailors and the fabric are in short supply and so the accountant at CS has correctly produced a linear programming model to help decide the optimal production mix.

The model is as follows:

Variables:

Let W = the number of work suits produced
 Let L = the number of lounge suits produced

Constraints

Tailors' time: $7W + 5L \leq 3500$ (hours) — this is line T on the diagram
Fabric: $2W + 2L \leq 1200$ (metres) — this is line F on the diagram
Production of work suits: $W \leq 400$ — this is line P on the diagram

Objective is to maximize contribution subject to:

$C = 48W + 40L$

On the diagram provided the accountant has correctly identified OABCD as the feasible region and point B as the optimal point.

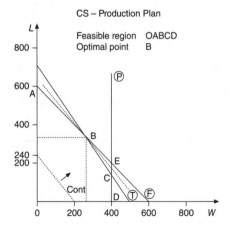

CS – Production Plan

Feasible region OABCD
Optimal point B

Required:

(a) Find by appropriate calculation the optimal production mix and related maximum contribution that could be earned by CS.

(4 marks)

(b) Calculate the shadow prices of the fabric per metre and the tailor time per hour.

(6 marks)

The tailors have offered to work an extra 500 hours provided that they are paid three times their normal rate of $1.50 per hour at $4.50 per hour.

Required:

(c) Briefly discuss whether CS should accept the offer of overtime at three times the normal rate.

(6 marks)

(d) Calculate the new optimum production plan if maximum demand for W falls to 200 units.

(4 marks)
(Total 20 marks)
ACCAF5 Performance Management

Question 25.6

Advanced: Formulation of an initial tableau and interpretation of final matrix using the Simplex method

Hint: Reverse the signs and ignore the entries of 0 and 1. You are not required to solve the model.

A chemical manufacturer is developing three fertilizer compounds for the agricultural industry. The product codes for the three products are X1, X2 and X3 and the relevant information is summarized below:

Chemical constituents: percentage make-up per tonne

	Nitrate	Phosphate	Potash	Filler
X1	10	10	20	60
X2	10	20	10	60
X3	20	10	10	60

Input prices per tonne

Nitrate	£150
Phosphate	£ 60
Potash	£120
Filler	£10

Maximum available input in tonnes per month

Nitrate	1 200
Phosphate	2 000
Potash	2 200
Filler	No limit

The fertilizers will be sold in bulk and managers have proposed the following prices per tonne.

X1	£83
X2	£81
X3	£81

The manufacturing costs of each type of fertilizer, excluding materials, are £11 per tonne.

You are required to:

(a) formulate the above data into a linear programming model so that the company may maximize contribution;

(4 marks)

(b) construct the initial Simplex tableau and state what is meant by 'slack variables' (Define X4, X5, X6 as the slack variables for X1, X2, and X3 respectively);

(2 marks)

(c) indicate, with explanations, which will be the 'entering variable' and 'leaving variable' in the first iteration;

(2 marks)

(d) interpret the final matrix of the simplex solution given below:

Basic Variable	X1	X2	X3	X4	X5	X6	Solution
X1	1	0	3	20	−10	0	4 000
X2	0	1	−1	−10	10	0	8 000
X6	0	0	−0.4	−3	1	1	600
Z	0	0	22	170	40	0	284 000

(8 marks)

(e) use the final matrix above to investigate:

  (i) the effect of an increase in nitrate of 100 tonnes per month;

  (ii) the effect of a minimum contract from an influential customer for 200 tonnes of X3 per month to be supplied.

(4 marks)
(Total 20 marks)
CIMA Stage 3 Management Accounting Techniques

Question 25.7

Advanced: Optimal output with a single limiting factor and interpretation of a final matrix

Hint: Reverse the signs in the final matrix.

(a) Corpach Ltd manufactures three products for which the sales maxima, for the forthcoming year, are estimated to be:

Product 1	Product 2	Product 3
£57 500	£96 000	£125 000

Summarized unit cost data are as follows:

	Product 1 (£)	Product 2 (£)	Product 3 (£)
Direct material cost	10.00	9.00	7.00
Variable processing costs	8.00	16.00	10.00
Fixed processing costs	2.50	5.00	4.00
	£20.50	30.00	£21.00

The allocation of fixed processing costs has been derived from last year's production levels and the figures may need revision if current output plans are different.

The established selling prices are:

	Product 1	Product 2	Product 3
	£23.00	£32.00	£25.00

The products are processed on machinery housed in three buildings:

Building A contains type A machines on which 9800 machine hours are estimated to be available in the forthcoming year. The fixed overheads for this building are £9800 p.a.

Building B1 contains type B machines on which 10 500 machine hours are estimated to be available in the forthcoming year.

Building B2 also contains type B machines and again 10 500 machine hours are estimated to be available in the forthcoming year.

The fixed overheads for the B1 and B2 buildings are, in total, £11 200 p.a.

The times required for one unit of output for each product on each type of machine, are as follows:

	Product 1	Product 2	Product 3
Type A machines	1 hour	2 hours	3 hours
Type B machines	1.5 hours	3 hours	1 hour

Assuming that Corpach Ltd wishes to maximize its profits for the ensuing year, you are required to determine the optimal production plan and the profit that this should produce.

(9 marks)

(b) Assume that, before the plan that you have prepared in part (a) is implemented, Corpach Ltd suffers a major fire which completely destroys building B2. The fire thus reduces the availability of type B machine time to 10 500 hours p.a. and the estimated fixed overhead for such machines to £8200. In all other respects the conditions set out in part (a) to this question continue to apply.

In his efforts to obtain a revised production plan the company's accountant makes use of a linear programming computer package. This package produces the following optimal tableau:

Z	X1	X2	X3	S1	S2	S3	S4	S5	
0	0	0	0	0.5	1	0	0.143	−0.429	1150
0	0	1	0	−0.5	0	0	−0.143	0.429	1850
0	0	0	0	0	0	1	−0.429	0.286	3800
0	0	0	1	0	0	0	0.429	−0.286	1200
0	1	0	0	1	0	0	0	0	2500
1	0	0	0	1.5	0	0	2.429	0.714	35050

In the above:

Z is the total contribution,

$X1$ is the budgeted output of product 1,

$X2$ is the budgeted output of product 2,

$X3$ is the budgeted output of product 3,

$S1$ is the unsatisfied demand for product 1,

$S2$ is the unsatisfied demand for product 2,

$S3$ is the unsatisfied demand for product 3,

$S4$ is the unutilized type A machine time,

$S5$ is the unutilized type B machine time.

The tableau is interpreted as follows:

Optimal plan – Make 2500 units of Product 1, 1850 units of Product 2, 1200 units of Product 3

Shadow prices – Product 1	£1.50 per unit
Type A machine time	£2.429 per hour
Type B machine time	£0.714 per hour.

Explain the meaning of the shadow prices and consider how the accountant might make use of them. Calculate the profit anticipated from the revised plan and comment on its variation from the profit that you calculated in your answer to part (a).

(9 marks)

(c) Explain why linear programming was not necessary for the facts as set out in part (a) whereas it was required for part (b).

(4 marks)
(Total 22 marks)
ACCA Level 2 Management Accounting

Part II
Solutions

An introduction to cost terms and concepts

Solutions to Chapter 2 questions

Question 2.1

Item (B) will be constant within the relevant range of output.

Item (C) will be constant per unit of output.

If output declines fixed costs per unit will increase. Total variable cost will fall in line with a fall in output and therefore item A is the correct answer.

Question 2.2

Answer = B

Question 2.3

Answer = B

Question 2.4

In Chapters 1 and 2 it was pointed out that a management accounting system should generate information to meet the following requirements:

(1) to allocate costs between cost of goods sold and inventories for internal and external profit measurement and inventory valuation;

(2) to provide relevant information to help managers to make better decisions;

(3) to provide information for planning, control and performance measurement.

The question relates to how costs can be classified for meeting the planning, control and decision-making requirements.

Planning relates to the annual budgeting and long-term processes described in Chapter 15. Within these processes costs can be classified by:

- *Behaviour* – By classifying costs into fixed, variable, semi-fixed and semi-variable categories the outcomes from different activity levels can be examined.
- *Function* – Functions are the different responsibility centres within the organization. The budget is built up by the functional levels so that everyone in the organization has a clear understanding of the role that their responsibility centre has in achieving the annual budget.
- *Expense type* – Classifying by expense types provides useful information on the nature, content and trend of different expense categories that is useful for planning how much should be authorized on spending within the different categories.
- *Controllability* – Classifying expenses by responsibility centres determines the individuals who are accountable for achieving the budget and who should thus be involved in setting the budget for the specific responsibility centres.

The management function of control consists of the measurement, reporting and the subsequent correction of performance in an attempt to ensure that a firm's objectives and plans are achieved. Within the control process costs can be classified by:

- *Behaviour* – Costs must be classified by behaviour for comparing actual and budgeted performance using flexible budgets. You should refer to Chapter 16 for a description of flexible budgeting.
- *Function* – For control, cost and revenues should be traced to the heads of the responsibility centres who are responsible for incurring them. For a description of this process you should refer to 'Responsibility Accounting' in Chapter 2.
- *Expense type* – This will ensure that like items are compared with one another when budget and actual performance are compared and trends in revenues and different expense categories are monitored.

- *Controllability* – Costs and revenues must be assigned to the responsibility heads who are made accountable for them so that effective control can be exercised.
- *Relevance* – Attention should only be focused on those expense categories where there are significant deviations from the budget. Insignificant deviations are not relevant for cost control. See 'Management by Exception' in Chapter 1 for a more detailed explanation of this point.

Decision-making involves choosing between alternative courses of actions. The following classifications are important for decision-making:

- *By behaviour* – Classification of costs by fixed, variable, semi-fixed and semi-variable is necessary for predicting future costs for alternative courses of action. In particular, classification is necessary for cost–volume–profit analysis and identifying break-even levels. You should refer to Chapter 8 for a more detailed discussion of these topics.
- *By expense type* – This is necessary to identify how different cost categories will change as a result of pursuing alternative courses of action.
- *By relevance* – For decision-making it is necessary to distinguish between relevant and irrelevant costs and revenues for alternative courses of action. For a more detailed explanation you should refer to 'Relevant and Irrelevant Costs and Revenues' in Chapter 2.
- It is apparent from the above discussion that costs should be classified in different ways for different purposes. This is explained in more detail in the section entitled 'The cost and management accounting information system' in Chapter 2.

Question 2.5

(a) A large proportion of non-manufacturing costs are of a discretionary nature. In respect of such costs, management has some significant range of discretion as to the amount it will budget for the particular activity in question. Examples of discretionary costs (sometimes called *managed* or *programmed costs*) include advertising, research and development, and training costs. There is no optimum relationship between inputs (as measured by the costs) and outputs (as measured by revenues or some other objective function) for these costs. Furthermore, they are not predetermined by some previous commitment. In effect, management can determine what quantity of service it wishes to purchase. For example, it can choose to spend small or large amounts on research and development or advertising. The great difficulty in controlling such costs is that there is no established method for determining the appropriate amount to be spent in particular periods.

For a description of fixed and variable costs see Chapter 2. Examples of fixed costs include depreciation of the factory building, supervisors' salaries and leasing charges. Examples of variable costs include direct materials, power and sales commissions.

(b) The £500 000 is a sunk cost and cannot be avoided. It is therefore not a relevant cost for decision-making purposes. The project should be continued because the incremented/relevant benefits exceed the incremental/relevant costs:

	(£000)
Incremental benefits	350
Incremental costs	200
Net incremental benefit	150

(c) An opportunity cost is a cost that measures the opportunity lost or sacrificed when the choice of one course of action requires that an alternative course of action be given up. The following are examples of opportunity costs:

(i) If scarce resources such as machine hours are required for a special contract then the opportunity cost represents the lost profit that would have been earned from the alternative use of the machine hours.

(ii) If an employee is paid £5 per hour and is charged out at £11 per hour for committed work then, if that employee is redirected to other work, the lost contribution of £6 per hour represents the opportunity cost of the employee's time.

The CIMA terminology defines a notional cost as: 'A hypothetical cost taken into account in a particular situation to represent a benefit enjoyed by an entity in respect of which no actual cost is incurred.' The following are examples of notional costs:

(i) interest on capital to represent the notional cost of using an asset rather than investing the capital elsewhere;

(ii) including rent as a cost for premises owned by the company so as to represent the lost rent income resulting from using the premises for business purposes.

Question 2.6

(a) See Chapter 2 for a description of opportunity costs. Out of pocket cost can be viewed as being equivalent to incremental or relevant costs as described in Chapter 2.

(b) Depreciation is not a relevant cost since it will be the same for both alternatives. It is assumed that tyres and miscellaneous represent the additional costs incurred in travelling to work. The relevant costs are:

Using the car to travel to work:	(£)
Petrol	128
Tyres and miscellaneous	52
	180
Contribution from passenger	120
Relevant cost	60
Using the train:	
Relevant cost	£188

(c)

	(£000)	(£000)	(%)
Sales		2 560.0	100
Direct materials	819.2		32
Direct wages	460.8		18
Variable production overhead	153.6		6
Variable administration/selling	76.8		3
Total variable cost		1 510.4	59
Contribution		1 049.6	41
Fixed production overhead[a]	768		30
Fixed administration/selling[b]	224		8.75
		992	
Profit		57.6	2.25

Notes:

[a] $100/80 \times £2\,560\,000 \times 0.24$

[b] $100/80 \times £2\,560\,000 \times 0.07$

Cost assignment

Solutions to Chapter 3 questions

Question 3.1

Budgeted overhead rate = £258750/11250 hours = £23 per machine hour

Overheads absorbed = £23 × 10980

Actual hours = £252540

Overheads incurred = £254692

Overheads absorbed = £252540

Under-absorbed overheads = £2152

Answer = A

Question 3.2

Overhead absorbed $275000(110000 × $2.5)

Overhead incurred $300000

Under absorbed = $25000

Answer = B

Question 3.3

Actual cost $108875

Overhead absorbed $105000 (30000 × $3.50)

Under absorbed $3875

Answer = A

Question 3.4

Budgeted machine hour rate = $3.60 ($180000/50000 hours)

Standard machine hours per unit = 1.25 (50000 hours/40000 units)

	$
Overheads incurred	178080
Overheads absorbed (38760 units × 1.25 hours × $3.60) =	174420
Under absorbed overheads	3660

Answer = (b)

Question 3.5

$$\text{Stores (S)} = 6300 + 0.05 \text{ Maintenance (M)}$$
$$M = 8450 + 0.1S$$

Rearranging the equations:

$$S = 6300 + 0.05M \text{ (1)}$$
$$-0.1S = 8450 - M \text{(2)}$$

Multiply equation (1) by 20 and (2) by 1

$$20S = 126000 + M$$
$$-0.1S = 8450 - M$$

$19.9S = 134450$

$S = £6756$

Substituting for S in equation (1)

$6756 = 6300 + 0.05M$

$0.05M = 456$

$M = £9126$

For production department 1, the total overheads

$= 17500 + (£6756 \times 60\%) + (9126 \times 75\%)$

$= £28398$

Answer = C

Question 3.6

(a) Calculation of department overhead rates

	Department P (£)	Department Q (£)	Department R (£)
Repairs and maintenance	42000	10000	10000
Depreciation	17000[a]	14000	9000
Consumable supplies	4500[b]	2700	1800
Wage-related costs	48250	26250	12500
Indirect labour	45000[a]	27000	18000
Canteen/rest/smoke room	15000[c]	9000	6000
Business rates and insurance	13000[d]	10400	2600
	184750	99350	55900
Direct labour hours	50000	30000	20000
Overhead absorption rate	£3.70	£3.31	£3.00

Notes:

The calculations for Department P are:

[a]Depreciation = £170000/£400000 × £40000.

[b]Consumable supplies = 50000/100000 × £9000.

[c]Canteen = 25/50 × £30000.

[d]Business rates insurance = 5000/10000 × £26000.

(b) Job 976: Sample quotation

		(£)	(£)
Direct materials			800.00
Direct labour	P (30 × £7.72[a])	231.60	
	Q (10 × £7.00[b])	70.00	
	R (5 × £5.00[c])	25.00	326.60
Overhead absorbed	P (30 × £3.70)	111.00	
	Q (10 × £3.31)	33.10	
	R (5 × £3.00)	15.00	159.10
Production cost			1285.70
Selling, distribution and administration costs (20% × £1285.70)			257.14
Total cost			1542.84
Profit margin (20% of selling price)			385.71
Selling price (£1542.84 × 100/800)			1928.55

Notes:

[a]£386000/50000.

[b]£210000/30000.

[c]£100000/20000.

(c)

	(£)
Direct materials	800.00
Direct labour	326.60
Prime cost	1 126.60
Overhead applied (125%)	1 408.25
Total cost	2 534.85

The auditor's system results in a higher cost for this quotation. However, other jobs will be undercosted with the previous system. The alternative (new) system will result in the reporting of more accurate job costs with some job costs being higher, and others being lower, than the present system. For a more detailed answer see the section on plant-wide (blanket) overhead rates in Chapter 3.

Question 3.7

(a)

Calculation of overhead absorption rates

	Machining (£000)	**Assembly** (£000)	**Finishing** (£000)	**Stores** (£000)	**Maintenance** (£000)
Allocated costs	600.00	250.00	150.00	100.00	80.00
Stores apportionment (10%)	40.00 (40%)	30.00 (30%)	20.00 (20%)	(100.00)	10.00
Maintenance apportionment	49.50 (55%)	18.00 (20%)	18.00 (20%)	4.50 (5%)	(90.00)
Stores apportionment[a]	2.00 (4/9)	1.50 (3/9)	1.00 (2/9)	(4.50)	
Total	691.50	299.50	189.00	—	—
Machine hours	50 000				
Labour hours		30 000	20 000		
Overhead absorption rates[b]	13.83	9.98	9.45		

Notes:

[a]Costs have become too small at this stage to justify apportioning 10 per cent of the costs to the maintenance department.

Therefore stores costs are apportioned in the ratio 40 : 30 : 20.

[b]Machine hours are the predominant activity in the machine department whereas labour hours are the predominant activity in the assembly and finishing departments. Therefore machine hours are used as the allocation base in the machining department and direct labour hours are used for the assembly and finishing departments.

(b)

Quotation for Job XX34

	(£)	(£)
Direct material		2 400.00
Direct labour		1 500.00
Overhead cost:		
Machining (45 machine hours at £13.83)	622.35	
Assembly (15 labour hours at £9.98)	149.70	
Finishing (12 labour hours at £9.45)	113.40	885.45
Total cost		4 785.45
Selling price (Profit margin = 20% of selling price		
∴ selling price = £4 785.45/0.8)		5 981.81

(c)

Overhead control account

	(£)		(£)
Overhead incurred	300 000	WIP control (30 700 hrs at £9.98)	306 386
Balance – over-recovery transferred to costing profit and loss account	6 386		
	306 386		306 386

(d) For the answer to this question see 'An illustration of the two-stage process for an ABC system' in Chapter 3. In particular, the answer should stress that cost centres will consist of activity cost centres rather than departmental centres. Separate cost driver rates would also be established for the service departments and the costs would be allocated to cost objects via cost driver rates rather than being reallocated to production departments and assigned within the production department rates. The answer should also stress that instead of using just two volume-based cost drivers (e.g. direct labour and machine hours) a variety of cost drivers would be used, including non-volume-based drivers such as number of set-ups and number of material issues. The answer could also stress that within the machining department a separate set-up activity centre might be established with costs being assigned using the number of set-ups as the cost driver. The current system includes the set-up costs within the machine hour overhead rate.

Question 3.8

(a)

	Department A	Department B
Allocated costs	£217 860	£374 450
Apportioned costs	45 150	58 820
Total departmental overheads	263 010	433 270
Overhead absorption rate	£19.16 (£263 010/13 730)	£26.89 (£433 270/16 110)

(b)

	Department A (£)	Department B (£)	Department C (£)
Allocated costs	219 917	387 181	103 254
Apportionment of 70% of Department C costs[a]	32 267	40 011	(72 278)
Apportionment of 30% of Department C costs[b]	11 555	19 421	(30 976)
Total departmental overheads	263 739	446 613	
Overheads charged to production	261 956[c]	455 866[d]	
Under-/over-recovery	1 783	(9 253)	

Notes:

[a]Allocated on the basis of actual machine hours

[b]Allocated on the basis of actual direct labour hours

[c]£19.16 × 13 672 actual machine hours

[d]£26.89 × 16 953 actual direct labour hours

(c) See Appendix 3.1 (Chapter 3) for the answer to this question.

Question 3.9

(a) *Year 1*

(1) Budgeted machine hours	132 500
(2) Budgeted fixed overheads	£2 411 500 (132 500 × £18.20)
(3) Actual machine hours	134 200 (£2 442 440/£18.20)
(4) Fixed overheads absorbed	£2 442 440
(5) Actual fixed overheads incurred	£2 317 461
Over-absorption of fixed overheads	£124 979 (5 − 4)

The section on 'Under- and over-recovery of fixed overheads' in Chapter 3 indicates that an under- or over-recovery will arise whenever actual activity or expenditure differs from budgeted activity or expenditure. Actual activity was 1700 hours in excess of budget and this will result in an over-recovery of fixed overheads of £30 940. Actual overheads incurred were £94 039 (£2 317 461 − £2 411 500) less than budget and this is the second factor explaining the over-absorption of fixed overheads.

Summary	(£)
Over-recovery due to actual expenditure being less than budgeted expenditure	94 039
Over-recovery due to actual activity exceeding budgeted activity	30 940
Total over-recovery of overhead for year 1	124 979

Year 2

(1) Budgeted machine hours (134 200 × 1.05)	140 910
(2) Budgeted fixed overheads	£2 620 926
(3) Fixed overhead rate (£2 620 926/140 900 hours)	£18.60
(4) Actual fixed overheads incurred	£2 695 721
(5) Fixed overheads absorbed (139 260 × £18.60)	£2 590 236
(6) Under-recovery of overhead for year 2 (4 – 5)	£105 485

Analysis of under-recovery of overhead	**(£)**
Under-recovery due to actual activity	
being less than budgeted activity (139 260 − 140 910) × £18.60	30 690
Under-recovery due to actual expenditure being greater	
than budgeted expenditure (£2 695 721 − £2 620 926	74 795
Total under-recovery for the year	105 485

Change in the overhead rate

Change in the rate (£18.60 − £18.20)/£18.20	= + 2.198%
This can be analyzed as follows:	
Increase in budgeted expenditure	= + 8.684%
(£2 620 926 − £2 411 500)/£2 411 500	
Increase in budgeted activity	
(140 910 hours − 132 500 hrs)/132 500	= + 6.347%

The increase of 2.198 per cent in the absorption rate is due to an expenditure increase of 8.684 per cent in budgeted expenditure partly offset by an increase in budgeted activity of 6.347 per cent over the 2 years.

Proof

$(1.08684/1.06347) − 1 = 0.02198 (2.198\%)$

(b) See 'Plant-wide (blanket) overhead rates' and 'Budgeted overhead rates' in Chapter 3 for the answers to these questions.

Question 3.10

(a) (i) and (ii) An activity increase of 150 hours (1650 – 1500) results in an increase in total overheads of £675. It is assumed that the increase in total overheads is due entirely to the increase in variable overheads arising from an increase in activity. Therefore the variable overhead rate is £4.50 (£675/150 hours) per machine hour. The cost structure is as follows:

1. Activity level (hours)	1 500	1 650	2 000
2. Variable overheads at £4.50 per hour	£6 750	£7 425	£9 000
3. Total overheads	£25 650	£26 325	£27 900
4. Fixed overheads (3 – 2)	£18 900	£18 900	£18 900

(iii) The fixed overhead rate is £10.50 (£15 − £4.50 variable rate)

$$\text{normal activity} = \text{fixed overheads (£18 900)/fixed overhead rate (£10.50)}$$
$$= 1800 \text{ machine hours}$$

(iv) Under-absorption = 100 machine hours (1800 − 1700) at £10.50 = £1050

(b) (i) A machine hour rate is recommended for the machine department because most of the overheads (e.g. depreciation and maintenance) are likely to be related to machine hours. For non-machine labour-intensive departments, such as the finishing department, overheads are likely to be related to direct labour hours rather than machine hours. Overheads are therefore charged to jobs performed in the finishing department using the direct labour hour method of recovery.

Calculation of overhead rates

	Machining department	**Finishing department**
Production overhead	£35 280	£12 480
Machine hours	11 200	
Direct labour hours		7 800
Machine hour overhead rate	£3.15	
Direct labour hour overhead rate		£1.60

(ii)

	Machining department	Finishing department
Direct materials	(£)	(£)
(189 × 1.1 × £2.35/0.9)	542.85	—
Direct labour[a]		
25 hours × £4	100.00	
28 hours × £4		112.00
Production overhead		
46 machine hours at £3.15	144.90	
28 direct labour hours at £1.60		44.80
	787.75	156.80

Total cost of job = £944.55 (£787.75 + £156.80)

Note:

[a]Overtime premiums are charged to overheads, and are therefore not included in the above job cost.

Question 3.11

(a)

$$\text{Overhead rate} = \frac{\text{Budgeted overhead}}{\text{Budgeted direct wages}} \times 100$$

$$= \frac{£225\,000}{£150\,000} \times 100$$

$$= \underline{150\%}$$

(b)

	(£)
Direct materials	190
Direct wages	170
Production overhead (150% × £170)	255
Production cost	615
Gross profit (1/3 × £615)	205
	820

(c) (i) Each department incurs different overhead costs. For example, the overhead costs of Department A are considerably higher than those of the other departments. A blanket overhead rate is only appropriate where jobs spend the same proportion of time in each department. See the section on blanket overhead rates in Chapter 3 for an explanation of why departmental overhead rates are preferable.

(ii) Department A machine-hour overhead rate:

$$\frac{£120\,000}{40\,000 \text{ machine hours}} = £3 \text{ per machine hour}$$

A machine-hour rate is preferable because machine hours appear to be the dominant activity. Also, most of the overheads incurred are likely to be related to machine hours rather than direct labour hours. Possibly one worker operates four machines since the ratio is 40 000 machine hours to 10 000 direct labour hours. If some jobs do not involve machinery but others do, then two separate cost centres should be established (one related to machinery and the other related to jobs which involve direct labour hours only).

Department B direct labour hour overhead rate:

$$\frac{£30\,000}{50\,000 \text{ direct labour hours}} = £0.60 \text{ per labour hour}$$

Because direct labour hours are five times greater than machine hours a direct labour hour overhead rate is recommended. A comparison of direct labour hours and direct wages for budget, actual and job 657 for Department B suggests that wage rate are not equal throughout the department. Therefore the direct wages percentage method is inappropriate.

Department C direct labour hour overhead rate:

$$\frac{£75\,000}{25\,000 \text{ direct labour hours}} = £3 \text{ per direct labour hour}$$

This method is chosen because it is related to time and machine hours are ruled out. A comparison of budgeted direct wages and labour hours for budget, actual and job 657 for Department C suggests that wage rates are equal at £1 per hour throughout the department. Therefore direct labour hours or direct wages percentage methods will produce the same results.

(d) Department A (40 machine hours × £3)   120
            B (40 labour hours × £0.60)   24
            C (10 labour hours × £3)   30
                                 174

(e) (i) *Current rate (actual wages × 150%):*

	Absorbed (£000s)	Actual (£000s)	Over/(under)-absorbed (£000s)
Department A	45	130	(85)
B	120	28	92
C	45	80	(35)
	210	238	(28)

(ii) *Proposed rates:*

	Absorbed (£000s)	Actual (£000s)	Over/(under)-absorbed (£000s)
Department A	135	130	5
B	27	28	(1)
C	90	80	10
	252	238	14

Question 3.12

(a) It is easier to allocate service department B first because it provides services to both of the other service departments.

	Centre 1 (£)	Centre 2 (£)	Service A (£)	Service B (£)	Service C (£)
	2 000	3 500	300	500	700
Service B	250 (50%)	100 (20%)	100 (20%)	(500)	50 (10%)
	2 250	3 600	400		750
Service A	180 (45%)	180 (45%)	(400)	40 (10%)	
	2 430	3 780		40	750
Service C	450 (60%)	300 (40%)			(750)
	2 880	4 080		40	
Service B	20 (50%)	8 (20%)	8 (20%)	(40)	4 (10%)
	2 900	4 080	8		4
Service A	4 (45%)	4 (45%)	(8)		
Service C (Balance shared equally)	2	2			(4)
Total	2 906	4 094			

(b) It would appear that the department is machine intensive so it is preferable to use machine hours. The overhead absorption rate per machine hour is £0.969 (£2906/3000 machine hours).

Question 3.13

Cost driver rates:
Set-up costs = $250 per set-up ($200 000/800)
Inspection/quality costs = $300 per test ($120 000/400)
Stores receiving = $140 per requisition ($252 000/1 800)

Product W cost per unit

	$	
Direct materials	2.50	
Direct labour	0.54	
Set-up costs	1.67	(15 000/150 units = 100 batches × $250 = $25 000/ 15 000 units)
Inspection/quality costs	1.00	100/2 = 50 × $300 = $15 000/15 000 units
Stores receiving costs	0.75	(80 × $140 = $11 200/15 000 units)
	6.46	

Question 3.14

(a) (i) *Direct apportionment*

	Heat (£000)	Maintenance (£000)	Steam (£000)	Processing (£000)	Assembly (£000)	Total (£000)
Allocation	90	300	240			630
Heat (4 : 5)	(90)			40	50	—
Maintenance (1 : 2)		(300)		100	200	—
Steam (2 : 1)			(240)	160	80	—
				300	330	630

With the direct method of allocation, inter-service department apportionments are ignored; service department costs are reapportioned to *production* departments only.

(ii) *Step-down method*

This method is the specified order of closing described in Appendix 3.1. There the service department that provided the largest proportion of services for other services was closed first. In this answer the service department providing the largest value of cost inputs to other service departments (namely the maintenance department) is closed first, and the department providing the second largest value of cost input to other service departments (namely steam) is closed next. Return charges are not made.

	Heat (£000)	Maintenance (£000)	Steam (£000)	Processing (£000)	Assembly (£000)	Total (£000)
Allocation	90	300	240			630
Maintenance[a]	30	(300)	45	75	150	
Steam[a]	60		(285)	150	75	
Heat[a]	(180)			80	100	
				305	32	630

Note:

[a]Proportions allocated to each department:

Maintenance = 3/30, 4.5/30, 7.5/30, 15/30

Steam = 192/912, 480/912, 240/912

Heat = 4/9, 5/9.

(iii) *Reciprocal method*

Either the algebraic method or the repeated distribution method can be used to take account of reciprocal service arrangements. Both are illustrated in this answer.

Algebraic method

Let

h = total cost of heating

m = total cost of maintenance

s = total cost of steam

Then

$h = 90 + (3/30)m + (192/960)s$

$m = 300 + (5/100)h + (48/960)s$

$s = 240 + (5/100)h + (4.5/30)m$

Expressing these equations in decimal form, we get:

$h = 90 + 0.10m + 0.2s$ (1)

$m = 300 + 0.05h + 0.05s$ (2)

$s = 240 + 0.05h + 0.15m$ (3)

Substituting for s,

$h = 90 + 0.10m + 0.2(240 + 0.05h + 0.15m)$

$m = 300 + 0.05h + 0.05(240 + 0.05h + 0.15m)$

Expanding these equations gives:

$h = 90 + 0.10m + 48 + 0.01h + 0.03m$

$m = 300 + 0.05h + 12 + 0.0025h + 0.0075m$

Rearranging,

$0.99h = 138 + 0.13m$ (4)

$0.9925m = 312 + 0.0525h$ (5)

Substituting in equation (4) for m,

$$0.99h = 138 + 0.13\frac{(312 + 0.0525h)}{0.9925}$$

$$0.99h = 138 + 40.866 + 0.0069h$$

$$h = \frac{138 + 40.866}{0.99 - 0.0069} = 181.941$$

Substituting for h in equation (5),

$$0.9925m = 312 + 0.0525 (181.941)$$

$$m = \frac{312 + 0.0525}{(181.941)} = 324.165$$

Substituting into equation (3),

$$s = 240 + 0.05 (181.941) + 0.15 (324.165) = 297.722$$

We now apportion the values of h, m and s to the production departments according to the basis of allocation specified:

	Processing (£000)	Assembly (£000)
Heat (181.941)	72.776 (40/100)	90.970 (50/100)
Maintenance (324.165)	81.041 (7.5/30)	162.082 (15/30)
Steam (297.722)	148.861 (480/960)	74.431 (240/960)
	302.678	327.483

Repeated distribution method

	Heat (£000)	Maintenance (£000)	Steam (£000)	Processing (£000)	Assembly (£000)
Allocation per question	90.00	300.00	240.00		
Heat reallocation	(90.00)	4.50 (5%)	4.50 (5%)	36.00 (40%)	45.00 (50%)
Maintenance reallocation	30.45 (10%)	(304.50)	45.67 (15%)	76.13 (25%)	152.25 (50%)
Steam reallocation	58.03 (20%)	14.51 (5%)	(290.17)	145.09 (50%)	72.54 (25%)
Heat reallocation	(88.48)	4.42 (5%)	4.42 (5%)	35.40 (40%)	44.24 (50%)
Maintenance reallocation	1.89 (10%)	(18.93)	2.84 (15%)	4.73 (25%)	9.47 (50%)
Steam reallocation	1.45 (20%)	0.36 (5%)	(7.26)	3.63 (50%)	1.82 (25%)
Heat reallocation	(3.34)	0.16 (5%)	0.17 (5%)	1.34 (40%)	1.67 (50%)
Maintenance reallocation		(0.52)		0.17	0.35
Steam[a]			(0.17)	0.11	0.06
				302.6	327.4

Note:

[a]At this stage the costs are so small that no further reallocations between service departments are justified. The costs of the maintenance department are reapportioned in the ratio 7.5 : 15, while those of the steam department are reapportioned in the ratio 480 : 240.

(b) The main problems encountered are as follows:

(i) The costs allocated to the service departments are the result of arbitrary apportionments. The costs are then reallocated from the service to production departments using further arbitrary allocations. Consequently, the associated costs attached to products will be arbitrary and dependent upon the selected apportionment methods.

(ii) If a substantial part of the service department costs are fixed and costs are allocated to production departments on the basis of usage, there is a danger that the resulting unit product costs will fail to distinguish between the fixed and variable cost categories. This could result in misleading information being used for short-term decisions.

(iii) If the responsibility accounting system allocates the actual costs of the service departments to the production departments, the production departments will be accountable for the inefficiencies arising in the service departments. Consequently, the production managers will be demotivated and the service department managers will not be motivated to be efficient because they will always be able to recover their costs.

Possible solutions include the following:

(i) Avoid the use of arbitrary apportionments and identify appropriate cost drivers for the main activities undertaken by the service/support departments using an activity-based costing (ABC) system. See Chapters 3 and 11 for an explanation of an ABC system.

(ii) Separate fixed and variable costs when reallocating service department costs to production departments.

(iii) Charge service department costs to production departments on the basis of actual usage at standard cost. If the production managers have no control over the usage of the service, the service department costs should be regarded as uncontrollable (see' Guidelines for applying the controllability principle' in Chapter 16 for a discussion of this point). The service department managers will be motivated to control costs if they are accountable for the difference between actual and standard usage multiplied by the standard cost.

(c) The answer should include a discussion of the following points:

(i) In today's production environment an increasing proportion of total costs are fixed, and short-term variable costs do not provide a useful measure of the cost of producing a product. Managers require an estimate of long-run product costs. The allocation of fixed costs to products provides a rough guide of a product's long-run cost. The answer should draw attention to the criticisms that Kaplan and Cooper (see Chapter 11) have made of traditional cost allocation methods and explain that an ABC system is an approach that has been recommended to overcome the problems of arbitrary overhead allocations.

(ii) It is a tradition in some industries (e.g. Government contracts) for selling prices to be based on full product costs plus a percentage profit margin.

(iii) Total manufacturing costs are required for stock valuation for external reporting. However, it is questionable whether costs computed for stock valuation ought to be used for decision-making.

(iv) It is sometimes claimed that fixed costs should be allocated to managers in order to draw their attention to those costs that the company incurs to support their activities. This is because the manager may be able to indirectly influence these costs, and should therefore be made aware of the sums which are involved. If this approach is adopted, controllable and non-controllable costs ought to be distinguished in the performance reports.

Accounting entries for a job costing system

Solutions to Chapter 4 questions

Question 4.1

Production will be charged at the most recent (higher prices) resulting in lower profits and stocks will consist of the earlier (lower prices). Therefore answer = A.

Question 4.2

(a) Purchases are 460 units and issues are 420 units resulting in a closing stock of 40 units. Therefore closing stock valuation = 40 units at the latest purchase price ($1.90) = $76. Therefore answer = D

(b) Answer = C (see outcomes for Example 4.1 in the text).

Question 4.3

The company's cost accounts are not integrated with the financial accounts. For a description of a non-integrated accounting system see 'Interlocking accounts' in Chapter 4. The following accounting entries are necessary:

Cost ledger control account

	(£)			(£)
Sales a/c	410 000	1.5.00	Balance b/f	302 000
Capital under construction a/c	50 150		Stores ledger a/c – Purchases	42 700
Balance c/f	237 500		Wages control a/c	124 000
			Production overhead a/c	152 350
			WIP a/c – Royalty	2 150
			Selling overhead a/c	22 000
			Profit	52 450
	697 650			697 650

Stores ledger control account

		(£)		(£)
1.5.00	Balance b/f	85 400	WIP a/c	63 400
	Cost ledger control a/c – Purchases	42 700	Production overhead a/c	1 450
			Capital a/c	7 650
			31.5.X0 Balance c/f	55 600
		£128 100		£128 100

Wages control account

	(£)		(£)
Cost ledger control a/c	124 000	Capital a/c	12 500
		Production	35 750
		WIP a/c	7 550
	£124 000		£124 000

Production overhead control account

	(£)		(£)
Stores ledger a/c	1450	Capital a/c	30000
Wages control a/c	35750	WIP a/c – Absorption (balancing figure)	152000
Cost ledger control a/c	152350	Costing P/L a/c (under absorption)	7550
	£189550		£189550

Work in progress control account

		(£)		(£)
1.5.00	Balance b/f	167350	Finished goods control a/c (balancing figure)	281300
	Stores ledger a/c – Issues	63400		
	Wages control a/c	75750	31.5.X0 Balance c/f [a]	179350
Production overhead absorbed		152000		
Cost ledger control a/c – Royalty		2150		
		£460650		£460650

Finished goods control account

		(£)		(£)
1.5.00	Balance b/f	49250	Cost sales a/c [b]	328000
WIP a/c		281300	31.5.X0 Balance c/f	2550
		£330550		£330550

Capital under construction account

	(£)		(£)
Stores ledger a/c	7650	Cost ledger control a/c	50150
Wages control a/c	12500		
Production overhead absorbed	30000		
	£50150		£50150

Sales account

	(£)		(£)
Costing P/L a/c	£410000	Cost ledger control a/c	£410000

Cost of sales account

	(£)		(£)
Finished goods a/c [b]	£328000	Cost P/L a/c	£328000

Selling overhead account

	(£)		(£)
Cost ledger control a/c	£22000	Costing P/L a/c	£22000

Costing profit and loss account

	(£)		(£)
Selling overhead a/c	22000	Sales a/c	410000
Production overhead (under absorbed)	7550		
Cost of sales a/c	328000		
Profit – Cost ledger control a/c	52450		
	£410000		£410000

Notes:

[a] Closing balance of work in progress = £167 350 (opening balance)

$$\frac{£12\,000}{£179\,350} \text{ (increase per question)}$$

[b] Transfer from finished goods stock to cost of sales account: £410 000 sales × (100/125) = £328 000.

Question 4.4

(a)

Raw materials stores account

	(£)		(£)
Balance b/d	49 500	Work in progress	104 800
Purchases	108 800	Loss due to flood to P&L a/c	2 400
		Balance c/d	51 100
	£158 300		£158 300
Balance b/d	51 100		

Work in progress control account

	(£)		(£)
Balance b/d	60 100	Finished goods	222 500
Raw materials	104 800	Balance c/d	56 970
Direct wages	40 200		
Production overhead	74 370		
	£279 470		£279 470
Balance b/d	56 970		

Finished goods control account

	(£)		(£)
Balance b/d	115 400	Cost of sales	212 100
Work in progress	222 500	Balance c/d	125 800
	£337 900		£337 900
Balance b/d	125 800		

Production overhead

	(£)		(£)
General ledger control	60 900	Work in progress	
Notional rent (3 × £4000)	12 000	(185% × £40 200)	74 370
Overhead over absorbed	1 470		
	£74 370		£74 370

General ledger control account

	(£)		(£)
Sales	440 000	Balance b/d	
Balance c/d	233 870	(49 500 + 60 100 + 115 400)	225 000
		Purchases	108 800
		Direct wages	40 200
		Production overhead	60 900
		Notional rent	12 000
		P & L a/c	226 970
		(profit for period: see(b))	
	673 870		673 870

(b) *Calculation of profit in cost accounts*

	(£)	(£)
Sales		440 000
Cost of sales	212 100	
Loss of stores	2 400	
Less overhead over-absorbed	214 500	
Profit	1 470	213 030
		226 970

Reconciliation statement[a]

	(£)	(£)	(£)
Profit as per cost accounts			226 970
Differences in stock values:			
Raw materials opening stock	1 500		
Raw materials closing stock	900		
WIP closing stock	1 030	3 430	
WIP opening stock	3 900		
Finished goods opening stock	4 600		
Finished goods closing stock	3 900	(12 400)	(8 970)
Add items not included in financial accounts:			
Notional rent			12 000
Profit as per financial accounts			230 000

Note:

[a]Stock valuations in the financial accounts may differ from the valuation in the cost accounts. For example, raw materials may be valued on a LIFO basis in the cost accounts, whereas FIFO or weighted average may be used in the financial accounts. WIP and finished stock may be valued on a marginal (variable costing) basis in the cost accounts, but the valuation may be based on an absorption costing basis in the financial accounts. To reconcile the profits, you should start with the profit from the cost accounts and consider what the impact would be on the profit calculation if the financial accounting stock valuations were used. If the opening stock valuation in the financial accounts exceeds the valuation in the cost accounts then adopting the financial accounting stock valuation will reduce the profits. If the closing stock valuation in the financial accounts exceeds the valuation in the cost accounts then adopting the financial accounting stock valuation will increase profits. Note that the notional rent is not included in the financial accounts and should therefore be deducted from the costing profit in the reconciliation statement.

(c) The over recovery of overhead could be apportioned between cost of goods sold for the current period and closing stocks. The justification for this is based on the assumption that the under/over recovery is due to incorrect estimates of activity and overhead expenditure, which leads to incorrect allocations being made to the cost of sales and closing stock accounts. The proposed adjustment is an attempt to rectify this incorrect allocation.

The alternative treatment is for the full amount of the under/over recovery to be written off to the cost accounting profit and loss account in the current period as a period cost. This is the treatment recommended by SSAP 9.

Question 4.5

(a)

Stores ledger control account

	(£)		(£)
Opening balance	60 140	Finished goods control a/c (1)	985 200
Cost ledger control a/c	93 106	Closing balance	58 046
	153 246		153 246

Production wages control account

	(£)		(£)
Cost ledger control a/c (2)	121 603	Finished goods control a/c	87 480
		Production overhead control a/c (2) (indirect wages)	34 123
	121 603		121 603

Production overhead control account

	(£)		(£)
Cost ledger control a/c	116 202	Finished goods control a/c (3)	61 236
Production wages control a/c (2)	34 123	Profit & loss a/c – fixed overhead (3)	90 195
Profit & loss a/c – over absorbed variable production overhead (3)	1 106		
	151 431		151 431

Finished goods control account

	(£)		(£)
Opening balance	147 890	Variable production cost of sales a/c (balance)	241 619
Stores ledger control a/c	95 200		
Production wages control a/c	87 480	Closing balance	150 187
Production overhead control a/c	61 236		
	391 806		391 806

Workings

(1)

	(Kg)	(£)
Opening stock	540	7 663
Purchases	1 100	15 840
	1 640	23 503

Issue price £23 503/1 640 = £14.33 per kg
Cost of material issues: Material Y = £14.33 × 1 164kg   =   £16 680
Other materials   =   £78 520
  £95 200

(2) *Analysis of wages*

	Direct labour (£)	Indirect labour (£)
Direct workers productive time (11 664 × £7.50)	87 480	
Direct workers unproductive time at £7.50 (12 215 hours – 11 664)		4 132.50
Overtime premium (1075 hours × £2.50)		2 687.50
Indirect workers basic time (4655 hours × £5.70)		26 533.50
Indirect workers overtime premium (405 hours × £1.90)		769.50
	87 480	34 123.00

Total wages for the period £121 603 (£87 480 + £34 123)

(3) *Analysis of overheads*

Production overheads	=	£150 325 (£116 202 + £34 123)
Fixed overheads	=	90 195 (60% × £150 325)
Variable overheads	=	60 130 (40% × £150 325)
Variable overheads absorbed	=	61 236 (70% of the direct labour cost of £87 480)
Over-absorbed overheads	=	1 106 (£61 236 – £60 130)

Note that with a marginal costing system fixed overheads are charged directly to the profit and loss account and not included in the product costs. Therefore they are not included in the finished stocks.

(b) See working (2) in part (a) for the answer to this question.

(c)

	(£)	(£)
Sales		479 462
Less: Variable production cost of sales	241 619	
Variable selling and administration overheads	38 575	
Over-absorbed variable production overheads	(1 106)	279 088
Contribution		200 374
Less: Fixed production overheads	90 195	
Fixed selling and administration overheads	74 360	164 655
Net profit		35 819

Question 4.6

(a)

Stores ledger card

Date		Kilos	Total value (£)	Average price per kilo (£)	
Opening balance		21 600	28 944	1.34	
1	Issue	(7 270)	(9 742)	1.34	
7	Purchase	17 400	23 490	—	
		31 730	42 692	1.3455	(£42 692/31 730)
8	Issue	(8 120)	(10 925)	1.3455	
15	Issue	(8 080)	(10 872)	1.3455	
20	Purchase	19 800	26 730	—	
		35 330	47 625	1.348	(£47 625/35 330)
22	Issue	(9 115)	(12 287)	1.348	
Closing balance		26 215	35 338	1.348	

Summary of transactions	(£)
Opening balance	28 944
Purchases	50 220
Issues	(43 826)
Closing balance	35 338

Raw material stock control account

	(£)		(£)
Opening balance	28 944	WIP	43 826
Purchases	50 220	Closing balance	35 338
	79 164		79 164

Production costs for the period:	(£)
Raw materials	43 826
Labour and overhead	35 407
	79 233
Cost per unit (£79 233/17 150 units)	£4.62

Units sold = opening stock (16 960) + production (17 150)
   − closing stock (17 080) = 17 030 units

Finished goods stock control account

	(£)		(£)
Opening balance	77 168	Cost of sales (difference/balancing figure)	77 491
Raw materials	43 826		
Labour and overhead	35 407	Closing balance (17 080 × £4.62)	78 910
	156 401		156 401

(b) The financial ledger control account is sometimes described as a cost control account or a general ledger adjustment account. For an explanation of the purpose of this account see 'Interlocking accounting' in Chapter 4.

(c) Budgeted production (units):

Sales	206 000
Add closing stock	18 128 (206 000 × 1.10 × 20/250)
Less opening stock	(17 080)
	207 048 units

For month 12 the raw material usage is 1.90 kilos per unit of output:

(7270 + 8120 + 8080 + 9115 = 32 585kg used)/17 150 units produced

∴ Budgeted material usage = 207 048 units × 1.9kg per unit

$$= 393 391kg$$

Budgeted material purchases

Budgeted usage	*393 391kg*
Add closing stock	22 230 (11 700 × 1.9)
Less opening stock	(26 215)
	389 406kg

Question 4.7

(a)

Raw material stock control account

	(£)		(£)
Opening balance	72 460	Finished goods (1)	608 400
Creditors	631 220	Closing balance	95 280
	703 680		703 680

Production overhead control account

	(£)		(£)
Bank/Creditors	549 630	Finished goods (3)	734 000
Wages (2)	192 970	P & L – under absorption (3)	8 600
	742 600		742 600

Finished goods stock control account

	(£)		(£)
Opening balance	183 560	Production cost of sales (5)	1 887 200
Raw materials	608 400	Closing balance (6)	225 960
Wages (4)	587 200		
Production overhead	734 000		
	2 113 160		2 113 160

Workings

(1) Raw materials issues:
Product A: 41 000 units at £7.20 per unit = £295 200
Product B: 27 000 units at £11.60 per unit = £313 200
£608 400

(2) Indirect labour charged to production overhead:
3 250 overtime premium hours at £2 per hour = £6 500 + £186 470 = £192 970

(3) Production overhead absorbed charged to finished goods:
Product A: 41 000 × 1 hour × £10 = £410 000
Product B: 27 000 × 1.2 hours × £10 = £324 000
£734 000

Production overhead under-absorbed = £549 630 + £192 970 − £734 000 = £8600

(4) Direct labour charge to finished goods stock:
Product A: 41 000 × 1 hour × £8 = £328 000
Product B: 27 000 × 1.2 hours × £8 = £259 200
£587 200

(5) Production cost of sales:

Cost of product A = £7.20 materials + £8 direct labour + £10 overhead
$$= £25.20$$

Cost of product B = £11.60 materials + £9.60 direct labour (1.2 hours × £8)
$$+ £12 \text{ overhead (1.2 hours} \times £10) = £33.20$$

Cost of sales: Product A = 38 000 units × £25.20 per unit   =   £957 600
Product B = 28 000 units × £33.20 per unit   =   £929 600
£1 887 200

(6) Valuation of closing stocks of finished goods:
Product A: 6200 units at £25.20 =   £156 240
Product B: 2100 units at £33.20 =   £69 720
£225 960

The above figure can also be derived from the balance of the account.

(b)

	Product A (£000)	Product B (£000)	Total (£000)
Sales	1 330	1 092	2 422
Production cost of sales	(957.6)	(929.6)	(1 887.2)
Gross profit (before adjustment)	372.4	162.4	534.8
Under-absorbed production overheads			(8.6)
Gross profit (after adjustment)			526.2
Non-production overheads			(394.7)
Net profit			131.5

(c) With a marginal costing system fixed production overheads are charged directly against profits whereas with an absorption costing system they are included in the product costs and therefore included in the stock valuations. This means that with absorption costing, cost of sales and profits will be affected by the changes in stocks. An increase in stocks will result in some of the fixed overheads incurred during the period being deferred to future periods, whereas with a decrease in stocks the opposite situation will apply. Thus, absorption costing profits will be higher than marginal costing profits when stocks increase and lower when stocks decrease. For a more detailed explanation of the difference in profits you should refer to 'Variable costing and absorption costing: a comparison of their impact on profit' in Chapter 7.

In this question there is a stock increase of 3000 units for product A resulting in absorption costing profits exceeding marginal costing profits by £20 400 (3000 units at £6.80 per unit fixed overhead). Conversely, for product B there is a 1000 units stock reduction resulting in marginal costing profits exceeding the absorption costing profits by £8160 (1000 units at £8.16 per unit fixed overhead). The overall impact is that absorption costing profits exceed marginal costing profits by £12 240.

Question 4.8

(a) A wages control account is a summary account which records total wages payable including employers' National Insurance contributions. The account is cleared by a credit and corresponding debits in respect of total wages costs charged to WIP and the overhead control account. The detail which supports the control account is maintained in subsidiary payroll records.

(b) (i)

	Dr (£)	Cr (£)
Wages control	122 300	
Bank		122 300
Wages control	58 160	
Employees' National Insurance		14 120
Employees' pension fund		
Contributions		7 200
Income tax		27 800
Court order retentions		1 840
Trade union subscriptions		1 200
Private health plans		6 000
	180 460	180 460

Production overhead control Dr	18 770	
Employer's National Insurance		18 770
	18 770	18 770

(ii)

Work in progress control:

Wages	77 460	
Overtime wages – direct	16 800	
Production overhead control:		
Overtime premium	9 000	
Shift premium	13 000	
Indirect wages	38 400	
Overtime wage – indirect	10 200	
Warehouse construction account	2 300	
Statutory sick pay	9 000	
Idle time	4 300	
Wages control		180 460
	180 460	180 460

Process costing

Solutions to Chapter 5 questions

Question 5.1

	Units
Opening stock	400
Input	3 000
	3 400
Closing stock	(200)
Actual losses (normal + abnormal)	(400)
Output	2 800

Answer = (a)

Question 5.2

Cost per equivalent unit (480 000/10 000) = $48

WIP equivalent units × cost per equivalent unit ($48) = $144 000

WIP equivalent units = 3000

Degree of completion = 3000/4000 = 75%

Answer = D

Question 5.3

Cost per unit = [($50 000 + $15 000 + 150% × $15 000) − (3000 × $1)]/17 000 = $4.9706

Cost of output = 18 500 × $4.9706 = $91 956

Answer = C

Question 5.4

Completed units less opening WIP equivalent units	4 000	(4 100 less 40% × 250 units)
Abnormal loss	275	
Closing WIP	45	(150 × 30%)
Equivalent units	4 320	

It is assumed that the short-cut method (see Appendix 5.1) will be used in respect of normal losses.

Answer = C

Question 5.5

(i)

	(kg)	(£)	*Process A account*	(kg)	(£)	(£)
Direct material	2 000	10 000	Normal loss	400	0.50	200
Direct labour		7 200	Process B	1 400	18.575	26 005
Process costs		8 400	Abnormal loss	200	18.575	3 715
Overhead		4 320				
	2 000	29 920		2 000		29 920

Unit cost = (£29 920 − £200)/1600 = £18.575

(ii)

Process B account

	(kg)	(£)		(kg)	(£)	(£)
Process A	1 400	26 005	Finished goods	2 620	21.75	56 989
Direct material	1 400	16 800	Normal loss	280	1.825	511
Direct labour		4 200	(10% × 2 800)			
Overhead		2 520				
Process costs		5 800				
		55 325				
Abnormal gain	100	2 175				
	2 900	57 500		2 900		57 500

Unit cost = (£55 325 − £511)/(2800 − 280) = £21.75

(iii)

Normal loss/gain account

	(kg)	(£)		(kg)	(£)
Process A	400	200	Bank (A)	400	200
Process B	280	511	Abnormal gain (B)	100	182.5
			Bank (B)	180	328.5
	680	711		680	711

(iv)

Abnormal loss/gain

	(£)		(£)
Process A	3 715	Process B	2 175
Normal loss/gain (B)	182.5	Bank	100
		Profit and loss	1 622.5
	3 897.5		3 897.5

(v)

Finished goods

	(£)	(£)
Process B		56 989

(vi)

Profit and loss account (extract)

	(£)	(£)
Abnormal loss/gain		1 622.5

Question 5.6

(a) Units completed = 8250 − Closing WIP (1600) = 6650

Calculation of number of equivalent units produced

	Completed units	Closing WIP	Total equivalent units
Previous process	6 650	1 600	8 250
Materials	6 650	1 600	8 250
Labour and overhead	6 650	960 (60%)	7 610

(b)

	(£)	Total equivalent units	Cost per unit (£)
Previous process cost	453 750	8 250	55
Materials	24 750	8 250	3
Labour and overheads	350 060	7 610	46
			104

(c)

<table>
<tr><th></th><th>Units</th><th colspan="2" align="center">Process account
(£)</th><th></th><th>Units</th><th>(£)</th></tr>
<tr><td>Input from previous process</td><td>8 250</td><td colspan="2">453 750</td><td>Finished goods^a</td><td>6 650</td><td>691 600</td></tr>
<tr><td></td><td></td><td colspan="2"></td><td>Closing WIP^b</td><td>1 600</td><td>136 960</td></tr>
<tr><td>Materials</td><td></td><td colspan="2">24 750</td><td></td><td></td><td></td></tr>
<tr><td>Labour and overheads</td><td></td><td colspan="2">350 060</td><td></td><td></td><td></td></tr>
<tr><td></td><td>8 250</td><td colspan="2">828 560</td><td></td><td>8 250</td><td>828 560</td></tr>
</table>

Note:

^aCost of completed production = 6650 units × £104 = £691 600

	(£)
^bClosing WIP: Previous process cost (1 600 × £55) =	88 000
Materials (1 600 × £3) =	4 800
Labour and overhead (960 × £46) =	44 160
	136 960

(d) See the introduction to Chapter 6 and 'Accounting for by-products' in Chapter 6 for the answer to this question.

Question 5.7

(a)

	Units
Input:	
Opening WIP	12 000
Transferred from process 1	95 000
	107 000
Output:	
Closing WIP	10 000
Normal loss	200
Completed units (balance)	96 800
	107 000

Statement of completed production and calculation of cost per unit (Process 2)

	Opening WIP (£)	Current cost (£)	Total cost (£)	Completed units	Closing WIP	Total equiv. units	Cost per unit (£)	WIP (£)
Previous process cost	13 440	107 790	121 230	96 800	10 000	106 800	1.135	11 350
Materials added	4 970	44 000	48 970	96 800	9 000	105 800	0.463	4 167
Conversion costs	3 120	51 480	54 600	96 800	7 000	103 800	0.526	3 682
	21 530	203 270	224 800				2 124	19 199
				Completed units (96 800 × £2.124)				205 601
								224 800

Note that the above answer is based on the short-cut approach described in Appendix 5.1

(b)

<table>
<tr><th></th><th>Units</th><th colspan="2" align="center">Process 2 account
(£)</th><th></th><th>Units</th><th>(£)</th></tr>
<tr><td>Opening WIP</td><td>12 000</td><td colspan="2">21 530</td><td>Finished goods</td><td>96 800</td><td>205 601</td></tr>
<tr><td>Transferred from process 1</td><td>95 000</td><td colspan="2">107 790</td><td>Normal loss</td><td>200</td><td>—</td></tr>
<tr><td>Materials</td><td></td><td colspan="2">44 000</td><td>Closing WIP</td><td>10 000</td><td>19 199</td></tr>
<tr><td>Conversion cost</td><td></td><td colspan="2">51 840</td><td></td><td></td><td></td></tr>
<tr><td></td><td>107 000</td><td colspan="2">224 800</td><td></td><td>107 000</td><td>224 800</td></tr>
</table>

(c) If losses are not expected to occur the loss would be abnormal. Because abnormal losses are not an inherent part of the production process and arise from inefficiencies they are not included in the process costs. Instead, they are charged with their full share of production costs and removed (credited) from the process account and reported separately as an abnormal loss. The abnormal loss is treated as a period cost and written off in the profit and loss account.

(d) Workings would be different because FIFO assumes that the opening WIP is the first group of units to be completed during the current period. The opening WIP is charged separately to completed production, and the cost per unit is based only on current period costs and production for the current period. This requires that opening WIP equivalent units are deducted from completed units to derive current period equivalent units. The cost per unit is derived from dividing current period costs by current period total equivalent units.

Question 5.8

(a)

Cost element	Current period costs (£)	Completed units less opening WIP equiv. units	Closing WIP equiv. units	Current total equiv. units	Cost per unit (£)
Materials	2 255	2 800	1 300	4 100	0.55
Conversion costs[a]	3 078	3 300	975	4 275	0.72
	5 333				
	(£)	(£)			

Completed production:		
Opening WIP (£540 + £355)	895	
Materials (2 800 × £0.55)	1 540	
Conversion cost (3 300 × £0.72)	2 376	
		4 811
Closing work in progress:		
Materials (1 300 × £0.55)	715	
Conversion cost (975 × £0.72)	702	
		1 417
		6 228

Note:

[a]Bonus = Current total equivalent units (4275) − Process 1 account expected output (4000)

= 275 units × £0.80 = £220

Labour cost = 6 men × 37 hours × £10 = £2220 + Bonus (£220) = £2440

Conversion cost = £2440 overhead + £638 labour = £3078

Process account			
	(£)		(£)
Opening WIP	895	Completed output	4 811
Materials	2 255	Closing WIP	1 417
Labour and overhead	3 078		
	6 228		6 228

(b)

(i) In most organizations the purchasing function is centralized and all goods are purchased by the purchasing department. To purchase goods, user departments complete a purchase requisition. This is a document requesting the purchasing department to purchase the goods listed on the document.

(ii) See 'Materials recording procedure' in Chapter 4 for the answer to this question.

Question 5.9

(a) Calculation of input for process 1

	(litres)	(£)
Opening stock	4 000	10 800
Receipts	20 000	61 000
Less closing stock	(8 000)	(24 200)
Process input	16 000	47 600

Output	(litres)
Completed units	8 000
Closing WIP	5 600
Normal loss (15% of input)	2 400
	16 000

Because input is equal to output, there are no abnormal gains or losses.

Calculation of cost per unit (Process 1)

The calculation (based on the short-cut method) is as follows:

Element of cost	(£)	Completed units	Closing WIP	Total equiv. units	Cost per unit (£)	WIP (£)
Materials	47 600	8 000	5 600	13 600	3.50	19 600
Conversion cost	21 350	8 000	4 200	12 200	1.75	7 350
					£5.25	£26 950

Completed units 8 000 × £5.25 = £42 000

Process 1 account − May

	(litres)	(£)		(litres)	(£)
Materials	16 000	47 600	Transfers to process 2	8 000	42 000
Labour		4 880	Normal loss	2 400	—
Direct expenses		4 270	Closing stock C/f	5 600	26 950
Overheads absorbed		12 200			
	16 000	68 950		16 000	68 950

With process 2, there is no closing WIP. Therefore it is unnecessary to express output in equivalent units. The cost per unit is calculated as follows:

$$\frac{\text{cost of production less scrap value of normal loss}}{\text{expected output}} = \frac{£54\,000^a}{(90\% \times 8000)} = £7.50$$

Note:

[a]Cost of production = transferred in cost from process 1 (42 000) + labour (£6000) + overhead (£6000).

Process 2 account – May

	Litres	(£)		Litres	(£)
Transferred from process 1	8 000	42 000	Finished goods store[b]	7 500	56 250
Labour		6 000	Normal loss	800	
Overheads absorbed		6 000	Closing stock	—	—
Abnormal gain[a]	300	2 250			
	8 300	56 250		8 300	56 250

	Litres	(£)
		Finished goods account
Ex Process 2	7 500	56 250

	(£)		Litres	(£)
		Abnormal gain account		
Profit and loss account	2 250	Process 2 account	300	2 250

Notes:

[a]Input = 8000 litres. Normal output = 90% × 8000 litres = 7200 litres. Actual output = 7500 litres. Abnormal gain = 300 litres × £7.50 per litre = £2250.

[b]7500 litres at £7.50 per litre.

(b) If the materials can be replaced then the loss to the company will consist of the replacement cost of materials. If the materials cannot be replaced then the loss will consist of the lost sales revenue less the costs not incurred as a result of not processing and selling 100 litres.

Question 5.10

(a) Expected output from an input of 39 300 sheets: 3 144 000 cans   (39 300 × 80)

   Less 1% rejects   31 440 cans

   Expected output after rejects   3 112 560 cans

The normal loss arising from the rejects (31 440 cans) is sold at £0.26 per kg. It is therefore necessary to express the rejects in terms of kilos of metal. Each sheet weighs 2 kilos but wastage in the form of offcuts is 2 per cent of input. Therefore the total weight of 80 cans is 1.96kg (0.98 × 2kg) and the weight of each can is 0.0245 kilos (1.96kg/80 cans). The weight of the normal loss arising from the rejects is 770.28kg (31 440 × 0.0245kg). The normal loss resulting from the offcuts is 1572kg (39 300 × 2kg × 0.02). Hence the total weight of the normal loss is 2342.28 kilos (1572kg + 770.28kg), with an expected sales value of £609 (2342.28kg × £0.26).

	(£)		(£)
		Process account	
Direct materials (39 300 × £2.50)	98 250	Finished goods (3 100 760 cans × £0.042[a])	130 232
		Normal loss	609
Direct labour and overheads	33 087	Abnormal loss (11 800kg[b] at £0.042[a])	496
	131 337		131 337

	(£)		(£)
		Abnormal loss account	
Process account	496	Sale proceeds[c]	75
		Profit and loss account	421
	496		496

Notes:

$$^{a}\text{Cost per unit} = \frac{£98\,250 + £33\,087 - £609}{\text{expected output (3 112 560 cans)}} = £0.042 \text{ per can}$$

[b]Expected output (3 112 560) − actual output (3 100 760 cans) = 11 800 cans

[c]Abnormal loss = 11 800 cans (3 112 560 − 3 100 760)

This will yield 289.1 kilos (11 800 × 0.0245 kilos) of metal with a sales value of £75 (289.1 × £0.26).

(b) (i) See 'Opening and closing work in progress' in Chapter 5 for the answer to this question.

   (ii) See 'Weighted average method' and 'First in, first out method' in Chapter 5 for the answer to this question.

Question 5.11

(a) It is assumed that the normal loss occurs at the start of the process and should be allocated to completed production and closing WIP. It is also assumed that process 2 conversion costs are not incurred when losses occur. Therefore losses should not be allocated to conversion costs.

Statement of input and output (units)

Input		Output	
Opening WIP	1 200	Completed output	105 400
Transferred from Process 1	112 000	WIP	1 600
		Normal loss (5% multi symbol 112 000)	5 600
		Abnormal loss (balance)	600
	113 200		113 200

Since the loss occurs at the start of the process it should be allocated over all units that have reached this point. Thus the normal loss should be allocated to all units of output. This can be achieved by adopting the short-cut method described in Chapter 5 whereby the normal loss is not included in the unit cost statement.

Calculation of cost per unit and cost of completed production (FIFO method)

	Current costs (£)	Completed units less opening WIP equiv. units	Abnormal loss	Closing WIP equiv. units	Current total equiv. units	Cost per unit (£)
Previous process cost	187 704					
Materials	47 972					
	235 676	104 200 (105 400 − 21 200)	600	1 600	106 400	2.215
Conversion costs	63 176	104 800 (105 400 − 600)	—	1 200	106 000	0.596
	298 852					2.811

	(£)	(£)
Cost of completed production:		
Opening WIP (given)	3 009	
Previous process cost and materials (104 200 × £2.215)	230 803	
Conversion cost (104 800 × £0.596)	62 461	296 273
Abnormal Loss (600 × £2.215)		1 329
Closing WIP:		
Previous process cost and materials (1 600 × £2.215)	3 544	
Conversion costs (1 200 × £0.596)	715	4 259
		301 861

Process 2 account

	(£)		(£)
Opening WIP	3 009		
Transfers from Process 1	187 704	Transfer to finished goods	296 273
Raw materials	47 972	Abnormal loss	1 329
Conversion costs	63 176	Closing WIP	4 259
	301 861		301 861

(b) If the loss occurs at the end of the process then the normal loss should only be charged to those units that have reached the end of the process. In other words, the cost of normal losses should not be allocated to closing WIP. To meet this requirement a separate column for normal losses is incorporated into the unit cost statement and the normal loss equivalent units are included in the calculation of total equivalent units. The cost of the normal loss should be calculated and added to the cost of completed production. For an illustration of the approach see 'Losses in process and partially completed units' in the appendix to Chapter 5.

Question 5.12

(a)

Production statement

Input:	Units
Opening WIP	20 000
Transfer from previous process	180 000
	200 000
Output:	
Closing WIP	18 000
Abnormal loss	60
Completed units (balance)	181 940
	200 000

Statement of equivalent production and calculation of cost of completed production and WIP

	Current costs (£)	Completed units less opening WIP equivalent units	Abnormal loss	Closing WIP equivalent units	Current total equivalent units	Cost per unit (£)
Previous process cost	394 200	161 940	60	18 000	180 000	2.19
Materials	110 520	167 940	60	16 200	184 200	0.60
Conversion cost	76 506	173 940	60	12 600	186 600	0.41
	581 226					3.20

	(£)	(£)
Cost of completed production:		
Opening WIP (given)	55 160	
Previous process cost (161 940 × £2.19)	354 649	
Materials (167 940 × £0.60)	100 764	
Conversion costs (173 940 × £0.41)	71 315	581 888
Cost of closing WIP:		
Previous process cost (18 000 × £2.19)	39 420	
Materials (16 200 × £0.60)	9 720	
Conversion costs (12 600 × £0.41)	5 166	54 306
Value of abnormal loss (60 × £3.20)		192
		636 386

Process 3 account

	(£)		(£)
Opening WIP	55 160	Transfer to finished goods	581 888
Transfer from process 2	394 200	stock	
Materials	110 520	Abnormal loss	192
Conversion costs	76 506	Closing WIP	54 306
	636 386		636 386

(b) Normal losses are unavoidable losses that are expected to occur under efficient operating conditions. They are an expected production cost and should be absorbed by the completed production whereas abnormal losses are not included in the process costs but are removed from the appropriate process account and reported separately as an abnormal loss. See the appendix to Chapter 5 for a more detailed explanation of the treatment of normal losses.

(c) If the weighted average method is used, both the units and value of WIP are merged with current period costs and production to calculate the average cost per unit. The weighted average cost per unit is then applied to all completed units, any abnormal losses and closing WIP equivalent units. In contrast, with the FIFO method the opening WIP is assumed to be the first group of units completed during the current period. The opening WIP is charged separately to completed production, and the cost per unit is based only on current costs and production for the period. The closing WIP is assumed to come from the new units that have been started during the period.

Question 5.13

The physical input and output to the process are as follows:

Input:	Rolls	Output:	Rolls
Opening WIP	1 000	Spoiled	550
Started from new	5 650	Closing WIP	800
Reworked	500	Completed (balance)	5 800
	7 150		7 150

The 5800 rolls will include the reworked output of 500 rolls, which is assumed to be completed during the period. Therefore the un-reworked output is 5300 rolls. It is assumed that the normal loss is 10 per cent of the un-reworked output of 5300 units. Hence the abnormal loss is 20 rolls (550 − 530 rolls). Because the question specifically states that the loss can be identified only at the end of the process, losses are not allocated to closing WIP. Therefore the short-cut method is not applied.

(a) Schedule of completed production and cost per roll

	Current cost	Un-reworked completed rolls less opening WIP equivalent rolls	Reworked equivalent rolls[a]	Normal loss	Abnormal loss	Closing WIP equivalent rolls	Total equivalent rolls	Cost per roll
Materials	72 085	4 300	300	530	20	640	5 790	12.4499
Labour	11 718	4 700	250	530	20	320	5 820	2.0134
Overheads[b]	41 013	4 700	250	530	20	320	5 820	7.0469
	124 816							21.5102

Notes:

[a]Reworked equivalent rolls refers to production for the current period only. Previous period costs are not included in the cost per unit calculation when the FIFO method is used.

[b]Note that overheads are charged to production at the rate of £3.50 per £1 of labour.

(b) *Allocation of costs*

	(£)
Completed units:	
Un-reworked completed rolls	
[(4300 × £12.4499) + (4700 × £2.0134) + (4700 × £7.0469)]	96 118
Reworked rolls	
[(300 × £12.4499) + (250 × £2.0134) + (250 × £7.0469)]	6 000
Cost of normal spoilage (530 × £21.5102)	11 400
Opening WIP (£12 000 + £4620 + £16 170[a])]	32 790
	146 308
Value of closing WIP	
[(640 × £12.4499) + (320 × £2.0134) + (320 × £7.0469)]	10 868
Cost of abnormal spoilage (20 × £21.5102)	430
	157 606

Note:

[a]Overhead costs at the rate of £3.50 per £1 of labour should be added to the value of the opening WIP.

(c) The advantages of converting to a standard costing system are as follows:

(i) Calculations of *actual* costs per unit for each period will not be required. Completed production and stocks can be valued at standard costs per unit for each element of cost.

(ii) Targets can be established and a detailed analysis of the variances can be presented. This process should enable costs to be more effectively controlled.

(d) Actual costs computed in (a) and (b) imply that cost-plus pricing is used. Possible disadvantages of this approach include:

    (i)   Prices based solely on costs ignore demand and the prices that competitors charge.

    (ii) Overheads will include fixed overheads, which are arbitrarily apportioned and may distort the pricing decision.

    (iii) Replacement costs are preferable to historic costs for pricing decisions. Standard costs represent future target costs and are therefore more suitable for decision-making than historic costs based on a FIFO system.

    For additional comments see 'Limitations of cost-plus pricing' in Chapter 10.

(e) The implications are:

    (i)   Replacement costs should be used for management accounting, but they will have to be adjusted for external reporting.

    (ii) Practical difficulties in using replacement costs. For example, it is necessary to constantly monitor the current market price for all stock items.

    (iii) The benefits from the use of replacement costs will depend upon the rate of inflation. The higher the rate of inflation, the greater the benefits.

Joint and by-product costing

Solutions to Chapter 6 questions

Question 6.1

	(£)
Joint costs apportioned to P (4500/9750 × £117 000) =	54 000
Further processing costs (4500 × £9) =	40 500
Total cost	94 500
Sales revenues (4050 × £25)	101 250
Profit	6 750

Answer = A

Question 6.2

Joint costs to be allocated =	$140 000 less by product revenues (3000 × $6) = $122 000
Sales value of X	= $125 000 (2500 × $50)
Sales value of Y	= $210 000 (3500 × $60)
Total sales value	= $335 000
Costs allocated to X	= ($125 000/$335 000 × $122 000) + $24 000 = $69 522
Costs allocated to Y	= ($210 000/335 000 × $122 000) + $46 000 = $122 478

Question 6.3

Total sales revenue	= £1 080 000 (£18 × 10 000 + £25 × 20 000 + £20 × 20 000)
Joint costs to be allocated	= £270 000 (277 000 total output cost − £2 × 3500 by-product sales revenue)
Costs allocated to product 3	= 270 000 × (£20 × 20 000)/£1 080 000 = £100 000
Unit cost of product 3	= £5 per unit (£100 000/20 000 units)

Answer = C

Question 6.4

(a)

	Product X (£)	Material B (£)
Apportionment of joint costs (W1)	35 400	106 200
Further processing costs	18 000	—
	53 400	106 200
Sales (W2)	50 400	180 000
Profit/(loss)	(3 000)	73 800
Profit/(loss) per kg (W3)	(0.33)	2.46

Workings:

(W1) X = (£141 600/40 000kg) × 10 000kg

B = (£141 600/40 000kg) × 30 000kg

(W2) X = 9000kg at £5.60, B = 30 000 × £6

(W3) X = £3000/9000kg, B = £73 800/30 000kg

(b) The answer should stress that a joint products costs cannot be considered in isolation from those of other joint products. If product X was abandoned the joint costs apportioned to X would still continue and would have to be absorbed by material B. Therefore no action should be taken on product X without also considering the implications for material B. Note that the process as a whole is profitable. The decision to discontinue product X should be based on a comparison of those costs which would be avoidable if X were discontinued with the lost sales revenue from product X. Joint costs apportionments are appropriate for stock valuation purposes but not for decision-making purposes.

(c) An alternative method is to apportion joint costs on the basis of net realizable value at split-off point. The calculations are as follows:

	Sales value	Costs beyond split-off point	Net-realizable value at split-off point	Joint cost apportionment
Product X	50 400	18 000	32 400	21 600 (W1)
Material A	180 000	—	180 000	120 000 (W2)
			212 400	141 600

Workings:
(W1)   (£32 400/£212 400) × £141 600
(W2)   (£180 000/£212 400) × £141 600

The revised profit calculation for product X is:

		(£)
Sales		50 400
Less joint costs	21 600	
Processing costs	18 000	39 600
Profit		10 800
Profit per kg		£1.20 (£10 800/9000kg)

Apportionment methods based on sales value normally ensure that if the process as a whole is profitable, then each of the joint products will be shown to be making a profit.

Consequently it is less likely that incorrect decisions will be made.

Question 6.5

(a) See Figure Q6.5

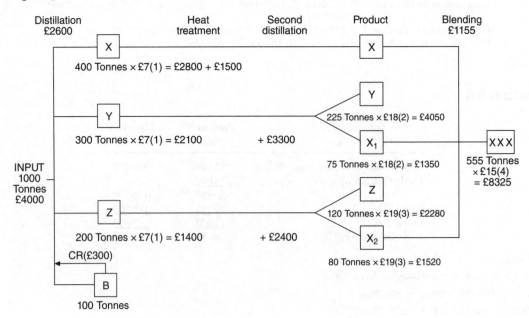

Figure Q6.5

Workings:

(W1)	(4000 + 2600 − 300)/900 = £7
(W2)	(2100 + 3300)/300 = £18
(W3)	(1400 + 2400)/200 = £19
(W4)	(2800 + 1500 + 1155 + 1350 + 1520)/555 = £15

(b)

Product	Output (tonnes)	Total cost (£)	Cost per tonne (£)
XXX	555	8 325	15
Y	225	4 050	18
Z	120	2 280	19

(c) An alternative treatment is to credit the income direct to the profit and loss account rather than crediting the proceeds to the process from which the byproduct was derived.

Question 6.6

(a) You can see from the question that the input is 240 000kg and the output is 190 000kg. It is assumed that the difference of 50 000kg is a normal loss in output which occurs at the start of processing. Therefore the loss should be charged to the completed production and WIP. By making no entry for normal losses in the cost per unit calculation the normal loss is automatically apportioned between completed units and WIP.

	Opening WIP (£)	Current cost (£)	Total cost (£)	Completed units	Closing WIP	Total equivalent units	Cost per unit (£)	WIP value (£)
Materials	20 000	75 000	95 000	160 000	30 000	190 000	0.50	15 000
Processing costs	12 000	96 000	108 000	160 000	20 000	180 000	0.60	12 000
			203 000				1.10	27 000
					Completed units (160 000 units × £1.10)			176 000
								203 000

(b) This question requires a comparison of incremental revenues and incremental costs. Note that the costs of process 1 are irrelevant to the decision since they will remain the same whichever of the two alternatives are selected. You should also note that further processing 120 000kg of the compound results in 240 000kg of Starcomp.

	(£)	(£)
Incremental sales revenue:		
Starcomp (120 000 × 2kg × £2)	480 000	
Compound (120 000 × £1.60)	192 000	288 000
Incremental costs:		
Materials	120 000	
Processing costs	120 000	240 000
Incremental profits		48 000

It is therefore worthwhile further processing the compound.

(c) The sales revenue should cover the additional costs of further processing the 40 000kg compound and the lost sales revenue from the 40 000kg compound if it is sold without further processing.

	(£)
Additional processing costs:	
Materials (£160 000 − £120 000)	40 000
Processing costs (£140 000 − £120 000)	20 000
Lost compound sales revenue (40 000 × £1.60)	64 000
	124 000

$$\text{Minimum selling price per kg of Starcomp} = \frac{£124\,000}{40\,000\text{kg} \times 2}$$
$$= £1.55$$

Question 6.7

(a) Operating statement for October

	(£)	(£)
Sales: Product A (80 000 × £5) =	400 000	
Product B (65 000 × £4) =	260 000	
Product C (75 000 × £9) =	675 000	1 335 000
Operating costs	1 300 000	
Less closing stock[a]	200 000	
		1 100 000
Profit		235 000

Note:

[a]Production for the period (kg):

	A	B	C	Total
Sales requirements	80 000	65 000	75 000	
Closing stock	20 000	15 000	5 000	
Production	100 000	80 000	80 000	260 000

$$\text{Cost per kg} = 260\,000\text{kg} = \frac{£1\,300\,000}{260\,000} = £5 \text{ per kg}$$

Therefore

Closing stock = 40 000kg at £5 per kg

(b) Evaluation of refining proposal

	A	B	C	Total (£)
Incremental revenue per kg (£)	12	10	11.50	
Variable cost per kg (£)	4	6	12.00	
Contribution per kg (£)	8	4	(0.50)	
Monthly production (kg)	100 000	80 000	80 000	
Monthly contribution (£)	800 000	320 000	(40 000)	1 080 000
Monthly fixed overheads (specific to B)		360 000		360 000
Contribution to refining general fixed costs (£)	800 000	(40 000)	(40 000)	720 000
Refining general fixed overheads				700 000
Monthly profit				20 000

(1) It is more profitable to sell C in its unrefined state and product B is only profitable in its refined state if monthly sales are in excess of 90 000kg (£360 000 fixed costs/£4 contribution per unit).

(2) If both products B and C are sold in their unrefined state then the refining process will yield a profit of £100 000 per month (£800 000 product A contribution less £700 000 fixed costs).

(3) The break-even point for the refining process if only product A were produced is 87 500kg (£700 000 fixed costs/£8 contribution per unit). Consequently if sales of A declined by 12½ per cent, the refining process will yield a loss. Note that 80 000kg of A were sold in October.

Question 6.8

(a) *Profit and loss account*

	W (£)	X (£)	Z (£)	Total (£)
Opening stock	—	—	8 640	8 640
Production cost	189 060	228 790	108 750	526 600
Less closing stock	(14 385)	(15 070)	(15 010)	(44 465)
Cost of sales	174 675	213 720	102 3810	490 775
Selling and administration costs	24 098	27 768	10 011	61 877

Total costs	198 773	241 488	112 391	552 652
Sales	240 975	277 680	100 110	618 765
Profit/(loss)	412 202	36 192	(12 281)	66 113

Workings

Joint process cost per kilo of output = £0.685 per kg (£509 640/744 000kg) Production cost for products W, X and Y:

$$\text{Product W} (276\,000\text{kg} \times £0.685) = £189\,060$$
$$\text{X} (334\,000\text{kg} \times £0.685) = £228\,790$$
$$\text{Y} (134\,000\text{kg} \times £0.685) = £91\,790$$

Closing stocks for products W and X:

$$\text{Product W} (21\,000\text{kg} \times £0.685) = £14\,385$$
$$\text{X} (22\,000\text{kg} \times £0.685) = £15\,070$$

Cost per kilo of product Z:

	(£)
Product Y (128 000kg × £0.685) =	87 680
Further processing costs	17 920
Less by-product sales (8 000 × £0.12) =	(960)
	104 640
Cost per kilo (£104 640/96 000kg)	£1.09
Closing stock of product Z (10 000kg × £1.09) =	£10 900
Add closing stock of input Y (6 000 × £0.685) =	£4 110
Closing stock relating to product Z	£15 010

Production cost relating to final product Z:

	(£)
Product Y (134 000kg × £0.685) =	91 790
Further processing costs	17 920
Less by-product costs	(960)
	108 750

(b) The joint costs are common and unavoidable to both alternatives, and are therefore not relevant for the decision under consideration. Further processing from an input of 128 000kg of Y has resulted in an output of 96 000kg of Z. Thus it requires 1.33kg of Y to produce 1kg of Z (128/96).

	(£)	
Revenue per kilo for product Z	1.065	(£100 110/94 000kg)
Sale proceeds at split-off point (1.33 × £0.62)	0.823	
Incremental revenue per kg from further processing	0.242	
Incremental costs of further processing	0.177	[(£17 920 − £960)/96 000]
Incremental profit from further processing	0.065	

It is assumed that selling and administration costs are fixed and will be unaffected by which alternative is selected. The company should therefore process Y further into product Z and not accept the offer from the other company to purchase the entire output of product Y.

(c) See 'Methods of allocating joint costs to joint products' in Chapter 6 for the answer to this question.

Question 6.9

(a) In a manufacturing organization product costs are required for stock valuation, the various types of decisions illustrated in Chapter 9 and pricing decisions (see 'Role of cost information in pricing decisions' in Chapter 10).

(b) The total net cost of the output for process 1 is calculated as follows:

	(£)
Materials (36 000kg at £1.50)	54 000
Labour	28 000
Overheads (120%)	33 600
	115 600
Less: Sale of waste (14 400kg at £0.30)	4 320
	111 280

Output for each category of fish is as follows:

Superior	3 600kg	
Special	7 200	
Standard	10 800	(50% × (36 000 − 14 400))
	21 600	

The allocation of costs based on weight and the resulting profits are as follows:

	Superior (£)	Special (£)	Standard (£)	Total (£)
Costs	18 547[a]	37 093[a]	55 640[a]	111 280
Sales	27 000	48 960	43 200	119 160
Profit/(Loss)	8 453	11 867	(12 440)	7 880

Note:
[a]Allocated pro-rata to output (e.g. Superior = £111 280 × 3600/21 600)

The allocation of costs based on market value and the resulting profits are as follows:

	Superior (£)	Special (£)	Standard (£)	Total (£)
Costs	25 215[b]	45 722[b]	40 343[b]	111 280
Sales	27 000	48 960	43 200	119 160
Profit/(Loss)	1 785	3 238	2 857	7 880

Note:
[b]Allocated in proportion to sales revenues (e.g. Superior = £111 280 × £27 000/119 160)

(c) Since all of the costs are joint and unavoidable in relation to all products, dropping a product with a reported loss will not result in any reduction in costs but sales revenues from the product will be forgone. Therefore, an individual loss-making product should not be dropped provided that the process as a whole is profitable. In the circumstances given in the question, the emphasis should be on whether the joint process as a whole is making a profit. In the question none of the products incur further processing costs that can be specifically attributed to them. Where this situation occurs, a joint product should be produced as long as the sales revenues from the product exceed the costs that are specifically attributable to the product (assuming that the joint process as a whole makes a profit).

(d) Further process is worthwhile as long as the incremental revenues exceed the incremental costs. The calculations are as follows:

	£ per kilo		
	Superior	Special	Standard
Incremental costs:			
Materials	0.10	0.10	0.10
Labour	0.60	0.60	0.60
Variable overhead	0.27	0.27	0.27
	0.97	0.97	0.97
Incremental revenue	1.20	0.70	1.20
Incremental contribution	0.23	(0.27)	0.23

The incremental revenues exceed the incremental costs for superior and standard. Special should not be further processed because the incremental revenues are insufficient to cover the incremental costs. Superior will generate a total contribution of £828 (3600kg × £0.23) and the total contribution from standard is £2484 (10 800kg × £0.23). Therefore, the total contribution from further processing is £3312. Further processing is profitable as long as the incremental contribution exceeds the fixed costs that are attributable to process 2 and that are avoidable. The fixed costs are not given but they would appear to exceed £3312. Assuming that the overhead rate has been derived from the output in (a) the total labour costs [included in the calculation in (d) are £12 960 (21 600kg × £0.60)]. Fixed costs would appear to be £17 496 (0.75 × 180 per cent × £12 960). The process would not appear to be worthwhile if all of the fixed costs can be avoided by not undertaking process 2.

Question 6.10

(a) Figure Q6.10 indicates that the relative sales value of each product is as follows:

	Boddie (£000)	Soull (£000)	Total (£000)
Total sales	8 400	36 000	44 400
Plus NRV of Threekeys		2 170(W1)	2 170
	8 400	38 170	416 570

Workings

(W1)   (280 000 litres × £8) − £70 000 delivery costs

Allocation of joint costs: *Workings*

$$\text{Boddie} = £840\,000 \left(\frac{8\,400}{46\,570} \times £4\,657\,000 \right)$$

$$\text{Soull} = \frac{£3\,817\,000}{4\,657\,000} \left(\frac{38\,170}{46\,570} \times £4\,657\,000 \right)$$

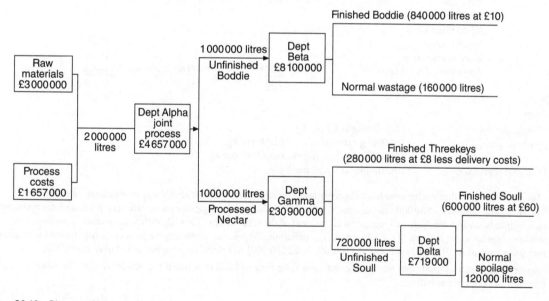

Figure Q6.10 Diagram of joint cost system

(b) *Profit and loss statement*

	Boddie (£000)	Soull (£000)	Threekeys (£000)	Total (£000)
Sales	8 400	36 000	2 240	46 640
Less specifically attributable costs:				
Department Beta	8 100			
Department Gamma		30 900		

Department Delta		719	
Delivery costs			70
Contribution to joint costs	300	4 381	2 170	6 851
Less apportioned joint costs	840	3 817	—	4 657
Profit/(loss)	(540)	564	2 170	2 194

(c) The incremental revenues are in excess of the incremental costs for all three products. In other words, each product provides a contribution towards the joint costs. Consequently, all three products should be produced.

Question 6.11

(a) *Preliminary workings*

The joint production process results in the production of garden fertilizer and synthetic fuel consisting of 80 per cent fertilizer and 20 per cent synthetic fuel. The question indicates that 1 600 000kg of fertilizer are produced. Therefore total output is 2 000 000kg, and synthetic fuel accounts for 20 per cent (400 000kg) of this output. The question also states that a wholesaler bought 160 000kg of the synthetic fuel, and the remaining fuel (400 000kg − 160 000kg = 240 000kg) was used to heat the company greenhouses. The greenhouses produce 5kg of fruit and vegetables per kg of fuel. Therefore 1 200 000kg of fruit and vegetables were produced during the period.

Summary profit statements

	Garden fertilizer (£000)	Synthetic fuel (£000)	Fruit and vegetables (£000)
Sales revenue/internal transfers[a]	4 800	560	600
Less costs:			
Internal transfers[a]			(336)
Joint costs[b]	(2 880)	(720)	
Variable packing costs		(192)	
Direct fixed costs		(40)	
Variable costs			(420)
Fixed labour costs			(100)
Apportioned fixed costs	(720)	(18)	(90)
Net profit/(Loss)	1 200	(410)	(346)

Notes:

[a] Garden fertilizer:	1 600 000kg at £3 per kg
Synthetic fuel:	160 000kg external sales at £1.40 per kg
	240 000kg internal transfers at £1.40 per kg
Fruit and vegetables:	1 200 000kg at £0.50 per kg

[b] The question states that the fertilizer has a contribution/sales ratio of 40 per cent after the apportionment of joint costs. Therefore joint costs of £2 880 000 (60 per cent × £4 800 000 sales) will be apportioned to fertilizers. Joint costs are apportioned on a weight basis, and synthetic fuel represents 20 per cent of the total weight. Thus £2 880 000 joint costs apportioned to fertilizers represents 80 per cent of the joint costs. The remaining 20 per cent represents the joint costs apportioned to synthetic fuel. Joint costs of £720 000 [20 per cent × (100/80) × £2 880 000] will therefore be apportioned to synthetic fuel.

(b) Apportioned joint and fixed costs are not relevant costs since they will still continue if the activity ceases. The relevant revenues and costs are as follows:

	(£)
Relevant revenues	224 000 (160 000kg at £1.40)
Less packing costs	(192 000)
avoidable fixed costs	(40 000)
Net benefit to company	(8 000)

The percentage reduction in avoidable fixed costs before the relevant revenues would be sufficient to cover these costs is 20 per cent (£8000/£40 000).

(c) The notional cost for internal transfers and the apportioned fixed costs would still continue if the fruit and vegetables activity were eliminated. These costs are therefore not relevant in determining the net benefit arising from fruit and vegetables. The calculation of the net benefit is as follows:

	(£)
Relevant revenues	600 000
Less variable costs	(420 000)
avoidable fixed labour costs	(100 000)
Net benefit	80 000

(d) Proposed output of synthetic fuel is 400 000kg, but there is a contracted requirement to supply a minimum of 100 000kg to the wholesaler. Consequently, the maximum output of fruit and vegetables is 1 500 000kg (300 000kg of synthetic fuel × 5kg). In determining the optimum price/output level the fixed costs will remain unchanged whatever price/output combination is selected. Internal transfers are a notional cost and do not represent any change in company cash outflows arising from the price/output decision. The price/output decision should be based on a comparison of the relevant revenues less incremental costs (variable costs) for each potential output level. In addition, using synthetic fuel for fruit and vegetable production results in a loss of contribution of £0.20 per kg (£1.40 − £1.20 packing) of synthetic fuel used. This opportunity cost is a relevant cost which should be included in the analysis. The net contributions for the relevant output levels are as follows:

Sales (000kg)	Contribution per kg[a] (£)	Total contribution (£)	Contribution forgone on fuel sales (£)	Net contribution (£)
1 200	0.15	180 000	0[b]	180 000
1 300	0.145	188 500	4 000[c]	184 500
1 400	0.135	189 000	8 000[d]	181 000
1 500	0.125	187 500	12 000[e]	175 500

The optimum output level is to sell 1 300 000kg of fruit and vegetables. This will require 260 000kg of synthetic fuel. Sales of synthetic fuel to the wholesaler will be restricted to 140 000kg.

Notes:

[a]Average selling price less variable cost of fruit and vegetable production (£420 000/1 200 000kg = £0.35 per kg).

[b]240 000kg of synthetic fuel used, resulting in 160 000kg being sold to the wholesaler. Therefore existing sales to the wholesaler of 160 000kg will be maintained.

[c]260 000kg of synthetic fuel used, resulting in 140 000kg being sold to the wholesaler. Therefore sales will decline by 20 000kg and the lost contribution will be £4000 (20 000kg × £0.20 per kg).

[d]280 000kg of synthetic fuel used, resulting in 120 000kg being sold to the wholesaler. Therefore lost contribution is £8000 (40 000kg × £0.20).

[e]300 000kg used, resulting in 100 000kg being sold to the wholesaler. Therefore the lost contribution is £12 000 (60 000kg × £0.20).

Question 6.12

(a) Figure Q6.12 shows a flowchart for an input of 100 litres of raw material A and 100 litres of raw material B. The variable costs for an input of 100 litres of raw materials for each product are shown below:

	(£)	(£)	Fertilizer P (£)	Fertilizer Q (£)
Raw materials:				
100 litres of A at £25 per 100 litres	25.00			
100 litres of B at £12 per 100 litres	12.00	37.00		
Mixing:				
200 litres at £3.75 per 100 litres	7.50			
Residue × (10 litres at £0.03)	(0.30)	7.20		
Distilling:				
190 litres at £5 per 100 litres	9.50			
By-product Y (57 litres × £0.04)	(2.28)	7.22		

	(£)	(£)	Fertilizer P (£)	Fertilizer Q (£)
Total joint costs		51.42	25.71[a]	25.71[a]
Raw material C (114 litres at £20 per 100 litres)			22.80	
Raw material D (57 litres at £55 per 100 litres)				31.35
Blending:				
P (171 litres at £7 per 100 litres)			11.97	
Q (114 litres at £7 per 100 litres)				7.98
Cans:				
P (57 cans at £0.32 per can)			18.24	
Q (19 cans at £0.50 per can)				9.50
Labels:				
P (57 cans at £3.33 per 1000 cans)			0.19	
Variable cost from 100 litres input of each raw material			78.91	74.54

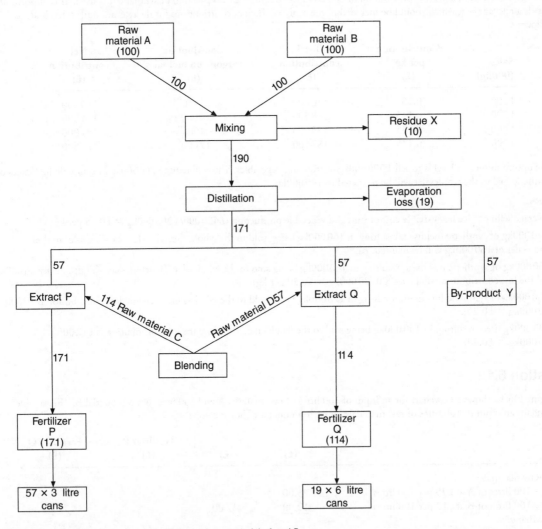

Figure Q6.12   Flowchart for an input of 100 litres of raw materials A and B

Output is restricted to 570 000 litres of Q. An input of 100 litres of raw materials A and B yields an output of 114 litres of Q. Therefore an input of 500 000 litres [570 000/(114/110)] of each raw material will yield an output of 570 000 litres of Q. An input to the joint process of 500 000 litres of each raw material will yield an output of 855 000 litres (171 × 5000) of P. The total manufacturing cost based on an input of 500 000 litres of each raw material is shown below:

	Fertilizer P (£)	Fertilizer Q (£)
Total variable cost: 5000 × £78.91	394550	
5000 × £74.54		372700
Mixing and distilling fixed costs	13000[a]	13000[a]
Blending fixed costs	19950[b]	13300[b]
(i) *Total manufacturing cost*	427500	399000

Notes:

[a]Joint costs are apportioned to the main products on the basis of the output from each process. The mixing and distilling processes yield identical outputs for each product. Therefore 50 per cent of the costs are apportioned to each product.

[b]Apportioned on the basis of an output of 171 litres of P and 114 litres of Q.

(i) *Manufacturing cost per litre*

$$\text{Fertilizer P} = £0.50 \ (£427\,500/855\,000 \text{ litres})$$
$$\text{Fertilizer Q} = £0.70 \ (£399\,000/570\,000 \text{ litres})$$

(ii) *List price per litre*

Costs and profit as a percentage of list price are:

	(%)
List price	100
Net selling price	75
Profit (20% − 75%)	15
Total cost (75% − 15%)	60
Selling and distribution (13.33% × 75%)	10
Manufacturing cost (60% − 10%)	50

List price per litre is, therefore, twice the manufacturing cost per litre:

$$P = £1.00$$
$$Q = £1.40$$

(iii) *Profit for the year*

$$P = £128\,250 \ (15\% \text{ of } £1) \times 855\,000 \text{ litres}$$
$$Q = £119\,700 \ (15\% \text{ of } £1.40) \times 570\,000 \text{ litres}$$

(b) Manufacturing joint product Q will also result in an additional output of P. The break-even point will depend on whether or not P is sold at split-off point as scrap or further processed and sold at the normal market price. The following analysis assumes that P is further processed and sold at the normal market price:

	(£)
Variable cost of producing 50000 litres of Q	
[(50000 × £372700)/570000]	32693
Variable selling costs of Q	2000
	34693
Contribution from sale of 75000 litres of P:	16500
75000 litres × £0.22[a]	
Net cost	18193

The selling price should at least cover the net cost per litre of £0.364 (£18193/50000 litres). Therefore the break-even selling price is £0.364 per litre.

Notes:
[a]Output of P is 1.5 times the output of Q (see the Flowchart). Therefore output of P is 75000 litres (50000 × 1.5)

Variable manufacturing cost per litre of P = £0.46
(394 500/855 000 litres)

Variable selling cost per litre of P = £0.07
[0.7 × (13.33% of £0.75)]

Selling price per litre = £0.75

Contribution per litre = £0.22

(c) There is no specific answer to this question. The recommendation should be based on price/demand relationships and the state of competition. The normal mark-up is 25 per cent on cost (20 per cent of selling price equals 25 per cent mark-up on cost).

$$\text{Selling price based on normal mark-up} = [1.25 \ (£18\,193)]/50\,000 \text{ litres}$$
$$= £0.455$$

The above price assumes that the additional output of P can be sold at the normal market price. If P cannot be sold then the following costs will be incurred:

	(£)
Variable costs of Q	34 693
Pre-separation variable costs previously apportioned to P:	
5000 at £25.71 per 100 = £128 550 (for 570 000 output)	
Pre-separation variable costs for an output of 50 000 litres	
[(£128 550/570 000) × 50 000]	11 276
	45 969

Minimum selling price = £0.919 (£45 969/50 000)

Note that pre-separation variable costs previously allocated to P will still be incurred if P is not produced. The recommended price will depend on the circumstances, competition, demand and the company's pricing policy.

Income effects of alternative cost accumulation systems

Solutions to Chapter 7 questions

Question 7.1

When production volume equals sales volume marginal (variable) and absorption costing profits will be identical. Production exceeds sales by 2000 units resulting in additional manufacturing overheads of £9000 (2000 × £63 000/14 000) being deferred as an expense and included in the closing stock valuation. Therefore profits will be £9000 lower with the variable costing system (i.e. £27 000) so the answer will be B.

Question 7.2

Fixed overhead = £250 per unit

Inventories decreased by 300 units resulting in an extra £75 000 (300 × £250) being charged as a production cost with an absorption costing system. Therefore profits will be £75 000 lower with an absorption costing system (i.e. Answer = (b))

Question 7.3

The profit difference is due to the fixed overheads being incorporated in the stock movements with the absorption costing system.

Profit difference = £9750 (£60 150 − £50 400)

Fixed overheads in stock movement = £9750

Physical stock movement = 1500 units

Fixed overhead rate per unit = £9750/1500 units = £6.50

Answer = (d)

Question 7.4

The difference between the marginal (variable) costing loss and the absorption costing profit is $5000. The absorption costing profit is higher indicating that there was an increase in inventories arising from production volume exceeding sales volume. Given that the fixed production cost is $2 per unit production will have exceeded sales by 2500 units ($5000/$2) so that actual production was 12 500 units. Therefore answer = D

Question 7.5

(a) Manufacturing cost per unit of output = variable cost (£6.40) + fixed cost (£92 000/20 000 = £4.60) = £11

Absorption costing profit statement

	(£000)
Sales (22 000 units at £14 per unit)	308.0
Manufacturing cost of sales (22 000 units × £11)	242.0
Manufacturing profit before adjustment	66.0
Overhead over-absorbed[a]	4.6
Manufacturing profit	70.6

Note:
[a]The normal activity that was used to establish the fixed over-head absorption rate was 20 000 units but actual production in period 2 was 21 000 units. Therefore a period cost adjustment is required because there is an over-absorption of fixed overheads of £4600 [(22 000 units − 21 000 units) × £4.60].

	(£000)
Sales	308.0
Variable cost of sales (22 000 units × £6.40)	140.8
Contribution to fixed costs	167.2
Less fixed overheads	92.0
Profit	75.2

(c) (i) Compared with period 1 profits are £34 800 higher in period 2 (£70 600 − £35 800). The reasons for the change are as follows:

	(£000)
Additional sales (7000 units at a profit of £3 per unit)	21 000
Difference in fixed overhead absorption (3000 units extra production at £4.60 per unit)[a]	13 800
Additional profit	34 800

Note:

[a]Because fixed overheads are absorbed on the basis of normal activity (20 000 units) there would have been an under-recovery of £9200 (2000 units × £4.60) in period 1 when production was 18 000 units. In period 2 production exceeds normal activity by 1000 units resulting in an over-recovery of £4600. The difference between the under and over-recovery of £13 800 (£9200 + £4600) represents a period cost adjustment that is reflected in an increase in profits of £13 800. In other words, the under-recovery of £9200 was not required in period 2 and in addition there was an over-recovery of £4600.

(ii) Additional profits reported by the marginal costing system are £4600 (£75 200 − £70 600). Because sales exceed production by 1000 units in period 2 there is a stock reduction of 1000 units. With an absorption costing system the stock reduction will result in a release of £4600 (1000 units at £4.60) fixed overheads as an expense during the current period. With a marginal costing system changes in stock levels do not have an impact on the fixed overhead that is treated as an expense for the period. Thus, absorption costing profits will be £4600 lower than marginal costing profits.

Question 7.6

(a)

January	Marginal costing (£)	(£)	(£)	Absorption costing (£)
Sales revenue (7000 units)		315 000		315 000
Less: Cost of sales (7000 units)				
Direct materials	77 000		77 000	
Direct labour	56 000		56 000	
Variable production overhead	28 000		28 000	
Variable selling overhead	35 000	196 000		
Fixed overhead (7000 × £3)			21 000	182 000
Contribution		119 000		
Gross profit				133 000
Over-absorption of fixed production overhead (1)				1 500
				134 500
Fixed production costs (2)	24 000			
Fixed selling costs (2)	16 000		16 000	
Variable selling costs			35 000	
Fixed admin costs (2)	24 000	64 000	24 000	75 000
Net profit		55 000		59 500

February	Marginal costing (£)	(£)	(£)	Absorption costing (£)
Sales revenue (8750 units)		393 750		393 750
Less: Cost of sales (8750 units)				
Direct materials	96 250		96 250	
Direct labour	70 000		70 000	
Variable production overhead	35 000		35 000	
Variable selling overhead	43 750	245 000		

February	Marginal costing (£)	(£)	(£)	Absorption costing (£)
Fixed overhead (8750 × £3)			26 250	227 500
Contribution		148 750		
Gross profit				166 250
Under-absorption of fixed production overhead				750
				165 500
Fixed production costs (2)				
Fixed selling costs (2)	24 000		16 000	
Variable selling costs	16 000		43 750	
Fixed admin costs (2)	24 000	64 000	24 000	83 750
Net profit		84 750		81 750

Workings:

(1) Fixed production overhead has been unitized on the basis of a normal monthly activity of 8000 units (96 000 units per annum). Therefore monthly production fixed overhead incurred is £24 000 (8000 × £3). In January actual production exceeds normal activity by 500 units so there is an over-absorption of £1500 resulting in a period cost adjustment that has a positive impact on profits. In February, production is 250 units below normal activity giving an under-absorption of production overheads of £750.

(2) With marginal costing fixed production overheads are treated as period costs and not assigned to products. Therefore the charge for fixed production overheads is £24 000 per month (see note 1). Both marginal and absorption costing systems treat non-manufacturing overheads as period costs. All of the non-manufacturing overheads have been unitized using a monthly activity level of 8000 units. Therefore the non-manufacturing fixed overheads incurred are as follows:

$$\text{Selling} = £16\,000\ (8000 \times £2)$$
$$\text{Administration} = £24\,000\ (8000 \times £3)$$

(b) In January additional profits of £4500 are reported by the absorption costing system. Because production exceeds sales by 1500 units in January there is a stock increase of 1500 units. With an absorption costing system the stock increase will result in £4500 (1500 units × £3) being incorporated in closing stocks and deferred as an expense to future periods. With a marginal costing system, changes in stock levels do not have an impact on the fixed overhead that is treated as an expense for the period. Thus, absorption costing profits will be £4500 higher than marginal costing profits. In February sales exceed production by 1000 units resulting in a stock reduction of 1000 units. With an absorption costing system the stock reduction will result in a release of £3000 (1000 units at £3) fixed overheads as an expense during the current period. Thus, absorption costing profits are £3000 lower than marginal costing profits.

(c) (i) Contribution per unit = Selling price (£45) − unit variable cost (£28) = £17

Break-even point (units) = Annual fixed costs (£64 000)/unit contribution (£17) = 3765 units

Break-even point (£ sales) = 3765 units × £45 selling price = £169 424

The above calculations are on a monthly basis. The sales value of the annual break-even point is £2 033 100 (£169 425 × 12).

(ii) Required contribution for an annual profit of £122 800

$$= \text{Fixed costs } (£64\,000 \times 12) + £122\,800$$
$$= £899\,800$$
$$\text{Required activity level} = \frac{\text{Required contribution } (£899\,800)}{\text{Unit contribution } (£17)}$$
$$= 52\,400 \text{ units}$$

(d) See 'Cost–volume–profit analysis assumptions' in Chapter 8 for the answer to this question.

Question 7.7

(a) *Preliminary calculations*

	January–June (£)	July–December (£)
Production overheads	90 000	30 000
(Over)/under-absorbed	(12 000)	12 000
	78 000	42 000
Change in overheads	36 000	
Change in production volume (units)	12 000	

	January–June (£)	July–December (£)
Production variable overhead rate per unit		£3
Fixed production overheads (£78 000 − (18 000 × £3)) £24 000		
Distribution costs	£45 000	£40 000
Decrease in costs		£5 000
Decrease in sales volume (units)		5 000
Distribution cost per unit sold		£1
Fixed distribution cost (£45 000 − (15 000 × £1))		£30 000

Unit costs are as follows:

	(£)	(£)
Selling price		36
Direct materials	6	
Direct labour	9	
Variable production overhead	3	
Variable distribution cost	1	19
Contribution		17

Note that the unit direct costs are derived by dividing the total cost by units produced.

Marginal costing profit statement

	January–June (£000)	(£000)	July–December (£000)	(£000)
Sales		540		360
Variable costs at £19 per unit sold		285		190
Contribution		255		170
Fixed costs:				
Production overhead	24		24	
Selling costs	50		50	
Distribution cost	30		30	
Administration	80	184	80	184
Profit		71		(14)

(b) Marginal costing stock valuation per unit = £18 per unit production variable cost.

Absorption costing stock valuation per unit = £20 per unit total production cost.

	January–June (£000)	July–December (£000)
Absorption costing profit	77	(22)
Fixed overheads in stock increase of 3 000 units	6	
Fixed overheads in stock decrease of 4 000 units		(8)
Marginal costing profit	71	14

(c) Absorption gross profit per unit sold = Annual gross profit (£400 000)/Annual sales (25 000 units)

= £16

	(£000)
Profit from January–June	77
Reduction in sales volume (5 000 × £16)	(80)
Difference in overhead recovery (£12 000 over recovery and £12 000 under recovery)	(24)
Reduction in distribution cost	5
	(22)

(d) Fixed cost £184 000 × 2 = £368 000

Contribution per unit   £17
Break-even point   21 647 units (Fixed costs/contribution per unit)

(e) See 'Some arguments in support of variable costing' in Chapter 7 for the answer to this question.

Question 7.8

(a) Fixed overhead rate per unit $= \dfrac{\text{Budgeted fixed overheads (£300 000)}}{\text{Budgeted production (40 000 units)}} = £7.50$

Absorption costing (FIFO) profit statement:

		(£000)
Sales (42 000 × £72) Less cost of sales:		3 024
Opening stock (2 000 × £30)	60	
Add production (46 000 × £52.50^a)	2 415	
	2 475	
Less closing stock (6 000 × £52.50)	315	2 160
		864
Add over-absorption of overheads^b		27
Profit		891

Notes:

^{a}Variable cost per unit = £2 070/46 000 = £45

^{b}Total cost per unit = £45 + £7.50 Fixed overhead = £52.50

Overhead absorbed (46 000 × £7.50)	= £345 000
Actual overhead incurred	= £318 000
Over-recovery	£27 000

Marginal costing (FIFO) profit statement:

	(£000)	(£000)
Sales		3 024
Less cost of sales:		
Opening stock (2 000 × £25)	50	
Add production (46 000 × £45)	2 070	
	2 120	
Less closing stock (6 000 × £45)	270	1 850
Contribution		1 174
Less fixed overheads incurred		318
Profit		856

Reconciliation:

Absorption profit exceeds marginal costing profit by £35 000 (£891 000 − £856 000). The difference is due to the fixed overheads carried forward in the stock valuations:

	(£)
Fixed overheads in closing stocks (6000 × £7.50)	45 000
Less fixed overheads in opening stocks (2000 × £5)	10 000
Fixed overheads included in stock movement	35 000

Absorption costing gives a higher profit because more of the fixed overheads are carried forward into the next accounting period than were brought forward from the last accounting period.

(b) *Absorption costing (AVECO) profit statement:*

	(£000)	(£000)
Sales		3 024
Opening stock plus production (48 000 × £51.56[a])	2 475	
Less closing stock (6 000 × £51.56)	309	2 166
		858
Add over-absorption of overheads		27
Profit		885

Marginal costing (AVECO) profit statement:

	(£000)	(£000)
Sales		3 024
Less cost of sales		
Opening stock plus production (48 000 × £44.17[b])	2 120	
Less closing stock (6 000 × £44.17)	265	1 855
Contribution		1 169
Less fixed overheads		318
Profit		851

Notes:

[a]With the AVECO method the opening stock is merged with the production of the current period to ascertain the average unit cost:

Opening stock (2000 × £30) + Production cost (£2 415 000) = £2 475 000
Average cost per unit = £2 475 000/48 000 units

[b]Average cost = (Production cost (£2 070 000) + Opening stock (50 000))/ 48 000 units.

Reconciliation:

	(£000)
Difference in profits (£885 − £851)	34
Fixed overheads in closing stocks (309 − 265)	44
Less fixed overheads in opening stock (2 000 × £5)	10
Fixed overheads included in stock movement	34

The variations in profits between (a) and (b) are £6000 for absorption costing and £5000 for marginal costing. With the FIFO method all of the lower cost brought forward from the previous period is charged as an expense against the current period. The closing stock is derived only from current period costs. With the AVECO method the opening stock is merged with the units produced in the current period and is thus allocated between cost of sales and closing stocks. Therefore some of the lower cost brought forward from the previous period is incorporated in the closing stock at the end of the period.

Question 7.9

(a) It is assumed that opening stock valuation in 2016 was determined on the basis of the old overhead rate of £2.10 per hour. The closing stock valuation for 2016 and the opening and closing valuations for 2017 are calculated on the basis of the new overhead rate of £3.60 per hour. In order to compare the 2016 and 2017 profits, it is necessary to restate the 2016 opening stock on the same basis as that which was used for 2017 stock valuations.

We are informed that the 2017 closing stock will be at the same physical level as the 2015 opening stock valuation. It should also be noted that the 2016 opening stock was twice as much as the 2015 equivalent. The 2015 valuation on the revised basis would have been £130 000, resulting in a 2016 revised valuation of £260 000. Consequently, the 2016 profits will be £60 000 (£260 000 − £200 000) lower when calculated on the revised basis.

From the 2016 estimate you can see that stocks increase and then decline in 2017. It appears that the company has over-produced in 2016 thus resulting in large opening stocks at the start of 2017. The effect of this is that more of the sales demand is met from opening stocks in 2017. Therefore production declines in 2017, thus resulting in an under recovery of £300 000 fixed overheads, which is charged as a period cost. On the other hand, the under recovery for 2016 is expected to be £150 000.

The reconciliation of 2013 and 2017 profits is as follows:

	(£)
2016 profits	128 750
Difference in opening stock valuation for 2016	(60 000)
Additional under recovery in 2017	(150 000)
Budgeted loss for 2017	(81 250)

(b) To prepare the profit and loss accounts on a marginal cost basis, it is necessary to analyze the production costs into the fixed and variable elements. The calculations are:

	2015 (£)	2016 (£)	2017 (£)
Total fixed overheads incurred	600 000	600 000	600 000
Less under recovery	300 000	150 000	300 000
Fixed overheads charged to production	300 000	450 000	300 000
Total production cost	1 000 000	975 000	650 000
Proportion fixed	3/10	6/13 (450/975)	6/13
Proportion variable (balance)	7/10	7/13	7/13

Profit and loss accounts (marginal cost basis)

	Actual 2015 (£)	(£)	(£)	Estimated 2016 (£)	(£)	Budget 2017 (£)	(£)
Sales		1 350 000		1 316 250			1 316 250
Opening finished goods stock at marginal cost	700 000[a]		140 000[a]		192 500[b]		
Variable factory cost	700 000[a]		525 000[b]		350 000[b]		
	770 000		665 000		542 500		
Closing finished goods stock at marginal cost	140 000[a]	630 000	192 500[b]	472 500	70 000[b]	472 500	
		720 000		843 750		843 750	
Fixed factory cost	600 000		600 000		600 000		
Administrative and financial costs	220 000		220 000		220 000		
		820 000		820 000		820 000	
Profit/(loss)		(£100 000)		£23 750		£23 750	

Notes:

[a] 7/10 × absorption cost figures given in the question.

[b] 7/13 × absorption cost figures given in the question.

(c) The under-absorption of overhead may be due to the fact that the firm is operating at a low level of activity. This may be due to a low demand for the firm's products. The increase in the overhead rate will cause the product costs to increase. When cost-plus pricing is used the selling price will also be increased. An increase in selling price may result in a further decline in demand. Cost-plus pricing ignores price/demand relationships. For a more detailed discussion of the answer required to this question see section on 'Limitations of cost-plus pricing' in Chapter 10.

(d) For an answer to this question see section on 'Reasons for using cost-based pricing formulae' in Chapter 10 and 'Some arguments in favour of absorption costing' in Chapter 7. Note that SSAP 9 requires that absorption costing (full costing) be used for external reporting.

Question 7.10

(a) Sales for the second six-monthly period have increased for department A, but profit has declined, whereas sales for department B have declined and profit has increased. This situation arises because stocks are valued on an absorption cost basis. With an absorption costing system, fixed overheads are included in the stock valuations, and this can result in the amount of fixed overhead charged as an expense being different from the amount of fixed overhead incurred during a period. The effect of including fixed overheads in the stock valuation is shown below:

	1 July–31 December		1 January–30 June	
	Department A	Department B	Department A	Department B
Fixed overheads brought forward in opening stock of finished goods[a]	36	112	72	96
Fixed overheads carried forward in closing stock of goods[b]	72	96	12	160
Profit increased by	36			64
Profit reduced by		16	60	
Net profit as per absorption costing profit and loss account	94	50	53	83
Profit prior to stock adjustment	58	66	113	19

Notes:

[a]Stocks are valued at factory cost with an absorption costing system. The opening stock valuation for Department A for the first six months is £60 000 based on a product cost of £20 per unit. Therefore opening stock comprises 3000 units. Fixed manufacturing overheads are charged to the product made in Department A at £12 per unit. Consequently, the stock valuation includes £36 000 for fixed overheads. The same approach is used to calculate the fixed overheads included in the opening stock valuation for the second period and Department B.

[b]Closing stock for Department B (first period) = 6000 units (£120 000/£20). Fixed overheads included in closing stock valuation = £72 000 (6000 units × £12).

The same approach is used to calculate fixed overheads included in the remaining stock valuations.

Comments

During the first six months for Department A, stocks are increasing so that the stock adjustment results in a reduction of the fixed overhead charge for the period of £36 000. Fixed manufacturing overheads of £132 000 have been incurred during the period. Therefore the total fixed manufacturing overhead charge for the period is £96 000. In the first period for Department B stocks are declining and the stock adjustment will result in an additional £16 000 fixed manufacturing overheads being included in the stock valuation. Consequently, the fixed manufacturing overhead charge for the period is £320 000 (£304 000 + £16 000). When stocks are increasing, the stock adjustment will have a favourable impact on profits (Department A, period 1), and when stocks are declining, the stock adjustment will have an adverse impact on profits (Department B, period 1).

In the second period stocks decline in Department A and the stock adjustment will have an adverse impact on profits, whereas in Department B stocks increase and this has a favourable impact on profit. When the two periods are compared, the stock adjustment has an adverse impact on the profits of Department A and a favourable impact on the profits of Department B. With an absorption costing system, profit is a function of sales and stock movements, and these stock movements can have an adverse impact on profits even when sales are increasing.

(b) Departmental profit and loss accounts (marginal costing basis)

	1 July–31 December		1 January–30 June	
	Department A (£000)	Department B (£000)	Department A (£000)	Department B (£000)
Sales revenue	300	750	375	675
Variable manufacturing costs:				
Direct material	52	114	30	132
Direct labour	26	76	15	88
Variable overheads	26	76	15	88
Variable factory cost of production	104	266	60	308
Add opening stock of finished goods	24	98	48	84
	128	364	108	392
Less closing stock of finished goods	48	84	8	140
Variable factory cost of goods sold	80	280	100	252
Total contribution	£220	£470	£275	£423
Less:				
Fixed factory overheads	132	304	132	304
Fixed administrative and selling costs	30	100	30	100
Net profit	58	66	113	19

Cost–volume–profit analysis
Solutions to Chapter 8 questions

Question 8.1

Break-even point in units = £18000 sales/unit selling price (£15) = 1200 units
Contribution per unit sold = £15 × 0.4 = £6
Profit when 1500 units are sold = (1500 − 1200) × £6 = £1800
Answer = B

Question 8.2

Variable costs are 60 per cent of the selling price and the variable cost per unit is £36 so the selling price per unit is £36/0.6 = £60
Contribution per unit = £24 (£60 × 0.4)
Break-even point = Fixed costs (£81 000)/contribution per unit (£24) = 3375 units
Margin of safety = 1625 units (5000 weekly sales − 3375 units break-even point)
Answer = A

Question 8.3

Variable costs are 60 per cent of the selling price and the variable cost per unit is £24 so the selling price per unit is £24/0.6 = £40
Contribution per unit = £16 (£40 × 0.4)
Break-even point = Fixed costs (£720 000)/contribution per unit (£16) = 45 000 units
Answer = D

Question 8.4

BEP = Fixed costs/PV ratio
PV ratio = Contribution/Sales = £275 000/£500 000 = 0.55
BEP = £165 000/0.55 = £300 000
Answer = (d)

Question 8.5

(a) See Figure Q8.5.
(b) See Chapter 8 for the answer to this question.
(c) The major limitations are:
   (i)   Costs and revenue may only be linear within a certain output range.
   (ii) In practice, it is difficult to separate fixed and variable costs, and the calculations will represent an approximation.
   (iii) It is assumed that profits are calculated on a variable costing basis.
   (iv) Analysis assumes a single product is sold or a constant sales mix is maintained.
(d) The advantages are:
   (i)   The information can be absorbed at a glance without the need for detailed figures.
   (ii) Essential features are emphasized.
   (iii) The graphical presentation can be easily understood by non-accountants.

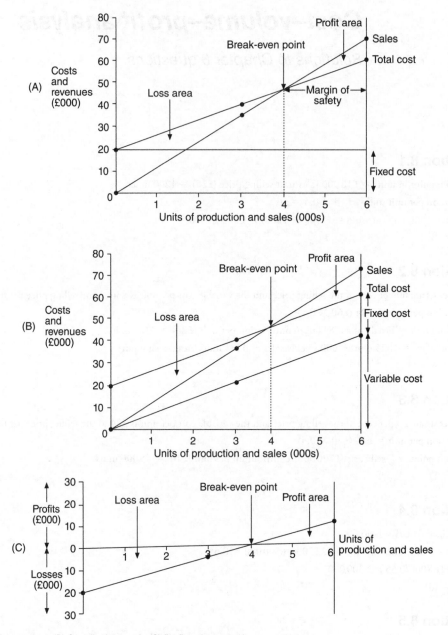

Figure Q8.5   (A) Break-even chart. (B) Contribution graph. (C) Profit–volume graph.

Question 8.6

(a)

$$\text{Break-even point} = \frac{\text{fixed costs } (£1\,212\,000)}{\text{average contribution per £ of sales } (£0.505)} = £2\,400\,000$$

Average contribution per £ of sales $= [0.7 \times (£1 - £0.45)] + [0.3 \times (£1 - £0.6)]$

(b) The graph (Figure Q8.6) is based on the following calculations:

Zero activity: loss $= £1\,212\,000$ (fixed costs)

£4 m existing sales: $(£4m \times £0.505) - £1\,212\,000 = £808\,000$ profit

£4 m revised sales: $(£4m \times £0.475) - £1\,212\,000 = £688\,000$ profit

Existing break-even point: $£2\,400\,000$

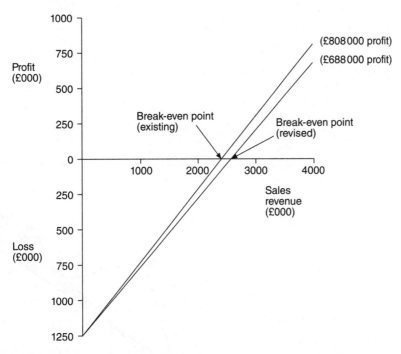

Figure Q8.6   Profit–volume chart

Revised break-even point: £2 551 579 (£1 212 000/£0.475)

Revised contribution per £ of sales: (0.5 × £0.55) + (0.5 × £0.40) = £0.475

(c)

$$\frac{\text{Required contribution}}{\text{Contribution per £ of sales}} = \frac{£455\,000 + £700\,000}{£0.55} = £2\,100\,000$$

Question 8.7

(a) See Figures Q8.7(A) and Q8.7(B) for the break-even charts.

(b) Both charts indicate that each product has three break-even points. With the Standard quality, profits are earned on sales from 80 000 to 99 999 units and above 140 000 units; whereas with the De Luxe quality, profits are earned on sales from 71 429 – 99 999 units and above 114 286 units. The charts therefore provide guidance regarding the level of sales at which to aim.

(c) *Expected unit sales*

Standard: (172 000 × 0.1) + (160 000 × 0.7) + (148 000 × 0.2) = 158 800

De Luxe: (195 500 × 0.3) + (156 500 × 0.5) + (109 500 × 0.2) = 158 800

Expected profits

	Standard (£)		De Luxe (£)	
Total contribution	397 000	(158 800 × £2.50)	555 800	(158 800 × £3.50)
Fixed costs	350 000		400 000	
Profit	47 000		155 800	

Margin of safety

Standard: expected sales volume (158 800) − break-even point (140 000)

= 18 800 units

De Luxe: expected sales volume (158 800) − break-even point (114 286)

= 44 514 units

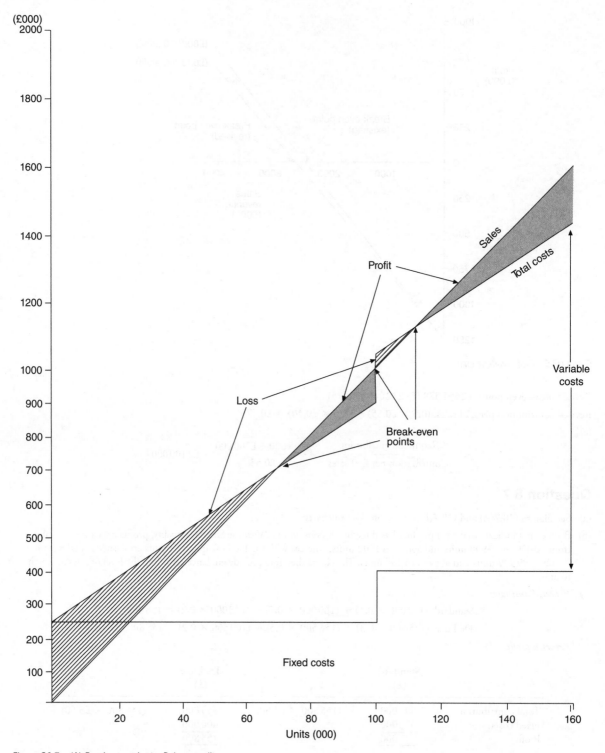

Figure Q8.7 (A) Break-even chart – Deluxe quality.

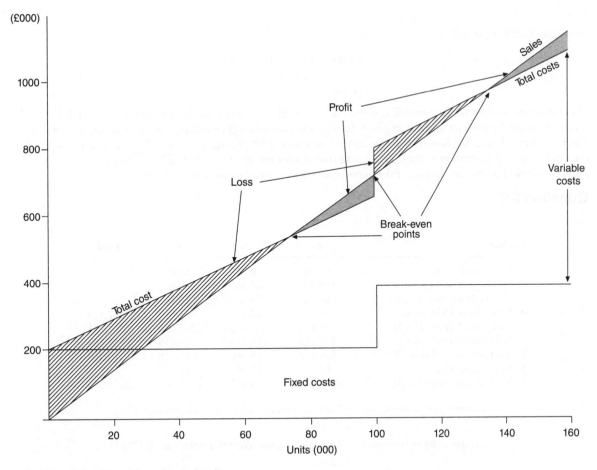

Figure Q8.7 (B) Break-even chart – Standard quality.

(d) The profit probability distributions for the products are:

Demand	Standard probability	Profits (£)	Demand	DeLuxe Probability	DeLuxe Profits/(loss) (£)
172 000	0.1	80 000	195 500	0.3	284 250
160 000	0.7	50 000	156 500	0.5	147 750
148 000	0.2	20 000	109 500	0.2	(16 750)

The De Luxe model has the higher expected profit, but is also more risky than the Standard product. There is a 0.2 probability that the De Luxe model will make a loss, whereas there is a zero probability that the Standard product will make a loss. The decision as to which product to produce will depend upon management's attitude towards risk and the future profitability from its other products. If the company is currently making a loss it may be inappropriate to choose the product that could make a loss. On the other hand, the rewards from the De Luxe model are much higher, and, if the company can survive if the worst outcome occurs, there is a strong argument for producing the De Luxe product.

Question 8.8

$$\text{Break-even point} = \frac{\text{Fixed costs}}{\text{Contribution per unit}}$$

Product X	25 000 units (£100 000/£4)
Product Y	25 000 units (£200 000/£8)
Company as a whole	57 692 units (£300 000/£5.20[a])

Note:

[a]Average contribution per unit

$$= \frac{(70\,000 \times £4) + (30\,000 \times £8)}{100\,000 \text{ units}}$$

$$= £5.20$$

The sum of the product break-even points is less than the break-even point for the company as a whole. It is incorrect to add the product break-even points because the sales mix will be different from the planned sales mix. The sum of the product break-even points assumes a sales mix of 50 per cent to X and 50 per cent to Y. The break-even point for the company as a whole assumes a planned sales mix of 70 per cent to X and 30 per cent to Y. CVP analysis will yield correct results only if the planned sales mix is equal to the actual sales mix.

Question 8.9

(a) (i)

Products	1	2	3	Total
1. Unit contribution	£1.31	£0.63	£1.87	
2. Specific fixed costs per unit	£0.49	£0.35	£0.62	
3. General fixed costs per unit	£0.46	£0.46	£0.46	
4. Sales volume (000s units)	98.2	42.1	111.8	252.1
5. Total contribution (1 × 4)	£128.642	£26.523	£209.066	£364.231
6. Total specific fixed costs (2 × 4)	£48.118	£14.735	£69.316	£132.169
7. Total general fixed costs (3 × 4)	£45.172	£19.366	£51.428	£115.966
8. Unit selling price	£2.92	£1.35	£2.83	
9. Total sales revenue (8 × 4)	£286.744	£56.835	£316.394	£659.973

Average contribution per unit = Total contribution (£364.231)/sales volume (252.1)

= £1.4448

Average selling price per unit = Total sales revenue (£659.973)/sales volume (252.1)

= £2.6179

$$\text{Break-even point (units)} = \frac{\text{Total fixed costs}}{\text{Average contribution per unit}}$$

= (£132.169 + £115.966)/£1.4448

= 171.743 units

Break-even point (sales value) = 171.743 units × average selling price (£2.6179)

= £449.606

Alternatively, the break-even point (sales value) can be calculated using the following formula:

$$\text{Break-even point} = \frac{\text{Fxed costs} (£132.169 + £115.966)}{\text{Total contribution} (£364.231)} \times \text{Total sales} (£659.973)$$

= £449.606

It is assumed that the question requires the calculation of the break-even point to cover both general and specific fixed costs. An alternative answer would have been to present details of the break-even point to cover only specific fixed costs.

(ii) The planned sales mix for Product 2 that was used to calculate the breakeven point in (i) is 42.1/252.1. Therefore the number of units of Product 2 at the break-even point is:

42.1/252.1 × 171 743 units = 28 681

(b) At the forecast sales volume the profit/contributions are as follows:

	(£000s)
Contributions to all fixed costs	26.523
Less specific fixed costs	14.735
Contribution to general fixed costs	11.788
Less share of general fixed costs	19.366
Net loss	7.578

Product 2 provides a contribution of £11788 towards general fixed costs and, unless savings in general fixed costs in excess of £11788 can be made if Product 2 is abandoned, it is still viable to produce Product 2. If the company ceases production of Product 2 it will lose a contribution of £11788 and total profits will decline by £11788. The company should investigate whether a greater contribution than £11788 can be generated from the resources. If this is not possible the company should continue production of Product 2.

Question 8.10

Task 1	(£)	(£)
Sales		2 106 000
Less variable cost of sales:		
Cost of beds	1 620 000	
Commission	210 600	
Transport	216 000	2 046 600
Contribution		59 400

Average contribution per bed sold = £59 400/5400 = £11

Fixed costs (£8450 + £10 000 + £40 000 + £40 000) = £98 450

$$\text{Break-even point (units)} = \frac{\text{Fixed costs (£98 450)}}{\text{Contribution per unit (£11)}} = 8950 \text{ beds}$$

Average selling price per unit (£2 106 000/5 400 beds) = £390

Break-even point (sales revenue) = 8950 beds at £390 = £3 490 500

Task 2

The letter should include the items listed in (a) to (e) below:

(a)

Required contribution:	(£)
Salary	36 550
Interest lost	15 000
Fixed costs shown in Task 1	98 450
	150 000
Less manager's salary saved	40 000
Total contribution	110 000

The minimum profit required to compensate for loss of salary and interest is £11 550 (£110 000 − £98 450 fixed costs).

(b) Required volume = Required contribution (£110 000)/Contribution per unit (£11) = 10 000 beds

(c) Average life of a bed = (9 years × 0.10) + (10 years × 0.60) + (11 years × 0.3) = 10.2 years

Total bed population = 44 880 households × 2.1 beds per market = 94 248

$$\text{Estimated annual demand} = \frac{94 248 \text{ beds}}{\text{Average replacement period (10.2 years)}}$$

$$= 9 240 \text{ beds}$$

(d) The proposal will not achieve the desired profit. Estimated annual sales are 9240 beds but 10 000 beds must be sold to achieve the desired profit. The shortfall of 760 beds will result in profit being £8360 (760 × £11) less than the desired profit.

(e) The estimate of maximum annual sales volume may prove to be inaccurate because of the following reasons:

(i) The population of Mytown may differ from the sample population. For example the population of Mytown might contain a greater proportion of elderly people or younger people with families. Either of these situations may result in the buying habits of the population of Mytown being different from the sample proportion.

(ii) The data are historic and do not take into account future changes such as an increase in wealth of the population, change in composition or a change in buying habits arising from different types of beds being marketed.

Task 3

This question requires a knowledge of the material covered in Chapter 9. Therefore you should delay attempting this question until you have understood the content of Chapter 9.

	A (£)	B (£)	C (£)	Total
Selling price	240	448	672	
Unit purchase cost	130	310	550	

	A (£)	B (£)	C (£)	Total
Carriage inwards	20	20	20	
Contribution	90	118	102	
Square metres per bed	3	4	5	
Contribution per square metre	£30	£29.50	£20.40	
Ranking	1	2	3	
Maximum demand	35	45	20	
Storage required (square metres)	105	180	100	385

Monthly sales schedule and statement of profitability:

	(£)	(£)
Contribution from sales of A (35 × £90)		3 150
Contribution from sales of B (45 × £118)		5 310
Contribution from sales of C (3^a × £102)		306
		8 766
Less specific avoidable fixed costs:		
Staff costs	3 780	
Departmental fixed overheads	2 000	5 780
Contribution to general fixed overheads		2 986
Less general fixed overheads		2 520
Departmental profit		466

Note:
[a]The balance of storage space available for Model C is 300 square metres
less the amount allocated to A and B (285 metres) = 15 metres. This will result
in the sales of three beds (15 metres/5 metres per bed).

Question 8.11

(a) *Analysis of semi-variable costs*[a]

$$\text{Method A: variable element} = \frac{\text{increase in costs}}{\text{increase in activity}} = \frac{£10\,000}{100\,000 \text{ copies}}$$

$$= £0.10 \text{ per copy}$$

fixed element = total semi-variable cost (£55 000) − variable cost
(£35 000) at an activity level of 350 000 copies

Therefore fixed element = £20 000

$$\text{Method B: variable element} = \frac{\text{increase in costs}}{\text{increase in activity}} = \frac{£5000}{100\,000 \text{ copies}}$$

$$= £0.05 \text{ per copy}$$

fixed element = total semi-variable cost (£47 500) − variable costs
(£17 500) at an activity level of 350 000 copies

Therefore element = £30 000

Note:
[a]The analysis is based on a comparison of total costs and activity levels at 350 000 and 450 000 copies per year.

Contribution per copy of new magazine

	Method A (£)	Method B (£)
Selling price	1.00	1.00
Variable cost (given)	(0.55)	(0.50)
Variable element of semi-variable cost	(0.10)	(0.05)
Lost contribution from existing magazine	(0.05)	(0.05)
Contribution	0.30	0.40

Calculation of net increase in company profits

	Method B			Method A		
Copies sold	500 000	400 000	600 000	500 000	400 000	600 000
Contribution per copy	£0.30	£0.30	£0.30	£0.40	£0.40	£0.40
Total contribution	£150 000	£120 000	£180 000	£200 000	£160 000	£240 000
Fixed costs[a]	£100 000	£100 000	£100 000	£150 000	£150 000	£150 000
Net increase in profit	£50 000	£20 000	£80 000	£50 000	£10 000	£90 000

Note:

[a] Method A = specific fixed costs (£80 000) + semi-variable element (£20 000)
= £100 000
Method B = specific fixed costs (£120 000) + semi-variable element (£30 000)
= £150 000

(b)
$$\text{Break-even point} = \frac{\text{fixed costs}}{\text{contribution per unit}}$$

Method A = £100 000/0.30 = 333 333 copies

Method B = £150 000/0.40 = 375 000 copies

The margin of safety is the difference between the anticipated sales and the break-even point sales:

Method A = 500 000 − 333 333 = 166 667 copies

Method B = 500 000 − 375 000 = 125 000 copies

(c) Method B has a higher break-even point and a higher contribution per copy sold. This implies that profits from Method B are more vulnerable to a decline in sales volume. However, higher profits are obtained with Method B when sales are high (see 600 000 copies in (B)).

The break-even point from the sale of the existing magazine is 160 000 copies (£80 000/£0.50) and the current level of monthly sales is 220 000 copies. Therefore sales can drop by 60 000 copies before break-even point is reached. For every ten copies sold of the new publication, sales of the existing publication will be reduced by one copy. Consequently, if more than 600 000 copies of the new publication are sold, the existing magazine will make a loss. If sales of the new magazine are expected to consistently exceed 600 000 copies then the viability of the existing magazine must be questioned.

Question 8.12

(a) (i) The opportunity costs of producing cassettes are the salary forgone of £1000 per month and the rental forgone of £400 per month.

(ii) The consultant's fees and development costs represent sunk costs.

(b) The following information can be obtained from the report.

	£10 selling price	£9 selling price
Sales quantity	7500–10 000 units	12 000–18 000 units
Fixed costs[a]	£13 525	£17 525
Profit at maximum sales[b]	£3 975	£4 975
Profit/(loss) at minimum sales[c]	(£400)	(£2 525)
Break-even point[d]	7 729 units	14 020 units
Margin of safety:		
Below maximum	2 271 units	3 980 units
Above minimum	229 units	2 020 units

Notes:

[a]Fixed production cost + £1400 opportunity cost

[b](10 000 units × £1.75 contribution) − £13 525 fixed costs = £3975 profit

(18 000 units × £1.25 contribution) − £17 525 fixed costs = £4975 profit

[c](7 500 units × £1.75 contribution) − £13 525 fixed costs = £400 loss

(12 000 units × £1.25 contribution) − £17 525 fixed costs = £2 525 loss

[d]Fixed costs/contribution per unit.

Conclusions

(i) The £10 selling price is less risky than the £9 selling price. With the £10 selling price, the maximum loss is lower and the break-even point is only 3 per cent above minimum sales (compared with 17 per cent for a £9 selling price).

(ii) The £9 selling price will yield the higher profits if maximum sales quantity is achieved.

(iii) In order to earn £3975 profits at a £9 selling price, we must sell 17 200 units (required contribution of 17 525 fixed costs plus £3975 divided by a contribution per unit of £1.25).

Additional information required

(i) Details of capital employed for each selling price.

(ii) Details of additional finance required to finance the working capital and the relevant interest cost so as to determine the cost of financing the working capital.

(iii) Estimated probability of units sold at different selling prices.

(iv) How long will the project remain viable?

(v) Details of range of possible costs. Are the cost figures given in the question certain?

Question 8.13

(a) *Impact of stitching elimination*

Loss of contribution from 10 per cent sales reduction	£135 000
(300 000 × 10% × £4.50)	
Production cost reduction (270 000 × £0.60)	£162 000
Net gain from the stitching elimination	£27 000

Note:

Contribution per unit − Fixed cost per unit (£1.50) = Net profit per unit (£3). Therefore contribution per unit = £4.50.

Use of plastic eyes

The reduction in sales volume arising from the stitching elimination also applies to the evaluation of the proposals for the change in type of eye and change in filling.

Glass eyes required for production = 540 000 (270 000 × 2)

Input required to allow for 5 per cent input losses (540 000/0.95 × £0.20) = £113 684

Plastic eyes required to allow for 10 per cent input losses	
(540 000/0.90 × £0.15) =	£90 000
Net saving from plastic eyes	£23 684

Use of scrap fabric for filling

Cost of synthetic filling (270 000/2000 × £80)	£10 800
Additional production cost of scrap fabric (270 000 × £0.05)	£13 500
Net increase in cost from use of scrap fabric	£2 700

The overall net increase in annual net profit arising from the implementation of the three proposals is £47 984 − (£27 000 + £23 684 − £2700)

(b)

Additional contribution from all three changes	
(£162 000 + £23 684 − £2700)/270 000 =	£0.678
Existing contribution	£4.50
Revised contribution per unit	£5.178

Number of toys required to give the same contribution prior to the changes:

(£4.50 × 300 000)/£5.178 = 260 718 toys

Therefore the reduction in sales required to leave net profit unchanged

$$= (300\,000 - 260\,718)/300\,000$$

$$= 13.1\%$$

(c) The report should indicate that answers to the following questions should be obtained before a final decision is taken:

(i) How accurate is the estimate of demand? Demand is predicted to fall by 10 per cent but the answer to (b) indicates that if demand falls by more than 13 per cent, profit will be lower if the changes are implemented.

(ii) Have all alternative courses of action been considered? For example, would a price reduction, or advertising and a sales promotion, stimulate demand and profits?

(iii) Will the change to using scrap fabric result in a loss of revenues from the sale of scrap?

(iv) Will the elimination of stitching result in redundancy payments and possible industrial action?

(v) Consideration should be given to eliminating stitching and using plastic eyes but not using scrap fabric for filling.

Question 8.14

(a) Actual patient days = 22 000 (£4.4 million/£200)

Bed occupancy = 75 per cent (22 000/29 200)

Profit/(Loss)	(£)	(£)
Total revenue		4 400 000
Variable costs		1 100 000
Contribution to direct and general fixed costs		3 300 000
Staffing costs: Supervisors	4 × £22 000	
Nurses	13 × £16 000	
Assistants	24 × £12 000	584 000
Fixed charges		1 650 000
Profit		1 066 000

Break-even point = Fixed costs (£584 000 + £1 650 000)/Contribution per patient day (£150)[a]

= 14 893 patient days.

The above calculation is based on the actual outcomes for the period. Because of the stepped nature of the fixed costs other break-even points can be calculated based on actual patient days for the period being less than 20 500 or over 23 000.

Note:

[a]£3 300 000/22 000 patient days.

(b) It is assumed that estimated bed occupancy will be at the previous year's level plus an extra 20 beds for 100 days giving an occupancy of 24 000 patient days [22 000 + (100 × 20)]. This will result in an estimated bed occupancy of 66 per cent [24 000/(100 × 365) = 66%].

	(£)	(£)
Total revenue (24 000 × £200)		4 800 000
Variable costs (24 000 × £50)		1 200 000
Contribution to direct and general fixed costs		3 600 000
Staffing costs: Supervisors	4 × £24 200	
Nurses	15 × £17 600	
Assistants	28 × £13 200	730 400
Fixed charges (£1 650 000 × 100/80)		2 062 500
Profit		807 100

(c) Attempting to cover the 100 days demand by increasing capacity by 20 beds for 365 days has resulted in a decline in the occupancy percentage from 75 per cent to 66 per cent. To meet the increased demand of 2000 patient days (100 days × 20 beds) extra capacity of 7300 potential patient days were provided (365 days × 20 beds). This has had a detrimental impact on the occupancy percentage. The extra contribution from the increased demand was £300 000 but this was offset by a higher allocation of fixed charges of £412 500 arising from the increase in bed capacity. The additional personnel costs arising from increases in stepped fixed costs and increased salaries further contributed to the reduction in profit.

Assuming that fixed costs (administration, security and property costs) will remain unchanged the extra demand has generated an additional contribution to these common and unavoidable fixed costs and should therefore increase the profit for the hospital as a whole. However, the way in which the fixed costs are allocated reduces the profit for the paediatric unit. A possible solution to overcome this problem is to make the units accountable for the contribution to unavoidable fixed costs (assumed to be contribution less staffing costs). Adopting this approach would result in a contribution to general fixed costs of £2716000 being reported and £2869000 in the following year. An alternative approach would be to allocate fixed costs on the basis of patient days rather than bed capacity. The danger with both approaches is that there is no incentive to encourage managers to restrict bed capacity.

(d) For organizations that have profit making objectives a reasonable financial return must be generated to satisfy the providers of the funds. However, for an organization to survive it must satisfy the objectives of other stakeholders (e.g. employees, customers and social objectives). Conflicts between financial and social objectives occur when a greater financial return can be achieved at the expense of poorer social provision or increased social provision can be obtained but this has a detrimental impact on meeting financial objectives. In a private healthcare organization higher profits might be obtained by charging higher fees and treating fewer patients compared with treating many patients at a lower fee. Thus financial objectives are being pursued at the expense of lower social provision. Determining the optimal balance between financial and social objectives represents a major problem for a private hospital. To ensure that an adequate level of social provision is provided, such as treating patients requiring expensive treatment, requires that the provision is provided within the public sector.

Question 8.15

(a)

	Estimated variable cost per unit Normal materials (£)	Cheaper grade materials (£)
Direct material	36.00	31.25
Direct labour	10.50	10.50
Variable overheads	10.50	10.50
	57.00	52.25
Wastage (5/95 × £52.25)		2.75
	57.00	55.00

Contribution from using normal grade of materials

Selling price (£)	80	84	88	90	92	96	100
Variable cost (£)	57	57	57	57	57	57	57
Unit contribution (£)	23	27	31	33	35	39	43
Demand (000)	25	23	21	20	19	17	15
Contribution to general fixed costs (£000)	575	621	651	660	665	663	645

Contribution from using cheaper grade of materials

Selling price (£)	80	84	88	90	92	96	100
Variable cost (£)	55	55	55	55	55	55	55
Unit contribution (£)	25	29	33	35	37	41	45
Demand (000)	25	23	21	20	19	17	15
Contribution to specific fixed costs (£000)	625	667	693	700	703	697	675
Specific fixed costs (£000)	30	30	30	30	30	30	30
Contribution to general fixed costs (£000)	595	637	663	670	673	667	645

The selling price that maximizes profit is £92 and the optimum output is 19000 units. For all levels of demand (other than 15000 units), profits are higher for the cheaper grade material. At 15000 units, profits are identical for both grades of materials.

If the reject rate for the cheaper grade of materials increased from 5 per cent to 6 per cent then at the optimum output level higher profits would be earned from using the normal grade of materials. Fixed inspection costs can increase by 10 per cent, and profits will still be higher with the cheaper grade materials for all output levels other than 15000 units. As long as demand is in excess of 15000 units (£30000 inspection costs/£2 variable cost saving), it is preferable to use the cheaper grade materials. Profits are not very sensitive to selling prices within the range £90–£96.

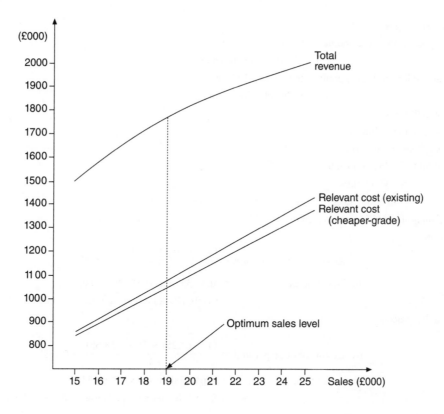

Figure Q8.15

(b) Total revenues and total costs are required to construct a cost–volume–profit graph (Figure Q8.13).

Demand (000)	25	23	21	20	19	17	15
Total revenue (£000)	2 000	1 932	1 848	1 800	1 748	1 632	1 500
Total variable cost (£000) (normal grade)	1 425	1 311	1 197	1 140	1 083	969	855
Total variable cost plus £30 000 inspection cost (cheaper grade)	1 405	1 295	1 185	1 130	1 075	965	855

The above costs and revenues are plotted on the CVP diagram, and optimum output is determined at the point where the difference between the total cost and revenue line is the greatest. This occurs at an output level of 19 000 units. The selling price with a demand of 19 000 units is £92.

Question 8.16

(a)

	Manual production		Computer-aided	
	Thingone (£)	Thingtwo (£)	Thingone (£)	Thingtwo (£)
Selling price	20	50	20.00	50.00
Variable production costs	(15)	(31)	(12.75)	(26.35)
Bad debts[a]	—	(2)	—	(2.00)
Finance cost[b]		(3)	—	(3.00)
Contribution	5	14	7.25	18.5
Fixed costs per month	£31 500		£43 500	

Notes:
[a] 4% of selling price
[b] 2% × £50 × 3 months

(i) *Thingone only is sold*

   Manual process break-even point = 6300 units (£31 500/£5)

   = £126 000 sales revenue

   Computer-aided break-even point = 6000 units (£43 500/£7.25)

   = £120 000 sales revenue

   Point of indifference:

   Let × = point of indifference

(ii) *Then indifference point is where:*

   $5x - 31\,500 = 7.25x - 43\,500$

   = 533.33 units

   = £106 667 sales revenue

(iii) *Sales of Thingone and Thingtwo in the ratio 4 : 1*

Manual process:

$$\text{average contribution per unit} = \frac{(4 \times £5)+(1 \times £14)}{5} = £6.80$$

break-even point = 4632.35 units (£31 500/£6.80)

= £120 441 sales revenue (4632.35 × £26 (W1))

Computer-aided process:

$$\text{average contribution per unit} = \frac{(4 \times £7.25) + (1 \times £18.65)}{5} = £9.53$$

break-even point = 4564.53 units (£43 500/£9.53)

= £118 678 sales revenue (4564.53 × £26 (W1))

Indifference point:

Let x = point of indifference

Then indifference point is where:

$$6.80x - 31\,500 = 9.53x - 43\,500$$

= 4395.60 units

= £114 286 sales revenue (4395.60 × £26 (W1))

Workings

(W1) Break-even point (sales revenue) = break-even point in units × average selling price per unit sold

$$\text{Therefore, average sales revenue per unit} = \frac{(4 \times £20) + (1 \times £50)}{5} = £26$$

(b) If Thingone alone is sold, budgeted sales are 4000 units, and break-even sales are 6000 units (computer-aided process) and 6300 units (manual process). Hence there is little point producing Thingone on its own. Even if the two products are substitutes, total budgeted sales are 6000 units, and Thingone is still not worth selling on its own. Only if sales are limited to £180 000 (budgeted sales revenue) is Thingone worth selling on its own. However, the assumption that the products are perfect substitutes and £180 000 sales can be generated is likely to be over-optimistic. In other words, the single-product policy is very risky.

Assuming that Thingone and Thingtwo are sold in the ratio of 4:1, the breakeven point is 4565 units using the computer-aided process. This consists of a sales mix of 3652 units of Thingone and 913 units of Thingtwo, representing individual margins of safety of 348 units and 1087 units when compared with the original budget. Launching both products is clearly the most profitable alternative.

It should be noted that the budgeted sales mix is in the ratio of 2:1, and this gives an average contribution per unit of £8 (manual process) and £11.05 (computer-aided process). The break-even point based on this sales mix is 3937 units for both the manual and computer-aided process, consisting of 2625 units of Thingone and 1312 units of Thingtwo. This represents a margin of safety of 1375 units of Thingone (34 per cent) and 688 units of Thingtwo (34 per cent). It is obviously better to sell Thingtwo in preference to Thingone. It is recommended that both products be sold and the computer-aided process be adopted.

(c) For the answer to this question see 'Pricing policies' in Chapter 10. In particular, the answer should stress the need to obtain demand estimates for different selling prices and cost estimates for various demand levels. The optimal *short-run* price is where profits are maximized. However, the final price selected should aim to maximize *long-run* profits and the answer should include a discussion of relevant pricing policies such as price skimming and pricing penetration policies. Competitors' reactions to different selling prices should also be considered.

Before demand estimates are made, market research should be undertaken to find customers' reaction to the new product. In addition, research should be undertaken to see whether a similar product is being developed or sold by other firms. This information might be obtained from trade magazines, market research or the company's sales staff. If a similar product is currently being sold, a decision must be made whether to compete on price or quality. The degree of interdependence of new and existing products must also be considered, and any lost sales from existing products should be included in the analysis. It may be necessary to differentiate the new product from existing products.

Measuring relevant costs and revenues for decision-making

Solutions to Chapter 9 questions

Question 9.1

The relevant cost of regularly used materials that will be replaced is the replacement cost ($600 \times £27$) = £16 200.

Answer = C

Question 9.2

If the company uses the equipment on the contract it will lose its current sale value of £2000 and incur additional disposal costs of £800 giving a total relevant cost of £2800.

Answer = D

Question 9.3

With throughput accounting direct labour and all overheads are assumed to be a fixed cost and contribution consists of sales less variable costs. The contribution per bottleneck minute is:

W = £17.66 (£159/9)

X = £13.00 (£130/10)

Y = £17.14 (£120/7)

The rankings are W, Y and X.

Question 9.4

(a)

	North East (£)	South Coast (£)
Material X from stock (i)	19 440	
Material Y from stock (ii)		49 600
Firm orders of material X (iii)	27 360	
Material X not yet ordered (iv)	60 000	
Material Z not yet ordered (v)		71 200
Labour (vi)	86 000	110 000
Site management (vii)	—	—
Staff accommodation and travel for site management (viii)	6 800	5 600
Plant rental received (ix)	(6 000)	—
Penalty clause (x)		28 000
	193 600	264 400
Contract price	288 000	352 000
Net benefit	94 400	87 600

(b) (i) If material X is not used on the North East contract the most beneficial use is to use it as a substitute material thus avoiding future purchases of £19 440 ($0.9 \times 21 600$). Therefore by using the stock quantity of material X the company will have to spend £19 440 on the other materials.

(ii) Material Y is in common use and the company should not dispose of it. Using the materials on the South Coast contract will mean that they will have to be replaced at a cost of £49 600 ($£24 800 \times 2$). Therefore the future cash flow impact of taking on the contract is £49 600.

(iii) It is assumed that with firm orders for materials it is not possible to cancel the purchase. Therefore the cost will occur whatever future alternative is selected. The materials will be used as a substitute material if they are not used on the contract and therefore, based on the same reasoning as note (i) above, the relevant cost is the purchase price of the substitute material (0.9 × £30 400).

(iv) The material has not been ordered and the cost will only be incurred if the contract is undertaken. Therefore additional cash flows of £60 000 will be incurred if the company takes on the North East contract.

(v) The same principles apply here as were explained in note (iv) and additional cash flows of £71 200 will be incurred only if the company takes on the South Coast contract.

(vi) It is assumed that labour is an incremental cost and therefore relevant.

(vii) The site management function is performed by staff at central headquarters. It is assumed that the total company costs in respect of site management will remain unchanged in the short term whatever contracts are taken on. Site management costs are therefore irrelevant.

(viii) The costs would be undertaken only if the contracts are undertaken. Therefore they are relevant costs.

(ix) If the North East contract is undertaken the company will be able to hire out surplus plant and obtain a £6000 cash inflow.

(x) If the South Coast contract is undertaken the company will have to withdraw from the North East contract and incur a penalty cost of £28 000.

(xi) The headquarter costs will continue whichever alternative is selected and they are not relevant costs.

(xii) It is assumed that there will be no differential cash flows relating to notional interest. However, if the interest costs associated with the contract differ then they would be relevant and should be included in the analysis.

(xiii) Depreciation is a sunk cost and irrelevant for decision-making.

Question 9.5

(a) *Note 1*

The cost of the engineering specification is based on three days multiplied by the salary and related employment costs of $500 per day. However, this is not a relevant value because the cost has already been incurred and is therefore a sunk cost. The relevant cost is zero.

Note 2

The cost of material A is based on 10 000 metres usage at $6.10 per metre derived from the weighted average of the historical cost of materials ($91 500/15 000). There would be no point selling the materials and replacing them at the higher cost. The relevant cost is the replacement cost (10 000 × $7 = $70 000).

Note 3

The direct cost of material B is based on 250 metre lengths being bought at a price of $10 per metre length. This is not the correct valuation because the sole supplier has a minimum order size of 300 metre lengths and the unused materials has no foreseeable use or net sales revenue. Therefore the relevant cost is $3000 (300 × $10) representing the cost of the minimum order of 300 lengths.

Note 4

The cost of the components is based on 500 units at the normal transfer price of $12 ($8 plus a 50 per cent markup) giving a total of $6000. However, the relevant cost to the M group is the variable cost of manufacturing the components plus any lost contribution from the reduction in external sales by HK. Therefore the total relevant cost is $4450. which is derived as follows:

$$350 \text{ components} \times \text{variable cost } (\$8) = \$2\,800$$
$$150 \text{ components} \times \text{variable cost } (\$8) + \text{lost contribution } (\$3) = \$1\,650$$

The external market price of $14 is not relevant because it is cheaper to manufacture internally.

Note 5

The $12 500 (1000 × $12.50) cost of direct labour is the cost of the existing employees. This is not the relevant cost. The relevant cost is $14 000 being the lower of recruiting engineers to do the work at $15 per hour or transferring the existing employees and recruiting replacements to do their work at $14 per hour.

Note 6

The cost of the supervisor is based on a monthly salary of $3500 (annual salary of $42 000/12 months) multiplied by 10 per cent. Since no additional supervisory costs will be involved the relevant cost is zero.

Note 7

The machine hire cost is based on five days multiplied by a hire charge of $500 per day. However, this is not the relevant cost because there is a lower cost option available. If the machine is hired at a monthly cost $5000 and then sub hired for $150 per day for 20 days the net cost of this option will be $2000. Therefore the relevant cost is $2000.

Note 8

The overhead cost value is $5.50 per hour based on estimated overhead costs ($220 000) divided by 40 000 hours (80 per cent of 50 000 hours). The cost estimate of $5500 is derived from multiplying 1000 hours of skilled labour at $5.50 per hour. These costs will be incurred whether the project goes ahead or not. Since no additional outlays will be incurred the relevant cost is zero.

The revised schedule of relevant costs is as follows:

	Note	$
Engineering specification	1	NIL
Direct material A	2	70 000
Direct material B	3	3 000
Components	4	4 450
Direct labour	5	14 000
Supervision	6	NIL
Machine hire	7	2 000
Overhead costs	8	NIL
Total		93 450

(b) Relevant costs represent short-run incremental costs specific to the order whereas the costs reported by routine practices represent estimated average long-run costs for financial accounting stock valuation and profit measurement purposes. For example, material A costs assigned to the contract are historical costs using the weighted average basis whereas relevant costs represent the change in future costs arising from undertaking the contract. The overhead costs are also allocated to meet financial accounting profit measurement and stock valuation requirements whereas the relevant costs represent the change in overhead spending arising from undertaking the contract.

(c) Undertaking the contract will result in one of the companies within the group (HK) not being able to meet the demand from existing customers. This could result in existing customers seeking alternative suppliers. A further issue is that temporary replacement workers will be paid a higher hourly rate than existing workers. This may result in conflicts and a decline in employee morale.

Question 9.6

(a)

	Note	$
Material D	1	1 520
Components	2	49 920
Direct labour	3	11 050
Specialist machine	4	10 000
Machine operating costs	5	12 000
Supervision	6	500
Development time	7	NIL
General fixed overhead	8	NIL
Total relevant cost		84 990

Notes:

1. Material D is in regular use and must be replaced so the relevant cost is its replacement cost. The original cost is not relevant because it is a sunk cost and the resale value is not relevant because CDF will not sell the materials and then replace them at a higher price.

2. CDF could obtain the components externally at a cost of $15 at a total price of $60 000 or they could be obtained from RDF. The transfer price from RDF is ($8 + 30%) + 20% = $12.48 per component. The internal cost to CDF is $12.48 × 4000 = $49 920. The opportunity cost to RDF is not relevant to CDF because the relevant cost is the price they have to pay to their supplier. Since this is lower than the external buying price the relevant cost for the contract is $49 920. Note that the quotation will be provided to CDF and will be based on the cost that it incurs since it appears to be an autonomous division within the group. Therefore the relevant costs for the quotation relate to divisional costs and not group costs.

3. The wages for the employees in department W will remain unchanged regardless of how the work is completed because they are working at 100 per cent capacity. Therefore their cost is irrelevant. The choice is between using employees from department Z at a cost of $15 per hour (total $12 750) or engaging sub-contract workers at a cost of $13 per hour (total $11 050). Since the use of sub-contract employees is the cheaper so the relevant cost is $11 050.

4. The following alternatives exist: (a) Hire at a cost of $15 000; (b) Buy the machine and then sell it after completion of the contract resulting in a net cost of $20 000; or (c) Buy and modify the machine thus avoiding the need to buy the other machine. This option has a net cost of $10 000 ($50 000 plus $5000 modifications less $45 000 cost of another machine). The lowest cost alternative is to buy the machine and then modify it so the relevant cost is $10 000.

5. The machine operating costs are future costs and therefore the relevant costs are $12 000.

6. The supervisor's salary is irrelevant, but the bonus needs to be included because it is an extra cost of undertaking the contract.

7. The development time has already been incurred. Therefore it is a sunk cost.

8. The absorption of general fixed overhead costs and depreciation are not relevant because they will be incurred whether or not the contract is undertaken.

(b) You should refer to the final two paragraphs in the section on 'Special pricing decisions' in Chapter 9 and the section in Chapter 10 titled 'A price-taking firm facing short-run product mix decisions.'

Question 9.7

(a)

	Note	$
Production director – meeting	1	NIL
Material A	2	1 375
Material B	3	360
Components	4	3 000
Direct labour	5	2 100
Machine hours	6	175
Fixed overhead	7	NIL
Total relevant cost		7 010

Notes:

1. This meeting has already taken place. This is a sunk cost and future costs will not change if the contract is undertaken.

2. Material A is in regular use so its relevant cost is the replacement cost. The historical cost is a sunk cost and the resale value is also not relevant since the company will not sell the materials and replace them at a higher price.

3. Material B will be purchased for the contract and therefore its purchase cost is the relevant cost. Only 30 litres are required but the minimum order quantity is 40 litres. RFT has no other use for this material and there is no indication that the unused 10 litres can be sold so the full cost of purchasing the 40 litres is the relevant cost.

4. The relevant cost is $50 each because this is the future expenditure that will be incurred as a result of the work being undertaken.

5. There is spare capacity of 75 hours that have a zero relevant cost. There are two choices for the remaining 160 hours: (a) use existing employees and pay them overtime at $14 per hour (total cost of $2240) or (b) engage the temporary staff at a cost of $1920 plus a supervision cost of $180. The latter is the cheaper alternative.

6. The machine is currently being leased and it has spare capacity. The lease cost will be incurred whether or not the contract is undertaken so the only relevant cost is the incremental running cost of $7 per hour.

7. Fixed overhead costs are incurred whether the work goes ahead or not so it is not a relevant cost.

(b) If HY has spare capacity the components will be produced for RFT using the unused capacity so there will be no opportunity cost and the variable cost will be the relevant cost. If HY does not have sufficient spare capacity to produce all of the components demanded by RFT then the cost of the capacity consists of the opportunity cost. This is equivalent to the contribution forgone by not being able to sell externally.

Question 9.8

(a) (i)

	Product I (£000)	Product II (£000)	Product III (£000)	Total (£000)
Sales	2475	3948	1520	7943
Contribution	1170	1692	532	3394
Attributable fixed costs	(275)	(337)	(296)	(908)
General fixed costs[a]	(520)	(829)	(319)	(1668)
	(795)	(1166)	(515)	(2576)
Profit	375	526	(83)	818
	= £1.60/unit	= £1.40/unit	= (£0.04/unit)	

Note:

[a] General fixed costs are allocated to products at 21 per cent of total sales revenue (£1668/£7943).

(ii) If Product III is discontinued it is assumed that variable costs and attributable (i.e. specific) fixed costs are avoidable. It is assumed that general fixed costs are common and unavoidable to all products and will remain unchanged if Product III is discontinued. However, it is possible that some general fixed costs may be avoidable in the longer term. The revised profits if Product III is discontinued will be:

	(£000s)
Contribution of Products I and II (£1170 + £1692)	2862
Attributable fixed costs (£275 + £337)	(612)
General fixed costs	(1668)
Profit	582

Profits will decline by £236000 (£818 − £582) if Product III is discontinued because A Ltd will no longer obtain a contribution of £236000 (£532 − £296) towards general fixed costs.

(iii) Extra sales of 15 385 units (£80 000 additional fixed costs/£5.20 unit contribution) will be required to cover the additional advertising expenditure. It is assumed that existing fixed costs will remain unchanged.

(iv) The revised unit contribution will be £3.45 (£9.45 − £6).

$$\text{Required sales} = \frac{£1\,692\,000 \text{ (existing total contribution)}}{£3.45 \text{ revised unit contribution}}$$

$$= 490\,435 \text{ units (an increase of 30.4 per cent over the budgeted sales of 376000 units)}$$

(b) The following factors will influence cost behaviour in response to changes in activity:

(i) The magnitude of the change in activity (more costs are likely to be affected when there is a large change in activity).

(ii) Type of expense (some expenses are directly variable with volume such as direct materials, whereas others are fixed or semi-fixed).

(iii) Management policy (some expenses are varied at the discretion of management, e.g. advertising).

(iv) The time period (in the long term, all costs can be changed in response to changes in activity whereas in the short term, some costs, e.g. salaries of supervisors, will remain unchanged).

Question 9.9

(a) If all of the resources required to produce component P are readily available the relevant costs will be as follows:

	$/unit
Direct labour (One hour @ $8/hour)	8.00
Direct material B (2kgs @ $5/kg)	10.00
Variable overhead (working 1):	
Direct labour (One hour @ $0.50/hour)	0.50
Machine hours (0.5 hours @ $0.25/hour)	0.125
	18.625

W1 Product J requires Two-and-a-half labour hours ($20/$8) so the labour related variable overhead rate is $0.50 per hour ($1.25/2.5 hours). Product J also requires One-and-a-half machine hours giving a machine related variable overhead rate of $0.25 per hour ($1.25/5 machine hours).

Assuming that all of the above resources are readily available the relevant cost of producing component P is less than the purchase price so the component should be produced internally. However, both materials A and B will be in scarce supply over the next ten weeks so it is necessary to examine how this will influence the optimum production programme of WZ. The following schedule compares the kilograms required to meet the planned production programme compared with the availability of materials:

Resource	Available	Total	J	K	L	M	P
Direct material A	21 000	20 150	2 200	3 700	0	14 250	0
Direct material B	24 000	31 050	2 200	0	8 850	19 000	1 000

Note that the above schedule is based on the maximum weekly demand plus existing contractual commitments. Material B is a binding constraint so the optimal production programme should be determined based on the ranking per unit of limiting factor (kg of material B).

	J $	L $	M $	P $
Selling price/buying cost	56	78	96	35
Direct labour	20	24	20	8
Material A	6	0	9	0
Material B	10	15	20	10
Overhead:				
Labour	1.25	1.50	1.25	0.50
Machinery	1.25	0.75	1	0.125
Contribution	17.50	36.75	44.75	16.375
Contribution/kg of material B	8.75	12.25	11.19	8.19
Rank	3	1	2	4

Note that product K is not included in the above ranking because it does not use material B. Therefore product K can be produced to meet maximum demand. Since the component is the lowest ranked usage of material B then WZ should continue to purchase the component so that the available resources can be used to manufacture products L, M and J.

(b) The optimum allocation of scarce resources is as follows:

Production		Kg used	Balance of kg unused
Contractual commitments for:	J	200	
	L	450	
	M	1 000	22 350
Maximum production of L (2 800 units)		8 400	13 950
Balance to M (3487.5 units)		22 350	—

(c) (i) For component P to be produced internally is will be necessary to reduce production of M., which currently yields a contribution of $11.19 per kg. To justify production of component P the purchase price will have to exceed the variable cost of $18.1625 plus the opportunity cost of scarce resources (2kg at $11.19 per kg) giving a purchase cost of $41. In other words, if you refer to the ranking of the scarce materials shown in part (b) the purchase price of P would have to be $41 to yield the same contribution per scarce factor of M.

(ii) Other factors to be considered include:
- the quality of the component produced internally compared with external supplies;
- the ability to resume supplies with the supplier when the constraint no longer applies.

(d) Objective function: Maximize C = 17.5J + 36.75L + 44.75M subject to:

$$2J + 1K + 0L + 3M < 21\,000 \text{ (Material A constraint)}$$
$$2J + 0K + 3L + 4M < 24\,000 \text{ (Material B constraint)}$$

Question 9.10

The following information represents a comparison of alternatives 1 and 2 with the sale of material XY.

Alternative 1: Conversion versus immediate sale	(£)	(£)	(£)
1. Sales revenue (900 units at £400) per unit			360 000
Less Relevant costs:			
2. Material XY opportunity cost		21 000	
3. Material A (600 units at £90)		54 000	
4. Material B (1 000 units at £45)		45 000	
5. Direct labour:			
Unskilled (5 000 hours at £6)	30 000		
Semi-skilled	nil		
Highly skilled (5 000 hours at £17)	85 000	115 000	
6. Variable overheads (15 000 hours at £1)		15 000	
7. Selling and delivery expenses		27 000	
Advertising		18 000	
8. Fixed overheads		—	295 000
Excess of relevant revenues			65 000
Alternative 2: Adaptation versus immediate sale			
9. Saving on purchase of sub-assembly:			
Normal spending (1 200 units at £900)		1 080 000	
Revised spending (900 units at £950)		855 000	225 000
Less relevant costs:			
2. Material XY opportunity cost		21 000	
10. Material C (1 000 units at £55)		55 000	
5. Direct labour:			
Unskilled (4 000 hours at £6)	24 000		
Semi-skilled	nil		
Skilled (4 000 hours at £16)	64 000	88 000	
6. Variable overheads (9 000 hours at £1)		9 000	
8. Fixed overheads		nil	173 000
Net relevant savings			52 000

Notes:

1. There will be additional sales revenue of £360 000 if alternative 1 is chosen.

2. Acceptance of either alternative 1 or 2 will mean a loss of revenue of £21 000 from the sale of the obsolete material XY. This is an opportunity cost, which must be covered whichever alternative is chosen. The original purchase cost of £75 000 for material XY is a sunk cost and is irrelevant.

3. Acceptance of alternative 1 will mean that material A must be replaced at an additional cost of £54 000.

4. Acceptance of alternative 1 will mean that material B will be diverted from the production of product Z. The excess of relevant revenues over relevant cost for product Z is £180 and each unit of product Z uses four units of material. The lost contribution (excluding the cost of material B which is incurred for both alternatives) will therefore be £45 for each unit of material B that is used in converting the raw materials into a specialized product.

5. Unskilled labour can be matched exactly to the company's production requirements. The acceptance of either alternative 1 or 2 will cause the company to incur additional unskilled labour costs of £6 for each hour of unskilled labour that is used. It is assumed that the semi-skilled labour would be retained and that there would be sufficient excess supply for either alternative at no extra cost to the company. In these circumstances semi-skilled labour will not have a relevant cost. Skilled labour is in short supply and can only be obtained by reducing production of product L, resulting in a lost contribution of £24 or £6 per hour of skilled labour. We have already established that the relevant cost for labour that is in short supply is the hourly labour cost plus the lost contribution per hour, so the relevant labour cost here will be £16 per hour.

6. It is assumed that for each direct labour hour of input variable overheads will increase by £1. As each alternative uses additional direct labour hours, variable overheads will increase, giving a relevant cost of £1 per direct labour hour.

7. As advertising selling and distribution expenses will be different if alternative 1 is chosen, these costs are clearly relevant to the decision.

8. The company's fixed overheads will remain the same whichever alternative is chosen, and so fixed overheads are not a relevant cost for either alternative.

9. The cost of purchasing the sub-assembly will be reduced by £225 000 if the second alternative is chosen, and so these savings are relevant to the decision.

10. The company will incur additional variable costs of £55 for each unit of material C that is manufactured, so the fixed overheads for material C are not a relevant cost.

When considering a problem such as this one, there are many different ways in which the information may be presented. The way in which we have dealt with the problem here is to compare each of the two stated alternatives with the other possibility of selling off material XY for its scrap value of £21 000. The above answer sets out the relevant information, and shows that of the three possibilities alternative 1 is to be preferred.

An alternative presentation of this information, which you may prefer, is as follows:

Sale of obsolete materials for scrap	Alternative 1	Alternative 2
Relevant revenues less relevant costs £21 000	£86 000	£73 000
Difference = £65 000		
Difference = £13 000		
	(£86 000 − £73 000)	

We show here *the sale of the obsolete materials as a separate alternative*, and so the opportunity cost of material XY, amounting to £21 000 (see item 2 in the answer) is not included in either alternative 1 or 2, since it is brought into the analysis under the heading 'Sale of obsolete materials for scrap' in the above alternative presentation. Consequently, in both alternatives 1 and 2 the relevant revenues less relevant costs figure is increased by £21 000. The differences between alternative 1 and 2 and the sale of the obsolete materials are still, however, £65 000 and £52 000 respectively, which gives an identical result to that obtained in the above solution.

Question 9.11

Preliminary calculations

Variable costs are quoted per acre, but selling prices are quoted per tonne. Therefore, it is necessary to calculate the planned sales revenue per acre. The calculation of the selling price and contribution per acre is as follows:

	Potatoes	Turnips	Parsnips	Carrots
(a) Yield per acre in tonnes	10	8	9	12
(b) Selling price per tonne	£100	£125	£150	£135
(c) Sales revenue per acre, (a) × (b)	£1 000	£1 000	£1 350	£1 620
(d) Variable cost per acre	£470	£510	£595	£660
(e) Contribution per acre	£530	£490	£755	£960

(a) (i) Profit statement for current year

	Potatoes	Turnips	Parsnips	Carrots	Total
(a) Acres	25	20	30	25	
(b) Contribution per acre	£530	£490	£755	£960	
(c) Total contribution (a × b)	£13 250	£9 800	£22 650	£24 000	£69 700
			Less fixed costs		£54 000
			profit		£15 700

(ii) Profit statement for recommended mix

| | Area A (45 acres) | | Area B (55 acres) | | |
	Potatoes	Turnips	Parsnips	Carrots	Total
(a) Contribution per acre	£530	£490	£755	£960	
(b) Ranking	1	2	2	1	
(c) Minimum sales requirements in acres[a]		5	4		
(d) Acres allocated[b]	40			51	
(e) Recommended mix (acres)	40	5	4	51	
(f) Total contribution, (a) × (e)	£21 200	£2 450	£3 020	£48 960	£75 630
				Less fixed costs	£54 000
				Profit	£21 630

Notes:

[a]The minimum sales requirement for turnips is 40 tonnes, and this will require the allocation of five acres (40 tonnes/8 tonnes yield per acre). The minimum sales requirement for parsnips is 36 tonnes, requiring the allocation of four acres (36 tonnes/9 tonnes yield per acre).

[b]Allocation of available acres to products on basis of a ranking that assumes that acres are the key factor.

(b) (i) Production should be concentrated on carrots, which have the highest contribution per acre (£960).

(ii)

	(£)
Contribution from 100 acres of carrots (100 × £960)	96 000
Fixed overhead	54 000
Profit from carrots	42 000

(iii)

$$\text{Break-even point in acres for carrots} = \frac{\text{fixed costs (£54 000)}}{\text{contribution per acre (£960)}}$$

$$= 56.25 \text{ acres}$$

Contribution in sales value for carrots = £91 125 (56.25 acres at £1620 sales revenue per acre).

Question 9.12

(a)

Product	W $/unit	R $/unit	X $/unit
Selling price	90	126	150
Variable costs	61	92	106
Contribution	29	34	44
Kgs of Material B	4	6	5
Contribution/kg of B	$7.35	$5.67	$8.80
Ranking	2nd	3rd	1st

The major customer order is for 400 units of each of W, R and X and therefore uses 6000kgs of material B (400 × (4 + 6 + 5)). This leaves 11 500kg of material B to be used for other sales.

Production plan:

Make (units)	500	250	1 600
Uses (kg of B)	2 000	1 500	8 000

Optimum plan (including major customer order) is therefore:

W	900 units
R	650 units
X	2 000 units

(b) In order to complete the order for the major customer, WRX will have to reduce sales of product R to other customers by 550 units (800 – 250) giving up a contribution of $18 700 (550 units × $34). These units can be produced and sold if the major customer's order is not met in full. To meet the unused demand of 550 units to other customers for R an additional 3300kg (550 units × 6kg) of material B is required. To ascertain the optimum number of units to be supplied to the major customer it is necessary to ascertain the contribution per kg of scarce material B from sales to the major customer.

Product	W $/unit	R $/unit	X $/unit
Selling price	80	116	140
Variable costs	61	92	106
Contribution	19	24	34
Kg of Material B	4	6	5
Contribution / kg of B	$4.75	$4.00	$6.80
Ranking	2nd	3rd	1st

WRX should reduce sales of the least profitable product (R) to the major customer by 400 units and this will provide 2400kg of material B. The remaining 900kg of material B can be obtained by reducing sales of product W by 225 units (900kg/4kg). This process will result in a loss of contribution of $13 875 [(400 × $24) + (225 × $19)]. The additional contribution from not meeting the major customer's order in full is $4825 ($18 700 − $13 875). Therefore the penalty value is $4825

(c) (i) The objective function is to maximize the contribution (C) 29w + 34r + 44x where:

w = number of units of W
r = number of units of R
x = number of units of X

And the constraints are:

Material B: 4w + 6r + 5x < = 11 500
Direct labour: 2w + 4r + 5x < = 5400
Demand W: 0 < = w < = 500
Demand R: 0 < = r < = 800
Demand X: 0 < = x < = 1600

Note that labour hours are the unused hours after allocating 400 units of each product to the major customer.

(c) (ii) Two constraints are binding:

Demand W − because the optimal solution is to produce 500 units of W

Direct labour hours − because the optimal solution uses 5 400 direct labour hours (500w uses 1000 hours and 880 × uses 4400 hours; total 5400 hours)

Question 9.13

(a) The total processing hours of the factory is 225 000 hours (18 hours × 5 days × 50 weeks × 50 production lines). The production capacity for all processes is as follows:

	Product A	Product B	Product C
Pressing	450 000	450 000	562 500
Stretching	900 000	562 500	900 000
Rolling	562 500	900 000	900 000

Note that the above are derived from dividing 225 000 hours by the processing time per metre (e.g. Pressing for product A = 225 000/0.5 hours). The bottleneck is the pressing process which has a lower capacity for each product. The other processes will probably be slowed to ensure smooth processing.

(b) TPAR for each product

	Product A	**Product B**	**Product C**
Selling price	70.0	60.0	27.0
Raw materials	3.0	2.5	1.8
Throughput	67.0	57.5	25.2
Throughput per bottleneck hour (W1)	134.0	115.0	63.0
Fixed costs per hour(W2)	90.0	90.0	90.0
TPAR	1.49	1.28	0.7
W1	(67/0.5 = 134)	(57.5/0.5 = 115)	(25.2/0.4 = 63)

W2 Total fixed costs ($18m) + Labour costs ($2.25m) = $20.25m
Fixed cost per bottleneck hour = $90 ($20.25m/225 000)

(c) (i) The TPAR of product C could be improved in the following ways:

- Increasing selling prices but this depends on the price/demand relationships. The company also operates in a competitive market but the company is selling all it can produce so an increase in selling price may be possible.
- Reducing material prices to increase the net throughput rate. Negotiating a long-term contract with a supplier or suppliers may enable Yam to reduce the purchase price in return for commitments with suppliers for large quantities of materials at regular intervals.
- Seeking to reduce fixed costs using the cost management techniques described in Chapter 21 (e.g. activity-based cost management). Alternative suppliers should also be investigated with a view to reducing the purchase cost of fixed resources.
- Increasing the speed of the bottleneck process will generate a greater rate of income provided that the extra production can be sold. Investment in automated machinery may speed up the process but the additional cost of the investment must be taken into account.

(ii) A TPAR of less than 1 indicates that the rate at which product C generates throughput (i.e. sales less material costs) is less than the rate at which it incurs fixed costs so production of product C is not justifiable in purely financial terms. However, the following factors should be considered prior to ceasing production of product C:

- Possible product interactions. Does the company need to offer a full production range? Will sales of other products decline if production of product C ceases?
- The alternative use of the spare capacity arising from ceasing production of product C.
- Throughput accounting assumes that all costs, apart from materials, are fixed. Some of the fixed costs are likely to be avoidable if production of product C is ceased. A detailed special study should be undertaken based on relevant cost principles, which examines the alternative use of the released capacity, to ascertain whether product C will yield a long term contribution to fixed costs.

Question 9.14

(a) Roadstar requires 0.16 hours (1 hour/6.25 units) and Everest 0.2 hours (1 hour/5 units) in the finishing department. A total of 38 000 hours are required to meet the demand (150 000 units of Roadstar × 0.16 hours plus 70 000 units of Everest × 0.2 hours). Therefore the finishing department hours are a bottleneck or limiting factor resource.

	Roadstar	**Everest**
Contribution per unit (£)	100 (200–100)	120 (280–160)
Hours per limiting factor	0.16	0.2
Contribution per limiting factor (£)	625	600

Ride should produce Roadstar until it has met the total demand and use any remaining hours to produce Everest. Thus 24 000 hours will be allocated to Roadstar (150 000 × 0.16 hours) and the remaining 6000 hours to Everest. This will enable 30 000 units of Everest (6000/0.2 hours) to be produced. The profit for the period is:

	(£000s)
Roadstar contribution	15 000 (150 000 × £100)
Everest contribution	3 600 (30 000 × £120)
Total contribution	18 600
Fixed costs	4 050
Profit	14 550

(b)

	Roadstar	Everest
Selling price − material cost (£)	120	180
Bottleneck hours utilized	0.16	0.20
Return per factory hour (£)	750 (£120/0.16)	900 (£180/0.2)
Cost per factory hour (£)	295 (£8 850 000/30 000)	295
Throughput accounting ratio (£)	2.54 (£750/£295)	3.05 (£900/£295)

Note:

That the cost per factory hour consists of total fixed costs (£4 800 000 + £4 050 000) divided by the hours available in the finishing department.

(c) Since Everest has the highest throughput ratio Ride should produce Everest until it has met the total demand and use any remaining hours to produce Roadstar. Thus 14 000 hours will be allocated to Everest (70 000 × 0.2 hours) and the remaining 16 000 hours to Roadstar. This will enable 100 000 units of Roadstar (16 000/0.16 hours) to be produced. The profit for the period is:

	(£000s)
Roadstar throughput return	12 000 (100 000 × £120)
Everest throughput return	12 600 (70 000 × £180)
Total throughput return	24 600
Fixed costs	8 850
Profit	15 750

(d) Contribution and throughput accounting differ in terms of their definition of variable cost. Contribution treats direct materials, direct labour and variable overheads as variable costs whereas throughput accounting assumes that only direct materials represent variable costs. Throughput accounting is more short-term oriented and assumes that direct labour and variable overheads cannot be avoided within a very short-term period (e.g. one month). In contrast, contribution assumes that the short-term represents a longer period than that assumed with throughput accounting and thus classifies direct labour and overheads as variable within this period (typically less than one year). The different interpretation of variable costs results in the contribution (selling price less material cost) used in throughput accounting being higher than that using the conventional analysis based on relevant cost principles. This is apparent from the question with the variable overheads of £4 800 000 being treated as variable in part (a) but fixed in the very short-term in part (b) where throughput accounting is applied.

It is apparent from the above discussion that the different interpretations of variable costs can yield different contributions per unit of bottleneck resource and thus result in a different recommended optimal product mix. Care must therefore be exercised in deciding which approach to use when they result in different optimal product mixes.

Pricing decisions and profitability analysis

Solutions to Chapter 10 questions

Question 10.1

(i)   Marginal cost (MC) = £15 per unit
      Profit is maximized when MC = MR giving:
      $15 = 50 - 0.05Q$
      $Q = 700$
      Price per unit (P) = $50 - (0.025 \times 700) = £32.50$
      Answer = D

(ii) When P = 20:
      $20 = 50 - 0.025Q$
      Therefore Q = 1200
      Total contribution = $1200 \times (£20 - £15) = £6000$
      Answer = D

Question 10.2

(a) *Computation of full costs and budgeted cost-plus selling price*

	EXE (£m)	WYE (£m)	Stores (£m)	Maintenance (£m)	Admin (£m)
Material	1.800	0.700	0.100	0.100	
Other variable	0.800	0.500	0.100	0.200	0.200
Gen factory	1.440	1.080	0.540	0.180	0.360
					0.560
Admin reallocation	0.224	0.168	0.112	0.056	(0.560)
Maintenance reallocation	0.268	0.134	0.134	(0.536)	
			0.986		
			(0.986)		
Stores	0.592	0.394			
	5.124	2.976			
Volume	150 000	70 000			
	(£)	(£)			
Full cost	34.16	42.51			
Mark up (25%)	8.54	10.63			
Price	42.70	53.14			

(b) (i) The incremental costs for the order consist of the variable costs. The calculation of the unit variable cost is as follows:

	EXE (£m)	WYE (£m)	Stores (£m)	Maintenance (£m)	Admin (£m)
Material	1.800	0.700	0.100	0.100	
Other variable	0.800	0.500	0.100	0.200	0.200
Admin	0.080	0.060	0.040	0.020	(0.200)
				0.320	
Maintenance	0.160	0.080	0.080	(0.320)	
			0.320		
Stores	0.192	0.128	(0.320)		
	3.032	1.468			
Volume	150 000	70 000			
	(£)	(£)			
Variable cost	20.21	20.97			

The proposed selling price exceeds the incremental cost and provides a contribution towards fixed costs and profits of £14.03 (£35 − £20.97) per unit thus giving a total contribution of £42 090. Given that the company has spare capacity no lost business will be involved and it appears that the order is a one-off short-term special order. Therefore the order is acceptable provided it does not have an impact on the selling price in the existing market or utilize capacity that has alternative uses. Given that the markets are segregated, the former would appear to be an unlikely event. However, if the order were to generate further regular business the longer-term cost considerations described in Chapter 10 should be taken into account in determining an acceptable long-run price.

(ii) The proposed selling price is £46.76 (full cost of £42.51 plus 10 per cent). This will generate a contribution of £25.79 (£46.76 − £20.97) per unit. Unutilized capacity is 30 000 units but the order is for 50 000 units. Therefore the order can only be met by reducing existing business by 20 000 units. The financial evaluation is as follows:

Increase in contribution from existing business (50 000 units at a contribution of £25.79)	£1 289 500
Lost contribution from existing business (20 000 units at a contribution of (£53.14 − £20.97))	643 400
Net increase in contribution	646 100

Before accepting the order the longer-term implications should be considered. The inability to meet the full demand from existing customers may result in a significant reduction in customer goodwill and the lost contribution from future sales to these customers may exceed the short-term gain of £646 100. Also the above analysis has not considered the alternative use of the un-utilized capacity of 30 000 units. If the cost savings from reducing the capacity exceed £646 100 for the period under consideration the order will not be worthwhile. The order will also result in the company operating at full capacity and it is possible that the cost structure may change if the company is operating outside its normal production range.

If the company does not rely on customer repeat orders and customer goodwill it is unlikely to be affected and the order would appear to be profitable. It is important, however, that long-term considerations are taken into account when evaluating the order. In particular, consideration should be given to the negotiation of a longer-term contract on both price and volume.

(c) See 'Alternative denominator level measures' in Chapter 7 and 'Selecting the cost driver denominator level' in Learning Note 10.1 on the open access website for the answer to this question.

Question 10.3

(a) For the answer to this question you should refer to Chapter 10. In particular the answer should discuss the role of cost information in the following situations:

(1) a price setting firm facing short-run pricing decisions;

(2) a price setting firm facing long-run decisions;

(3) a price taker firm facing short-run product-mix decisions;

(4) a price taker firm facing long-run decisions.

(b) *Calculation of variable overhead absorption rates*

	Moulding (£000)	Finishing (£000)	General factory (£000)
Allocated overheads	1 600	500	1 050
Reallocation of General Factory based on machine hours	600	450	(1 050)
	2 200	950	
Machine hours	800	600	
Variable overhead rate per hour	£2.75	£1.583	

Calculation of fixed overhead absorption rates

	Moulding (£000)	Finishing (£000)	General factory (£000)
Allocated overheads	2 500	850	1 750
Reallocation of general factory based on machine hours	1 050	700	(1 750)
	3 550	1 550	
Machine hours	800	600	
Variable overhead rate per hour	£4.4375	£2.583	

Calculation of full manufacturing cost

			(£)
Direct material			9.00
Direct labour	20.00	(2 × £10)	
	33.00	(3 × £11.00)	53.00
Variable overheads	11.00	(4 × £2.75)	
	4.75	(3 × £1.583)	15.75
Variable manufacturing cost			77.75
Fixed overheads	17.75	(4 × £4.4375)	
	7.75	(3 × £2.583)	25.50
Full manufacturing cost			103.25

Prices based on full manufacturing cost

25% mark up = £129.06

30% mark up = £134.22

35% mark up = £139.39

Minimum prices based on short-term variable cost and incremental cost are as follows:

Variable cost = £77.75

Incremental cost = £86.10 (£77.75 plus specific fixed costs of £8.35)

The specific fixed cost per unit is calculated by dividing the fixed costs of £167 000 by the estimated sales volume (10% × 200 000).

(c) The cost information is more likely to provide a general guide to the pricing decision but the final pricing decision will be influenced by the prices of competitors' products (£125 − £135). The full cost prices indicate prices within a range of £129 − £139. The variable/incremental price indicates a minimum short-run price that may be appropriate if the company wishes to pursue a price skimming policy. Given that the product is an improvement on competitors, a price in the region of £135 would seem to be appropriate but the final decision should be based on marketing considerations drawing off the knowledge of the marketing staff. The role of the cost information has been to indicate that a price within this range should provide a reasonable margin and contribution to general fixed costs.

Question 10.4

(a) (i) The total contribution at each selling price for product K is:

Selling price/unit ($)	100	85	80	75	
Contribution/unit ($)	62	47	42	37	
Demand (units)	600	800	1 200	1 400	
Total contribution ($)	37 200	37 600	50 400	51 800	
Capacity remaining to produce L				600	standard hours
Product L Maximum production				480	units

In order to maximize contribution during the maturity stage product K should be sold at $75 per unit.

(ii) At a selling price of $100 demand is 1000 units. Each increase or decrease in price of $10 results in a corresponding decrease or increase in demand of 200 units. Therefore, if the selling price were increased to $150, demand would be zero. To increase demand by one unit, selling price must be reduced by $0.05 ($10/200 units). Thus the maximum selling price (SP) for an output of x units is $SP = \$150 - \$0.05x$ so for an output of 480 units:

$$SP = \$150 - (480 \times 0.05) = \$126.$$

(b) See 'pricing policies' in Chapter 10 for the answer to this question. The answer should also point out that it is appropriate to use a price skimming policy for product M since it is an innovative product that is likely to change the entire market.

(c) In the growth stage, production costs per unit are likely to decline because of economies of scale and the impact of the learning and experience curves (see Chapter 23). In the maturity stage unit production costs are likely to remain fairly constant because the learning effect will have ended and the workforce will be experienced in the operating processes. In the decline stage production costs per unit may increase due to lower volumes.

Because the product is innovative with low competition the initial price during the early growth stage will be high in an attempt to recover the development costs of the product. Competitors will be attracted to the product by its high price and will seek to compete with it by introducing similar products. To deter competitors entering the market the company should reduce its price during the growth stage of the product's life cycle. Price reductions during this stage may also be implemented to make it more affordable to other market segments. As the product enters the maturity stage the price will need to be lowered so as to provide a minimal contribution to fixed costs. Fixed costs should have been covered at earlier stages of life cycle so the focus will be on marginal rather than full cost pricing.

Question 10.5

(a) The question states that fixed manufacturing costs are absorbed into the unit costs by a charge of 200 per cent of variable cost. Therefore unit variable cost is one third of total unit cost.

Contribution per processing hour

	Product A (£)	Product B (£)	Product C (£)
Selling price	20	31	39
Variable cost	6	8	10
Production contribution	14	23	29
Contribution per processing hour	14	23	14.50
Ranking	3	1	2

Optimal programme

	Output	Hours used	Contribution (£)
Product B	8 000	8 000	184 000
C	2 000	4 000	58 000
A	1 500	1 500	21 000
			263 000

Existing programme

	Output	Hours used	Contribution (£)
Product A	6 000	6 000	84 000
B	6 000	6 000	138 000
C	750	1 500	21 750
			243 750

Contribution and profits will increase by £19 250 if the optimal production programme is implemented. An additional hour of processing would be used to increase product A by one unit, thus increasing contribution by £14. Therefore the shadow price (or opportunity cost) of one scarce processing hour is £14.

Capacity is limited to 13 500 hours. It is therefore necessary to allocate output on the basis of marginal contribution per hour. Products A and B each require one processing hour, whereas product C requires two processing hours. To simplify the calculations, hours are allocated in 2000 blocks. Consequently, the allocation of the first 2000 hours will yield a marginal contribution of £37 000 from A, £52 000 from B and £29 500 from C. Note that an output of 2000 units of C will require 4000 processing hours, and will yield a contribution of £59 000. Therefore the contribution from 2000 hours will be £29 500. In other words, the marginal contributions for A and B in the above schedule are expressed in terms of blocks of 2000 hours, whereas the marginal contribution for C is expressed in terms of blocks of 4000 hours. To express the marginal contribution of C in terms of blocks of 2000 hours, it is necessary to divide the final column of the above schedule by 2.

Processing hours are allocated as follows:

	Hours		Marginal contribution (£)
Product B	first	2 000	52 000
B	next	2 000	48 000
B	2 000		44 000
B	2 000		40 000
A	2 000		37 000
B	2 000		36 000
A	1 500	(balance)	24 250[a]
	13 500		281 250

Note:

[a]3500 × (£23.50 − £6) − £37 000 = £24 250

The optimum output is £10 000 units of product B at a selling price of £30 and 3500 units of A at a selling price of £23.50, and contribution will be maximized at £281 250. It is assumed that it is company policy to change selling prices only in steps of £1.

(b)

Demand	Price (£)	Product A Total contribution (£000)	Marginal contribution (£000)
2 000	24.50	37	37
4 000	23.50	70	33
6 000	22.50	99	29
8 000	21.50	124	25
10 000	20.50	145	21
12 000	19.50	162	17
14 000	18.50	175	13

Demand	**Price** (£)	**Product B** Total contribution (£000)	**Marginal contribution** (£000)
2 000	34	52	52
4 000	33	100	48
6 000	32	144	44
8 000	31	184	40
10 000	30	220	36
12 000	29	252	32
14 000	28	280	28

Demand	**Price** (£)	**Product C** Total contribution (£000)	**Marginal contribution** (£000)
2 000	39.50	59	59
4 000	39.00	116	57
6 000	38.50	171	55
8 000	38.00	224	53
10 000	37.50	275	51
12 000	37.00	324	49
14 000	36.50	371	47

Question 10.6

(a) At present the selling price is $45 and demand is 130 000 units. Each increase or decrease in price of $1 results in a corresponding decrease or increase in demand of 10 000 units. Therefore if the selling price was increased to $58, demand would be zero. To increase demand by one unit the selling price must be reduced by $0.0001 ($1/10 000) so the maximum selling price for an output of x units is:

$$SP = \$58 - 0.0001x$$

The total revenue for an output of x units is $\$58x - \$0.0001x^2$

Therefore marginal revenue (MR) $= 58 - 0.0002x$

Marginal cost (MC) $= \$18.75$ (Total variable costs/annual production)

MR = MC where $58 - 0.0002x = 18.75$

so $x = 196 250$

Therefore SP at the optimal output level $= 58 - 0.0001(196 250) = \$38.375$

Annual contribution $= \$19.625 \times 196 250$ units $= \$3 851 406.25$	
Less annual fixed overhead costs	$3 60 000.00
Annual profit	$3 491 406.25

(b) (i) If the actual direct material cost per unit declined marginal cost per unit would decline but the selling price equation would remain unchanged. When the reduction in marginal cost is incorporated in the calculations in (a) the optimum output would increase and the optimum selling price would decline. The opposite would apply if there was an increase in the direct material cost per unit.

(ii) Since fixed costs would remain constant and are not relevant to the calculations in (a) any change in the fixed overhead cost would have no effect on the optimal selling price and quantity.

Question 10.7

(a) (i) If the selling price is £200, demand will be zero. To increase demand by one unit, selling price must be reduced by £1/1000 units or £0.001. Hence the maximum selling price attainable for an output of x units is:

$$P = £200 - 0.001x$$

At an output level of 100 000 units,

$$P = £200 - £0.001 \times 10 000$$
$$= £100 \text{ per unit}$$

Total contribution at an output level of 100 000 units

$$
\begin{array}{ll}
100\,000 \times (£100 - £50) & 5\,000\,000 \\
\text{Less fixed costs } (100\,000 \times £25) & 2\,500\,000 \\
\text{Profit} & 2\,500\,000
\end{array}
$$

(ii) Profit is maximized where MC = MR

$$MC = £50 \text{ per unit variable cost (given)}$$

$$MR = \frac{dTR}{dx}$$

$$TR = x(200 - 0.001x)$$

$$= 200x - 0.001x^2$$

$$\frac{dTR}{dx} = 200 - 0.002x$$

Therefore optimum output is where $50 = 200 - 0.002x$ (i.e. where MC = MR). And so

$$150 = 0.002x$$

That is,

$$x = 75\,000 \text{ units}$$

At an output level of 75 000 units, the selling price is $£200 - (£0.001 \times 75\,000) = £125$. Therefore profit at 75 000 units:

	(£)
Contribution (75 000 × £75)	5 625 000
Less fixed costs	2 500 000
	3 125 000

(b) (i) Revised fixed costs = £3 000 000.

The optimal output level will not be affected by a change in fixed costs. Therefore the selling price should not be changed. Profit will decline by £500 000.

(ii) Revised marginal cost = £60.

$$\text{The new optimum is where } 60 = 200 - 0.002x$$
$$0.002x = 140$$
$$\text{Therefore } x = 70\,000 \text{ unit}$$
$$\text{At this output level, } P = £200 - £0.001 \times 70\,000$$
$$= £130$$

(c) Profit before advertising expenditure:

	(£)
Total contribution [70 000 × (£130 − £60)]	4 900 000
Less fixed costs	3 000 000
Profit	1 900 000

After the introduction of the advertising expenditure:

$$P = 210 - 0.001x$$
$$TR = x(210 - 0.001x)$$
$$= 210x - 0.001x^2$$
$$\text{Therefore MR} = 210 - 0.002x$$

$$\text{The revised optimum output is where } 60 = 210 - 0.002x$$
$$0.002x = 150$$
$$x = 75\,000$$

The optimum price at this output level is where $P = £210 - £0.001 \times 75\,000$
$$= £135$$

	(£)
Total contribution [75 000 × (£135 − £60)]	5 625 000
Revised fixed costs	4 000 000
Profit	1 625 000

Therefore profits will decline by £275 000 if the advertising campaign is undertaken.

(d) The original budgeted output of 100 000 units was higher than the optimum output level. The solution to (a) (ii) indicates that the optimum output level is achieved by reducing production to 75 000 units and increasing the selling price to £125. Beyond an output level of 75 000 units, marginal cost per unit is in excess of marginal revenue. This is because selling price is reduced in order to expand output. Consequently, marginal revenue declines and is less than marginal cost. This means that profits decline when output is in excess of 75 000 units. This analysis is based on the following assumptions:

(i) The demand schedule can be predicted accurately.

(ii) Marginal cost per unit is constant at all output levels.

(iii) Fixed costs are constant throughout the entire output range.

The analysis also showed that the change in fixed costs had no effect on the MR and MC function, so that the optimum output level and price did not change. When MC increases, the effect is to decrease output level and increase price.

The effect of the advertising campaign is to shift the demand curve to the right, thus causing sales demand to be higher at each selling price or the selling price to be higher at each demand level. However, the increased advertising costs are in excess of the additional revenue, thus resulting in a reduction in profits.

Question 10.8

(i) When the product moves from the introduction to the growth stage the product will have less of a novelty appeal as competitors introduce their versions of the product so PT may wish to discourage competitors from entering the market by lowering the price and this will reduce product profitability. Also the price reduction should make the product more attractive to customers in different market segments thus increasing demand and sales growth.

The move from the introduction to the growth stage should result in a reduction in unit costs because of reduced material costs from bulk buying, reduced labour costs arising from increased efficiency due to the learning effect and lower unit fixed costs arising from fixed production costs being spread over a greater volume.

(ii) The move from the growth stage to the maturity stage means that the product has become established and the selling price is likely to be fairly constant but periodically special offers may be made to tempt customers to buy the product. Unit production costs are likely to be fairly constant as there will be no further benefits arising from economies of scale.

Question 10.9

Several factors should be considered in the determination of pricing policy. The most important is price elasticity of demand, but if price is to be set in order to maximize profits then knowledge of cost structures and cost behaviour will also be of great importance. Knowledge of price–demand relationships and costs at different output levels is necessary to determine the optimum price. This is the price that results in marginal revenue being equal to marginal cost. The emphasis should be placed on providing information on the effect of changes in output on total cost rather than providing average unit cost information.

When cost information is presented using absorption costing, the resulting selling price calculation will be a function of the overhead apportionments and recovery methods used and the assumed volume of production. At best, the calculated selling price will only be appropriate for one level of production, and a different selling price would be produced for different output levels. Single cost figures calculated using absorption costing also fail to supply information on the effect of changes in output on total cost. For other disadvantages that appear when absorption costing is used in the determination of pricing policy see 'Limitations of cost-plus pricing' in Chapter 10.

The advantage claimed from the use of absorption costing in price determination is that all manufacturing costs are included in the cost per unit calculation, so that no major manufacturing cost is overlooked. With variable costing, there is a danger that output will be priced to earn a low contribution that is insufficient to cover total fixed costs. Also, the use of production facilities entails an opportunity cost from the alternative use of capacity forgone. The fixed cost per unit of capacity used can be regarded as an attempt to approximate the opportunity cost from the use of productive capacity. In spite of these claimed advantages, the presentation of relevant costs for pricing decisions (see Chapter 10) is likely to be preferable to information based on absorption cost.

Question 10.10

(a) See Chapters 9–11 for the answer to this question. In particular, the answer should indicate:

   (i) Information presented to the product manager should be *future* costs, not past costs.

   (ii) *Incremental* cost and revenue information should be presented, and the excess of incremental revenues over incremental costs compared for different selling price and sales quantity levels. Costs that are common to all alternatives are not relevant for decision-making purposes.

   (iii) Decisions involve a choice between alternatives, and this implies that a choice leads to forgoing *opportunities*. Therefore relevant cost information for a pricing decision should include future cash costs and imputed (opportunity) cost.

   (iv) *Sunk costs* are past costs and not relevant to the pricing decision.

   (v) Pricing decisions should be based on estimates of demand schedules and a comparison of marginal revenues and costs.

(b) See 'Reasons for using cost-based pricing formulae' in Chapter 10 for the answer to this question. Note that overhead allocation is an attempt to provide an estimate of the long-run costs of producing a product.

(c) There is no specific answer to this question. The author's views on this question are expressed in Chapters 10 and 11.

Question 10.11

(a) Short-run profits are maximized at the output level where marginal revenue equals marginal cost. The optimum selling price is that which corresponds to the optimal output level (see Figure 10.3 in Learning Note 10.1 on the website). From Figure 10.3 you will see that, with imperfect competition (no pricing decision is necessary with perfect competition), firms are faced with a downward-sloping demand curve. The highest selling price will apply to the first unit sold, but Figure 10.3 indicates that it is unlikely that this will be at the point where marginal revenue equals marginal cost.

(b) The objective is to maximize total contribution not unit contribution. Contribution per unit sold is the difference between marginal revenue and marginal cost. It is unlikely that contribution per unit will remain constant over the entire range of output. In Chapter 8 we noted that variable cost per unit and selling price per unit may change in relation to output. With a downward-sloping demand curve, marginal revenue will decline, thus causing contribution per unit to decline as output is increased. From Figure 10.3 in Learning Note 10.1 we can see that profit is maximized where $MR = MC$. This is not at the point where unit contribution (difference between marginal revenue and marginal cost) is the greatest.

(c) Joint costs are allocated on an arbitrary basis, and costs that include arbitrary allocations are inappropriate for product, project or divisional comparisons. Performance should be judged on the basis of comparisons between controllable costs and revenues. With profit centres, measures such as controllable residual income should be used, whereas contribution should be used for comparing products.

(d) This statement presumably refers to the use of cost-plus pricing methods. If prices are set completely on a cost-plus basis then accounting information will determine the selling price. Consequently, the marketing and production people might feel that they have no influence in determining selling prices with pricing dominated by a concern for recovering full costs. If cost-plus pricing is used in a rigid way then marketing and production people may well consider the statement in the question to be correct. Cost information should be used in a flexible manner, and is one of several variables that should be used in determining selling prices. If this approach is adopted then the statement in the question will be incorrect.

(e) Management accounting should not be constrained by the requirements of external reporting. The emphasis should be on assembling financial information so as to help managers make good decisions and to plan and control activities effectively. In Chapter 7 we noted that there are strong arguments for adopting a system of variable costing in preference to absorption costing. If management accounts were consistent with SSAP 9 then the financial information might motivate managers to make wrong decisions.

(f) All costs must be covered in the long run if a firm is to be profitable. Therefore the objective should be to recover R and D expenditure in the long-run. R and D expenditure should be regarded as a pool of fixed costs to which products should generate sufficient contribution. Giant Steps Ltd should not rely on a policy of recovering R and D in relation to expenditure on each individual product. Price/demand relationships for some products might mean that the associated R and D cannot be recovered, while other products might be able to recover more than their fair share. Once a product is launched, only the incremental costs are relevant to the pricing decision. The objective should be to obtain a selling price in excess of relevant short-run costs and to provide a contribution to fixed costs and profit. R and D should be regarded as part of the pool of fixed costs to be recovered.

Activity-based costing

Solutions to Chapter 11 questions

Question 11.1

Budgeted number of batches per product:

D =	1 000	(100 000/100)
R =	2 000	(100 000/50)
P =	2 000	(50 000/25)
	5 000	

Budgeted machine set-ups:

D =	3 000	(1 000 × 3)
R =	8 000	(2 000 × 4)
P =	12 000	(2 000 × 6)
	23 000	

Budgeted cost per set-up = £150 000/23 000 = £6.52 Budgeted set-up cost per unit of R = (£6.52 × 4)/50 = £0.52 Answer = A

Question 11.2

(a) Total machine hours = (120 × 4 hrs) + (100 × 3 hrs) + (80 × 2 hrs) + (120 × 3 hrs) = 1300 hrs

$$\text{Machine hour overhead rate} = \frac{£10\,430 + £5\,250 + £3\,600 + £2\,100 + £4\,620}{1\,300\text{ hrs}} = £20\text{ per machine hour}$$

Product	A (£)	B (£)	C (£)	D (£)
Direct material	40	50	30	60
Direct labour	28	21	14	21
Overheads at £20 per machine hour	80	60	40	60
	148	131	84	141
Units of output	120	100	80	120
Total cost	£17 760	£13 100	£6 720	£16 920

(b)

Costs	(£)	Cost driver	cost driver transactions	cost per unit (£)
Machine department	10 430	Machine hours	1 300 hours	8.02
Set-up costs	5 250	Production runs	21	250
Stores receiving	3 600	Requisitions raised	80 (4 × 20)	45
Inspection/quality control	2 100	Production runs	21	100
Materials handling	4 620	Number of orders executed	42	110

Note:

Number of production runs = Total output (420 units)/20 units per set-up.

Number of orders executed = Total output (420 units)/10 units per order.

The total costs for each product are computed by multiplying the cost driver rate per unit by the quantity of the cost driver consumed by each product.

	A	**B**	**C**	**D**
Prime costs	8 160 (£68 × 120)	7 100	3 520	9 720
Set ups	1 500 (£250 × 6)	1 250 (£250 × 5)	1 000	1 500
stores/receiving	900 (£45 × 20)	900	900	900
Inspection/quality	600 (£100 × 6)	500	400	600
Handling despatch	1 320 (£110 × 12)	1 100 (£110 × 10)	880	1 320
Machine dept cost*	3 851	2 407	1 284	2 888
Total costs	16 331	13 257	7 984	16 928

Note:

*A = 120 units × 4 hrs × £8.02: B = 100 units × 3 hrs × £8.02

(c) Cost per unit

Costs from (a)	148.00	131.00	84.00	141.00
Costs from (b)	136.09	132.57	99.80	141.07
Difference	(11.91)	1.57	15.80	0.07

Product A is over-costed with the traditional system. Products B and C are under-costed and similar costs are reported with Product D. It is claimed that ABC more accurately measures resources consumed by products. Where cost-plus pricing is used, the transfer to an ABC system will result in different product prices. If activity based costs are used for stock valuations then stock valuations and reported profits will differ.

Question 11.3

(a) The calculation of the cost driver rates is as follows:

Machine maintenance

$$\$100\,000/[(1\,500 \times 3) + (2\,500 \times 2) + (4\,000 \times 3)] = \$4.65 \text{ per machine hour}$$

Machine setups

$$\$70\,000/[\{(1\,500/50) \times 2\} + \{(2\,500/100) \times 3\} + \{(4\,000/500) \times 1\}] = \$489.51 \text{ per setup}$$

Purchasing

$$\$90\,000/[\{(1\,500/50) \times 4\} + \{(2\,500/100) \times 4\} + \{(4\,000/500) \times 6\}] = \$335.82 \text{ per order}$$

Material handling

$$\$60\,000/[\{(1\,500/50) \times 10\} + \{(2\,500/100) \times 5\} + \{(4\,000/500) \times 4\}] = \$131.29 \text{ per movement}$$

Other costs

$$\$80\,000/((1\,500 \times 2) + (2\,500 \times 4) + (4\,000 \times 3)) = \$3.20 \text{ per labour hour}$$

Product	**X**	**Y**	**Z**
Batch costs:			
Machine setup	979	1 468.5	489.5
Purchasing	1 343	1 343	2 015
Material handling	1 313	656.5	525
	3 635	3 468	3 029.5
Batch size	50	100	500
Unitised batch costs	72.70	34.68	6.06
Machine maintenance	13.95	9.30	13.95
Other overhead costs	6.40	12.80	9.60
Production overhead cost	93.05	56.78	29.61

(b) Pareto analysis is also known as the 80 : 20 rule, which means 80 per cent of the production overhead costs are caused by 20 per cent of the factors influencing total cost. W has identified $320 000 (80 per cent) out of the total of $400 000 are linked these with just four cost drivers. The remaining $80 000 is assumed to be caused by a number of other factors. By focusing attention on controlling these four cost causes W will be concentrating on controlling 80 per cent of the overhead costs.

Question 11.4

Cost driver rates:

Accounts preparation and advice	580 000/18 000 hours = $32.22 per hour
Requesting missing information	30 000/250 times = $120 per request
Issuing fee payment reminders	15 000/400 times = $37.50 per reminder
Holding client meetings	60 000/250 meetings = $240 per meeting
Travelling to clients	40 000/10 000 miles = $4 per mile

Client costs:

	Client		
	A	**B**	**C**
	$	**$**	**$**
Accounts preparation and advice	32 222	8 055	10 955
Requesting missing information	480	1 200	720
Issuing fee payment reminders	75	300	375
Holding client meetings	960	240	480
Travelling to clients	600	2 400	0
Total costs	34 337	12 195	12 530
Total costs on original basis*	40 280	10 070	13 695
Client fees − new basis	41 204	14 634	15 036
Client fees − original basis	48 336	12 084	16 434
Increase/(Decrease)	(7 132)	2 550	(1 398)

*$725 000/18 000 hours = $40.28 per hour

Question 11.5

(a) The calculation of the overhead costs using the current system for each of the procedures is as follows:

	Hip $	Knee $	Shoulder $	Total $
Sales revenue	$8 000 × 600 = $4 800 000	$10 000 × 800 = $8 000 000	$6 000 × 400 = $2 400 000	$15 200 000
Overheads				$9 880 000
Overheads / sales revenue				65%
Cost per procedure	$8 000 × 65% $5 200	$10 000 × 65% $6 500	$6 000 × 65% $3 900	

Profitability analysis using the current system

	Hip $	Knee $	Shoulder $
Fee charged to patient	8 000	10 000	6 000
Surgeon's fee	(1 200)	(1 800)	(1 500)
Fee for follow-up consultations	(24)	(15)	(30)
Medical supplies	(400)	(200)	(300)
Overhead cost	(5 200)	(6 500)	(3 900)
Profit per procedure	1 176	1 485	270

Fees for follow-up consultations are calculated as follows:

Hip – $300 per consultation × 8% = $24

Knee – $300 per consultation × 5% = $15

Shoulder – $300 per consultation × 10% = $30

(b) Calculation of cost driver rates

Activity	Cost driver	Overheads $000	No. of cost drivers	Cost per driver $
Theatre preparation for each session	Number of theatre preparations	864	$(600/2 + 800/1 + 400/4)$ $= 1\,200$	$720 per theatre preparation
Operating theatre usage	procedure time	1449	$(600 \times 2 \text{ hrs}) + (800 \times 1.2 \text{ hrs})$ $+ (400 \times 1.5 \text{ hrs}) = 2\,760$	$525 per hour
Nursing and ancillary services	In-patient days	5428	$(600 \times 3) + (800 \times 2)$ $+ (400 \times 1) = 3\,800$	$1\,428 per day
Administration	Sales revenue	1216	$15\,200\,000$	$0.08 per $ sales revenue
Other Overheads	Number of procedures	923	$(600 + 800 + 400) = 1\,800$	$513 per procedure

ABC overhead cost per procedure

	Hip	Knee	Joint
Theatre preparation for each session	$720/2 = $360	$720/1 = $720	$720/4 = $180
Operating theatre usage	$($525 \times 2$) = $1\,050	$($525 \times 1.2$) = $630	$($525 \times 1.5$) = $788
Nursing and ancillary services	$($1\,428 \times 3$) = $4\,284	$($1\,428 \times 2$) = $2\,856	$($1\,428 \times 1$) = $1\,428
Administration	$(8\,000 \times 0.08) = $640	$(10\,000 \times 0.08) = $800	$(6\,000 \times 0.08) = $480
Other overheads	$513	$513	$513
Total overhead cost per procedure	$6\,847	$5\,519	$3\,389

Profit per procedure

	Hip ($)	Knee ($)	Joint ($)
Fees charged to patients	8000	10000	6000
Surgeon's fee	(1200)	(1800)	(1500)
Fee for follow-up consultations	(24)	(15)	(30)
Medical supplies	(400)	(200)	(300)
Overhead cost	(6847)	(5519)	(3389)
Profit per procedure	(471)	2466	781

(c) The answer should include the following points:
- the generation of more accurate product/service costs resulting in improved decision-making;
- improved cost management by focusing on activity cost management (see Chapter 21);
- more accurate profitability analysis (note that with the existing costing system the profitability analysis reports that hip replacements are profitable whereas the ABC system reports a loss);
- more accurate cost information for pricing decisions.

Question 11.6

(a) (i) Fixed production overheads = $69.6m

Budgeted machine hours = $(1\,000 \times 100) + (1\,200 \times 200) + (800 \times 300) = 580\,000$

Machine hour fixed production overhead absorption rate = $69m/580\,000 = $120 per machine hour

Profit statement using current absorption costing system

	Superior $000	Deluxe $000	Ultra $000
Sales	54000	86400	102000
Direct material	17600	27400	40200
Direct labour	10700	13400	16600
Production overhead	12000	28800	28800
Gross profit	13700	16800	16400

Note that the production overhead is allocated on the basis of the number of machine hours per boat.

(a) (ii)

Activity cost driver usage

Cost Driver	Number of cost drivers
Machine hours	$(1\,000 \times 100) + (1\,200 \times 200) + (800 \times 300) = 580\,000$
Number of set ups	$(1\,000/5) + (1\,200/4) + (800/2) = 900$
Number of quality inspections	$(200 \times 10) + (300 \times 20) + (400 \times 30) = 20\,000$
Number of component deliveries	$500 + 600 + 800 = 1\,900$
Number of issues from stores	$4\,000 + 5\,000 + 7\,000 = 16\,000$

Profit statement using ABC

	Superior $000	Deluxe $000	Ultra $000
Sales	54 000	86 400	102 000
Direct material	17 600	27 400	40 200
Direct labour	10 700	13 400	16 600
Machining	2 400	5 760	5 760
	$(13\,920/580 \times 100)$	$(13\,920/580 \times 240)$	$(13\,920/580 \times 240)$
Set ups	5 316	7 973	10 631
	$(23\,920/900 \times 200)$	$(23\,920/900 \times 300)$	$(23\,920/900 \times 400)$
Quality inspections	1 414	4 242	8 484
	$(14\,140/20 \times 2)$	$(14\,140/20 \times 6)$	$(14\,140/20 \times 12)$
Stores receiving	1 800	2 160	2 880
	$(6\,840/1\,900 \times 500)$	$(6\,840/1\,900 \times 600)$	$(6\,840/1\,900 \times 800)$
Stores issuing	2 695	3 369	4 716
	$(10\,780/16 \times 4)$	$(10\,780/16 \times 5)$	$(10\,780/16 \times 7)$
Gross profit	12 075	22 096	12 729

(b) See 'A comparison of traditional and ABC systems' for the answer to this question. The answer should point out that ABC systems produce more accurate costs because they rely on a greater number of cost centres and a greater number and variety of second-stage cost drivers.

(c) The establishment of more accurate product costs using ABC should enable managers to make better product mix decisions. The product profitability analysis *per unit* with the existing traditional costing system is:

	Superior	Deluxe	Ultra
Selling price per unit	$54 000	$72 000	$127 500
Gross profit per unit	$13 700	$14 000	$20 500
Gross margin	25.4%	19.4%	16.1%

The profitability analysis *per unit* with the ABC system is:

	Superior	Deluxe	Ultra
Selling price per unit	$54 000	$72 000	$127 500
Gross profit per unit	$12 075	$18 413	$15 911
Gross margin	22.4%	25.6%	12.5%

Managers should review the product mix based on the above analysis. ABC can be extended beyond product costing to activity based cost management (see Chapter 21). For example, ABC gives more detailed information about how costs are incurred and the potential for cost reduction by reducing activity levels.

Question 11.7

(a) Profit per machine

	Small $	Medium $	Large $
Copy charge per machine	(60 000 × $0.03)	(120 000 × 0.04)	(180 000 × $0.05)
	1 800	4 800	9 000
Cost of parts per machine	($100 × 5)	($300 × 7)	($400 × 14)
	(500)	(2 100)	(5 600)
Labour cost per machine	($60 × 5)	($80 × 7)	($100 × 14)
	(300)	(560)	(1 400)
Overhead cost	(324)	(864)	(1 620)
Profit per machine	676	1 276	380

Overhead cost workings

	Small $	Medium $	Large $	Total $
Sales revenue	$1 800 × 300 = $540 000	$4 800 × 800 = $3 840 000	$9 000 × 500 = $4 500 000	$8 880 000
Overheads				$1 596 000
Overheads/sales revenue				18%
Cost per machine	$1 800 × 18% $324	$4 800 ×18% $864	$9 000 × 18% $1 620	

(b) Cost driver rates

Activity	Cost Driver	Overheads $000	No. of cost drivers	Cost per driver $
Customer account handling	Number of customers	126	(300/2)+ (800/2) + (500/2) = 800	$157.50 per customer
Planned maintenance scheduling	Number of planned maintenance visits	480	(300 × 4) + (800 × 6) + (500 ×12) = 12 000	$40 per planned maintenance visit
Unplanned maintenance scheduling	Number of unplanned maintenance visits	147	(300 × 1) + (800 × 1) + (500 × 2) = 2 100	$70 per unplanned maintenance visit
Spare part procurement	Number of purchase orders	243	(500 + 1 200 + 1 000) = 2 700	$90 per purchase order
Other overheads	Number of machines	600	(300 + 800 + 500) = 1 600	$375 per machine

Overhead cost per machine

	Small	Medium	Large
Customer account handling	($157.50/2) = $79	($157.50/2) = $79	($157.50/2) = $79
Planned maintenance scheduling	($40×4) = $160	($40 × 6) = $240	$40 × 12 = $480
Unplanned maintenance scheduling	($70 × 1) = $70	($70 ×1) = $70	($70 × 2) = $140
Spare part procurement	($90 × 500/300) = $150	($90 × 1 200/800) = $135	($90 × 1 000/500) = $180
Other overheads	$375	$375	$375
Total overhead cost per machine	$834	$899	$1 254

Profit per machine

	Small $	Medium $	Large $
Copy charge per machine	1 800	4 800	9 000
Parts and labour per machine	(800)	(2 660)	(7 000)
Overhead cost per machine	(834)	(899)	(1 254)
Profit per machine using ABC	166	1 241	746

(c) By using cause-and-effect assignments ABC assigns overhead costs more accurately to cost objects and this results in improved levels of accuracy in term of determining product costs and profitability analysis. In the example ABC has resulted in different levels of profit for each of the product groups. Small photocopies are less profitable than suggested by the traditional system, medium machines generate similar profits and higher profits are reported for the large machines under the ABC system. This information will enable management to make better product mix and pricing decisions. ABC can be extended beyond product costing to activity based cost management (see Chapter 21). For example, ABC gives more detailed information about how costs are incurred and the potential for cost reduction by reducing activity levels.

Question 11.8

(a) The costs and associated prices for the GC and the EX using labour hours to allocate overheads are:

	GC ($)	EX ($)
Materials	3 500	8 500
Labour: 300 hours at $15 per hour	4 500	
500 hours at $15 per hour		7 500
Overheads[1]:		
300 hours at $10 per hour	3 000	
500 hours at $10 per hour		5 000
	11 000	20 500
Profit margin (50%)	5 500	10 250
Quoted price	16 500	30 750

Note:

[1]$400 000 total overheads/40 000 direct labour hours

(b) The costs and quoted prices using ABC to assign overheads are:

	GC ($)	EX ($)
Materials	3 500	8 000
Labour: 300 hours at $15 per hour	4 500	
500 hours at $15 per hour		7 500
Overheads[1]		
Supervisor	180	1 080
Planners	280	1 400
Property	1 800	3 000
	10 260	20 980
Profit margin (50%)	5 130	10 490
Quoted price	15 390	31 470

Note:

[1]The overheads assigned to GC and EX are calculated as follows:

	Costs	Number of drivers	Cost per driver
Supervisor	90 000	500	180
Planners	70 000	250	280
Property	240 000	40 000	6

	Supervisor ($)	Planner ($)	Property ($)
Cost per unit of cost driver	180	280	6
GC	180 ($180 × 1)	280 ($280 × 1)	1 800 ($6 × 300)
EX	1 080 ($180 × 6)	1 400 ($280 × 5)	3 000 ($6 × 500)

(c) The ABC systems provides a more accurate measure of resources consumed by the different services and it is therefore preferable that costs generated by ABC should be used as an input to the pricing decision. It is important to note that any cost-plus generated selling price should represent the starting point in the process of negotiating the final price. The price should be adjusted upwards or downwards after taking account of the number of sales orders on hand, the extent of competition, demand, the importance of the customer in terms of future sales and the policy relating to customer relations. In other words, management should adjust the mark-up based on the state of sales demand and other factors that are of vital importance in determining the final pricing decision.

The cost-plus price based on the ABC system suggests a reduction in price and this would seem to be appropriate for GC given that demand is less than expected. However, the ABC system suggests that the price of EX should be slightly increased and this may be justifiable given that the failure to win contracts may not be applicable to EX.

The company appears to use cost-plus pricing in a rigid manner. More emphasis should be given to adopting a more flexible approach and taking demand into account. The reasons for failing to win contracts should be investigated. It is possible that failure to win contracts may relate to the quality of work or the reputation and reliability of the builder. If the investigation indicates that the success of quotes is price sensitive consideration could be given to obtaining a greater number of contracts and establishing a reputation in the industry by adopting a pricing penetration policy (see 'Pricing Policies' in Chapter 10).

(d) If marginal costs are used as a basis for cost-plus pricing only the incremental cost (direct labour, direct materials and any variable overheads) are assigned to products and a greater percentage profit margin than the current 50 per cent should be added to cover a contribution to both fixed overheads and profit. Marginal costs are likely to be more understandable by managers and customers but they represent only partial costs. Also by adding a larger percentage profit margin the company is, in effect, recovering overheads on the basis of a percentage on variable cost. This is just as arbitrary as a traditional costing system. Arbitrary allocations can be substantially reduced by adopting ABC. The choice of the costing system for assigning overheads should be influenced by the percentage and magnitude of overheads in the cost structure and the diversity of the activities undertaken by the company.

Decision-making under conditions of risk and uncertainty

Solutions to Chapter 12 questions

Question 12.1

(i) Regret matrix

Customer reaction	Agreement A $	Agreement B $	Agreement C $
Strong	12 100	19 900	0
Moderate	0	7 500	2 100
Weak	0	3 700	5 100

The maximum regret if Agreement A is chosen is $12 100
The maximum regret if Agreement B is chosen is $19 900
The maximum regret if Agreement C is chosen is $5 100

To minimize the maximum regret the manager will choose Agreement C.

(ii) A risk averse decision maker seeks to avoid risky outcomes and faced with a choice between two alternatives with identical expected values will choose the less risky alternative.

Question 12.2

The decision tree is shown in Figure Q12.2. The company is faced with choosing between three alternatives at the decision point (represented by the box labelled 1 in the diagram). The circles represent the possible outcomes that can occur and the probabilities of these outcomes are shown on the lines emanating from the circles. Note that for the first alternative (undertaking the survey) the

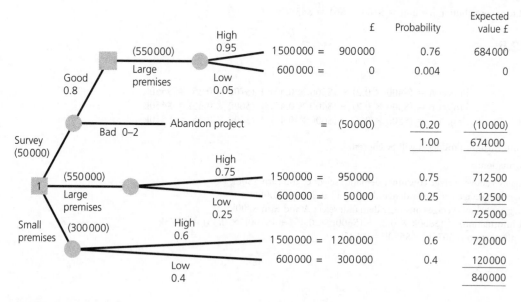

Figure Q12.2   Decision tree

probabilities for the two branches in the top right hand corner of the diagram are derived from the joint probabilities of two events occurring (i.e. the multiplication of the probability of one event occurring by the probability of the other event occurring). Therefore the probabilities are 0.76 (0.95 × 0.8), 0.004 (0.8 × 0.05) and 0.2 (1 × 0.2).

The highest expected value is £840 000 for the third alternative (build the small premises without any survey) and, based on the expected value decision rule, this alternative should be chosen.

Question 12.3

(i) The expected values ($000) are:

$$Project\ A\ (\$400 \times 0.3) + (\$500 \times 0.5) + (\$600 \times 0.2) = \$490$$
$$Project\ B\ (\$300 \times 0.3) + (\$350 \times 0.5) + (\$400 \times 0.2) = \$345$$
$$Project\ C\ (\$500 \times 0.3) + (\$450 \times 0.5) + (\$650 \times 0.2) = \$505$$

(ii) Value of perfect information ($000)

$$If\ demand\ is\ weak\ select\ Project\ C = (\$500 \times 0.3) = \$150$$
$$If\ demand\ is\ average\ select\ Project\ A = (\$500 \times 0.5) = \$250$$
$$If\ demand\ is\ good\ select\ Project\ C = (\$650 \times 0.2) = \$130$$
$$The\ value\ of\ perfect\ information\ is\ (\$150 + \$250 + \$130 = \$530 - \$505) = \$25$$

Question 12.4

(i) The following outcomes will yield a contribution in excess of $39 per unit:

$$\$80 - \$40 = \$40\ Joint\ probability\ is\ 0.25 \times 0.20 = 0.05$$
$$\$100 - \$40 = \$60\ Joint\ probability\ is\ 0.30 \times 0.20 = 0.06$$
$$\$100 - \$60 = \$40\ Joint\ probability\ is\ 0.30 \times 0.55 = 0.165$$
$$\$120 - \$40 = \$80\ Joint\ probability\ is\ 0.45 \times 0.20 = 0.09$$
$$\$120 - \$60 = \$60\ Joint\ probability\ is\ 0.45 \times 0.55 = 0.2475$$
$$\$120 - \$80 = \$40\ Joint\ probability\ is\ 0.45 \times 0.25 = 0.1125$$
$$\underline{0.725}$$

(ii) Expected value of selling price per unit
($80 × 0.25) + ($100 × 0.30) + ($120 × 0.45) = $104

Expected value of variable cost per unit
($40 × 0.20) + ($60 × 0.55) + ($80 × 0.25) = $61

Expected value of contribution per unit = $104 − $61 = $43

Question 12.5

Expected values:

$$Project\ A = (\$400 \times 0.2) + (\$500 \times 0.45) + (\$700 \times 0.35) = \$550k$$
$$Project\ B = (\$300 \times 0.2) + (\$400 \times 0.45) + (\$600 \times 0.35) = \$450k$$
$$Project\ C = (\$800 \times 0.2) + (\$600 \times 0.45) + (\$300 \times 0.35) = \$550k$$

Without perfect information Product A will be chosen.

With perfect information:

If the research suggests above average consumer demand: select C and earn $800k
If the research suggests average consumer demand: select C and earn $600k
If the research suggests below average consumer demand: select A and earn $700k
EV (with perfect information) = ($800k × 0.2) + ($600k × 0.45) + ($700k × 0.35) = $675k
Value of perfect information is $675k − $550k = $125k

Question 12.6

Consumer reaction	Project A expected value	Project B expected value	Project C expected value
	$000s	$000s	$000s
Strong	250	400	300
Good	100	120	150
Weak	70	49	35
Expected value	420	569	485

Project B is the best choice (without the benefit of perfect information) since it has the highest expected value (EV) of $569 000.

With perfect information:

If research reveals strong consumer reaction: select B — with an outcome of $1 600k
If research reveals good consumer reaction: select C — with an outcome of $375k
If research reveals weak consumer reaction: select A — with an outcome of $200k
EV (with perfect information) = ($1 600 × 0.25) + ($375 × 0.40) + ($200 × 0.35) = $620k
Value of perfect information is $620 000 − $569 000 = $51 000

Question 12.7

(a) *Profit and Loss Statement for Period Ending 31 May 2015*

	(£)
Revenue (14 400 000 journeys):	1 440 000
0 − 3 miles (7 200 000 × £0.20)	1 296 000
4 − 5 miles (4 320 000 × £0.30)	1 440 000
Over 5 miles (2 880 000 × £0.50)	720 000
Juvenile fares (4 800 000 × £0.15)	480 000
Senior citizen fares (4 800 000 × £0.10)	5 376 000
Advertising revenue	250 000
	5 626 000
Less: Variable costs (20 routes × 4 buses × 150 miles × 330 days × £0.75)	(2 970 000)
Fixed costs	(1 750 000)
Net profit	906 000

(b) Assuming the same passenger mix as 2015 the weighted average fare per passenger for year ending 31 May 2016 is (£5 376 000 × 1.05)/24 000 000 = £0.2352.

The break-even point is where:

Total revenue from fares + Advertising revenue = Total cost Let x = number of passenger journeys
Break-even point: $0.2352x + £250 000 = (2 970 000 + £1 750 000)\ 1.1$

$$0.2352x = £4 942 000$$
$$x = 21 011 905$$

Maximum capacity utilization = 40 000 000 passenger journeys (24 000 000/0.6)
Break-even capacity utilization = 21 011 905/40 000 000 = 52.5%

(c) (i) *Expected value and probability estimates for 2016*

%	Capacity Utilization (Probability)	Revenue Fares (£000)	Revenue Adverts (£000)	Inflation (%)	Inflation (Probability)	Costs (£000)	Combined probability	Net profit (£000)	Expected value (£000)
70	0.1	6585.6[a]	250	8	0.3	5097.6[b]	0.03	1738.0	52.14
		6585.6	250	10	0.6	5192.0[b]	0.06	1643.6	98.62
		6585.6	250	12	0.1	5286.4[b]	0.01	1549.2	15.49
60	0.5	5644.8[a]	250	8	0.3	5097.6	0.15	797.2	119.58
		5644.8	250	10	0.6	5192.0	0.30	702.8	210.84
		5644.8	250	12	0.1	5286.4	0.05	608.4	30.42

Capacity Utilization %	(Probability)	Revenue Fares (£000)	Adverts (£000)	(%)	Inflation (Probability)	Costs (£000)	Combined probability	Net profit (£000)	Expected value (£000)
50	0.4	4704.0[a]	250	8	0.3	5097.6	0.12	−143.6	−17.23
		4704.0	250	10	0.6	5192.0	0.24	−238.0	−57.12
		4704.0	250	12	0.1	5286.4	0.04	−332.4	−13.30
							1.00		439.44

Notes:

[a] Fare revenues at 60 per cent capacity for 2015 were £5 376 000. Assuming 5 per cent inflation fare revenues for 2016 at 60 per cent capacity will be £5 644 800 (£5 376 000 × 1.05). At 70 per cent and 50 per cent capacity utilization fare revenues will be as follows:

$$70\% = 70/60 \times £5\,644\,800 = £6\,585\,600$$
$$50\% = 50/60 \times £5\,644\,800 = £4\,704\,000$$

[b] Variable costs vary with bus miles which are assumed to remain unchanged. Predicted costs at the different inflation levels are as follows:

$$8\% = (£2\,970\,000 + £1\,750\,000)1.08 = £5\,097\,600$$
$$10\% = (£2\,970\,000 + £1\,750\,000)1.10 = £5\,192\,000$$
$$12\% = (£2\,970\,000 + £1\,750\,000)1.12 = £5\,286\,400$$

(ii) The answer to this question requires the preparation of a cumulative probability distribution that measures the cumulative probability of profits/(losses) being greater than specified levels.

Cumulative probability distribution

Losses greater than £300 000	= 0.04 probability
Probability of a loss occurring	= 0.40
Profits greater than £600 000	= 0.60
Profits greater than £700 000	= 0.55
Profits greater than £800 000	= 0.10
Profits greater than £1 500 000	= 0.10

(d) The following factors have not been incorporated into the analysis:

(i) Change in the passenger mix.

(ii) Changes in the number of routes and the number of days operation per year.

(iii) Changes in fare structure such as off-peak travel or further concessions for juveniles and senior citizens.

(iv) Changes in cost levels due to factors other than inflation (e.g. more efficient operating methods).

Question 12.8

(a)

	70	80	90
Selling price (£)	70	80	90
Maximum demand (£)	75 000	60 000	40 000
Maximum revenue (£)	5 250 000	4 800 000	3 600 000
Total variable cost (£)	3 750 000	3 000 000	2 000 000
Fixed costs (£)	800 000	800 000	800 000
R & D cost (£)	250 000	250 000	250 000
	4 800 000	4 050 000	3 050 000
Estimated profit (£)	450 000	750 000	550 000

The above analysis is based on the maximum sales demand. On this basis, the analysis indicates that profits are maximized at an output level of 60 000 units when the selling price is £80. It is preferable to use the 'most likely' demand level and to incorporate uncertainty around the 'most likely' demand into the analysis.

(b) For a selling price of £90 there are three different demand levels, and for each demand level there are three different outcomes for actual unit variable cost. Therefore there are nine possible outcomes. The contribution and probability of each outcome is presented in the following schedule:

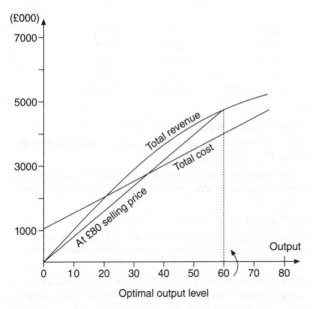

Figure Q12.8

(1)	(2)	(3) Unit variable cost (£)	(4)	(5) Unit contribution (£)	(6) Total contribution (£000)	(7) Joint probability (2 × 4)	(8) Weighted outcome (6 × 7) (£000)
Demand (000)	Probability		Probability				
20	0.2	60	0.2	30	600	0.04	24.00
20	0.2	55	0.7	35	700	0.14	98.00
20	0.2	50	0.1	40	800	0.02	16.00
35	0.7	60	0.2	30	1 050	0.14	147.00
35	0.7	55	0.7	35	1 225	0.49	600.25
35	0.7	50	0.1	40	1 400	0.07	98.00
40	0.1	60	0.2	30	1 200	0.02	24.00
40	0.1	55	0.7	35	1 400	0.07	98.00
40	0.1	50	0.1	40	1 600	0.01	16.00
						1.00	1121.25

	(£)
Expected total contribution	1 121 250
Fixed costs	1 050 000
Expected profit	71 250

(c) To compare the three selling prices, it is necessary to summarize the information in part (b) for a £90 selling price in the same way as part (c) of the question. Note that fixed costs are deducted from the total contribution column in the schedule presented in (b) to produce the following statement:

		Prices under review		
		£70	£80	£90
Probability of a loss				
Greater than or equal to	£500 000	0.02	0	0
	£300 000	0.07	0.05	0.18
	£100 000	0.61	0.08	0.20
	0	0.61	0.10	0.34

Probability of a profit				
Greater than or equal to	0	0.39	0.91	0.80
	£100 000	0.33	0.52	0.66
	£300 000	0.03	0.04	0.15
	£500 000	0	0.01	0.01
Expected profit		Loss (£550 750)	£68 500	£71 250

The following items should be included in the memorandum:

(i) The £90 selling price has the largest expected profit, but there is also a 0.34 probability of not making a profit.

(ii) Selling price of £80 may be preferable, because there is only a 0.10 probability of not making a profit. A selling price of £80 is least risky, and the expected value is only slightly lower than the £90 selling price.

(iii) Subjective probability distributions provide details of the uncertainty surrounding the estimates and enable the decision-maker to select the course of action that is related to his personal risk/profit trade-off (see Chapter 12 for an explanation of this).

(iv) Subjective probabilities are subject to all the disadvantages of any subjective estimate (e.g. bias).

(v) Calculations are based on discrete probabilities. For example, this implies that there is a 0.7 probability that demand will be exactly 35 000. A more realistic interpretation is that 35 000 represents the mid-point of demand falling within a certain range.

(d) If the increase in fixed costs represents an additional cost resulting from an increase in volume then this incremental cost is relevant to the pricing decision. If the fixed costs represent an apportionment then it is not relevant. Nevertheless, we noted in Chapter 10 that selling prices should be sufficient to cover the common and unavoidable long-run fixed costs.

The research and development expenditure is a sunk cost, and is not a relevant cost as far as the pricing decision is concerned. However, the pricing policy of the company may be to recover the research and development expenditure in the selling price. The amount recovered per unit sold should be a policy decision. Note that the decision to write off research and development in one year instead of three will affect the reported profits.

Question 12.9

Figure 12.9 shows the decision tree relating to the question:

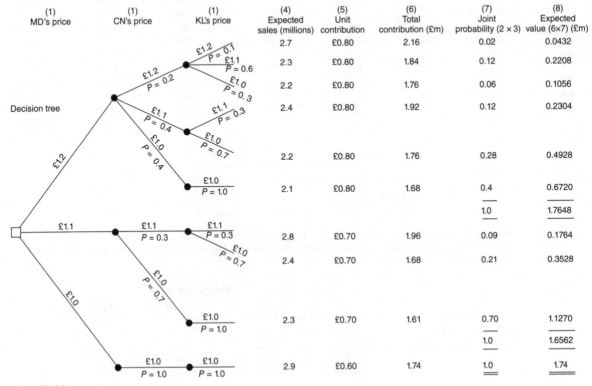

Figure Q12.9

The variable cost per litre is as follows:

	(£)
Direct materials	0.12
Direct wages	0.24
Indirect wages etc. ($16^2/3\% \times £0.24$)	0.04
	0.40

and the range of contributions are:

£0.80 for a selling price of £1.20
£0.70 for a selling price of £1.10
£0.60 for a selling price of £1.00

The decision tree indicating the possible outcomes presented in Figure Q12.8 shows that the expected value of the contribution is maximized at a selling price of £1.20. Fixed costs are common and unavoidable to all alternatives, and are therefore not included in the analysis. However, management might prefer the certain contribution of £1.74 million at a selling price of £1.00. From columns 6 and 7 of the decision tree it can be seen that there is a 0.60 probability that contribution will be in excess of £1.74 million when a selling price of £1.20 is implemented. The final decision depends on management's attitude towards risk.

Question 12.10

(a) *Budgeted net profit/loss outcomes for year ending 30 June*

Client days	Fee per client day (£)	Variable cost per client day (£)	Contribution per client day (£)	Total contrib. per year (£)
15750	180	95	85	1338750
15750	180	85	95	1496250
15750	180	70	110	1732500
13125	200	95	105	1378125
13125	200	85	115	1509375
13125	200	70	130	1706250
10500	220	95	125	1312500
10500	220	85	135	1417500
10500	220	70	150	1575000

(b) The *maximax* rule looks for the largest contribution from all outcomes. In this case the decision maker will choose a client fee of £180 per day where there is a possibility of a contribution of £1732500.

The *maximin* rule looks for the strategy which will maximize the minimum possible contribution. In this case the decision maker will choose client fee of £200 per day where the lowest contribution is £1378125. This is better than the worst possible outcome from client fees per day of £180 or £220 which will provide contribution of £1338750 and £1312500 respectively.

The *minimax regret* rule requires the choice of the strategy which will minimize the maximum regret from making the wrong decision. Regret represents the opportunity lost from making the wrong decision.

The calculations in part (a) are used to list the opportunity losses in the following regret matrix:

	State of nature		
	Low variable cost of £70	Most likely variable cost of £85	High variable cost of £95
Choose a fee of £180	0	£13125	£39375
Choose a fee of £200	£26250	0	0
Choose a fee of £220	£157500	£91875	£65625

At a variable cost of £70 the maximum contribution is £1732500 derived from a fee of £180. Therefore there will be no opportunity loss. At a fee of £200 the opportunity loss is £26250 (£1732500 − £1706250) and at the £220 fee the opportunity loss is £157500 (£1732500 − £1575000). The same approach is used to calculate the opportunity losses at variable costs of £85 and £95.

The maximum regrets for each fee are as follows:

	(£)
£180	39 375
£200	26 250
£220	157 500

The minimum regret is £26 250 and adopting a minimum regret strategy will result in choosing the £200 fee per day alternative.

(c)

$$\text{The expected value of variable cost} = £95 \times 0.1 + £85 \times 0.6 + £70 \times 0.3 = £81.50$$

For each client fee strategy the expected value of budget contribution for the year is calculated as follows:

$$* \text{ fee of } £180 : 15\,750\,(180 - 81.50) = £1\,551\,375$$
$$* \text{ fee of } £200 : 13\,125\,(200 - 81.50) = £1\,555\,312.50$$
$$* \text{ fee of } £220 : 10\,500\,(220 - 81.50) = £1\,454\,250$$

A client fee of £200 per day is required to give the maximum expected value contribution of £1 555 312.50. Note that there is virtually no difference between this and the contribution where a fee of £180 per day is used.

(d) Profit can be increased by making cost savings provided that such actions do not result in a fall in demand and a reduction in revenues. Alternatively, investments may be made that will increase the level of service and thus demand. Profits will increase if the extra revenues exceed the increase in costs. The balanced scorecard approach to performance measurement and the determinants of performance measurement relating to service organizations described in Learning Note 22.1 on the open access website can be used to identify appropriate performance areas for the health centre. The performance areas identified in Exhibit LN 22.1 in Learning Note 22.1 include quality of service, flexibility, resource utilization and innovation. Each of these areas is discussed below.

(i) Quality of service may be improved by upgrading facilities such as a cafeteria, free daily newspapers and better waiting room facilities. This may increase demand and generate additional revenues which exceed the cost increases.

(ii) Flexibility of service may be improved by providing additional sports/exercise facilities that are not currently available. In addition, additional exercise and dietary consultants who can provide services that are not currently available.

(iii) Resource utilization may be improved by better scheduling relating to the use of the exercise equipment and staff time and extending the opening hours. The aim should be to provide at least the same level of service with fewer resources.

(iv) Innovation may take the form of new services such as an extension of the range of health advice that can be provided and introducing online booking systems which can be directly accessed by the clients.

Question 12.11

The answer should distinguish between risk and uncertainty (see 'Risk and uncertainty' in Chapter 12). The three approaches that apply where meaningful estimates of probabilities cannot be determined should be described. These approaches (maximin, maximax and regret criteria) are described in Chapter 12.

Where meaningful estimates of probabilities can be assigned then uncertainty can be classified as risk and expected values for different alternatives can be calculated. Expected values can be supplemented with measures of risk (measures of dispersion) of the different alternatives. The standard deviation and coefficient of variation are two measures that are described in Chapter 12.

The answer should describe the different attitudes to risk (see Chapter 12) and point out that a risk neutral decision-maker will choose the alternative with the highest expected value, a risk averse individual is likely to focus on alternatives with low risk measures and risk seeing individuals will focus on alternatives that have a greatest probability of maximizing the outcomes even though they have high levels of risk.

Capital investment decisions: appraisal methods

Solutions to Chapter 13 questions

Question 13.1

At 13 per cent NPV is estimated to be -10

Using interpolation: $10\% + [50/60 \times (10\% - 13\%)] = 12.5\%$

Answer = C

Question 13.2

Let x = the annual perpetuity.

$5000 = x + x/.08$

$5000 = 13.5\,x$

Note that the perpetuity formula is based on the assumption that the cash flow starts at the end of the first period.

Value of annual perpetuity = $5000/13.5 = \$370$

Answer = A

Question 13.3

The semi-annual interest rate is 2 per cent and if this is compounded semi-annually we can use the compound interest formula to determine the annual effective rate (AER) AER = $(1.02)^2 - 1 = 0.0404$ or 4.04%

The four-year interest rate is 20 per cent so formula 13.7 can be used to determine the annual effective rate:

AER = $_4\sqrt{1.20} - 1 = 0.0466 = 4.66\%$

Answer = C

Question 13.4

Market value (\$108.06) = PV of interest payments at 6 per cent + PV of redemption (100×0.840)

PV of interest payments at 6 per cent for three years = \$24.06

Annuity factor for three years at 6 per cent = 2.673

Interest payment = \$24.06/2.673 = \$9

Coupon rate = \$9/\$100 = 9%

Question 13.5

The PV of a perpetuity = Annual cash flow/cost of capital where the cash flows start at the *end* of the first year. Here the cash flows start at the beginning of the first year so:

PV = \$4 000 + \$4 000/0.12 = \$37 333

Question 13.6

Year(s)	Description	Cash flow	Discount factor (3%)	Present value $	Discount factor (6%)	Present value $
0	Purchase	103	1.000	(103.00)	1.000	(103.00)
1–4	Interest	6	3.717	22.30	3.465	20.79
4	Redemption	100	0.888	88.80	0.792	79.20
NPV				8.10		(3.01)

By interpolation

3% + (($8.10/($8.10 + $3.01)) × 3) = 5.19%

The bond's yield to maturity is 5.19%

Question 13.7

Year(s)	Description	Cash flow $	Discount factor (4%)	Present value $
1−4	Interest	6	3.630	21.78
4	Redemption	100	0.855	85.50
0	Market value			107.28

The current expected market value of the bond is therefore $107.28

Question 13.8

It is necessary to find the annuity factor where the initial investment will be equal to the net cash inflows.

$281 000 × four year annuity factor = $800 000

Four year annuity factor = $800 000/$281 000 = 2.847

The four year annuity factor for 15 per cent = 2.855

The four year annuity factor for 16 per cent = 2.798

The maximum discount rate at which the project will be financially viable is therefore 15 per cent.

Question 13.9

(a) Net present values:

Year	0% NPV (£)	Discount Factor	10% NPV (£)	Discount Factor	20% NPV (£)
0	(142 700)	1 000	(142 700)	1.000	(142 700)
1	51 000	0.909	46 359	0.833	42 483
2	62 000	0.826	51 212	0.694	43 028
3	73 000	0.751	54 823	0.579	42 267
NPV	43 300		9 694		(14 922)

(b)

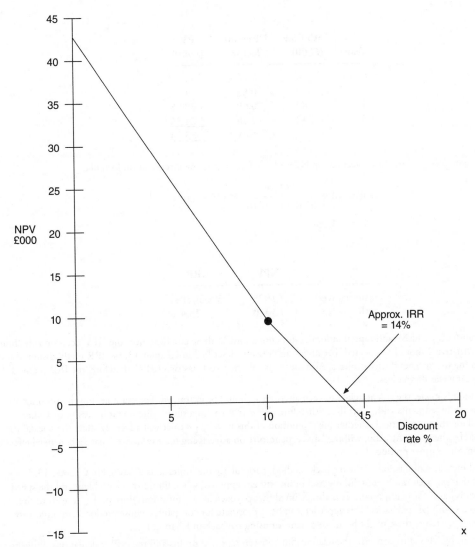

Question 13.10

(a) *Alternative 1*

NPV:

Year	Cash flow (£000)	Discount factor	PV (£000)
0	−100	1.00	−100
1	+255	0.83	+211.65
2	−157.5	0.69	−108.675
		NPV =	2.975

IRR: The cash flow sign changes after year 1, which implies that the project will have two IRRs. Using the interpolation method, the NPV will be zero at a cost of capital of 5 per cent and 50 per cent. Therefore the IRRs are 5 per cent and 50 per cent.

Alternative 2

NPV:

Year	Cash flow (£000)	Discount factor	PV (£000)
0	−50	1.00	−50
1	0	0.83	0
2	+42	0.69	+28.98
3	+42	0.58	+24.36
		NPV =	+3.34

IRR: At a 25 per cent discount rate the project has an NPV of −1.616. Using the interpolation formula:

$$IRR = 20 + \frac{3340}{3340-(-1616)} \times (25 - 20)$$

$$= 23.4\%$$

Summary

	NPV	IRR
Alternative 1	£2 975	5% or 50%
Alternative 2	£3 340	23.4%

(b) The projects are mutually exclusive and capital rationing does not apply. In these circumstances the NPV decision rule should be applied and alternative 2 should be selected. Because of the reasons described in Chapter 13, the IRR method should not be used for evaluating mutually exclusive projects. Also, note that alternative 1 has two IRRs. Therefore, the IRR method cannot be used to rank the alternatives.

Before a final decision is made, the risk attached to each alternative should be examined. For example, novelty products are generally high-risk investments with short lives. Therefore alternative 1 with a shorter life might be less risky. Other considerations include the possibility of whether the promotion of this novelty product will adversely affect the sales of the other products sold by the company. Also, will the large expenditure on advertising for alternative 1 have a beneficial effect on the sales of the company's other products?

(c) The answer should include a discussion of the payback method, particularly the limitations discussed in Chapter 13. It should be stressed that payback can be a useful method of investment appraisal when liquidity is a problem and the speed of a project's return is particularly important. It is also claimed that payback allows for uncertainty in that it leads to the acceptance of projects with fast paybacks. This approach can be appropriate for companies whose products are subject to uncertain short lives. Therefore there might be an argument for using payback in Khan Ltd.

The second comment by Mr Court concerns the relationship between reported profits and the NPV calculations. Projects ranked by the NPV method can give different rankings to projects that are ranked by their impact on the reported profits of the company. The NPV method results in the maximization of the present value of future cash flows and is the correct decision rule. If investors give priority to reported profits in valuing shares (even if reported profits do not give an indication of the true economic performance of the company) then Mr Court's comments on the importance of a project's impact on reported profits might lead to the acceptance of alternative 1. However, if investors are aware of the deficiencies of published reported profits and are aware of the company's future plans and cash flows then share values will be based on PV of future cash flows. This is consistent with the NPV rule.

Question 13.11

(a) (i)

Project 1

Current contribution = $10 950k (20 000 passengers × $1.50 × 365 days)
Revised contribution = $11 388k (20 000 × 1.20 × $1.30 × 365)
Incremental contribution in year 1 = $438k ($11 388k − $10 950k)
NPV = Incremental cash flows [($438k − $100k) × 3.993] − investment outlay (1000) = $349.6

Project 2

Expected passengers for year 1 = (6 000 × 50%) + (9 000 × 30%) + (12 000 × 20%) = 8 100

Expected contribution for year 1 = 8 100 × $1.50 × 365 days = $4 435k

Additional fixed costs (excluding depreciation) per annum = $3 500k − ($5 000 000/5) = $2 500k

Net Present Value

	Year 0 $000	Year 1 $000	Year 2 $000	Year 3 $000	Year 4 $000	Year 5 $000
Initial Investment	(5 000)					
Working capital	(1 000)					1 000
Expected contribution		4 435	4 568	4 705	4 846	4 991
Fixed costs		(2 500)	(2 500)	(2 500)	(2 500)	(2 500)
Net cash flows	(6 000)	1 935	2 068	2 205	2 346	3 491
Discount Factor @ 8%	1.000	0.926	0.857	0.794	0.735	0.681
Present value	(6 000)	1 792	1 772	1 751	1 724	2 377
Net present value						3 416

Project 2 should be accepted because it has the higher NPV.

(a) (ii)

The following factors should be considered before a final decision is made:

- Project 2 has higher risk in terms of the increased number of passengers on the new routes being critical to the success of the project.
- The initial investment for project 2 is significantly higher so it is important to ensure that sufficient capital can be raised.
- Potential competitor reaction on the new routes should be considered.

(b)

The NPVs will be identical when the following requirement is met for project 2:

PV of annual contribution − PV of fixed costs ($9 982.5k) − initial outlay ($6 000k) = 349.6k

Let x = annual contribution for year 1 for project 1

$x(0.926) + 1.03x (0.857) + 1.03x^2 (0.794) + 1.03x^3 (0.735) + 1.03x^4 (0.681) = \$16 332.1k$

$0.926x + 0.883x + 0842x + 0.803x + 0.766x = \$16 332.1k$

$4.22x = \$16 332.1$

$x = \$3 870k$

Expected contribution for year 1 = passenger numbers × $1.50 × 365 days = $3 870k Passenger numbers = 7 068

Assuming that the 3 per cent annual increase is maintained, if passenger numbers in year 1 reduce by more than 1 032 (12.7%) the NPV of Project 2 will be less than that of Project 1 and therefore the choice will be to accept Project 1.

D, C and B which will use $90 000 of the available funding. The remaining $20 000 can be used for part of project A.

Question 13.12

(a) *Attending 6 training courses per year*

Year	Travel and accommodation etc. (£000's)[a]	Course costs (£000's)[a]	Total cash flows (£000's)	Discount factor	Present value (£000's)
1	522.00	70.50	592.50	0.877	519.62
2	548.10	72.26	620.36	0.769	477.06
3	575.51	74.07	649.58	0.675	438.47
4	604.29	75.92	680.21	0.592	402.68
5	634.50	77.82	712.32	0.519	369.69
					2 207.52

Note:
[a]Travel etc. = £870 $\times$ 100 delegates $\times$ 6 courses = £522 000
Courses = £11 750 $\times$ 6 courses = £70 500
Travel etc. Year 2 = £522 (1.05), Year 3 = £522 $(1.05)^2$ and so on.
Course costs Year 2 = £70.5 (1.025), Year 3 = £70.5 $(1.025)^2$ and so on.

Proposed e-learning solution

Year	0 (£000's)	1 (£000's)	2 (£000's)	3 (£000's)	4 (£000's)	5 (£000's)
Hardware[a]	1 500					(50)
Software	35	35	35	35	35	
Technical manager and trainers (30 + 12)[b]		42	44.52	47.19	50.02	53.02
Camera and sound		24	24	25.44	26.97	28.59
Broadband connection		30	28.50	27.08	25.73	24.44
		131	132.02	134.71	137.72	56.05
Discount factor	1.000	0.877	0.769	0.675	0.592	0.519
Present value	1 535	114.89	101.52	90.93	81.53	29.09

Total present value = £1 953 257

Notes:

[a]Depreciation is not a relevant cost and should not be included in the analysis.

[b]The technical manager will have to be replaced resulting in an incremental cash flow of £20 000 per annum.

The e-learning solution should be recommended since this has the lowest present value.

(b) (i) Note that equivalent annual costs/cash flows are explained in Learning Note 14.1 on the open access website accompanying this book. To answer this question it is necessary to separate those costs that are variable with the number of delegates and those that are fixed and thus do not change with the number of candidates. It is assumed that six courses will be provided per year. For the course attendance alternative, the course costs are fixed and travel, etc. is variable with the number of delegates. Separate present values must be calculated for course costs and travel, etc. If you discount the second and third columns for the course attendance alternative you will find that the present values are £1 954 800 (variable cost) and £252 720 (fixed cost). Dividing both of these items by an annuity factor for five years at 14 per cent (3.433) gives annual equivalent costs of £569 415 (variable costs) and £73 615 (fixed cost).

For the e-learning costs alternative, the broadband connection is variable with the number of delegates and the remaining costs are fixed. The respective present values are £94 421 (variable) and £1 858 836 (fixed) giving equivalent annual costs of £27 504 (variable) and £541 461 (fixed). Therefore, the additional annual equivalent fixed costs for the e-learning alternative are £467 846. The savings in annual equivalent variable costs from this alternative are £541 911 (£569 415 − £27 504) per 100 delegates or £5419 per delegate. Therefore the minimum number of delegates required to achieve the fixed cost savings is 86.33 (£467 846/£5419).

(ii) The required number of delegates to break even is 87 per cent. This is a very high required take-up rate and so the company must ensure that virtually all of the delegates will favour this method of delivery.

Question 13.13

(a) The expected number of passengers is derived from the demand at each exchange rate:

Expected demand at 1.52€/£ = 0.33(500 + 460 + 420) = 460
Expected demand at 1.54€/£ = 0.33(550 + 520 + 450) = 506.67
Expected demand at 1.65€/£ = 0.33(600 + 580 + 500) = 560
Expected demand = 0.2(460) + 0.5(506.67) + 0:3(560) = 513.335 per train (or 1026.7 per day).

(b) Cash flows: in-house option

Year	1	2	3	4	5
Sales[a]	748 440	748 440	748 440	748 440	748 440
Variable costs[b]	(501 455)	(501 455)	(501 455)	(501 455)	(501 455)
Contribution	246 985	246 985	246 985	246 985	246 985
Labour costs[c]	(74 844)	(78 586)	(82 516)	(86 641)	(90 973)
Purchase and insurance[d]	(37 422)	(37 422)	(37 422)	(37 422)	(37 422)
Asset sale/purchase		(500 000)			280 000
Net cash flow	134 719	(369 023)	127 047	122 922	398 590
Discount factor at 12%	0 893	0 797	0.712	0.636	0.567
Present value	120 304	(294 111)	90 457	78 178	226 000

Net present value = £220 828

Cash flows: contract out option

Year	0	1	2	3	4	5
Contract fee[f]		(90 000)	(90 000)	(90 000)	(90 000)	(90 000)
Asset purchase/sale	650 000					
Purchase and insurance[e]		(16 422)	(16 422)	(16 422)	(16 422)	(16 422)
Net cash flow	650 000	(106 422)	(106 422)	(106 422)	(106 422)	(106 422)
Discount factor	1.0	0.893	0.797	0.712	0.636	0.567
Present value	650 000	(95 035)	(84 818)	(75 772)	(67 684)	(60 341)

Net present value = £266 350

The contract out option is preferred because it has the higher NPV of £45 522.

Notes:

[a]Sales revenues = 0.45 × 513.335 × £9 × 360 = £748 440

[b]Direct materials = 0.55 × £748 440 = £411 642

Variable overhead = 0.12 × £748 440 = £89 813 Variable costs = £501 455

[c]Labour costs = 0.10 × £748 440 = £74 844 for year 1, Year 2 = £74 844 (1.05), Year 3 = £74 844 $(1.05)^2$

[d]Purchase and insurance = 0.05 × £748 440 = £37 422 (for in-house provision)

[e]Purchase and insurance = £37 422 − £21 000 = £16 422 (for contracting out)

[f]Provision of catering service by outside supplier = £250 × 360 days = £90 000

[g]Gross catering receipts are £2079 per day (£748 440/360) do not exceed £2200 so the 5 per cent commission does not apply

[h]Depreciation is not a cash flow and is therefore not a relevant cost.

(c) A 10 per cent increase in sales would increase the annual contribution by £24 699 giving an increase in present value of £89 040 (£24 699 × 3.605 discount factor at 12 per cent). The present value of the additional costs is £36 050 (£10 000 × 3.605) resulting in an increase in NPV of £52 990. This exceeds the NPV of £45 522 from changing to the contracting out alternative. However, the revised annual sales per day would be £2287 (£2079 × 1.10), thus enabling the company to receive 5 per cent of gross sales receipts once sales exceed £2200 per day. The company would therefore receive £41 164 per annum (5 per cent × £748 440 sales × 1.10). This would result in the contracting out alternative having the higher NPV. The choice is highly dependent on future sales being in excess of £2200 per day.

(d) The answer should draw attention to the difficulties in deriving probabilities and using past data to estimate probabilities based on the view that the past is indicative of the future. The outcome using probabilities represents an average outcome, which may be unlikely to occur. Also expected values ignore risk. For a more detailed discussion of these points you should refer to the sections on probabilities, probability distributions and expected value and measuring the amount of uncertainty in Chapter 12.

(e) The following non-financial factors need to be taken into account:

(1) The loss of ability to control the quality and reliability of the service if the service is contracted out. These factors may influence the number of passengers choosing to travel with Amber plc.

(2) Impact on staff morale as a result of the reduction in labour costs. Existing staff may be concerned that their jobs are under threat and may leave the company.

(3) The difficulty and high costs of changing back to in-service provision once the company has contracted out the service.

(4) Willingness of the supplier to respond to changes in market demand.

Question 13.14

(a) *NPV calculations*

	Cash flows (£m)	Years	Discount factor	PV (£m)
Initial outlay	(40)	t_0	1.0000	(40.000)
Disposal value	10	t_{10}	0.2472	2.472
Retraining costs[a]	(10)	$t_{0,1}$	1.8696	(18.696)
Annual cost savings	12	t_1-t_{10}	5.0190	60.228
Rental income	2	t_{1-10}	5.0190	10.038
Software	(4)	t_{1-10}	5.0190	(20.076)
Reduction in working capital	5	t_0	1.0000	5.000
NPV				(1.034)

It is assumed that taxation should be ignored.

Note:

[a]The question implies that retraining costs do not occur at the end of the year. It is therefore assumed that the cash flows occur at the start of years 1 and 2 (that is, t_0 and t_1).

Calculation of accounting rate of return

	(£m)
Year 1 incremental profits:	
Annual cost savings	12
Retraining costs (20m/10 years)	(2)
Rental income	2
Software	(4)
Depreciation of equipment (40 – 10)/10 years	(3)
Increase in profits	5

	(£m)
Year 1 incremental capital investment:	
Initial outlay	40
Capitalized retraining costs	20
Reduction in working capital	(5)
	55

It is assumed that ROI is calculated based on the opening written-down value:

$$ROI = 5/55 = 9.1\%$$

The proposed investment fails to meet either of the company's investment criteria and would be rejected.

(b) The answer should include a discussion of the following:

(i) A theoretical explanation of the NPV rule and a justification for its use. In perfect capital markets a positive NPV reflects the increase in the market value of a company arising from acceptance of the project.

(ii) An explanation of the impact of market imperfections on the NPV rule. For NPV to represent the increase in shareholders' value resulting from acceptance of an investment, it is necessary for investors to be aware of the project's existence and also the projected future cash flows. This implies that the efficient market hypothesis applies in its strong form and that changes in short-run reported profits do not affect market prices.

(iii) In imperfect markets shareholders lack information regarding projected future cash flows. Consequently, they may use short-run reported profits and ROI as an indication of potential future cash flows. In such circumstances changes in reported profits will affect share prices. Hence management have reacted to this situation by considering the impact of a project's acceptance on reported ROI.

(iv) Widespread use of ROI and payback in the UK and USA.

(v) Shareholders and financial analysts tend to monitor short-run profits and ROI and use these measures as an input that determines their estimates of future share prices. It is therefore not surprising that companies consider the implications of their investment decisions on reported short-run profits and ROI.

(c) The answer should include a discussion of the specific problems that arise in evaluating investments in advanced manufacturing technologies (AMTs) and an explanation of why the financial appraisal might incorrectly reject such investments. In particular, it is claimed that many of the benefits from investing in AMTs are difficult to quantify and tend not to be included in the analysis (e.g. improved product quality). It is also claimed that inflation is incorrectly dealt with and that excessive discount rates are applied which overcompensate for risk.

A further reason that has been cited why companies under-invest in AMTs is that they fail to properly evaluate the relevant alternatives. There is a danger that the investment will be compared incorrectly against an alternative that assumes a continuation of the current market share, selling prices and costs- in other words, the status quo. However, the status quo is unlikely to apply, since competitors are also likely to invest in the new technology. In this situation the investment should be compared with the alternative of not investing, based on assuming a situation of declining cash flow.

The answer should also stress that taxation has not been incorporated into the analysis. In addition, the project has been discounted at the company's normal cost of capital of 15 per cent. This rate is only justified if the risk of the project is equivalent to the average risk of the firm's existing assets.

Capital investment decisions: the impact of capital rationing, taxation, inflation and risk

Solutions to Chapter 14 questions

Question 14.1

Discounted value of cash inflow = $100k × 3.791 = $379.1k

Sensitivity = $320k/$379.1k = 84.4%

Answer = C

Question 14.2

Net Present Value of the project = $180 000

Present value of the annual cash outflow = $100 000 × 3.312 = $331 200

Sensitivity = $180 000/$331 200 = 54.3%

Answer = A

Question 14.3

You should refer to Learning Note 14.1 on the CourseMate online resources that accompany this book for an explanation of the annualized equivalent method.

		Van A		Van B	
Year	Discount Factor @ 8%	Cash Flows $	Present Value $	Cash Flows $	Present value $
0	1.000	(25 000)	(25 000)	(30 000)	(30 000)
1	0.926	(2 000)	(1 852)	(3 000)	(2 778)
2	0.857	(2 000)	(1 714)	(3 000)	(2 571)
3	0.794	(3 000)	(2 382)	(3 000)	(2 382)
4	0.735	5 000	3 675	(4 000)	(2 940)
5	0.681			6 000	4 086
Present Value			(27 273)		(36 585)

Cumulative discount factors   3.312 (4 years)   3.993 (5 years)

Equivalent annual cost (PV/cum. disc. factor) $8 234 (van A), $9 162 (van B)

Van A should be replaced because it has the lowest annual equivalent cost

Question 14.4

(a) Expected value of the annual sales = (4m × 0.2) + (£5m × 0.4) + (£7m × 0.3) + (£10m × 0.1) = £5.9m

The market research survey (note vii) is a sunk cost.

Cash flows £'000s	Year 0	1	2	3	4	5	6
Purchase of company	(400)						
Legal/professional		(20)	(20)	(20)	(20)	(20)	

Cash flows £'000s	Year 0	1	2	3	4	5	6
Lease rentals		(12)	(12)	(12)	(12)	(12)	
Studio hire		(540)	(540)	(702)	(702)	(702)	
Camera hire		(120)	(120)	(120)	(120)	(120)	
Technical staff		(1560)	(1716)	(1888)	(2077)	(2285)	
Screenplay		(150)	(173)	(199)	(229)	(263)	
Actors' salaries		(2100)	(2310)	(2541)	(2795)	(3074)	
Costumes/wardrobe		(180)	(180)	(180)	(180)	(180)	
Non production staff wages		(60)	(66)	(73)	(80)	(88)	
Set design		(450)	(450)	(450)	(450)	(450)	
Lost income from office accommodation		(20)	(20)	(20)	(20)	(20)	
Sales		5900	6195	6505	6830	7172	
Cash flow before tax	(400)	688	588	300	145	(42)	
Tax		—	(227)	(194)	(99)	(48)	14
Net cash flow	(400)	688	361	106	46	(90)	14
Disc. factor	1	0.877	0.769	0.675	0.592	0.519	0.456
PV cash flow	(400)	603	278	72	27	(47)	6

NPV = £539 000

(b) Limitations of expected values include:

   (1) Expected values represent average outcomes based on the assumption that decisions will be repeated but a specific investment decision is likely to occur once so the average outcome is unlikely to occur.

   (2) Deriving probabilities is highly subjective.

   (3) Expected values do not take into account the range of outcomes. A probability distribution is likely to provide more meaningful information.

For a more detailed discussion of the above points you should refer to the sections on probability distributions and expected values and measuring the amount of uncertainty in Chapter 12.

(c) (i) See 'Profitability index' in Chapter 14 for the answer to this question.

   (ii) Profitability index = Present value/investment outlay

$$\text{Profitability index for the filmmaking acquisition} = \frac{\text{NPV (£539 000)} + \text{Investment outlay (£400 000)}}{\text{Investment outlay (£400 000)}}$$

$$= 2.347$$

Investment X present value:

   $(200 \times 0.877) + (200 \times 0.769) + (150 \times 0.675) + (100 \times 0.592) + (100 \times 0.519) + (100 \times 0.456) = £587$

Profitability index = £587/200 = 2.935

Investment Y present value:

   $(80 \times 0.877) + (80 \times 0.769) + (40 \times 0.675) + (40 \times 0.592) + (40 \times 0.519) + (40 \times 0.456) = £221$

Profitability index = £221/100 = 2.21

Given that projects are indivisible the choice is between:

   (1) Investing in X and Y, yielding an NPV of £508 000 (587 + 221 − 300 investment outlay). The un-utilized funds of £100 000 can only be reinvested to obtain a zero NPV.

   (2) Investing all of the £400 000 in the filmmaking company yielding an NPV of £539 000.

The company should choose to invest in the filmmaking company.

   (iii) For a discussion of the limitations of the profitability index you should refer to the final paragraph in the section on capital rationing in Chapter 14. In addition, the answer should point out that the profitability index does not take into account:

   (1) How projects interact to reduce risk or to provide a strategic alignment such as the vertical integration that may occur with the purchase of the filmmaking company.

   (2) Problems can occur when projects are indivisible and the strict application of this method can result in misleading decisions. For example, investment X has the highest profitability index but it is clearly preferable to not invest in this project since it will not lead to the maximization of NPV when funds are restricted to £400 000.

(d) See 'Taxation and investment decisions' in Chapter 14 for the answer to this question.

Question 14.5

(a) It is assumed that all of the cash flows will increase at the general rate of inflation so that estimates in current prices at the time of appraising the investment will be equal to real cash flows. Real cash flows must be discounted at a real discount rate but the question includes a nominal required rate of return (i.e. discount rate). Therefore we must convert the nominal discount rate to a real discount rate using the following formula:

$$1 + \text{nominal rate} = (1 + \text{real rate}) \times (1 + \text{anticipated rate of inflation})$$

so that $(1 + \text{real rate}) = 1 + \text{nominal rate}/(1 + \text{anticipated rate of inflation})$

giving a real rate of 8 per cent $(1.14/1.055) = 1.08$

$$\text{Contribution per box sold} = £20 - (£8 + £2 + £1.50 + £2) = £6.50$$

Allocated fixed overheads do not represent incremental cash flows and are therefore not relevant to the decision. The annual cash flows are 150 000 boxes $\times$ £6.50 $\times$ $(1 - \text{corporate tax rate} (0.33)) = £653 250$. The annual cash flows are constant so the cumulative discount (i.e. annuity tables) in Appendix 2 of the text can be used.

$$\text{NPV} = (£653\,250 \times 3.993) - £2m = £608\,428$$

$\text{IRR} = (\text{annual cash flows}) \times (\text{the cumulative discount factor at x\% for five years}) - \text{investment outlay} = 0$

so that IRR is where the cumulative discount factor at x% for five years = Investment outlay $(£2m)/£653\,250 = 3.062$.

If you examine the five-year row in Appendix 2 you will find that the figure closest to 3.062 appears between 18 and 20 per cent. Therefore the IRR is approximately 19 per cent.

Because the project has a positive NPV and the IRR exceeds the real cost of capital of 8 per cent the project is acceptable.

(b) See 'Sensitivity analysis' in Chapter 14 for the answer to this question.

(c) (i) *Price (P)*

$$\text{NPV} = 0 = 0.15m(P - £13.50)(1 - 0.33)(AF_{8\%,\,5}) - £2m$$
$$= 0 = (0.15mP - £2025m)\,2.675 - £2m$$
$$= 0 = £0.401mP - 5.417m - 2m$$
$$0.401mP = 7.417m$$
$$P = £18.50$$

Therefore the price can drop by £1.50 (or 7.5 per cent) before NPV becomes negative.

Note:

$AF_{8\%,\,5} = $ Annuity factor at 8 per cent for five years

(ii) *Volume (V)*

$$\text{NPV} = 0 = V(£20 - £13.50)\,(1 - 0.33)\,(AF_{8\%,\,5}) - £2m$$
$$= 0 = £6.50V(2.675) - £2m$$
$$= 0 = £17.3875V - £2m$$
$$V = £2m/17.3875$$
$$V = 115\,025$$

Therefore volume can drop by 34 975 boxes (150 000 − 115 025) or 23 per cent before NPV becomes negative.

The results suggest that the NPV of the project is more sensitive to price variations than to changes in volume. The company therefore should review the estimated price to ensure that it is confident that prices will not decline by more than seven per cent. If prices decline by more than seven per cent, and the other variables remain unchanged, the project will yield a negative NPV. Consideration should be given to advertising to ensure that demand is maintained at the proposed price but it should be noted that NPV will decline by the amount spent on advertising.

Question 14.6

Advanced

The expected value of number of visitors per year is:

$$(1.2m \times 30\%) + (0.8m \times 50\%) + (0.6m \times 20\%) = 880k$$

Contribution per visitor = $35 ($60 − $25)

Total contribution for year 1 = $35 \times 880k \times 1.04 = $32\,032k$. The total contributions for the remaining years are calculated by inflating the year 1 figure by 4 per cent per annum.

Year 1 Fixed maintenance costs = $200k \times 1.04 = $208k$. Maintenance costs for the remaining years are calculated by inflating the year 1 figure by 4 per cent per annum.

Cash Flows

	Year 1 $000	Year 2 $000	Year 3 $000	Year 4 $000	Year 5 $000
Contribution	32 032	33 313	34 646	36 032	37 473
Lease costs	(500)	(500)	(500)	(500)	(500)
Maintenance costs	(208)	(216)	(225)	(234)	(243)
Net cash flows	31 324	32 597	33 921	35 298	36 730

Taxation

	Year 1 $000	Year 2 $000	Year 3 $000	Year 4 $000	Year 5 $000
Net cash flows	31 324	32 597	33 921	35 298	36 730
Tax Depreciation	(30 000)	(22 500)	(16 875)	(12 656)	12 031
Taxable profit	1 324	10 097	17 046	22 642	48 761
Taxation @ 30%	(397)	(3 029)	(5 114)	(6 793)	(14 628)

Note that the tax depreciation (WDAs) are calculated at 25 per cent on a reducing balance basis:

Year 1 = 0.25 × $120m, Year 2 = 0.25 × ($120m − $30m), Year 3 = 0.25 × ($120m − $52.5m), Year 4 = 0.25 × ($120m − $69.375m), Year 5 = Net cost of $70m − accumulated depreciation of $82 031 resulting in a balancing charge of $12 031m)

Net present value

	Year 0 $000	Year 1 $000	Year 2 $000	Year 3 $000	Year 4 $000	Year 5 $000	Year 6 $000
Structure cost	(120 000)					50 000	
Net cash flows	0	31 324	32 597	33 921	35 298	36 730	
Tax payment	0	(198)	(1 514)	(2 557)	(3 396)	(7 314)	
Tax payment		0	(199)	(1 515)	(2 557)	(3 397)	(7 314)
Net cash flow after tax	(120 000)	31 126	30 884	29 849	29 345	76 019	(7 314)
Discount factors @ 12%	1.000	0.893	0.797	0.712	0.636	0.567	0.507
Present value	(120 000)	27 796	24 615	21 252	18 663	43 103	(3 708)

The project should be accepted since it has a positive NPV of $11 721.

(b) (i)

Net cash flow after tax	(120 000)	31 126	30 884	29 849	29 345	76 019	(7 314)
Discount factors @ 20%	1.000	0.833	0.694	0.579	0.482	0.402	0.335
Present value	(120 000)	25 928	21 433	17 283	14 144	30 560	(2 450)

NPV = − $13 102

By interpolation

IRR = 12% + ($11 721/($11 721 + $13 102)) × (20% − 12%)

IRR = 12% + 3.78%

IRR = 15.78%

(ii)

Year	Cash flow	Cumulative cash flow
0	(120 000)	(120 000)
1	31 126	(88 874)
2	30 884	(57 990)
3	29 849	(28 141)
4	29 345	1 204

Payback period = 3 years + ((28 141/29 345) × 12)
= 3 years 11.5 months

(c) See 'The effects of inflation on capital investment decisions' in Chapter 14 for the answer to this question. Note that the terms 'money cost of capital and real cost of capital' are equivalent to the terms 'money and real rate of returns' used in the text.

Question 14.7

Advanced

(a) Other cash fixed costs are $2.6m per annum ($10.6m − $8m depreciation)

$$\text{Annual depreciation} = (\$60m - \$12m)/6 = \$8m$$

The expected future costs of external environmental failure cost savings are:

$$(\$18m \times 0.3) + (\$12m \times 0.25) + (\$10m \times 0.35) + (\$5m \times 0.1) = \$12.4m$$

Expected Savings = $20m − $12.4m = $7.6m per annum

The net cash flows for years 1 – 6 are:

$$\$18.1m - \$1.5m \text{ fixed maintenance costs} - \$2.6m \text{ other fixed costs} = \$14.0m$$

Taxation

	Year 1 $m	Year 2 $m	Year 3 $m	Year 4 $m	Year 5 $m	Year 6 $m
Net cash flows	14	14	14	14	14	14
Tax Depreciation	(15)	(11.3)	(8.4)	(6.3)	(4.8)	(2.2)
Taxable profit	(1)	2.7	5.6	7.7	9.2	11.8
Taxation @ 30%	0.3	(0.8)	(1.7)	(2.3)	(2.8)	(3.5)

Note that the tax depreciation (WDAs) are calculated at 25 per cent on a reducing balance basis:

Year 1 = 0.25 × $60m, Year 2 = 0.25 × ($60m − $15m), Year 3 = 0.25 × ($60m − $26.3m), Year 4 = 0.25 × ($60m − $34.7m), Year 5 = 0.25 × ($60m − $41m), Year 6 = Net cost of $48m − accumulated depreciation of $45.8 resulting in a balancing allowance of $2.2m).

Net present value

	Year 0 $m	Year 1 $m	Year 2 $m	Year 3 $m	Year 4 $m	Year 5 $m	Year 6 $m	Year 7 $m
Investment/residual value	(60)						12	
Net cash flows		14	14	14	14	14	14	
Tax payment		0.2	(0.4)	(0.9)	(1.2)	(1.4)	(1.8)	
Tax payment			0.1	(0.4)	(0.8)	(1.1)	(1.4)	(1.7)
Net cash flow after tax	(60)	14.2	13.7	12.7	12.0	11.5	22.8	(1.7)
Discount factors @ 12%	1.000	0.893	0.797	0.712	0.636	0.567	0.507	0.452
Present value	(60)	12.7	10.9	9.0	7.6	6.5	11.6	(0.8)

The project has a negative NPV of $2.5m and should be rejected.

(b) (i)

Payback

Year	Cash flows $m	Cumulative cash flows $m
0	(60)	(60)
1	14.2	(45.8)
2	13.7	(32.1)
3	12.7	(19.4)
4	12.0	(7.4)
5	11.5	4.1
6	22.8	26.9
7	(1.7)	25.2

$$\text{Payback period} = 4 \text{ years} + ((7.4/11.5) \times 12)$$
$$= 4 \text{ years } 8 \text{ months}$$

(ii) See 'Payback method' in Chapter 13 for the answer to this question.

(c) There following environmental factors that are difficult to quantify should be taken into account:
- The potential impact on the image of the company and future sales from being seen as an environmentally friendly company.
- The pressure from government and other stakeholders to improve environmental management.
- Potential benefits relating to the external social environmental costs arising from pollution and its impact on health care and the global environment.

Question 14.8

Advanced

Investment costs

$200 000 per limousine × 20 = $4 000 000
Residual value = $30 000 × 20 = $600 000

Fixed costs

Depreciation per per annum = ($200 000 − $30 000)/5 = $34 000
Other fixed costs (excluding depreciation) per annum
$45 000 − $34 000 = $11 000 per limousine
$11 000 × 20 limousines = $220 000
Administration costs = $300 000
The head office and garaging charges are not relevant costs.

Contribution for years 1 – 5

Contribution per limousine per day = $500 ($800 − $300)

Total contribution per day = $500 × 20 = $10 000

Total contribution per year:

Year 1 = 260 days × $10 000 = $2 600 000
Year 2 = 270 days × $10 000 = $2 700 000
Year 3 = 280 days × $10 000 = $2 800 000
Year 4 = 290 days × $10 000 = $2 900 000
Year 5 = 300 days × $10 000 = $3 000 000

Cash flows

	Year 1 $k	Year 2 $k	Year 3 $k	Year 4 $k	Year 5 $k
Contribution	2 600	2 700	2 800	2 900	3 000
Other fixed operating costs	(220)	(220)	(220)	(220)	(220)
Administration costs	(300)	(300)	(300)	(300)	(300)
Net cash flows	2 080	2 180	2 280	2 380	2 480

Taxation

	Year 1 $k	Year 2 $k	Year 3 $k	Year 4 $k	Year 5 $k
Net cash flows	2 080	2 180	2 280	2 380	2 480
Tax Depreciation	(1 000)	(750)	(563)	(422)	(665)
Taxable profit	1 080	1 430	1 717	1 958	1 815
Taxation @ 30%	324	429	515	587	545

Note that the tax depreciation (WDA's) are calculated at 25 per cent on a reducing balance basis:

Year 1 = 0.25 × $4m, Year 2 = 0.25 × ($4m − $1m), Year 3 = 0.25 × ($4m − $1.75m), Year 4 = 0.25 × ($4m − $2.313m), Year 5 = Net cost of $3.4m − accumulated depreciation of $2.735 resulting in a balancing allowance of $0.665m).

Net present value

	Year 0 $k	Year 1 $k	Year 2 $k	Year 3 $k	Year 4 $k	Year 5 $k	Year 6 $k
Investment/residual value	(4 000)					600	
Net cash flows		2 080	2 180	2 280	2 380	2 480	
Tax payment		(162)	(215)	(258)	(294)	(273)	
Tax payment			(162)	(214)	(257)	(293)	(272)
Net cash flow after tax	(4 000)	1 918	1 803	1 808	1 829	2 514	(272)
Discount factors @ 12%	1.000	0.893	0.797	0.712	0.636	0.567	0.507
Present value	(4 000)	1 713	1 437	1 287	1 163	1 425	(138)

The investment has a positive NPV of $2 887 000 and should therefore be undertaken.

(b) You should refer to Learning Note 14.1 on the CourseMate online resources that accompany this book for an explanation of the annualized equivalent method.

		Replace after Year 1		Replace after Year 2		Replace after Year 3	
Year	Discount Factor @ 12%	Cash flows $	Present value $	Cash flows $	Present value $	Cash flows $	Present value $
0	1.00	(30 000)	(30 000)	(30 000)	(30 000)	(30 000)	(30 000)
1	0.893	19 500	17 414	(1 500)	(1 340)	(1 500)	(1 340)
2	0.797			12 300	9 803	(2 700)	(2 152)
3	0.712					5 400	3 845
Net present value			(12 586)		(21 537)		(29 647)
Cumulative discount factor			0.893		1.690		2.402
Annualized equivalent			(14 094)		(12 744)		(12 343)

Since the lowest annualized equivalent cost occurs when the vehicles are kept for three years the optimum replacement cycle is to replace the vehicles every three years.

(c) The annualized equivalent method assumes that identical assets are replaced each time and that this process continues until a common time horizon is reached for the potential replacement periods under consideration. This assumption ignores changing technology and the possibility of replacing assets with more efficient up to date models. The method also ignores the impact of inflation which may differ for each replacement period.

Question 14.9

(a) *Calculation of expected NPV (£000)*

Year	0	1	2	3	4	5	6
Investment outlay	(1 500)						
Sales at £2 per unit		3 000	3 000	3 000	3 000	3 000	3 000
Variable costs at £1.59 per unit[a]		2 385	2 385	2 385	2 385	2 385	2 385
Taxable cash flows		615	615	615	615	615	615
Tax at 35%		215	215	215	215	215	215
Net cash flow[b]	(1 500)	400	400	400	400	400	400

NPV at a discount rate of 8%[c] = (£400 × 4.623) − £1500 = £349 200

Notes:

[a]Unit variable cost = Purchase cost (£1.50 × 40%) + copyright fee (20% × £3.95) + £0.20 additional variable cost.

[b]Market research is a sunk cost.

[c]See part (b) of the answer for an explanation of why a discount rate of 8 per cent has been used. Note that the financing costs are incorporated in the discount rate and should not be included in the cash flows as this would lead to double counting.

(b) Assuming that the company wishes to maintain its current capital structure the specific cost of financing the project should not be used as a discount rate. The project has been financed by a bank loan but this will result in less borrowing being used in the future as the company re-balances its finance to achieve the target capital structure. To reflect the company's target capital structure the weighted average cost of capital (WACC) should be used.

The money WACC should be used only if the cash flows are expressed in money/nominal terms (i.e. adjusted for inflation). Current cash flows have been used to calculate NPV. Current cash flows are equivalent to real cash flow when all cash flows increase at the general rate of inflation. This situation occurs in this question and therefore the cash flows are equivalent to real cash flows. Thus the real WACC of capital should be used to discount the cash flows.

The WACC represents the discount rate applicable for the company as a whole and reflects the average risk of all of the company's assets. If the project has a different level of risk from the average risk of the assets of the company as a whole, the existing WACC will not represent the appropriate discount rate. In this situation a separate risk adjusted discount rate should be used.

It is also assumed that all of the cash flows increase at the general rate of inflation. If the cash flows are subject to different rates of inflation it will be incorrect to use current prices. If this situation occurs the cash flows should be adjusted by their specific rates of inflation and a nominal discount rate should be used.

(c) (i) *Initial outlay*

The NPV of the project is £349 200. Therefore the investment outlay could increase by £349 200 before NPV becomes negative. This represents a percentage increase of 23.28 per cent (£349.2/£1500 × 100).

Annual contribution

Let x = annual contribution

With a corporate tax rate of 35 per cent the annual contribution at which NPV will be zero can be calculated from the following formula:

$(1 - 0.35) \, 4.623x - £1500 = 0$
$3.005x - 1500 \qquad\qquad = 0$
$x = 1500/3.005 \qquad\quad = £499.16$

Therefore annual contribution can decline from the existing figure of £615 000 to £499 160. A percentage decrease of 18.83 per cent (£115.84/£615 × 100). Note that 4.623 and check text has Appendix B £1500 in the above formula represents the cumulative discount factor and the investment outlay.

The life of the agreement

Let x = annuity factor at 8 per cent

NPV will be zero where

$400x - £1500 = 0$
$\qquad\quad x = 3.75$

From the annuity table shown in Appendix B of the text:

PV of annuity for four years at 8 per cent = 3.312
PV of annuity for five years at 8 per cent = 3.993

Extrapolating, the PV annuity factor is:

$$4 \text{ years} + \frac{3.75 - 3.312}{3.993 - 3.312} \times 1 \text{ year} = 4.643 \text{ years}$$

This represents a reduction of 22.61% [(6 − 4.643)/6 years × 100]

Discount rate

Let x = PV of annuity for six years

NPV will be zero where:

$$400x = 1500$$
$$x = 3.75$$

From the annuity tables (Appendix B) 15 per cent has a PV annuity factor of 3.784 and 16 per cent is 3.685. Thus the discount rate at which NPV will be zero is approximately 15.5 per cent. This represents an increase of 93.75 per cent [(15.5 − 8)/8 × 100]. The above calculations indicate that the annual contribution is the most sensitive variable.

(d) See 'Sensitivity Analysis' in Chapter 14 for an outline of the limitations of sensitivity analysis.

(e) Possible additional information includes:

(i) Is the agreement likely to be renewed after six years?

(ii) Are competitors likely to enter the market and what impact would this have on the sales volume and price?

(iii) How accurate are the estimated cash flows?

(iv) How reliable is the supplier who supplies microfiche readers? Can the microfiche readers be obtained from any other source or is the company dependent upon the one supplier?

The budgeting process

Solutions to Chapter 15 questions

Question 15.1

	Kg
Materials required to meet production requirements (7 200 × 3kg)	21 600
Add budgeted closing stock	500
Less opening stock	(400)
Budgeted purchases	21 700

Answer = D

Question 15.2

Materials usage

12 000 units × 4kg = 48 000kg

Opening inventory = 3 000kg

Closing inventory = 12 000/12 × 4kg × 1.1 = 4 400kg

Material purchases budget (kg)	
Material usage	48 000kg
Plus closing inventory	4 400kg
Less opening inventory	(3 000)kg
	49 400kg

Material purchases budget ($)		
49 000kg × $8	=	$392 000
400kg × $7.50	=	$3 000
Total		$395 000

Question 15.3

(a) For a description of six objectives of budgeting (planning, coordination, communication, motivation, control and performance evaluation) see 'the multiple functions of budgets' in Chapter 15.

(b) See 'participation in the budgeting and target setting process' in Chapter 16 for the answer to this question. In particular the following items should be included for each of the objectives:

Planning – Should be more accurate since budgets are prepared by managers for areas within their control so the managers should have greater knowledge of the activities.

Coordination – Encourages communication between budgetees and their superiors thus making the budgeting process more effective.

Communication – The budget negotiation process required with participation will ensure that the objectives of the budgets are communicated to all budget holders. See 'negotiation of budgets' in Chapter 15 for a more detailed answer.

Motivation – Managers are more likely to strive to achieve budgets that they have been involved in setting but care should be taken that budgetees do not deliberately set targets that are too easy to achieve.

Control – comparison of actual with budget is essential whether or not participation is used. Budgetees are more motivated to take appropriate remedial action if actual outcomes differ from targets that they have been involved in setting.

Performance evaluation – Managers will be more likely to accept the evaluation as fair when they are compared with targets the budgetees have been involved in setting.

Question 15.4

The main advantage of incremental budgets is that they are simple to prepare, not too time consuming and impose a limit on spending. With incremental budgets the current budgeted allowance for existing activities is taken as the base level for preparing the budget. The base level is then adjusted for known changes and inflation. Therefore the cost of past activities becomes fixed and any inefficiencies or wastage is incorporated in the budgets. The incremental approach can also encourage budget holders to spend this year's budget to ensure that next year's budget will be as high as possible. The incremental approach therefore does not encourage managers to focus on the efficiency and effectiveness of activities undertaken.

Question 15.5

Zero based budgeting (ZBB) is best suited to allocating resources and controlling discretionary costs such as research and development costs. The major disadvantages of ZBB are that it is very costly and time consuming to implement.

ZBB involves:

- a description of each organizational activity in a decision package;
- the evaluation and ranking of decision packages in order of priority;
- allocation of resources based on order of priority up to the spending cut-off level.

The process of identifying decision packages and determining their purpose, cost and benefits is extremely time-consuming. Requesting funds for projects that do not have clearly defined benefits is difficult to implement in practice. Also there are often too many decision packages to evaluate and there is frequently insufficient information to enable them to be ranked.

A possible solution is to approximate the principles of ZBB rather than applying the full-scale approach using priority-based incremental budgets. Priority incremental budgets require managers to specify what incremental activities or changes would occur if their budgets were increased or decreased by a specified percentage (say 10 per cent). Budget allocations are made by comparing the change in costs with the change in benefits. Priority incremental budgets thus represent an economical compromise between ZBB and incremental budgeting.

Question 15.6

(a) Incremental budgeting uses the previous year's budget as the starting point for the preparation of next year's budget. It is assumed that the basic structure of the budget will remain unchanged and that adjustments will be made to allow for changes in volume, efficiency and price levels. The budget is therefore concerned with increments to operations that will occur during the period and the focus is on existing use of resources rather than considering alternative strategies for the future budget period. Incremental budgeting suffers from the following weaknesses:

(i) it perpetuates past inefficiencies;

(ii) there is insufficient focus on improving efficiency and effectiveness;

(iii) the resource allocation tends to be based on existing strategies rather than considering future strategies;

(iv) it tends to focus excessively on the short term and often leads to arbitrary cuts being made in order to achieve short-term financial targets.

(b) See 'Activity-based budgeting' in Chapter 15 for the answer to this question. In particular, the answer should stress that:

(i) the focus is on managing activities;

(ii) the focus is on the resources that are required for undertaking activities and identifying those activity resources that are unutilized or which are insufficient to meet the requirements specified in the budget;

(iii) attention is given to eliminating non-value-added activities;

(iv) the focus is on the control of the causes of costs (i.e. the cost drivers).

For a more detailed discussion of some of the above points you should also refer to 'Activity-based management' in Chapter 21.

Question 15.7

(a) *Cumbersome process*

The answer to the first comment in the question should include a very brief summary of 'Stages in the budgeting process' in Chapter 15. The process involves detailed negotiations between the budget holders and their superiors and the accountancy staff.

Because the process is very time consuming it must be started well before the start of the budget year. Subsequent changes in the environment, and the fact that the outcomes reflected in the master budget may not meet financial targets, may necessitate budget revisions and a repeat of the negotiation process. The renegotiating stage may well be omitted because of time constraints. Instead, across the board cost reductions may be imposed to meet the budget targets.

Concentration on short-term financial control

Short-term financial targets are normally set for the budget year and the budget is used as the mechanism for achieving the targets. Budget adjustments are made to ensure that the targets are achieved often with little consideration being given to the impact such adjustments will have on the longer-term plans.

Undesirable motivation effects on managers

Managers are often rewarded or punished based on their budget performance in terms of achieving or exceeding the budget. There is a danger that the budget will be viewed as a punitive device rather than as an aid to managers in managing their areas of responsibility. This can result in dysfunctional consequences such as attempting to build slack into the budgeting system by overstating costs and understating revenues. Alternatively, cuts may be made in discretionary expenses which could have adverse long-term consequences. The overriding aim becomes to achieve the budget, even if this is done in a manner that is not in the organization's best interests.

Emphasizing formal organizational structure

Budgets are normally structured around functional responsibility centres, such as departments and business units. A functional structure is likely to encourage bureaucracy and slow responses to environmental and competitive changes. There is a danger that there will be a lack of goal congruence and that managers may focus on their own departments to the detriment of the organization. Also if budgets are extended to the lower levels of the organization employees will focus excessively on meeting the budget and this may constrain their activities in terms of the flexibility that is required when dealing with customers.

(b) *Cumbersome process*

Managers could be given greater flexibility on how they will meet their targets. For example, top management might agree specific targets with the managers and the managers given authority to achieve the targets in their own way. Detailed budgets are not required and the emphasis is placed on managers achieving their overall targets.

Another alternative is to reduce the budget planning period by implementing a system of continuous or rolling budgets.

Concentration on short-term financial control

This might be overcome by placing more stress on a manager's long-term performance and adopting a profit-conscious style of budget evaluation (see 'Side effects from using accounting information for performance evaluation' in Chapter 16) and also placing more emphasis on participative budgeting (see 'Participation in the budget process' in Chapter 16). Attention should also be given to widening the performance measurement system and focusing on key result areas that deal with both short-term and long-term considerations. In particular a balanced scorecard approach (see Chapter 22) might be adopted.

Undesirable motivation effects on managers

The same points as those made above (i.e. profit-conscious style of evaluation, participative budgeting and a broader range of performance measures) also apply here. In addition, the rewards and punishment system must be changed so that it is linked to a range of performance criteria rather than being dominated by short-term financial budget performance. Consideration could also be given to changing the reward system from focusing on responsibility centre performance to rewards being based on overall company performance.

Emphasizing formal organizational structure

Here the answer could discuss activity-based budgeting with the emphasis being on activity centres and business processes, rather than functional responsibility centres that normally consist of departments. For a discussion of these issues you should refer to 'Activity-based budgeting' in Chapter 15 and 'Activity-based cost management' in Chapter 21. Consideration should also be given to converting cost centres to profit centres and establishing a system of internal transfer prices. This would encourage managers to focus more widely on profits rather than just costs. Finally, budgets should not be extended to lower levels of the organization and more emphasis should be given to empowering employees to manage their own activities (see 'Employee empowerment' in Chapter 1).

Question 15.8

(a) See 'Incremental budgeting' and 'Zero-based budgeting' in Chapter 15 for the answer to this question. Note that incremental budgeting is described within the section on activity-based budgeting.

(b) The answer should draw off the material within the section on zero-based budgeting and point out that projects should be identified as decision packages and ranked on a cost versus benefits basis with resources allocated according to the ranking up to the spending cut-off level.

(c) See 'Activity-based budgeting' in Chapter 15 for the answer to this question.

Question 15.9

Production Budget in units

	Quarter 1	Quarter 2	Quarter 3	Quarter 4	Total
Required by Sales	2250	2050	1650	2050	8000
Plus required Closing inventory	615	495	615	375	375
Less opening inventory	−675	−615	−495	−615	−675
Production Budget	2190	1930	1770	1810	7700

Raw Materials purchases budget

Material B	Quarter 1 kg	Quarter 2 kg	Quarter 3 kg	Quarter 4 kg	Total kg
Required by production	6570	5790	5310	5430	23100
Plus required Closing inventory	2605.50	2389.50	2443.50	2011.50	2011.50
Less opening inventory	−2956.50	−2605.50	−2389.50	−2443.50	−2956.50
Material Purchases Budget	6219	5574	5364	4998	22155
Value	£43533	£39018	£37548	£34986	£155085

(b) If material A is in short supply the company will need to obtain an alternative source of supply or find a substitute material. If they are unable to do this they will need to use limiting factor analysis (see Chapter 9) to determine the optimum output level. In this situation sales will not be the limiting factor and the production budget will become the key budget factor in the budget preparation process.

(c) It is assumed that the flexible budget statement does not require the inclusion of direct materials. The statement is as follows:

Operating Statement

	Fixed Budget	Flexed Budget	Actual	Flexible Budget Variance
Activity	7700	7250	7250	
Overheads	£	£	£	£
Variable	168000	158182	185000	26818 advance
Fixed	112000	112000	105000	7000 favourable
Labour				
Skilled	462000	435000	568750	133750 adverse
Semi-skilled	415800	391500	332400	59100 favourable
	1157800	1096682	1191150	94468 adverse

Note that the fixed and variable overheads for the fixed budget are respectively £112000 (40% × £240000) and £168000 (60% × £240000). The variable overhead rate per unit of output is £21.818 (£168000/7700 units). This rate per unit is multiplied by 7250 units to obtain the flexible budget allowance for variable overheads.

(d) See 'zero-based budgeting' (ZBB) in Chapter 15 for the answer to this question. In particular, the answer should point out that with incremental budgeting the budget process uses the previous year's budget or actual results and adjusts for anticipated changes in the budget period. Thus past inefficiencies are incorporated in the budget. In contrast, ZBB starts from base zero and requires each cost element to be specifically justified as if the budgeted activities were being undertaken for the first time.

(e) See 'the budget process' in Chapter 15 for the answer to this question. The answer should point out that rolling budgets are particularly useful when it is difficult to forecast future costs/activities accurately. Given that the company is experiencing an increase in competition and a shortage of raw materials it may need to react speedily to these factors in terms of competitive responses and sourcing alternative supplies. In these circumstances rolling budgets may be preferable.

Question 15.10

(a) *Workings*

Budgeted sales (units and value)

Product	Units	Price	Value (£)
F1	34 000	£50.00	1 700 000
F2	58 000	£30.00	1 740 000
			3 440 000

Budgeted production (units)

Product	Sales	Stock increase	Production
F1	34 000	1 000	35 000
F2	58 000	2 000	60 000

(i) Component purchase and usage budget (units and value)

Product	Component C3	Component C4	Total
F1	280 000u	140 000u	
F2	240 000u	180 000u	
	520 000u	320 000u	
Value	£650 000	£576 000	£1 226 000

(ii) Direct labour budget (hours and value)

Product	Assembly	Finishing	Total
F1	17 500 hours	7 000 hours	
F2	15 000 hours	10 000 hours	
	32 500	17 000	
Value	£325 500	£204 000	£5 29 000

(iii) Departmental manufacturing overhead recovery rates

	Assembly	Finishing
Total overhead cost per month	£617 500	£204 000
Total direct labour hours	32 500	17 000
Overhead rate (per direct labour hour)	£19.00	£12.00

(iv) Selling overhead recovery rate

Total overhead cost per month	£344 000
Total sales value (month 9)	£3 440 000
Selling overhead rate	10%

(v) Closing stock budget

Product	Units	Cost[a] £	Value £
F1	1 000	36.50	36 500
F2	2 000	21.65	43 300
			79 800

Note:

[a]See part (b) for the calculation of the cost per unit

(b) Standard unit costs for month 9

			F1 £/unit		F2 £/unit
			Product		
Material	C3	8 × £1.25	10.00	4 × £1.25	5.00
	C4	4 × £1.80	7.20	3 × £1.80	5.40
Labour	Assembly	30/60 × £10	5.00	15/60 × £10	2.50
	Finishing	12/60 × £12	2.40	10/60 × £12	2.00
M'fg. overhead	Assembly	30/60 × £19	9.50	15/60 × £19	4.75
	Finishing	12/60 × £12	2.40	10/60 × £12	2.00
Manufacturing	cost		36.50		21.65
Selling overhead (10 per cent of selling price)			5.00		3.00
Total cost			41.50		24.65
Selling price			50.00		30.00
Profit			8.50		5.35

(c) Budgeted profit and loss account for month 9

	(£)
Components	1 226 000
Direct labour	529 000
Manufacturing overhead	821 500
Subtotal	2 576 500
Less closing stock	79 800
Cost of sales	2 496 700
Selling overhead	344 000
Total cost	2 840 700
Sales	3 440 000
Net profit	599 300

(d) The company currently uses an absorption costing system but computes predetermined overhead rates on a monthly basis. It is preferable to calculate a predetermined overhead rate at annual intervals. This is because a large amount of overheads are likely to be fixed in the short-term whereas activity will fluctuate from month to month, giving large fluctuations in overhead rates if monthly rates are used. An average, annualized rate based on the relationship of total annual overhead to total annual activity is more representative of typical relationships between total costs and volume/activity than a monthly rate. For a more detailed discussion of these issues you should refer to 'Budgeted overhead rates' in Chapter 3.

Question 15.11

(a) *Raw materials:*

(Units)	March	April	May	June
Opening stock	100	110	115	110
Add: Purchases	80	80	85	85
	180	190	200	195
Less: Used in production	70	75	90	90
Closing stock	110	115	110	105
(Units) *Finished production*:				
Opening stock	110	100	91	85
Add: Production	70	75	90	90
	180	175	181	175
Less: Sales	80	84	96	94
Closing stock	100	91	85	81

(b) *Sales*:

					Total
(at £219 per unit) *Production cost:*	£17 520	£18 396	£21 024	£20 586	£77 526
Raw materials (using FIFO)	3 024 (1)	3 321 (2)	4 050	4 050	14 445
Wages and variable costs	4 550	4 875	5 850	5 850	21 125
	£7 574	£8 196	£9 900	£9 900	£35 570

Debtors:

Closing debtors = May + June sales = £41 610

Creditors:

June purchases 85 units × £45 £3825

Notes:

(1) 70 units × £4320/100 units = £3024.

(2) (30 units × £4320/100 units + (45 units × £45) = £3321.

Closing stocks:

Raw materials 105 units × £45	£4725
Finished goods 81 units × £110[1]	£8910

Note:

[1]Materials (£45) + Labour and Variable Overhead (£65). It is assumed that stocks are valued on a variable costing basis.

(c) *Cash budget:*

	March (£)	April (£)	May (£)	June (£)
Balance b/fwd	6 790	4 820	5 545	132 415
Add: Receipts				
Debtors (two months' credit)	7 680	10 400	17 520	18 396
Loan	—	—	120 000	—
	(A) 14 470	15 220	143 065	150 811
Payments:				
Creditors (one month's credit)	3 900	3 600	3 600	3 825
		(80 × £45)		
Wages and variable overheads	4 550	4 875	5 850	5 850
Fixed overheads	1 200	1 200	1 200	1 200
Machinery	—	—	—	112 000
Interim dividend	—	—	—	12 500
	(B) 9 650	9 675	10 650	135 375
Balance c/fwd	(A) − (B) 4 820	5 545	132 415	£15 436

(d) *Master budget:*

Budgeted trading and profit and loss account for the four months to 30 June

	(£)	(£)
Sales		77 526
Cost of sales: Opening stock finished goods	10 450	
Add: Production cost	35 570	
	46 020	
Less: Closing stock finished goods	8 910	37 110
		40 416
Less: *Expenses*		
Fixed overheads (4 × £1 200)	4 800	
Depreciation		
Machinery and equipment	15 733	
Motor vehicles	3 500	

Loan interest (2/12 × 71/2% of £120 000)	1 500		25 533	
			14 883	
Less: Interim dividends			12 500	
			2 383	
Add: Profit and loss account balance b/fwd			40 840	
			£43 223	

Budgeted balance sheet as at 30 June

	Cost (£)	Depreciation to date (£)	Net (£)
Fixed assets			
Land and buildings	500 000	—	500 000
Machinery and equipment	236 000	100 233	135 767
Motor vehicles	42 000	19 900	22 100
	778 000	120 133	657 867
Current assets			
Stock of raw materials		4 725	
Stock of finished goods		8 910	
Debtors		41 610	
Cash and bank balances		15 436	
		70 681	
Less: Current liabilities			
Creditors	3 825		
Loan interest owing	1 500	5 325	65 356
			£723 223

	(£)
Capital employed	
Ordinary share capital £1 shares (fully paid)	500 000
Share premium	60 000
Profit and loss account	43 233
	603 223
Secured loan (71/2%)	120 000
	£723 223

(e) See the section of cash budgets in Chapter 15 for possible ways to improve cash management.

Question 15.12

(a) (i) *Cash budget for weeks 1–6*

	Week 1 (£)	Week 2 (£)	Week 3 (£)	Week 4 (£)	Week 5 (£)	Week 6 (£)
Receipts from debtors[a]	24 000	24 000	28 200	25 800	19 800	5 400
Payments:						
To material suppliers[b]	8 000	12 500	6 000	nil	nil	nil
To direct workers[c]	3 200	4 200	2 800	nil	nil	nil
For variable overheads[d]	4 800	3 200	nil	nil	nil	nil
For fixed overhead[e]	8 300	8 300	6 800	6 800	6 800	6 800
Total payments	24 300	28 200	15 600	6 800	6 800	6 800
Net movement	(300)	(4 200)	12 600	19 000	13 000	(1 400)
Opening balance (week 1 given)	1 000	700	(3 500)	9 100	28 100	41 100
Closing balance	700	(3 500)	9 100	28 100	41 100	39 700

Notes:
[a]Debtors:

	Week 1	Week 2	Week 3	Week 4	Week 5	Week 6
Units sold*	400	500	400	300	—	—
Sales (£)	24 000	30 000	24 000	18 000	—	—
Cash received (70 per cent)		16 800	21 000	16 800	12 600	
(30 per cent)			7 200	9 000	7 200	5 400
Given	24 000	7 200				
Total receipts (£)	24 000	24 000	28 200	25 800	19 800	5 400

*Sales in week 4 = opening stock (600 units) + production in weeks 1 and 2 (1000 units) less sales in weeks 1–3 (1300 units) = 300 units.

[b]Creditors:

	Week 1 (£)	Week 2 (£)	Week 3	Week 4	Week 5	Week 6
Materials consumed at £15	9 000	6 000	—	—	—	—
Increase in stocks	3 500	—				
Materials purchased	12 500	6 000				
Payment to suppliers (given)	8 000	12 500	6 000	nil	nil	nil

[c]Wages:

	Week 1 (£)	Week 2 (£)	Week 3 (£)	Week 4	Week 5	Week 6
Wages consumed at £7	4 200	2 800	nil	nil	nil	nil
Wages paid	3 200 (given)	4 200	2 800	—	—	—

[d]Variable overhead payment = budgeted production X budgeted cost per unit.

[e]Fixed overhead payments for weeks 1–2 = fixed overhead per week (£9000) less weekly depreciation (£700).

Fixed overhead payments for weeks 3–6 = £8300 normal payment less £1500 per week.

(ii) *Comments*

(1) Finance will be required to meet the cash deficit in week 2, but a lowering of the budgeted material stocks at the end of week 1 would reduce the amount of cash to be borrowed at the end of week 2.

(2) The surplus cash after the end of week 2 should be invested on a short-term basis.

(3) After week 6, there will be no cash receipts, but cash outflows will be £6800 per week. The closing balance of £39 700 at the end of week 6 will be sufficient to finance outflows for a further five or six weeks (£39 700/£6800 per week).

(b) The answer should include a discussion of the matching concept, emphasizing that revenues and expenses may not be attributed to the period when the associated cash inflows and outflows occur. Also, some items of expense do not affect cash outflow (e.g. depreciation).

Question 15.13

Task 1

Alderley Ltd Budget Statements 13 weeks to 4 April

(a) Production budget

	Elgar units	Holst units
Budgeted sales volume	845	1 235
Add closing stock[a]	78	266
Less Opening stock	(163)	(361)
Units of production	760	1 140

(b) Material purchases budget

	Elgar kg	Holst kg	Total kg
Material consumed	5 320 (760 × 7)	9 120 (1 140 × 8)	14 440
Add raw material closing stock[b]			2 888
Less raw material opening stock			(2 328)
Purchases (kg)			15 000

(c) Purchases (£) (1500 × £12) £180 000

(d) Production labour budget

	Elgar hours	Holst hours	Total hours
Standard hours produced[c]	6 080	5 700	11 780
Productivity adjustment (5/95 × 11 780)			620
Total hours employed			12 400
Normal hours employed[d]			11 544
Overtime hours			856

(e) Labour cost

	£
Normal hours (11 544 × £8)	92 352
Overtime (856 × £8 × 125%)	8 560
Total	100 912

Notes:

[a]Number of days per period = 13 weeks × 5 days = 65

Stock: Elgar = (6/65) × 845 = 78, Holst = (14/65) × 1 235 = 266

[b](13/65) × (5 320 + 9 120) = 2 888

[c]Elgar 760 × 8 hours = 6 080, Holst 1140 × 5 hours = 5 700

[d]24 employees × 37 hours × 13 weeks = 11 544.

Task 2

(a) Four ways of forecasting future sales volume are:

(i) Where the number of customers is small it is possible to interview them to ascertain what their likely demand will be over the forecasting period.

(ii) Produce estimates based on the opinion of executives and sales personnel. For example, sales personnel may be asked to estimate the sales of each product to their customers, or regional sales managers may estimate the total sales for each of their regions.

(iii) Market research may be necessary where it is intended to develop new products or new markets. This may involve interviews with existing and potential customers in order to estimate potential demand.

(iv) Estimates involving statistical techniques that incorporate general business and market conditions and past growth in sales.

(b) Interviewing customers and basing estimates on the opinions of sales personnel are likely to be more appropriate for existing products and customers involving repeat sales. Market research is appropriate for new products or markets and where the market is large and anticipated revenues are likely to be sufficient to justify the cost of undertaking the research.

Statistical estimates derived from past data are likely to be appropriate where conditions are likely to be stable and past demand patterns are likely to be repeated through time. This method is most suited to existing products or markets where sufficient data is available to establish a trend in demand.

(c) The major limitation of interviewing customers is that they may not be prepared to divulge the information if their future plans are commercially sensitive. There is also no guarantee that the orders will be placed with Alderley Ltd. They may place their orders with competitors.

Where estimates are derived from sales personnel there is a danger that they might produce over-optimistic estimates in order to obtain a favourable performance rating at the budget setting stage. Alternatively, if their future performance is judged by their ability to achieve the budgeted sales they may be motivated to underestimate sales demand.

Market research is expensive and may produce unreliable estimates if inexperienced researchers are used. Also small samples are often used which may not be indicative of the population and this can result in inaccurate estimates.

Statistical estimates will produce poor demand estimates where insufficient past data is available, demand is unstable over time and the future environment is likely to be significantly different from the past. Statistical estimates are likely to be inappropriate for new products and new markets where past data is unavailable.

Question 15.14

(a) The following points should be included in the answer:

Budget preparation

A brief discussion of budget participation (see Chapter 16) and an indication that some element of participation is generally considered desirable. The lack of consultation and involvement with the departmental manager should be addressed.

Implication of the increase in volume

A fixed budget is being operated for cost control and performance evaluation but the number of visits was 12000 compared with a budget of 10000. For those items of expense that vary with the number of visits (such as wages, travel expenses and consumables), it is inappropriate to compare the actual costs of visiting 12000 clients with a budget of 10000 clients. The current report draws attention to this invalid comparison. There is a need to implement flexible budgets (see Chapter 16) instead of fixed budgets.

Controllability

Some of the costs in the report are not controllable by the departmental manager. Adopting the controllability principle (see Chapter 16), non-controllable costs should either be excluded from the report or shown in a separate section indicating that they are not directly controllable by the departmental manager. At present the departmental manager appears to be held accountable for expenses (e.g. allocated administrative costs) that he/she cannot directly influence.

Funding allocation

As indicated by the director it is important that the department keeps within its funding allocation to ensure that costs are controlled. For fixed expenses, such as the salary of the supervisor, managers should ensure that costs do not exceed the original (fixed) budget but for variable expenses the costs should not exceed the flexed budget for the actual level of activity. Increased expenditure should only be permitted if more funds are allocated from local or central government.

Social aspects

Social aspects generally cannot be expressed in financial terms but they must not be lost sight of in the pursuit of only those items that are incorporated in the budget. Where budget amounts are allocated to social aspects it is important that managers seek to use these funds, since under-spending represents a failure to pursue objectives expressed in the budget. The main difficulty with expenses relating to social aspects is that there is not any clear input–output relationship, so it can be difficult to ascertain whether the funds are being utilized efficiently.

Other aspects

The focus of the report is entirely on financial aspects. Non-financial measures should also be incorporated such as total staff hours worked, feedback on client satisfaction on the service provided and the frequency of visits. These aspects can be vital to the success of the service and the present system does not appear to highlight them. Consideration also should be given to incorporating additional columns in the report that compare the actual against budget for the year to date so that the focus is not only on the most recent period. Also the lack of consultation and the apparent authoritarian manner in the way that the report is being used warrants attention, since this is likely to result in harmful behavioural consequences.

(b) The answer should draw off the material within the section on zero-based budgeting (ZBB), pointing out its claimed advantages. In addition, the answer should draw attention to the weaknesses of conventional budgets in the form of incremental budgets (an explanation can be found at the beginning of the section on activity-based budgeting). Finally, the problems associated with implementing ZBB should be described with an indication that for this organization it may be more appropriate to approximate the principles of ZBB using a more simplistic form of priority-based budgeting.

Question 15.15

(a) Cost driver rates:

$$W\frac{£160\,000}{(20 \times 4) + (30 \times 5) + (15 \times 2) + (40 \times 3) + (25 \times 1)} = £395$$

$$X\frac{£130\,000}{(20 \times 3) + (30 \times 2) + (15 \times 5) + (40 \times 1) + (25 \times 4)} = £388$$

$$Y\frac{£80\,000}{(20 \times 3) + (30 \times 3) + (15 \times 2) + (40 \times 4) + (25 \times 2)} = £205$$

$$Z\frac{£200\,000}{(20 \times 4) + (30 \times 6) + (15 \times 8) + (40 \times 2) + (25 \times 3)} = £373$$

Actual activities during October:

W $(18 \times 4) + (33 \times 5) + (16 \times 2) + (35 \times 3) + (28 \times 1) = 402$

X $(18 \times 3) + (33 \times 2) + (16 \times 5) + (35 \times 1) + (28 \times 4) = 347$

Y $(18 \times 3) + (33 \times 3) + (16 \times 2) + (35 \times 4) + (28 \times 2) = 381$

Z $(18 \times 4) + (33 \times 6) + (16 \times 8) + (35 \times 2) + (28 \times 3) = 552$

Budget control statement

Activity	Original budget (£000)	Flexible budget (£000)	Actual costs (£000)	Variance (£000)
W	160	159 (402 × £395)	158	1F
X	130	135 (347 × £388)	139	4A
Y	80	78 (381 × £205)	73	5F
Z	200	206 (552 × £374)	206	0
	570	578	576	2F

(b) For the answer to this question see the points listed at the end of the section on the factors influencing the effectiveness of participation in Chapter 16.

(c) A fixed budget represents the original budget set at the beginning of the period based upon the planned level of activity. A flexible budget represents a budget that is adjusted to reflect what the budget would have been, based on the actual level of activity that occurred during the period. Flexible budgets are appropriate for those costs that are expected to vary with activity. Therefore actual expenditure should be compared with a flexible budget. Fixed budgets are more appropriate for controlling discretionary items of expenditure. Examples include advertising and research and development. These items do not vary with activity and there is no obvious level of optimum spending. Also the budget represents a commitment or policy decision to allocate a specific amount of funds to spend on these items. Thus under-spending may be considered undesirable because it represents a failure to pursue management commitments of spending to be incurred during the budget period.

(d) y = Total cost for the period

a = Variable cost per unit of activity

b = Fixed costs for the period

x = Activity level for the period.

For a more detailed explanation of the above terms you should refer to the first section in Chapter 23.

Management control systems

Solutions to Chapter 16 questions

Question 16.1

(a) See Chapter 16 for the answer to this question. In particular, your answer should stress:

(i) The need for a system of responsibility accounting based on a clear definition of a manager's authority and responsibility.

(ii) The production of performance reports at frequent intervals comparing actual and budget costs for individual expense items. Variances should be analyzed according to whether they are controllable or non-controllable by the manager.

(iii) The managers should participate in the setting of budgets and standards.

(iv) The system should ensure that variances are investigated, causes found and remedial action is taken.

(v) An effective cost control system must not be used as a punitive device, but should be seen as a system that helps managers to control their costs more effectively.

(b) Possible problems include:

(i) Difficulties in setting standards for non-repetitive work.

(ii) Non-acceptance by budgetees if they view the system as a punitive device to judge their performance.

(iii) Isolating variances where interdependencies exist.

Question 16.2

(a) See 'Planning', 'Motivation' and 'Performance evaluation' in the section on the multiple functions of budgets in Chapter 15 for the answer to this question. The answer should emphasize that the role of motivation is to encourage goal congruence between the company and the employees.

(b) See 'Conflicting roles of budgets' in Chapter 15 for an explanation of how the planning and motivation roles can conflict. Prior to the commencement of the budget period, management should prepare budgets that represent targets to be achieved based upon anticipated environmental variables. It is possible that at the end of the budget period the *actual* environmental variables will be different from those envisaged when the budget was prepared. Therefore actual performance will be determined by the actual environmental variables, but the plans reflected in the budget may be based on different environmental variables. It is inappropriate to compare actual performance based on one set of environmental variables with budgeted performance based on another set of environmental variables. Consequently, a budget that is used for planning purposes will be in conflict with one that is used for performance evaluation.

The conflict between motivation and evaluation is described by Barrett and Fraser (1977) (see Bibliography in main text) as follows:

> 'In many situations the budget that is most effective in the evaluation role might be called an ex-post facto budget. It is one that considers the impact of uncontrollable or unforeseeable events, and it is constructed or adjusted after the fact.
>
> The potential role conflict between the motivation and evaluation roles involves the impact on motivation of using an ex-post facto standard in the evaluation process. Managers are unlikely to be totally committed to achieving the budget's objectives if they know that the performance standards by which they are to be judged may change.'

In other words, for evaluation purposes the budget might be adjusted to reflect changes in environmental variables. If a manager expects that the budget will be changed for evaluation purposes, there is a danger that he or she will not be as highly motivated to achieve the original budget.

(c) (i) The planning and motivation conflict might be resolved by setting two budgets. A budget based on most likely outcomes could be set for planning purposes and a separate, more demanding budget could be used for motivation purposes.

(ii) The planning and evaluation role conflict can be resolved by comparing actual performance with an ex-post budget. See 'Ex-post variance analysis' in Chapter 18 for an illustration of how this conflict can be resolved.

(iii) Barrett and Fraser (1977) suggest the following approach for resolving the motivation and evaluation conflict:

'The conflict between the motivation and evaluation roles can also be reduced by using "adjustable budgets". These are operational budgets whose objectives can be modified under predetermined sets of circumstances. Thus revision is possible during the operating period and the performance standard can be changed.

In one company that uses such a budgeting system, managers commit themselves to a budget with the understanding that, if there are substantial changes in any of five key economic or environmental variables, top management will revise the budget and new performance criteria will be set. This company automatically makes budget revisions whenever there are significant changes in any of these five variables. Naturally, the threshold that triggers a new budget will depend on the relative importance of each variable. With this system, managers know they are expected to meet their budgets. The budget retains its motivating characteristics because it represents objectives that are possible to achieve. Uncontrollable events are not allowed to affect budgeted objectives in such a way that they stand little chance of being met. Yet revisions that are made do not have to adversely affect commitment, since revisions are agreed to in advance and procedures for making them are structured into the overall budgeting system.'

A more detailed answer to this question can be found in Barrett and Fraser (1977).

Question 16.3

(a) The answer should include a discussion of the following points:

(i) Constant pressure from top management for greater production may result in the creation of anti-management work groups and reduced efficiency, so that budgetees can protect themselves against what they consider to be increasingly stringent targets.

(ii) Non-acceptance of budgets if the budgetees have not been allowed to participate in setting the budgets.

(iii) Negative attitudes if the budget is considered to be a punitive control device instead of a system to help managers do a better job. The negative attitudes might take the form of reducing cooperation between departments and also with the accounting department. Steps might be taken to ensure that costs do not fall below budget, so that the budget will not be reduced next year. There is a danger that data will be falsified, and more effort will be directed to finding excuses for failing to achieve the budget than trying to control or reduce costs.

(iv) Managers might try and achieve the budget at all costs even if this results in actions that are not in the best interests of the organization, e.g. delaying maintenance costs.

(v) Organizational atmosphere may become one of competition and conflict rather than one of cooperation and conciliation.

(vi) Suspicion and mistrust of top management, resulting in the whole budgeting process being undermined.

(vii) Belief that the system of evaluation is unjust and widespread worry and tension by the budgetees. Tension might be relieved by falsifying information, blaming others or absenteeism.

(b) For the answer to this question see 'Dealing with the distorting effects of uncontrollable factors before (and after) the measurement period' in Chapter 16.

Question 16.4

The answer should include a discussion of the following:

(i) The impact of targets on performance.

(ii) The use of accounting control techniques for performance evaluation.

(iii) Participation in the budgeting and standard setting process.

(iv) Bias in the budget process.

(v) Management use of budgets and the role of the accountant in the education process.

See Chapter 16 for a discussion of each of the above items.

Question 16.5

(a) See Chapter 16 for the answer to this question.

(b) For the answer to this question see 'Dealing with the distorting effects of uncontrollable factors before (and after) the measurement period', 'Participation in the budget and target setting process' and 'Side effects from using accounting information for performance evaluation' in Chapter 16.

(c) Feedback takes the form of control reports issued by the accountant to the managers responsible for controlling inputs. Effective control requires that corrective action be taken so that actual outputs conform to planned outputs in the future. In order to assist managers in controlling activities, the performance reports should highlight those areas that do not conform to plan. The performance reports should also provide clues as to why the actual outputs differ from the planned outputs. Feedback information is necessary to provoke corrective managerial action.

It should be noted that accounting reports of performance also have a direct effect on motivation by giving the department manager knowledge of performance. Knowledge of results has been shown in various psychological experiments to lead to improved performance. This is partly because it conveys information that can be used for acting more effectively on the next trial; but also partly because knowledge of results motivates through satisfying the achievement need. It appears that communicating knowledge of results acts as a reward or punishment. It can serve either to reinforce or extinguish previous employee behaviours.

(d) The purpose of goal congruence is to encourage an individual manager's goals to be in agreement with the organization's goals. For a description of this process see 'Goal congruence' in Chapter 16.

Question 16.6

See 'Participation in the budget and target setting process' for the answer to this question.

Question 16.7

See 'Setting financial performance targets' in Chapter 16 for the answer to this question.

Question 16.8

(a) For the answer to this question see 'Setting financial performance targets' in Chapter 16. In particular, the answer should stress that a tight budget is preferable for motivation purposes, whereas for planning and control purposes an expected target should be set that management believes will be achieved. Consequently, a conflict occurs between the motivational and management reporting objectives.

(b) The levels of efficiency that may be incorporated in the standards used in budgetary control and/or standard costing include the following:

    (i) *Perfection:* Standards based on perfection are termed 'ideal standards'. Ideal standards have no motivational advantages and are unsatisfactory for planning and control purposes.

    (ii) *Tight standards:* These standards represent targets that are set at a level of performance that is difficult, but not impossible, for budgetees to achieve. Tight standards should increase aspiration levels and actual performance. Because tight standards may not be achieved, they are unsatisfactory for planning and control purposes.

    (iii) *Expected performance:* Expected performance standards are based on the level of efficiency expected to be attained. One advantage of expected standards is that variances indicate deviations from management's expectations. A further advantage is that expected standards can be used for planning purposes. Expected standards are likely to be unsatisfactory for motivational purposes, since they may not provide a challenging target.

    (iv) *Loose standards:* With loose standards, the level of efficiency implied by the standard is less than expected. Loose standards are poor motivators and are unsatisfactory for planning and control purposes.

(c) see 'Participation in the budgeting and target setting process' in Chapter 16 for the answer to this question.

Question 16.9

(a) For a discussion of feedback and feedforward controls see Chapter 16. The remaining terms are also discussed in Chapter 16.

(b) For the answer to this question see 'Dealing with the distorting effects of uncontrollable factors before (and after) the measurement period', 'Participation in the budget and target setting process' and 'Side effects from using accounting information for performance evaluation' in Chapter 16.

Question 16.10

(a) For an explanation of responsibility accounting you should refer to 'The nature of management accounting control systems' in Chapter 16. Potential difficulties in operating a system of responsibility accounting include:

    (1) identification of specific areas of responsibility where actions can be influenced by two or more persons resulting in the problem of joint responsibility occurring. It therefore becomes difficult to ascertain which managers should be held accountable for the outcomes;

(2) distinguishing between those items which managers can control and for which they should be held accountable and those items over which they have no control and for which they are not held accountable (see 'The controllability principle' in Chapter 16);

(3) determining how challenging the targets should be (see 'Setting financial performance targets' in Chapter 16);

(4) determining how much influence managers should have in setting financial performance targets (see 'Setting financial performance targets' in Chapter 16);

(5) choosing an appropriate mix of financial and non-financial measures to be included in the performance report and seeking to avoid some of the harmful side-effects of controls (see 'Harmful side-effects of controls' in Chapter 16).

(b) see 'Feedback and feedforward controls' in Chapter 16 for the answer to this question.

(c) (i) The budget acts as a resource allocation device by determining the total resources available for a non-profit organization and allocating these resources within the budget process to the different programmes or activities (e.g. between spending on education, care of the elderly, or leisure provision within a municipal authority). The budget planning process specifies where and how the available funds should be spent during the current period.

(ii) When the master budgets (and thus the budgets making up the master budget) have been reviewed by the appropriate top management committee, they represent the formal approval for each budget manager to carry out the plans contained in his/her budget. At the end of the appropriate budget period, actual expenditure will be compared against the budget authorization. For example, a school may be allocated with a budgeted sum to spend on part-time teaching staff. At the end of the period actual spending will be compared against the budget and the head will be held accountable for any difference.

(iii) For the answer to this question see 'Control' within the section on multiple functions of budgets in Chapter 15. An example of the control process is provided in 'Line item budgets' within the section on the budgeting process in non-profit-making organizations in Chapter 15.

Question 16.11

(a) The desirable attributes of a suitable measure of activity for flexing the budget are as follows:

(i) The selected measure should exert a major influence on the cost of the activity. The objective is to flex the budget to ascertain the costs that should be incurred for the actual level of activity. Therefore the costs of the activity and the measure selected should be highly correlated.

(ii) The measure selected should not be affected by factors other than volume. For example, if direct labour cost is selected as the activity measure then an increase in wage rates will cause labour cost to increase even when activity remains constant.

(iii) The measure should be easily understood. Complicated indexes are unlikely to be satisfactory.

(iv) The measure should be easily obtainable without too much cost.

(v) The measure should be based on output rather than input in order to ensure that managers do not obtain larger budget allowances for being inefficient.

(b) Because the activities of a service or overhead department tend not to be repetitive, it is unlikely that a system of standard costing can be justified. Output will be fairly diverse, and it may not be possible to find a single output measure that is highly correlated with costs. It might be necessary to flex the budget on inputs rather than outputs. Also, several variables are likely to cause changes in cost rather than a single measure of output, and an accurate flexible budget may require the use of multiple regression techniques. However, because multiple regression measures might not be easily obtainable and understood, a single input measure may be preferable.

It may be necessary to use several measures of activity within a cost centre for the different costs. For example, machine maintenance costs might be flexed according to machine hours, and lighting and heating costs might be flexed according to labour hours of input.

(c) Suitable measures include the following:

(i) *Standard hours of output:* This measure is suitable when output is sufficiently standardized to enable standard labour times to be established for each activity. It is unsatisfactory where labour efficiency is unlikely to be constant or output is too diverse to enable standard time to be established.

(ii) *Direct labour hours of input:* This measure is suitable where costs are highly correlated with labour hours of input, output cannot be measured in standard hours and labour efficiency is fairly constant. It is unsatisfactory if these conditions do not hold, because labour hours will be an unsatisfactory guide to output.

(iii) *Direct labour costs:* This measure is suitable where the same conditions apply as those specified in (ii) and the wage rates are not consistently changing. If these conditions do not apply then it will be unsatisfactory.

Question 16.12

(a) See 'Setting financial performance targets' in Chapter 16 for the answer to this question.

(b) See 'Participation in the budgeting and target setting process' in Chapter 16 for the answer to this question.

(c) Management by exception is based on the principle that accounting reports should highlight those activities that do not conform to plans, so that managers can devote their scarce time to focusing on these items. Effective control requires that corrective action be taken so that actual outcomes conform to planned outcomes. These principles are based on the following assumptions:

    (i) Valid targets and budgets can be set.

    (ii) Suitable performance measures exist that enable divergences from plans to be correctly measured.

    (iii) Plans and divergences from plan are communicated to the individuals who are responsible for implementing the plan.

    (iv) Performance reports correctly distinguish those items that are controllable by a manager from those that are non-controllable.

    (v) Feedback information is translated into corrective action.

    (vi) Management intervention is not required where no adverse variances exist.

    (vii) Divergences from plan can only be remedied by corrective action. Management by exception as an effective system of routine reporting will depend on the extent to which the above conditions hold. The system will have to be supplemented by informal controls to the extent that the above conditions do not hold. Management by exception can only be a very effective means of control if behavioural factors are taken into account when interpreting the divergences from plan. Otherwise there is a danger that other systems of control will have a greater influence on future performance.

(d) The answer should include the following:

    (i) An explanation of why it is considered necessary to distinguish between controllable and uncontrollable costs at the responsibility level.

    (ii) Difficulty in assigning variances to responsibility centres when dual responsibilities apply or interdependencies exist.

    (iii) Possible dysfunctional consequences that might occur when a manager's performance is measured by his or her success in controlling only those items that have been designated as controllable by him or her.

    (iv) Arguments for including those uncontrollable items that a manager might be able to influence in a separate section of the performance report.

The above items are discussed in 'The controllability principle' in Chapter 16.

(e) Budget statements should not be expressed only in monetary terms. This is because all aspects of performance relating to a firm's goals cannot be expressed in monetary terms. Therefore budgetary statements should be supplemented by non-monetary measures. Monetary gains can be made at the expense of items that cannot easily be measured in monetary terms but that may be critical to an organization's long-term profitability. For example, monetary gains can be made by hierarchical pressure to cut costs, but such gains might be at the expense of adverse motivational changes, increased labour turnover and reduced product quality. The long-term costs of these items might be far in excess of the cost-cutting benefits.

A range of non-monetary measures is presented in the balanced scorecard (see Chapter 22). Some qualitative variables (e.g. measurement of attitudes) are difficult to measure, but judgements based on interviews can be made. The inclusion of behavioural and qualitative factors in budget statements more accurately reflects the complexity of managerial performance in relation to a number of objectives rather than a single monetary objective. The difficulty with incorporating qualitative variables into budget statements is not sufficient grounds for expressing budget statements only in monetary terms.

Question 16.13

Task 1

Reclamation Division Performance Report – four weeks to 31 May:

Original budget	250 tonnes
Actual output	200 tonnes

	Budget based on 200 tonnes	Actual	Variance	Comments
Controllable expenses:				
Wages and social security costs[a]	43 936	46 133	2 197A	
Fuel[b]	15 000	15 500	500A	
Consumables[c]	2 000	2 100	100A	
Power[d]	1 500	1 590	90A	
Directly attributable overheads[e]	20 000	21 000	1 000A	
	82 436	86 323	3 887A	
Non-controllable expenses:				
Plant maintenance[e]	5 950	6 900	950A	
Central services[e]	6 850	7 300	450A	
	12 800	14 200	1 400A	
Total	95 236	100 523	5 287A	

Notes:

[a] 6 employees × 4 teams × 42 hours per week × £7.50 per hour × 4 weeks = £30 240 + (40% × £30 240) + (200 tonnes × £8) = £43 936.

[b] 200 tonnes × £75

[c] 200 tonnes × £10

[d] £500 + (£5 × 200) = £1500

[e] It is assumed that directly attributable expenses, plant maintenance and central services are non-variable expenses.

Task 2

(a) (i) Past knowledge can provide useful information on future outcomes but ideally budgets ought to be based on the most up-to-date information. Budgeting should be related to the current environment and the use of past information that is two years old can only be justified where the operating conditions and environment are expected to remain unchanged.

(ii) For motivation and planning purposes budgets should represent targets based on what we are proposing to do. For control purposes budgets should be flexed based on what was actually done so that actual costs for actual output can be compared with budgeted costs for the actual output. This ensures that valid comparisons will be made.

(iii) For variable expenses the original budget should be reduced in proportion to reduced output in order to reflect cost behaviour. Fixed costs are not adjusted since they are unaffected in the short-term by output changes. Flexible budgeting ensures that like is being compared with like so that reduced output does not increase the probability that favourable cost variances will be reported. However, if less was produced because of actual sales being less than budget this will result in an adverse sales variance and possibly an adverse profit variance.

(iv) Plant maintenance costs are apportioned on the basis of capital values and therefore newer equipment (with higher written-down values) will be charged with a higher maintenance cost. Such an approach does not provide a meaningful estimate of maintenance resources consumed by departments since older equipment is likely to be more expensive to maintain. The method of recharging should be reviewed and ideally based on estimated usage according to maintenance records. The charging of the overspending by the maintenance department to user departments is questionable since this masks inefficiencies. Ideally, maintenance department costs should be recharged based on actual usage at budgeted cost and the maintenance department made accountable for the adverse spending (price) variance.

(v) The comments do not explain the causes of the variances and are presented in a negative tone. No comments are made, nor is any praise given, for the favourable variances.

(vi) Not all variances should be investigated. The decision to investigate should depend on both their absolute and relative size and the likely benefits arising from an investigation.

(vii) Central service costs are not controllable by divisional managers. However, even though the divisional manager cannot control these costs there is an argument for including them as non-controllable costs in the performance report. The justification for this is that divisional managers are made aware of central service costs and may put pressure on central service staff to control such costs more effectively. It should be made clear to divisional managers that they are not accountable for any non-controllable expenses that are included in their performance reports.

Question 16.14

(a)

Performance report for the quarter ending October

	Budget	Flexed Budget	Actual	Variance	
Sales units	12000	13000	13000		
Production units	14000	13500	13500		
	$000	*$000*	*$000*	*$000*	
Sales	360	390	385	5	A
Direct materials	70	67.5	69	1.5	A
Direct labour	140	135	132	3	F
Variable overhead	42	40.5	43	2.5	A
Fixed overhead	84	84	85	1	A
Inventory adjustment	(48)	(12)	(12)	0	
Cost of sales	288	315	317	2	A
Gross Profit	72	75	68	7	A

Note that the variable cost items have been derived by multiplying the original budget by 13500/14000. The inventory adjustment relates to the actual increase in inventory (500 unit) compared with the original budgeted increase of 2000 units. Therefore the flexed budget is one quarter of the original budget.

(b) The original statement compared the original budgeted revenues and costs with actual revenues and costs. The resulting variances are not very meaningful as to why the differences occurred. For effective performance appraisal it is important that the figures are compared on a 'like for like' basis. It is inappropriate to compare the actual costs of producing 13500 units with the budgeted costs of producing 14000 units.

The flexible budget does not analyze the variances by areas of responsibility and control. For example, the total direct materials variance should be analyzed by the price and usage elements because these variances will be the responsibility of different managers.

Question 16.15

Task 1 (a)

		Calculation of unit variable costs		
	Original budget	Revised budget	Difference	Variable unit cost[a]
Units	24000	20000	4000	
Variable costs				
Material	216000	180000	£36000	£9
Labour	288000	240000	£48000	£12
Semi-variable costs				
Heat, light and power	31000	27000	£4000	£1
Analysis of heat, light and power				
Variable cost	£24000	£20000		
Total cost	£31000	£27000		
Fixed cost	£7000	£7000		

Note:

[a]Unit variable cost = change in total cost/change in volume

Task 1 (b)

Rivermede Ltd – flexible budget statement for the year ended 31 May

	Revised budget	Actual results		Variance
Production and sales (units)	22 000	22 000		
Variable costs	(£)	(£)		(£)
Material 22 000 × £9	198 000	214 320	(£206 800 + £7 520)	6 320(A)
Labour 22 000 × £12	264 000	255 200		8 800(F)
Semi-variable cost				
Heat, light and power (22 000 × £1) + £7 000	29 000	25 880	(£33 400 − £7 520)	3 120(F)
Fixed costs				
Rent, rates and depreciation	40 000	38 000		2 000(F)
	531 000	533 400		2 400(A)

Task 2 (a)

The original statement compares the actual cost of producing 22 000 units with a budget for 20 000 units. This is not comparing like with like. The flexible budget shows what budgeted costs would have been for the actual production level of 22 000 units. Because actual production was greater than budgeted production of 20 000 units variable costs are likely to be higher and this comparison will result in an adverse effect on variable cost variances. The fact that overall variances are smaller when comparisons are made with the flexible budget is due to flexing the budget and not to participative budgeting.

Task 2 (b)

The report should indicate that favourable variances may have arisen for the following reasons:

(i) Controllable factors due to the more efficient usage of direct labour and heating, light and power.

(ii) Budget participation may have resulted in the creation of slack through an overstatement of budgeted costs.

(iii) Uncontrollable factors such as a reduction in the prices charged to Rivermede for rent and rates.

Task 2 (c)

The report should include the following items:

(i) The increased sales may have been due to a general increase in demand rather than the effort of the salesforce.

(ii) The original budget of 24 000 units may have been over-estimated or the revised budget of 20 000 units may have been understated due to the sales director creating slack by deliberately understating demand.

Question 16.16

Task 1 (a)

For the next year x takes on a value of 9.

Therefore annual demand $(y) = 640 + (40 \times 9) = 1000$

weekly demand $= 1000/25 = 40$ holidays

Task 1 (b)

Weaknesses of the least squares regression formula include:

(i) The formula assumes a linear relationship based on time but demand for holidays may not be a linear function of time.

(ii) Seasonal variations are ignored. Demand may vary throughout the holiday season with some holiday weeks being more popular than others.

(iii) It ignores changes in holidaymakers' tastes such as a change in demand from short haul to long haul or ten-day holidays to short-break holidays.

(iv) Cyclical fluctuations are ignored. Demand for holidays is likely to vary depending on the state of the economy, such as boom or recession.

Linear regression is covered in Chapter 23.

Task 2 (a)

Revised cost statement 10 days ended 27 November

Flexed budget	Note	Budget (£)	Actual (£)	Variance (£)	
Aircraft seats	1	18 000	18 600	600	A
Coach hire		5 000	4 700	300	F
Hotel rooms	2	14 300	14 200	100	F
Meals	3	4 560	4 600	40	A
Tour guide		1 800	1 700	100	F
Advertising		2 000	1 800	200	F
		45 660	45 600	60	F

Notes:

1. £450 × 40 because purchases are in blocks of 20 seats

2. £70 × 10 days × 34 tourists × 0.5   £11 900
    £60 × 10 days × 4 tourists   £2 400
                                          £14 300

3. £12 × 10 days × 38 tourists

Task 2 (b)

The original budget is a fixed budget based on the anticipated demand when the budget was set. If actual demand is different from anticipated demand a fixed budget is inappropriate for control purposes because it does not ensure that like is compared with like. See the answer to Question 16.15 for an explanation of this point. The revised flexible budget shows what costs should have been for the volume of passengers taken on the holiday. This ensures that a more meaningful comparison of budget and actual costs is made.

Task 2 (c)

The factors to be taken into account in deciding whether or not to investigate individual variances is examined in Chapter 18. The following factors should be considered:

(i)   the absolute amount of the variance;

(ii) the relative amount of the variance expressed as a percentage of budgeted costs;

(iii) the trend in variances by examining the cumulative variances for the period;

(iv) whether or not the variance is controllable;

(v)   the cost and benefits from investigating the variance.

For a more detailed discussion of the above points you should refer to Chapter 18.

Standard costing and variance analysis 1

Solutions to Chapter 17 questions

Question 17.1

The question requires the standard profit for actual sales (not the budgeted profit) so the sales volume variance is not part of the reconciliation.

Answer = $108 000 + $2000 − $3000 + $7000 − $5000 = $109 000 = C

Question 17.2

The fixed overhead expenditure variance is not relevant to a reconciliation of budgeted and actual contributions because fixed costs are not included in the calculation of the contribution to profits and fixed overheads. The sales volume contribution variance has already been taken into account in arriving at the standard contribution on actual sales ($40 000). Therefore the only variance that needs to be taken into account is the favourable sales price variance so the answer is $41 000 [40 000 + 1000]

Answer = D

Question 17.3

(a) The labour rate variance is:

26 000 × 2.8 ($10.00 − $10.40) = $29 120 A

(b) The labour efficiency variance is:

(26 000 × (3.0 − 2.8)) × $10.00 = $52 000 F

Question 17.4

Standard cost = 31 000 repairs × 24/60 hours × $10.60 = $131 440

Actual cost = $134 540 (standard cost plus adverse labour variance of $3100)

Actual labour hours = 12 400 (31 000 repairs × 0.4 hours) given that actual hours are the same as the standard hours due to a zero labour efficiency variance

Actual wage rate = $10.85 ($134 540/12 400 hours)

Answer = C

Question 17.5

(a) *Standard cost of output produced (18 000 units)*

	(£)
Direct materials	864 000
Direct labour	630 000
Variable production overhead	180 000
Fixed production overhead	900 000
	2 574 000

(b)

	Standard cost of output (£)	Variances (£)	Actual cost (£)
Direct materials	864 000		
Price variance[a]		76 000 (F)	
Usage variance[b]		48 000 (A)	
Actual cost			836 000
Direct labour	630 000		
Rate variance[c]		16 800 (A)	
Efficiency variance[d]		42 000 (F)	
Actual cost			604 800
Variable production overhead	180 000		
Expenditure variance[e]		4 000 (A)	
Efficiency variance[f]		12 000 (F)	
Actual cost			172 000
Fixed production overhead	900 000		
Expenditure variance[g]		30 000 (A)	
Volume variance[h]		100 000 (A)	
Actual cost			1 030 000
	2 574 000	68 800 (A)	2 642 800

Notes:

[a](Standard price − Actual price) × Actual quantity

(£12 − £836 000/76 000) × 76 000 = £76 000 (F)

[b](Standard quantity − Actual quantity) × Standard price

(18 000 × 4kg = 72 000 − 76 000) × £12 = £48 000 (A)

[c](Standard rate − Actual rate) × Actual hours

(£7 − £604 800/84 000) × 84 000 = £16 800 (A)

[d](Standard hours − Actual hours) × Standard rate

(18 000 × 5 hours = 90 000 − 84 000) × £7 = £42 000 (F)

[e](Actual hours × Standard rate) − Actual cost

(84 000 × £2) = £168 000 − £172 000 = £4000 (A)

[f](Standard hours − Actual hours) × Standard rate

(18 000 × 5 hours = 90 000 − 84 000) × £2 = £12 000 (F)

[g]Budgeted fixed overheads − Actual fixed overheads

(20 000 × £50 = £1 000 000 − £1 030 000) = £30 000 (A)

[h](Actual output − Budgeted output) × Standard rate

(18 000 − 20 000) × £50 = £100 000 (A)

(c) The statement in (b) can be used to provide a detailed explanation as to why actual cost exceeded standard cost by £68 800 for the output achieved. The statement provides attention-directing information by highlighting those areas that require further investigation. Thus management can concentrate their scarce time on focusing on those areas that are not proceeding according to plan. By investigating variances, management can pinpoint inefficiencies and take steps to avoid them re-occurring. Alternatively, the investigation may indicate that the current standards are inappropriate and need changing to take account of the changed circumstances. This may result in an alteration in the plans or more up-to-date information for decision-making.

Question 17.6

Budgeted fixed overhead rate per unit of output = $10 (Two hours at $5 per hour)

Since the actual fixed overheads absorbed were $60 000 actual output must have been 6000 units ($60 000/$10).

Variance analysis

The sales price and sales volume valances are given in the question. The workings for the cost variances are as follows:

Direct material price = (18 600 × $4) − $70 680

= $3720 favourable

Direct material usage = [(6000 × 3) − 18 600] × $4

= $2400 adverse

Direct labour rate = (11 500 × $10) − $128 800

= $13 800 adverse

Direct labour efficiency = [(6000 × 2) − 11 500] × $10

= $5000 favourable

Variable overhead expenditure = (11 500 × $4) − $47 150

= $1150 adverse

Variable overhead efficiency = [(6000 × 2) − 11 500] × $4

= $2000 favourable

Fixed overhead expenditure = $50 000 − $57 000

= $7000 adverse

Fixed overhead volume = (6000 − 5000) × $10

= $10 000 favourable

The price variances are calculated as follows:

(SP − AP) AQ giving:

(SP × AQ) − actual cost.

SP for materials is calculated by dividing the budgeted cost of resources ($600 000) by the budgeted activity level (50 000 units) multiplied by the SQ per unit of output (3kg) giving a SP of $4. The SPs for labour and overheads are calculated using the same approach.

Reconciliation statement

			$
Budgeted profit			84 000
Sales volume variance			4 200 (A)
Standard profit on actual sales			79 800
Selling price variance			34 200 (A)
			45 600

	Adverse	**Favourable**	
Direct material price		3 720	
Direct material usage	2 400		
Direct labour rate	13 800		
Direct labour efficiency		5 000	
Variable overhead expenditure	1 150		
Variable overhead efficiency		2 000	
Fixed overhead expenditure	7 000		
Fixed overhead volume		10 000	
Totals	24 350	20 720	3 630 (A)
Actual profit			41 970

Question 17.7

Reconciliation Statement for February			$	
Budgeted variable production cost (1100 units)			148 500	
Planning variance (labour rate)			2 475	adv
Revised budgeted variable production cost			150 975	
	$ Fav	$ Adv		
Materials price		11 540		
Materials usage	8 300			
Labour rate		2 065		
Labour idle time		4 347		
Labour efficiency	567			
Variable overhead expenditure		3 000		
Variable overhead efficiency	1 000			
Total variances	9 867	20 952	11 085	adv
Actual variable production cost			162 060	

Workings

Planning variance = $49 500 × 5% = $2475

Material price = ($10 × 5770) − $69 240 = $11 540A

Material usage = [1100 × 6kg) − 5770kg] × $10 = $8300F

Labour rate = (standard rate of $9.45 × 5900) − $57 820 = $2065A

Labour efficiency = [(1100 × 5) − (5900 − 460)] × $9.45 = $567F

Labour idle time = 460 hours at $9.45 per hour = $4347A

Variable overhead expenditure = (6400 × $5) − $35 000 = $3000A

Variable overhead efficiency = [(1100 × 6) − 6400] × $5 = $1000F

Question 17.8

(a)

$$\text{Wage rate variance} = (SP − AP)AH = (SP × AH) − (AP × AH)$$
$$= (£14 × 53 \text{ workers} × 13 \text{ weeks} × 40 \text{ hours}) − £386 540$$
$$= £700A$$

$$\text{Labour efficiency} = (SH − AH) SP$$
$$SH (\text{Standard hours}) = (35 000 × 0.4 \text{ hours}) + (25 000 × 0.56 \text{ hours})$$
$$= 28 000$$
$$AH(\text{Actual hours}) = 53 \text{ workers} × 13 \text{ weeks} × 40 \text{ hours} = 27 560$$
$$\text{Variance} = (28 000 − 25 760) × £14 = £6160A$$

(b)

$$\text{Material price variance} = (SP) − AP)AQ$$
$$= (AQ × SP) − (AQ × AP)$$
£430F (given) $$= 47 000 SP − £85 110$$
$$SP (\text{Standard price}) = \frac{£430 + 85 110}{47 000}$$
$$= £1.82$$

$$\text{Material usage variance} = (SQ − AQ)SP$$
$$= (SQ × SP) − (AQ × SP)$$
£320.32A (given) $$= £1.82 SQ − (33 426 × £1.82)$$
− £320.32A $$= £1.82 SQ − £60 835.32$$

$$\text{£1.82 SQ} = \text{£60 515}$$
$$\text{SQ} = \text{£60 515/£1.82} = 33 250$$

Note that SQ = Actual production (35 000 units) × Standard usage

Therefore 35 000 × Standard usage = 33 250

Standard usage = 33 250/35 000

= 0.95kg per unit of component X

(c) For the answer to this question you should refer to the detailed illustration of the budget process shown in Chapter 15. In particular, the answer should indicate that if sales are the limiting factor the production budget should be linked to the sales budget. Once the production budget has been established for the two components, the production quantity of each component multiplied by the standard usage of material A per unit of component output determines the required quantity of material to meet the production requirements. The budgeted purchase quantity of material A consists of the quantity to meet the production usage requirements plus or minus an adjustment to take account of any planned change in the level of raw material stock.

Question 17.9

Standard product cost for one unit of product XY

	(£)
Direct materials (8kg (W2) at £1.50 (W1) per kg)	12.00
Direct wages (two hours (W4) at £10 (W3) per hour)	20.00
Variable overhead (two hours (W4) at £1 (W5) per hour)	2.00
	34.00

Workings

(W1) Actual quantity of materials purchased at standard price is £225 000 (actual cost plus favourable material price variance).

Therefore standard price = £1.50 (£225 000/150 000kg)

(W2) Material usage variance = 6000kg (£9000/£1.50 standard price).

Therefore standard quantity for actual production = 144 000kg (150 000 − 6000kg).

Therefore standard quantity per unit = 8kg (144 000kg/18 000 units)

(W3) Actual hours worked at standard rate = £320 000 (£328 000 − £8000).

Therefore standard rate per hour = £10 (£320 000/32 000 hours).

(W4) Labour efficiency variance = 4000 hours (£40 000/£10).

Therefore standard hours for actual production = 36 000 hours (32 000 + 4000).

Therefore standard hours per unit = two hours (36 000 hours/18 000 units).

(W5) Actual hours worked at the standard variable overhead rate is £32 000 (£38 000 actual variable overheads less £6000 favourable expenditure variance).

Therefore, standard variable overhead rate = £1 (£32 000/32 000 hours).

Question 17.10

(a) (i) *Sales margin volume variance (Marginal costing):*

(Actual volume − Budgeted volume) × Standard contribution margin per unit

(9500 − 10 000) × Standard margin (SM) = £7500A

500 SM = 7500

Standard margin = £15

(ii) *Sales margin volume variance (Absorption costing):*

(Actual volume − Budgeted volume) × Standard profit margin per unit

(9500 − 10 000) × Standard margin (SM) = £4500A

500 SM = £4500

Standard profit margin per unit = £9

(iii) *Fixed overhead volume variance:*

(Actual production − Budgeted production) × Standard rate

(9700 − 10 000) × Standard rate = £1800A

Standard fixed overhead rate per unit = £6

Budgeted fixed overheads = 10 000 units × £6 = £60 000

Fixed overhead expenditure variance   = £2500F

Actual fixed overheads (£60 000 − £2500) = £57 500

(b) Absorption costing unitizes fixed overheads and treats them as product costs whereas marginal costing does not charge fixed overheads to products. Instead, the total amount of fixed overheads is charged as an expense (period cost) for the period. A fixed overhead volume variance only occurs with an absorption costing system. Because marginal costing does not unitize fixed costs, product margins are expressed as contribution margins whereas absorption costing expresses margins as profit margins. For a more detailed answer you should refer to the section on standard absorption costing in Chapter 17.

(c) See the section on volume variance in Chapter 17 for the answer to this question.

(d) See an illustration of ABC and traditional product costing systems in Chapter 11 and the section on activity-based cost management in Chapter 21 for the answer to this question.

Standard costing and variance analysis 2: further aspects

Solutions to Chapter 18 questions

Question 18.1

(a) *Variance analysis*

Material price = (standard price − actual price) × actual purchases

X   = (£20 − £20.50) × 9000

             = £4500A

Y   = (£6 − £5.50) × 5000

             = £2500F

Material usage = (standard usage − actual usage) × standard price

X   = (800 × 10kg − 7800kg) × £20

             = £4000F

Y   = (800 × 5 litres − 4300 litres) × £6

             = £1800A

Wage rate = [standard rate (£14) − actual rate (£57750/4200)] × actual hours (4200)

       = £1050F

Labour efficiency = [standard hours(800 × 5 hrs) − actual hours (4200)] × standard rate (£14)

       = £2800A

Fixed overhead expenditure = budgeted cost(10 800/12 × £50) − actual cost (£47 000)

               = £2000A

Volume efficiency = [standard hours (800 × 5 hrs) − actual hours (4200)] × (£50/5 hours)

        = £2000A

Volume capacity[a] = [actual hours (4200) − budgeted hours[b] (4500)] × FOAR (£50/5 hours)

        = £3000A

Notes:

[a]Note that the CIMA Terminology (at the time of setting the examination) described the volume variance as being equivalent to the volume capacity variance.

[b]Budgeted hours = monthly budgeted output (10 800/12) × 5 hours

(b)

Stores control

	(£)		(£)
K Ltd: X (AQ × SP)	180 000	WIP: (SQ × SP)	160 000
C Ltd: Y (AQ × SP)	30 000	WIP: (SQ × SP)	24 000
Material usage variance (X)	4 000	Material usage variance (Y)	1 800
		Balance	28 200
	£214 000		£214 000

Wages control account

	(£)		(£)
Cash	53 750	Wages owing b/fwd	6 000
PAYE and NI	5 000	Labour efficiency	2 800
Accrued wages	5 000	WIP (SQ × SP)	56 000
Wage rate variance	1 050		
	£64 800		£64 800

WIP control account

	(£)		(£)
Stores control: X	160 000	Finished goods control a/c	280 000
Y	24 000		
Wages control	56 000		
Fixed overhead	40 000		
	£280 000		£280 000

Fixed overhead control

	(£)		(£)
Expense creditors	33 000	WIP (SQ × SP)	40 000
Depreciation provision	14 000	Expenditure variance 2 000	
		Efficiency variance 2 000	
		Capacity variance 3 000	
	£47 000		£47 000

Finished goods control

	(£)		(£)
WIP control	£280 000	Cost of sales	£280 000

Cost of sales

	(£)		(£)
Finished goods control	£280 000	Profit and loss (P/L)	£280 000

Material price variance

	(£)		(£)
K Ltd: X	4 500	C Ltd: Y	2 500
		P/L	2 000
	£4 500		£4 500

Material usage variance

	(£)		(£)
Stores control: Y	1 800	Stores control X	£4 000
P/L	2 200		
	£ 4 000		£4 000

Labour rate variance

	(£)		(£)
P/L	£2 800	Wages control	£2 800

Labour efficiency variance

	(£)		(£)
Wages control	£1 200	P/L	£1 200

Fixed overhead expenditure variance

	(£)		(£)
Overhead control	2 000	P/L	2 000

Fixed overhead efficiency variance

	(£)		(£)
Overhead control	2 000	P/L	2 000

Fixed overhead capacity variance

	(£)		(£)
Overhead control	£3 000	P/L	£3 000

Sales

	(£)		(£)
P/L	352 000	Debtors	352 000

K Limited

			(£)
		Stores control	180 000
		Price variance account	4 500

C plc

	(£)		(£)
Price variance account	2 500	Stores control	30 000

Expense creditors

			(£)
		Fixed overhead control	33 000

Provision for depreciation

			(£)
		Fixed overhead control	14 000

Profit and loss account

	(£)	(£)	(£)
Sales			352 000
Cost of sales			280 000
			72 000
Variances	(F)	(A)	
Material price	—	2 200	
usage	2 000	—	
Labour rate	1 050	—	
efficiency	—	2 800	
Overhead expenditure	—	2 000	
efficiency	—	2 000	
volume	—	3 000	
	3 250	11 800	8 550
Gross profit			63 450

(c) The difference of £250 in the accounts is due to the fact that the material price variance has been calculated on purchases (instead of usage) and written off as a period cost. In the question the raw material stocks are recorded at actual cost, and therefore the £250 is included in the stock valuation and will be recorded as an expense next period.

Question 18.2

(a)

Reconciliation statement

Budgeted profit (W1)			206750
Sales mix profit margin variances (W2):			
Product B	26250F		
Product C	28219A	1969A	
Sales quantity profit variances (W3):			
Product B	13750F		
Product C	12094F	25844F	23875F
Standard profit on actual sales			230625
Selling price variances:			
Product B 3000 ($110 − $100)	30000F		
Product C 1500 ($105 − $107.50)	3750A		26250F
Direct material price variance:			
((25600kg × $5) − $124800)	3200F		
Direct material usage variance:			
((3000 × 5kg) + (1500 × 7kg)) − 25600kg) × $5	500A	2700F	
Direct labour rate variance:			
(9140 × $7) − $67980	4000A		
Direct labour efficiency variance:			
((3000 × 2hrs) + (1500 × 1.5 hours)) − 9140) × $7	6230A	10230A	
Variable overhead expenditure variance:			
(9140 hours × $1.50) − $14300	590A		
Variable overhead efficiency variance			
((3000 × 2hrs) + (1500 × 1.5 hours)) − 9140) × $1.5	1335A	1925A	
Fixed overhead expenditure variance:			
((2200 × $8) + (1800 × $6)) − $27000	1400F		
Fixed overhead volume variance:			
Product B: (3000 − 2200) × $8	6400F		
Product C: (1500 − 1800) × $6	1800A	6000F	3455A
Actual profit (W4)			253420

Workings:

W1 Standard selling price per unit B: $50 × 2 = $100, C: $53.75 × 2 = $107.50

Budgeted profit for the period

	Product B	Product C	Total
Sales (units)	2200	1800	
Budgeted profit per unit	$50	$53.75	
Total budgeted profit	$110000	$96750	$206750

W2 Sales mix profit margin variances

	Actual sales @ standard mix (units)	Actual sales @ actual mix (units)	Variance (units)	Standard profit $	Variance $
Product B	2475	3000	525F	50.00	26250F
Product C	2025	1500	525A	53.75	28219A
	4500	4500			1969A

W3 Sales quantity profit variances

	Actual sales @ standard mix (units)	Budget sales @ standard mix (units)	Variance (units)	Standard profit $	Variance $
Product B	2 475	2 200	275F	50.00	13 750F
Product C	2 025	1 800	225F	53.75	12 094F
	4 500	4 000	500F		25 844F

W4 Actual profit for the period

		$	$
Sales	$(3\,000 \times \$110) + (1\,500 \times \$105)$		487 500
Direct materials		124 800	
Direct labour		67 980	
Variable production overheads		14 300	
Fixed production overheads		27 000	
Total production cost			234 080
Actual profit			253 420

(b) The separation of the sales volume margin variance into the quantity and mix variance explains how sales volume is affected by a change in the total volume of sales and a change in the relative mix of products. The sales quantity margin variance indicates that if the original planned sales mix had been maintained for the actual sales volume of 4500 units, profits would have increased by $25 844. However because the actual sales mix differed from the budgeted sales mix there was an adverse mix variance of $1969 so profits only increased by the sales volume variance of $23 875. The adverse mix variance arose because there was an increase in the percentage of units sold of lowest profit margin (B) and a decrease in the percentage sold of the highest profit margin product (C). The separation into the quantity and mix components demonstrates that increasing sales volume may not be as beneficial as sales being made in the most profitable mix of products.

(c) For the answer to this question you should refer to learning notes 18.4 and 18.5 on the CourseMate online resources that accompany this book.

Question 18.3

(a)

Reconciliation statement for February

Standard material cost	$78 \times \$210$	$16 380
Material price variance – Raw material A	$2\,800 \text{ litres} \times (\$1.40 - \$1.50)$	$280 A
Material price variance – Raw material B	$2\,700 \text{ litres} \times (\$1.20 - \$1.30)$	$270 A
Material price variance – Raw material C	$1\,000 \text{ litres} \times (\$3.65 - \$4.00)$	$350 A
Material price variance – Raw material D	$1\,900 \text{ litres} \times (\$2.60 - \$2.50)$	$190 F
Material mix variance – Raw material A	See workings	$784 A
Material mix variance – Raw material B	See workings	$648 A
Material mix variance – Raw material C	See workings	$1 314 A
Material mix variance – Raw material D	See workings	$3 796 F
Material yield variance	See workings	$420 A
Actual material cost		$16 460

Material mix variance

Raw material	Actual input @ standard mix litres	Actual input @ actual mix litres	Variance litres	Standard cost $	Variance $
A	2 240	2 800	560 A	1.40	784A
B	2 160	2 700	540 A	1.20	648A
C	640	1 000	360 A	3.65	1 314A
D	3 360	1 900	1 460 F	2.60	3 796F
	8 400	8 400			1 050F

For an input of 105 litres the expected output is 100 litres. The actual input for the period was 8400 litres so the expected output is 8000 litres (8400/1.05).

Therefore there is an adverse yield variance of $420 (200 litres × $2.10 standard cost per litre of output).

(b) The following factors should be considered when deciding whether to investigate the variance:

- the size of the variance;
- the cost of investigation compared with the potential benefits from investigation;
- the likelihood that the variance is due to uncontrollable factors or an assignable cause (see Chapter 18)

(c) Direct labour rate planning variance:

(7800 litres output × 8/100 hours) × ($24 − $26) = $1248 A
Direct labour rate operational variance
(640 hours at the $26 revised standard hourly) − $16 500 = $140 F
Direct labour efficiency operational variance
[(7800 × 8/100) − 640] × $26 = $416 A

(d) See 'Ex-post variance analysis' in Chapter 18 for the answer to this question.

Question 18.4

(a) (i) Sales price variance = (actual price − standard price) × actual volume

	Actual price $	Standard price $	Difference $	Actual volume	Sales price variance $
Plasma TVs	330	350	−20	750	15 000 A
LCD TVs	290	300	−10	650	6 500 A
					21 500 A

Sales volume contribution variance = (actual sales volume − budgeted sales volume) × standard margin

	Actual sales volume	Budgeted sales volume	Difference	Standard margin $	Sales volume variance $
Plasma TVs	750	590	160	190	30 400 F
LCD TVs	650	590	60	180	10 800 F
	1 400	1 180			41 200 F

(ii) Material planning variance = (original target price − general market price at time of purchase) × quantity purchased
($60 − $85) × 1400 = $35 000 A.
Material price operational variance = (general market price at time of purchase − actual price paid) × quantity purchased.
($85 − $80) × 1400 = $7000 F.

(iii) Wage rate variance = (std rate per hour − actual rate per hour) × actual hours worked.

Actual hours worked by temporary workers:
Total hours required assuming staff were fully efficient = (750 × 2) + (650 × 1.5) = 2475.
Permanent staff provided 2200 hours resulting in an excess of 275 hours.
Temporary workers took twice as long so 550 hours (275 × 2) were worked

The wage rate variance relates solely to temporary workers.

Wage rate variance = ($14 − $18) × 550 = $2200 A.

Labour efficiency variance = (std hours for actual production − actual hours worked) × std rate.

(275 − 550) × $14 = $3850 A.

(b) The original variance analysis shown in the question reports an adverse material price variance of $28 000. This variance will be used to evaluate the purchasing department even though it is not a reliable indicator of the purchasing department's efficiency. This is because market conditions can change resulting in an increase in price. The change in market conditions is not within the control of the purchasing department.

Analyzing the materials price variance into its planning and operational components provides more meaningful information for performance evaluation since the planning variance is uncontrollable by the planning department and the operational variance is controllable. The planning variance provides useful feedback information on how successful management are in estimating future prices. The operational variance is a more meaningful indication of the purchasing department's efficiency given the market conditions that prevailed at the time. Incorporating factors that the purchasing department cannot control adversely effects the motivation of departmental staff.

Question 18.5

(a) Actual sales were 960 units giving a total revenue of $76 800. Therefore the actual selling price of $80 ($76 800/960) is identical to the budgeted selling price so the sales margin price variance is zero. The sales margin volume variance is the difference between the actual sales volume (960 units) and the budgeted sales volume (1000 units) giving an adverse variance of $1760 (40 units × $44 contribution). This variance, however, can be divided into a planning variance based on the difference between the original budget (1000 units) and the revised budget taking into account the revised market share (1000 × 0.9 = 900 units) and an operational (controllable) variance. The calculations are:

Planning variance = 100 units at $44 unit contribution = $4400A

Operational variance = Actual sales (960) − Revised budget (900) × $44 = $2640F

The cost variances are calculated as follows:

Material price (SP − AP) × AQ = ($3 − $3.05) × 3648 = $182 A

Material usage (SQ − AQ) × SP = (3840 − 3648) × $3 = $576 F

Labour efficiency (SH − AH) × SR = (1920 − 1824) × $10 = $960 F

Variable overhead efficiency (SH − AH) × SR = (1920 − 1824) × $2 = $192 F

Variable overhead expenditure = (Flexed budget − actual cost) = $3648 − $3283 = $365 F

Reconciliation Statement	$	$
Budgeted sales revenue	80 000	
Budgeted standard variable cost	(36 000)	
Budgeted contribution		44 000
Sales contribution variances		
Operational (controllable)	2 640	
Planning (uncontrollable)	(4 400)	(1 760)
		42 240
Variable cost variances		
Materials		
– price	(182)	
– usage	576	394
Labour efficiency		960
Variable overhead		
– efficiency	192	
– expenditure	365	557
Actual contribution		44 151

(b) Standard costing as a control mechanism may be incompatible with TQM because:

- TQM relies on a culture of continuous improvement within an organization where the focus is on quality rather than quantity relationships. Traditional variance analysis focuses on quantity rather than quality. This can result in lower grade of materials or labour being used to report favourable variances and this is inconsistent with TQM.
- With standard costing standards tend to represent targets to be achieved rather than encouraging a focus of continuous improvement, which is a feature of TQM. Thus with TQM regular small changes (improvements) to the targets are required and this may be incompatible with standard costing.
- Standard costing systems may be based on standard costs that incorporate allowances for waste whereas TQM seeks to eliminate waste.

- Traditional standard costing emphasizes responsibility accounting whereas inter-departmental coordination is emphasized with TQM.

The above issues should therefore be examined to ascertain the contribution that standard costing makes when TQM is introduced to ensure that they are not incompatible.

Question 18.6

(a)

Variance	Actual quantity in stand. Mix	Actual quantity in actual mix	Difference	Standard price	
A	450 litres	600 litres	+150 litres	$30	$4 500 A
B	337.5 litres	250 litres	−87.5 litres	$30	$2 625 F
C	562.5 litres	500 litres	−62.5 litres	$15	$937.50 F

Total $937.50A

Note that the revised standard price of $30 for material B is used in the above calculation. Each 1.2 litres of input (0.4 + 0.3 + 0.5) should yield 1 litre of output so an actual input of 1350 litres should yield an output of 1125 litres (1350/1.2). Actual output is 1000 litres resulting in a shortfall of 125 litres so the yield variance is $3562.50 adverse (125 × $28.50).

(b) The total material usage variance consists of an adverse mix variance of $937.50 plus adverse yield variance of $3562.50. The Production Manager's decision to substitute some of chemical B with chemical A to avoid the increased in price appears to have had an adverse impact on the yield and mix variances. This may have been due to the mix of chemicals no longer being optimum. There was a significant increase in the input required to produce 1000 litres of output, possibly because the mix of chemicals being used was no longer optimum. The adverse mix variance has occurred the manager used chemical A instead of chemical B, but A was originally the most expensive chemical and cost as much per litre as the revised price of chemical B that it replaced.

The purchasing department should be responsible for the effect of price changes rather than the Production Manager. Also the manager may not have the authority to change the mix without consulting the company's chemical advisors since the alternative mix may not result in the optimum quality of output.

Question 18.7

(a) (i)

Variance	Actual sales in actual mix	Actual sales in stand. Mix	Difference	Standard contribution	
DVD	3 000	2 800	+200	$25	$5 000 F
Blu-ray	1 200	1 400	−200	$95	$19 000 A
	4 200	4 200			$14 000 A

(a) (ii) The sales volume profit variance relates only to Blu-ray players because the actual and revised budget volumes of DVD players are the same.

Therefore the variance is 300 players × $95 = $28 500 A

(b) The change in market size is not within the control of the sales manager so any variances relating to market size represent planning variances. However, variances arising from changes in the selling prices and market shares would be within the control of the sales manager and treated as operating variances.

The market size variance compares the original and revised market sizes. This is unchanged for DVD players but the variance for the Blu-ray players is $47 500 (500 players × $95). The manager's performance will be distorted if the planning variance and revised market share is not taken into account. The favourable volume variance of $19 000 referred to in the sales manager's email consists of a favourable planning variance of $47 500 and an adverse operational volume variance of $28 500. Thus the manager has not been responsible for the favourable performance.

Question 18.8

(a)

		Superb	Excellent	Good	Total
1.	Budget sales (units)	30 000	50 000	20 000	100 000
2.	Actual sales (units) in std. proportions	28 800	48 000	19 200	96 000

	Superb	Excellent	Good	Total
3. Actual sales (units)	36 000	42 000	18 000	96 000
Standard unit valuations:				
4. Selling price (£)	100	80	70	
5. Contribution (£)	60	55	48	
6. Profit (£)	35	30	23	
Sales volume variance:				
On turnover basis				
$(3 - 1) \times 4$ (£)	600 000(F)	640 000(A)	140 000(A)	180 000(A)
On contribution basis				
$(3 - 1) \times 5$ (£)	360 000(F)	440 000(A)	96 000(A)	176 000(A)
On profit basis				
$(3 - 1) \times 6$ (£)	210 000(F)	240 000(A)	46 000(A)	76 000(A)

Note:

Fixed cost per unit = £2 500 000/100 000 units = £25

(b) The answer should:

(i) Explain the limitations of using sales revenues to value the sales variances (see 'Sales variances' in Chapter 17).

(ii) Point out the limitations of using a net profit margin derived from unitizing fixed costs. Fixed costs remain unchanged in the short term with variations in sales volumes. Therefore total profits will change by the sales volumes multiplied by the contribution per unit sold and not the net profit per unit sold.

(iii) Argue in favour of using contribution margins based on the point made in (ii) above. Contribution most closely represents the changes in cash flows. Also contribution does not involve arbitrary apportionments of fixed overheads and thus avoids the reporting of misleading sales variances.

(c) Sales mix variance

	Actual sales volume	Actual sales volume in budgeted proportions	Difference	Standard contribution margin (£)	Sales margin mix variance (£)
Superb	36 000	28 800 (30%)	−7 200	60	+432 000
Excellent	42 000	48 000 (50%)	+6 000	55	−330 000
Good	18 000	19 200 (20%)	+1 200	48	−57 600
					+44 400F

Sales quantity variance

	Actual sales volume in budgeted proportions	Budgeted sales quantity	Difference	Standard contribution margin (£)	Sales quantity variance (£)
Superb	28 800 (30%)	30 000	−1 200	60	−72 000
Excellent	48 000 (50%)	50 000	−2 000	55	−110 000
Good	19 200 (20%)	20 000	−800	48	−38 400
					−220 400A

(d) See 'Criticisms of sales margin variances' in Chapter 18 for the answer to this question.

(e) (i)

	Original standard (£)	Revised standard (£)	Actual (£)
Selling price	100	94.00	90
Variable cost	40	38.80	38
Unit contribution	60	55.20	52

Reconciliation of actual with original budget (Ex-post variance analysis)

		£
Original budget (30 000 × £60)		1 800 000
Planning variances:		
Sales price (30 000 × £6)	180 000A	
Variable cost (30 000 × £1.20)	36 000F	144 000A
Revised ex-post budgeted contribution		1 656 000
Operational variances		
Sales volume (6000 × £55.20)	331 200F	
Sales price (36 000 × £4)	44 000A	
Variable cost (36 000 × £0.80)	28 800F	216 000F
Actual contribution (36 000 × £52)		1 872 000

(ii) For the answer to this question see '*Expost* variance analysis' in Chapter 18.

Question 18.9

(a) The question relates to the role of standard costing in a modern manufacturing environment. For the answer to this question see 'The future role of standard costing' and 'The role of standard costing when ABC has been implemented' in Learning Notes 18.4 and 18.5 on the open access website.

(b) The expenditure variance is the difference between the budgeted fixed overheads (£100 000) and the actual fixed overheads (£102 300). For more detailed cost control the variance should be disaggregated by the individual categories of fixed overheads.

The budgeted capacity measured in direct labour hours of input were 10 000 but actual hours were 11 000. The extra hours of input should have enabled an extra 1000 hours of overheads to be absorbed at a budgeted rate of £10 per hour. Therefore a favourable variance of £10 000 is reported.

Budgeted standard hours for each unit of output is 0.10 hours (10 000 hours/100 000 units). Therefore for an actual output of 105 000 units the target hours are 10 500 (105 000 × 0.10 hours) but the actual hours were 11 000. This has resulted in a failure to recover £5000 overheads (500 hours × £10).

For a more detailed discussion of the above variances and a discussion of their usefulness you should refer to the sections in Chapter 17 on fixed overhead expenditure, volume capacity and volume efficiency variances.

(c) (i) It is assumed that material handling expenditure fluctuates in the longer term with the number of orders executed. The variance has been derived adopting a flexible budgeting approach using the number of orders as the cost driver as follows:

Budgeted materials handling overheads (5500 orders at a budgeted rate of £30 000/5000)	£33 000
Actual materials handling expenditure	£30 800
Variance (favourable)	£2 200

The variance therefore indicates that the actual expenditure is £2200 less than expected for the actual level of activity. The same approach is used to calculate the expenditure variance for set ups:

Budgeted set up overheads (2600 production runs at a budgeted rate of £70 000/2800)	£65 000
Actual set up expenditure	£71 500
Variance (adverse)	£6 500

The variance indicates that the actual expenditure is £6500 more than expected for the actual level of activity.

The efficiency variances compare the standard/budgeted cost driver usage for the actual output with the actual usage valued at the standard cost driver rate. The material handling overhead efficiency variance is calculated as follows:

Standard usage for actual output (5000/100 000 × 105 000 units = 5250 orders)

Actual number of orders (5500)

Adverse variance = 250 orders at £30 000/5000 per order = £1500 A

The variance indicates that 250 orders more than expected were executed at £6 per order.

The calculation of the set up efficiency variance is as follows:

Standard usage for actual output (2800/100 000 × 105 000 units = 2940 set ups)

Actual number of set ups (2600)

Favourable variance = 340 set ups at £70 000/2800 = £8500

The variance indicates that 340 less set ups than expected were required at £25 per set up.

(ii) Presumably the company has introduced ABC because there was no cause-and-effect relationship between the previous cost drivers used by the traditional cost system and the overhead expenditure. Hence there is a need for the standard costing system to support the decision-making and cost management applications which would have been instrumental in introducing ABC. Failure to change the standard costing system to be consistent with the ABC system would have undermined the ABC system. Where reported variances prompt actions such as decisions to change the production processes/methods it is important that decisions are based on cost driver rates that are the causes of the overheads being incurred.

For further discussion of aspects relating to (c) (i) and (c) (ii) you should refer to 'The role of standard costing when ABC has been implemented' in Chapter 18.

Question 18.10

(a) (i)

		(£)
Material price variance:		
(standard price − actual price) × actual quantity		
[£0.05 − (£45/1000)] × 105 000		525F
Material usage variance:		
(standard quantity − actual quantity) × standard price		
(100 000 − 105 000) × £0.05		250A
	Total variance	275F

(ii)

	Dr (£)	Cr (£)
Dr Stores ledger control account (AQ × SP)	5 250	
Cr Creditors control account (AQ × AP)		4 725
Cr Material price variance account		525
Dr Work in progress (SQ × SP)	5 000	
Dr Material usage variance account	250	
Cr Stores ledger control account (AQ × SP)		5 250

(iii) On the basis of the above calculations, the buyer would receive a bonus of £52.50 (10% × £525) and the production manager would not receive any bonus. It could be argued that the joint price/usage variance should be separated if the variances are to be used as the basis for calculating bonuses. (For a discussion of joint price/usage variances see Chapter 17.)

The revised analysis would be as follows:

	(£)
Pure price variance:	
(standard price − actual price) × standard quantity (£0.05 − £0.045) × 100 000	500F
Joint price/usage variance:	
(standard price − actual price) × excess usage	
(£0.05 − £0.045) × 5 000	25F

Buyer's viewpoint

At the purchasing stage the buyer can influence both quality and price. Consequently, the buyer can obtain favourable price variances by purchasing inferior quality materials at less than standard price. The adverse effects in terms of excess usage, because of the purchase of inferior quality of materials, are passed on to the production manager and the buyer gains from the price reduction. Indeed, if the joint price/usage is not isolated (see above), the buyer gains if production uses materials in excess of standard. Therefore the bonus system might encourage the buyer to purchase inferior quality materials, which results in an overall adverse *total* material cost variance and inferior product quality. In summary, the bonus system appears to be biased in favour of the buyer at the expense of the production manager.

Production manager's viewpoint

The isolation of the joint price/usage variance might encourage the buyer not to purchase inferior quality materials, and this will be to the production manager's advantage. Nevertheless, the problem of the control of material quality still exists. The production manager would need to ensure that the quality of material purchased is in line with the quality built into the standard. Therefore some monitoring device is necessary. If variations do occur, the quantity standard should be adjusted for the purpose of performance reporting and bonus assessment.

Company's viewpoint

The objective of the bonus system is to encourage goal congruence and increase motivation. Interdependencies exist between the two responsibility centres, and it is doubtful that the bonus system encourages goal congruence or improves motivation. If the quality of materials that can be purchased from the various suppliers does not vary then the adverse effects of the bonus system will be reduced. Nevertheless, interdependencies will still exist between the responsibility centres. One solution might be to base the bonuses of both managers on the *total* material cost variance. In addition, standards should be regularly reviewed and participation by both managers in setting the standards encouraged.

(b) (i) The minimum present value of expected savings that would have to be made in future months in order to justify making an investigation is where

$$IC + (P \times CC) = Px$$

where IC = investigation costs; P = probability that process is out of control;
CC = correction cost, x = present value of expected savings if process is out of control

Therefore £50 + (0.5 × £100) = 0.5x

$$0.5x = £100$$
$$x = £200$$

Therefore the minimum present value of expected savings that would have to be made is £200.

(ii) The standard cost will probably represent the mean value, and random variations around the mean value can be expected to occur even when the process is under control. Therefore it is unlikely that the £500 variance will be eliminated completely, because a proportion of the variance simply reflects the randomness of the variables affecting the standard.

If the process is found to be out of control, the corrective action will only confine variances to the normal acceptable range of standard outcomes. If the £500 is an extreme deviation from the standard then it is likely that the potential savings from investigation will be insignificant.

(iii) Applying the notation used in (i), the firm will be indifferent about whether to conduct an investigation when the expected savings resulting from correction are equal to the expected cost of correction. That is, where

$$IC + (P \times CC) = Px$$

if x = £600 then

$$50 + P \times 100 = P \times 600$$
$$500P = 50$$
$$P = 10\%$$

if x = 250 then

$$50 + P \times 100 = P \times 250$$
$$150P = 50$$
$$P = 33\%$$

STANDARD COSTING AND VARIANCE ANALYSIS 2: FURTHER ASPECTS

Divisional financial performance measures

Solutions to Chapter 19 questions

Question 19.1

Residual income ($36 000) = Profit − cost of capital (12% × $200 000)

Profit $60 000

ROI = Profit ($60 000)/200 000 = 30%

Answer = A

Question 19.2

(a) If divisional budgets are set by a central planning department and imposed on divisional managers then it is true that divisional independence is pseudo-independence. However, if budget guidelines and goals are set by the central planning department and divisional managers are given a large degree of freedom in the setting of budgets and conduct of operations then it is incorrect to claim that pseudo-independence exists.

One of the reasons for creating a divisionalized organization structure is to improve motivation by the delegation of responsibility to divisional managers, thus giving them greater freedom over the control of their activities. Nevertheless, complete independence cannot be granted, since this would destroy the very idea that divisions are an integral part of a single business. The granting of freedom to divisions in conducting their operations can be allowed only if certain limits are applied within which that freedom can be exercised. This normally takes the form of the presentation of budgets by divisions to corporate management for approval. By adopting this approach, divisions pay a modest price for the extensive powers of decentralized decision-making.

As long as budgets are not imposed by the central planning department, and divisions are allowed to determine their own budgets within the guidelines set, then divisional managers will have greater independence than the managers of centralized organizations.

(b) The answer should consist of a discussion of divisional profit, return on capital employed and residual income. A discussion of each of these items is presented in Chapter 19.

Question 19.3

(a) Examples of the types of decisions that should be transferred to the new divisional managers include:

   (i) Product decisions such as product mix, promotion and pricing.

   (ii) Employment decisions, except perhaps for the appointment of senior managers.

   (iii) Short-term operating decisions of all kinds. Examples include production scheduling, subcontracting and direction of marketing effort.

   (iv) Capital expenditure and disinvestment decisions (with some constraints).

   (v) Short-term financing decisions (with some constraints).

(b) The following decisions might be retained at company head office:

   (i) Strategic investment decisions that are critical to the survival of the company as a whole.

   (ii) Certain financing decisions that require an overall view be taken. For example, borrowing commitments and the level of financial gearing should be determined for the group as a whole.

   (iii) Appointment of top management.

   (iv) Sourcing decisions such as bulk buying of raw materials if corporate interests are best served by centralized buying.

   (v) Capital expenditure decisions above certain limits.

   (vi) Common services that are required by all profit centres. Corporate interests might best be served by operating centralized service departments such as an industrial relations department. Possible benefits include reduced costs and the extra benefits of specialization.

(vii) Arbitration decisions on transfer pricing disputes.

(viii) Decisions on items which benefit the company rather than an individual division, e.g. taxation and computer applications.

(c) The answer to this question should focus on the importance of designing performance reports which encourage goal congruence. For a discussion of this topic see Chapter 19.

Question 19.4

(a) The following factors should be considered:

(i) *Definition of profit:* The question states that the measure should be used for performance measurement. It is therefore necessary to define 'controllable profit' for the companies. Clearly, apportionment of group headquarters expenditure should be excluded from the calculation of controllable profit. If investment decisions are made by the companies then depreciation should be included as a controllable expense. Otherwise, companies can increase controllable profit by substituting capital equipment for direct labour when this is not in the best interest of the group as a whole.

(ii) *Definition of capital employed:* There are many different definitions of capital employed, and it is important that the same basis of measurement be used for comparing the performance of the different companies. Capital employed might be defined as total assets or net assets. All assets that are controlled by the companies should be included in the valuation. If debtors are controlled by the companies but not included in the capital employed then there is a danger that managers might lengthen the credit period to increase sales even when this is not in the best interests of the group. The benefits from the increased credit period accrue to the companies, but the increased investment is not reflected in the capital employed.

(iii) *Valuation of capital employed:* Capital employed can be valued on an historical cost basis, or an alternative method such as replacement cost might be used. If historical cost is used then assets might be valued at written-down value or gross value. Both approaches can result in misleading comparisons. If written-down value is used then an asset that yields a constant profit will show an annual increase in ROCE because the written-down value will decline over the asset's life. Therefore those companies with old assets and low written-down values might incorrectly show higher ROCE calculations. For a more detailed discussion of this topic see 'The impact of depreciation' in Chapter 19.

(iv) *Alternative accounting methods:* For comparisons, it is important that the same accounting methods be applied to all companies within the group. For example, one company may capitalize major expense items such as advertising, lease rentals, and research and development expenditure, whereas another company might not capitalize these items. For example, if company A capitalizes lease payments and company B does not then the accounting treatment will result in the capital employed of company B being understated and consequently ROCE overstated.

(b) A single ROCE might not be an adequate measure because:

(i) Companies operate in different industries and a single ROCE measure might not give an adequate measure of performance. For example, if companies A and B have ROCEs of 20 per cent and 10 per cent, respectively, one might conclude that company A has produced the better performance. However, the industry ROCEs might be 25 per cent for the industry in which A operates and 5 per cent for the industry in which B operates. Relative to industry performance, company B has performed better than company A. The ROCE should therefore be compared with other companies and supplemented by other measures such as percentage market shares.

(ii) Companies with a high existing ROCE might reject projects whose returns are in excess of the cost of capital but less than existing ROCE. Such companies might be reluctant to expand and be content with a high ROCE and low absolute profits. The ROCE should be supplemented with a measure of absolute profits (e.g. residual income) and details of investment in new projects. This would indicate whether or not the companies were restricting growth in order to preserve their existing high ROCE.

(iii) Concentration on short-run ROCE at the expense of long-run profitability. For an illustration of points that could be considered here see 'Addressing the dysfunctional consequences of short-term financial measures' in Chapter 19.

Question 19.5

(a) For cost control and performance measurement purposes it is necessary to measure performance at frequent intervals. Managers tend to be evaluated on short-term (monthly, quarterly or even yearly) performance measures such as residual income (RI) or return on investment (ROI). Such short-term performance measures focus only on the performance for the particular control period. If a great deal of stress is placed on managers meeting short-term performance measure targets, there is a danger that they will take action that will improve short-term performance but that will not maximize long-term profits. For example, by skimping on expenditure on advertising, customer services, maintenance, and training and staff development costs, it is possible to improve short-term performance. However, such actions may not maximize long-term profits.

Ideally, performance measures ought to be based on future results that can be expected from a manager's actions during a period. This would involve a comparison of the present value of future cash flows at the start and end of the period, and a manager's performance would be based on the increase in present value during the period. Such a system is not feasible, given the difficulty in predicting and measuring outcomes from current actions.

ROI and RI represent single summary measures of performance. It is virtually impossible to capture in summary financial measures all the variables that measure the success of a manager. It is therefore important that accountants broaden their reporting systems to include additional non-financial measures of performance that give clues to future outcomes from present actions.

It is probably impossible to design performance measures which will ensure that maximizing the short-run performance measure will also maximize long-term performance. Some steps, however, can be taken to improve the short-term performance measures so that they minimize the potential conflict. For example, during times of rising prices, short-term performance measures can be distorted if no attempt is made to adjust for the changing price levels. ROI has a number of deficiencies. In particular, it encourages managers to accept only those investments that are in excess of the current ROI, and this can lead to the rejection of profitable projects. Such actions can be reduced by replacing ROI with RI as the performance measure. However, merely changing from ROI to RI will not eliminate the short-run versus long-run conflicts.

(b) One suggestion that has been made to overcome the conflict between short-term and long-term measures is for accountants to broaden their reporting systems and include non-financial performance measures in the performance reports. For example, obtaining feedback from customers regarding the quality of service encourages managers not to skimp on reducing the quality of service in order to save costs in the short term. For a discussion of the potential contribution from including non-financial measures in the reporting system see 'Addressing the dysfunctional consequences of short-term financial performance measures' in Chapter 19.

Other suggestions have focused on refining the financial measures so that they will reduce the potential for conflict between actions that improve short-term performance at the expense of long-term performance. For a description of these suggestions see 'The impact of depreciation' and 'The effect of performance measurement on capital investment decisions' in Chapter 19.

Question 19.6

(a) (i) Return on capital employed, residual income and economic value added (EVA) should be considered as potential measures. The superiority of EVA or residual income over return on capital employed (see Chapter 19) should be discussed. The objective is to select a performance measure that is consistent with the NPV rule. Residual income is the long-run counterpart of the NPV rule, but it may lead to decisions that are not consistent with the NPV rule if managers base their decisions on short-term measures. Problems occur with both return on capital employed and residual income in terms of bases that should be used for asset valuations. Current values are preferable to historical costs.

(ii) Ideally, market performance measures should indicate sales achievement in relation to the market, competitors and previous performance. Target market shares or unit sales should be established for each product or product range. Actual market shares and unit sales should be compared with targets and previous periods. Trends in market shares should be compared with overall market trends and product life cycles.

(iii) Productivity is concerned with the efficiency of converting physical inputs into physical outputs. Therefore the performance measure should be a physical one. Possible performance measures include output per direct labour hour and output per machine hour. Where divisions produce a variety of products, output could be expressed in standard hours. If monetary measures are used then changes in price levels should be eliminated. In addition to *total* measures of output for each division, performance measures should also be computed for individual products. Output measures should be compared with targets, previous periods and with other divisions.

(iv) Possible measures of the ability of divisions to offer up-to-date product ranges include:

(1) number of new products launched in previous periods;

(2) expenditure on product development.

Quality and reliability might be measured in terms of:

(1) percentage of projects rejected;

(2) comparison of target and actual market shares;

(3) comparisons with competitors' products;

(4) customer surveys.

The performance measures should be compared with previous periods, targets and competitors (if this is possible). Some of the measures may be difficult to express in quantitative terms, and a subjective evaluation may be necessary.

(v) Responsibility towards employees might be reflected by the following measures:

(1) rate of labour turnover;

(2) level of absenteeism.

Additional information is also necessary to explain the reasons for high labour turnover and absenteeism. Possible reasons might be identified by regularly undertaking attitude surveys on such issues as:

(1) payment systems;

(2) management style;

(3) degree of participation;

(4) working conditions.

Other proxy measures that might be used include:

(1) number of promotions to different employee and management grades;

(2) number of grievance procedures processed;

(3) number of applications received per vacancy;

(4) training expenditure per employee;

(5) number of accidents reported per period.

The above measures should be compared with previous periods and targets.

(vi) It is extremely difficult to assess whether a firm is considered to be a socially responsible citizen within the community. Possible areas of interaction between the firm and the local community include:

(1) employment;

(2) environmental effects;

(3) involvement in community affairs;

(4) provision of recreational and social facilities.

Surveys should be undertaken locally in order to assess the attitude of the population to each of the above areas. Possible quantitative measures include:

(1) amount of financial support given to charities, sports organizations and educational establishments;

(2) amounts spent on anti-pollution measures;

(3) number of complaints received from members of the local community.

(vii) Possible growth measures include comparisons over time (in absolute terms and percentage changes) of the following:

(1) total sales revenue;

(2) profit (expressed in terms of residual income);

(3) total assets;

(4) total employees;

(5) total market share.

Price changes should be removed where appropriate. Comparisons should be made with other divisions, comparable firms and the industry as a whole. Survival in the long term depends on an acceptable level of profitability.

Therefore appropriate profitability measures should be used. The degree of divisional autonomy might be measured in terms of an assessment of the central controls imposed by central headquarters. (For example: what are the limits on the amounts of capital expenditure decisions that divisions can determine independently?)

(b) A single performance measure underestimates the multi-faceted nature of organizational goals. It might be claimed that a profitability measure is sufficiently general to incorporate the other goals. For example, maintaining high market shares, increasing productivity, offering an up-to-date product range, being a responsible employee, and growth tend to result in increased profitability. To this extent a profitability measure might best capture the multi-faceted nature of organizational goals. Nevertheless the profitability goal alone cannot be expected to capture the complexity of organizational goals. Firms pursue a variety of goals, and for this reason there are strong arguments for using multiple performance measures when evaluating organizational performance. For a further discussion of organizational goals see 'The decision-making process' in Chapter 1.

Question 19.7

(a) For the answer to this question you should refer to Chapter 22, which contains a full description of the balanced scorecard.

(b)

Division A ROI:

Net profit = $44.6m × 28% = $12.488m

ROI = $12.488m/$82.8m = 15.08%

Division B ROI

Net profit = $21.8m $\times$ 33% = $7.194m

ROI = $7.194m/$40.6m = 17.72%

Division A Residual income:

Divisional profit = $12.488m

Capital employed = $82.8m

Imputed interest charge = $82.8m $\times$ 12% = 9.936m

Residual income = $12.488m $-$ $9.936m = $2.552m.

Division B Residual income

Divisional profit = $7.194m

Capital employed = $40.6m

Imputed interest charge = $40.6m $\times$ 12% = $4.872m

Residual income = $7.194 $-$ $4.872 = $2.322m.

If a decision about whether to proceed with the investments is made based on ROI it is likely that the manager of Division A will reject the proposal whereas the manager of Division B will accept the proposal. This is because each division currently has a ROI of 16 per cent and since Division A's investment has a ROI of 15.08 per cent, it would result in a reduction of the division's overall ROI to less than 16 per cent. Division B's investment has a ROI of 17.72 per cent and this is higher than its current 16 per cent, so this would result in an increase in its overall ROI. If residual income is used to evaluate managerial performance both divisions will report an increase in residual income and would proceed with the investments.

Both investments yield a ROI in excess of the cost of capital and this suggests that it is best for the company as a whole if both investments are undertaken. Ideally the decision should be based on a NPV evaluation but there is insufficient information in the question to calculate the NPV's. Therefore from the company's point of view the decision should be made to invest if the estimated ROI exceeds the cost of capital. Using ROI to evaluate performance results in a lack of goal congruence for Division A whereas residual income encourages goal congruence for both divisions.

Question 19.8

The investment has a positive net present value and therefore should be accepted. However, since the bonus of the manager of the Northern Hotel is determined by the hotel's ROI this may influence the manager's decision whether to undertake the new investment. The net assets values of the new investment, profits and ROI (i.e. return on net assets) are as follows:

	Incremental net assets $000	Incremental profit $000	RONA %
2015	750	110	14.7
2016	700	120	17.1
2017	650	155	23.8
2018	600	145	24.2
2019	550	130	23.6

The above calculations show that the investment yields a return in excess of the cost of capital of 10 per cent in all years but it is not until 2017 that it yields a return greater than the current return of 20 per cent. Therefore the overall ROI of the hotel will decline in the first two years and there is a danger that the manager may not proceed with the investment because it will adversely affect the bonus receivable in the immediate future.

Question 19.9

(a) The annual ROI and residual income calculations for each plant are as follows:

	2015	2016	2017	2018	Total
Aromatic					
(1) Net cash flow (£m)	2.4	2.4	2.4	2.4	9.6
(2) Depreciation	1.6	1.6	1.6	1.6	
(3) Profit	0.8	0.8	0.8	0.8	3.2

(4) Cost of capital (16 per cent of 6)	(1.02)	(0.77)	(0.51)	(0.26)	
(5) Residual income	(0.22)	0.03	0.29	0.54	
(6) Opening WDV of asset	6.4	4.8	3.2	1.6	
(7) ROI (Row 3/Row 6)	12.5%	16.67%	25%	50%	
Zoman					
(1) Net cash flow	2.6	2.2	1.5	1.0	7.3
(2) Depreciation	1.3	1.3	1.3	1.3	
(3) Profit	1.3	0.9	0.2	(0.3)	2.1
(4) Cost of capital (16 per cent)	(0.83)	(0.62)	(0.42)	(0.21)	
(5) Residual income	0.47	0.28	(0.22)	(0.51)	
(6) Opening WDV of asset	5.2	3.9	2.6	1.3	
(7) ROI	25%	23%	7.7%	(23%)	

The answer should indicate:

(i) Over the whole life of the project both ROI and residual income (RI) favour the Aromatic plant. The average ROI and RI figures are 25 per cent and £0.16 million (£0.64m/4) for the Aromatic plant and 20 per cent and £0.005 million (£0.02m/4) for the Zoman plant. The ROI calculations are based on expressing the average profits as a percentage of the average investment (defined as one-half of the initial capital investment).

(ii) An explanation that Mr Elton will favour the Zoman plant because it yields a higher ROI and RI over the first two years. Mr Elton will probably focus on a two-year time horizon because of his personal circumstances, since choosing the Aromatic plant is likely to result in him losing his bonus. Therefore he will choose the plant with the lower NPV and there will be a lack of goal congruence.

(iii) Suggestions as to how alternative accounting techniques can assist in reconciling the conflict between accounting performance measures and DCF techniques:

(1) Avoiding short-term evaluations and evaluating performance at the end of the project's life. Thus bonuses would be awarded with hindsight.

(2) Use alternative asset valuations other than historic cost (e.g. replacement cost).

(3) Choose alternative depreciation methods that are most consistent with NPV calculations (e.g. annuity depreciation).

(4) Incorporate a range of variables (both financial and non-financial when evaluating managerial performance) that give a better indication of future results that can be expected from current actions.

(b) Managers may use pre-tax profits to evaluate divisional performance because it is assumed that taxation is non-controllable. Taxation payable is based on total group profits and present and past capital expenditure rather than individual divisional profitability. After-tax cash flows are used to appraise capital investments because the focus is on decision-making and accepting those projects that earn a return in excess of the investors' opportunity cost of capital. To do this IRRs and NPVs should be based on after-tax cash flows.

The following potential problems can arise:

(i) Managers may ignore the taxation impact at the decision-making stage because it is not considered when evaluating their performance.

(ii) Confusion and demotivation can occur when different criteria are used for decision-making and performance evaluation.

Possible solutions include evaluating divisional profitability after taxes or evaluating performance based on a comparison of budgeted and actual cash flows. Adopting the latter approach is an attempt to ensure that the same criteria is used for decision-making and performance evaluation.

(c) Steps that can be taken to avoid dysfunctional behaviour include:

(i) Not placing too much emphasis on short-term performance measures and placing greater emphasis on the long term by adopting a profit-conscious style of evaluation.

(ii) Focusing on controllable residual income or economic value-added combined with asset valuations derived from depreciation models that are consistent with NPV calculations. Alternatively, performance evaluation might be based on a comparison of budgeted and actual cash flows. The budgeted cash flows should be based on cash flows that are used to appraise capital investments (see Learning Note 19.1 on the CourseMate online resources).

(iii) Supplementing financial performance measures with non-financial measures when evaluating performance (see 'addressing the dysfunctional consequences of short-term financial measures' in Chapter 19).

Question 19.10

(a)

Summary statement I (Straight-line depreciation)

Year	1 (£000)	2 (£000)	3 (£000)	4 (£000)	5 (£000)
Investment at start of year	600	480	360	240	120
Net cash flow (40 per cent of sales)	200	200	200	200	200
Less: Depreciation	120	120	120	120	120
Net profit	80	80	80	80	80
Less: Interest on capital[a]	96	76.8	57.6	38.4	19.2
Residue income	(16)	3.2	22.4	41.6	60.8
ROCE[b]	13.3%	16.7%	22.2%	33.3%	66.7%

Notes:

[a]16 per cent of investment at the start of the year.

[b]Net profit expressed as a percentage of the investment at the start of the year.

Calculation of annuity depreciation

Year	(1) Annual repayment (£000)	(2) 16% interest on capital outstanding (£000)	(3) = (1) − (2) Capital repayment (£000)	(4) = (4) − (3) Capital outstanding (£000)
0				600.0
1	183.24	96.0	87.24	512.76
2	183.24	82.04	101.20	411.56
3	183.24	65.85	117.39	294.17
4	183.24	47.07	136.17	158.00
5	183.24	25.28	158.00	—

For an explanation of the calculations see Learning Note 19.1 on the website. Note that the annual repayment is determined by dividing the investment of £600 000 by the cumulative discount factor for five years at 16 per cent (3.274 shown in Appendix B).

Summary statement 2 (Annuity depreciation)

Year	1 (£000)	2 (£000)	3 (£000)	4 (£000)	5 (£000)
Investment at start of year	600	512.76	411.56	294.17	158.00
Net cash flow	200	200	200	200	200
Depreciation	87.24	101.20	117.39	136.17	158.00
Net profit	112.76	98.80	82.61	63.83	42.0
Imputed interest	96.00	82.04	65.85	47.07	25.28
Residual income	16.76	16.76	16.76	16.76	16.72
ROCE	18.8%	19.3%	20.1%	21.7%	26.6%

(b) (i) Management are motivated to focus only on the outcomes of the first year for any new project because of the criterion used for performance measurement and investment decisions. When straight-line depreciation is used residual income is negative and the ROCE of 13.3 per cent is less than the target return of 20 per cent. Therefore if the focus is only on the performance measures for the first year the project will be rejected even though residual income and ROCE rise steadily throughout the five-year period.

When annuity depreciation is used residual income is positive and constant for each year of the project's life and therefore the proposal would be accepted if the residual income method is used. ROCE is 18.8 per cent and this is less than the target return of 20 per cent and the project would be rejected using this method. However, ROCE ranges from 18.8 per cent to 26.6 per cent when annuity depreciation is used, compared with 13.3 per cent to 66.7 per cent with straight-line depreciation. Therefore, when compared with straight-line depreciation annuity depreciation does not distort ROCE to the same extent.

(ii) NPV = £200 000 cumulative discount factor for five years at 16 per cent (3.274) − Investment outlay £600 000

= £54 800

The project has a positive NPV and should be accepted. Residual income is the long-run counterpart of NPV. The present value of residual income of £16760 per year for five years discounted at 16 per cent is approximately £54800. When cash flows are constant and the annuity method of depreciation is used residual income will also be constant. For a more detailed discussion of the relationship between residual income and NPV see Learning Note 19.1 on the website.

(c) (i)

	Year 1 (straight-line depreciation) (£000)	Year 1 (annuity depreciation) (£000)
Investment at beginning of year	600	600
Net cash flow (40% × £700 000)	280	280
Less: Depreciation (see part (a))	(120)	(87.3)
Profit	160	192.7
Less: Interest on capital	(96)	(96)
Residual income	64	96.7
ROCE	26.7%	32.1%

(ii) *Discounted cash flow approach:*

Year	Physical (£000)	Discount factor at 16%	DCF (£000)
0	(600)	1.000	(600)
1	280	0.862	241.36
2	200	0.743	148.60
3	200	0.641	128.20
4	120	0.552	66.24
5	80	0.476	38.08
		NPV	22.48

(iii) Adopting the criteria used by management both projects yield a positive residual income and a ROCE in excess of the target return in the first year using either straight-line or annuity methods of depreciation. The project therefore will be accepted. The project also has a positive NPV and, in this situation, the criteria used by management will be consistent with the NPV decision model. The decline in NPV reflects the fact that sales revenue has declined over the five-year period.

Question 19.11

(a) To compute EVA, adjustments must be made to the conventional after tax profit measures of $44m and $55m shown in the question. Normally an adjustment is made to convert conventional financial accounting depreciation to an estimate of economic depreciation, but the question indicates that profits have already been computed using economic depreciation. Non-cash expenses are added back since the adjusted profit attempts to approximate cash flow after taking into account economic depreciation. Net interest is also added back because the returns required by the providers of funds will be reflected in the cost of capital deduction. Note that net interest is added back because interest will have been allowed as an expense in determining the taxation payment.

The capital employed used to calculate EVA should be based on adjustments that seek to approximate book economic value at the start of each period. Because insufficient information is given, the book value of shareholders funds plus medium and long-term loans at the end of 2014 is used as the starting point to determine economic capital employed at the beginning of 2015.

	2014 ($m)	2015 ($m)
Adjusted profit	56.6 (44 + 10 + (4·0 × 65))	68.9 (55 + 10 + (6 × 0.65))
Capital employed	233 (223 + 10)	260 (250 + 10)

The weighted average cost of capital should be based on the target capital structure. The calculation is as follows:

$$2014 = (15\% \times 0.6) + (9\% \times 0.65 \times 0.4) = 11.34\%$$
$$2015 = (17\% \times 0.6) + (10\% \times 0.65 \times 0.4) = 12.8\%$$
$$\text{EVA } 2014 = 56.6 - (233 \times 0.1134) = \$30.18m$$
$$\text{EVA } 2015 = 68.9 - (260 \times 0.128) = \$35.62$$

The EVA measures indicate that the company has added significant value in both years and achieved a satisfactory level of performance.

(b) The present value of EVA from an investment approximates the NPV of the investment. For an explanation of this point you should refer to 'The effect of performance measurement on capital investment decisions' in Chapter 19.

(c) Advantages of EVA include:

(1) Because some discretionary expenses are capitalized the harmful side-effects of financial measures described in Chapters 16 and 19 are reduced.

(2) EVA is consistent with maximizing shareholders funds.

(3) EVA is easily understood by managers.

(4) EVA can also be linked to managerial bonus schemes and motivate managers to take decisions that increase shareholder value.

Disadvantages of EVA include:

(1) The EVA computation can be complicated when many adjustments are required.

(2) EVA is difficult to use for inter-firm and inter-divisional comparisons because it is not a ratio measure.

(3) If economic depreciation is not used, the short-term measure can conflict with the long-term measure (see 'The effect of performance measurement on capital investment decisions' in Chapter 19).

(4) Economic depreciation is difficult to estimate and conflicts with generally accepted accounting principles which may hinder its acceptance by financial managers.

Question 19.12

(a) The answer to this question should include much of the content included in the section entitled 'economic value-added' in Chapter 19. In addition, the answer should include the following points:

(i) Some of the revenue expenditure, such as research and development and advertising, provide future benefits over several years but financial accounting requirements often require such expenditure to be written off in the year in which they are incurred. This understates the value added during a particular period.

(ii) The profits computed to meet financial accounting requirements do not take into account the cost of equity finance provided by the shareholders. The only cost of capital that is taken into account is interest on borrowed funds (i.e. the cost of debt finance). Profits should reflect the cost of both debt and equity finance.

(iii) A better measure of the managers' ability to create value is to adjust the traditional financial statements for those expenses that are likely to provide benefits in future periods. The economic value-added measure attempts to meet this requirement.

The following comments relate to the treatment of specific adjustments:

Research and development
The expenditure of £2.1 million is added back because it represents an investment that will yield future benefits. Therefore it should be capitalized and allocated to the future periods based on the benefits received in the particular period. The expenditure of £17.4m is added back, based on the assumption that the company is continuing to benefit from such expenditures that have previously been written off against profits. There should be an element of this expenditure written off as depreciation based on the value that has been eroded during the period.

Advertising
Advertising expenditure adds value by supporting future sales arising from increasing customer awareness and brand loyalty. Based on the same justification as research and development expenditure, advertising should be capitalized for the EVA calculation and added back to profits. The £10.5m added back in the balance sheet reflects the costs incurred in building up future income. Some of this cost should be depreciated based on the value of future benefits eroded during the period.

Interest and borrowings
The aim is to ascertain whether value is being added for the shareholders in the sense of whether the funds invested in the business generate a return in excess of the opportunity cost of capital (see Chapter 14). To do this a profit figure is calculated that initially does not include any charges for the cost of capital. Interest on borrowings is therefore added back to avoid the situation where the cost of capital on debt finance is included in the traditional profit calculation whereas the cost of equity capital is not. To ascertain the total source of funds invested in the business, borrowings are added back to the capital base in the balance sheet. The required return (i.e. the opportunity cost of capital) of £17.5m on the resulting capital base is calculated and compared with the adjusted profit of £16.1m generated from the funds. This comparison captures the cost of both debt and equity and indicates that value-added is a negative figure.

Goodwill
Goodwill refers to the price paid for the business in excess of the current cost of net assets. Goodwill payments should therefore add value to the company. Hence the amount written off is added back to profits since it represents part of the intangible asset value of the business. The cumulative write-off of £40.7m is added back in order to provide a more realistic value of the capital base from which a return should be generated. This is because it represents an element of the value of the business. The value of goodwill should be regularly reviewed and the amount eroded written off against profits.

(b) *Revised divisional profit statements*

	Division A (£m)	Division B (£m)	Division C (£m)	Head office (£m)	Total (£m)
Profit before interest and tax	5.7	5.6	5.8	(1.9)	15.2
Add back:					
Advertising	2.3				2.3
Research and development		2.1			2.1
Goodwill[a]		0.3	1.0		1.3
Allocation of head office expenses[b]	(0.4)	(0.3)	(1.2)	1.9	
Less tax paid[c]	(2.0)	(1.6)	(1.2)		(4.8)
Revised profit	5.6	6.1	4.4		16.1

Revised balance sheet

	Division A (£m)	Division B (£m)	Division C (£m)	Head office (£m)	Total (£m)
Total assets less current liabilities	27.1	23.9	23.2	3.2	77.4
Add back:					
Advertising	10.5				10.5
Research and development		17.4			17.4
Goodwill		10.3	30.4		40.7
Head office net assets[d]	0.7	0.5	2.0	(3.2)	
Revised capital base	38.3	52.1	55.6		146.0
Cost of capital at 12 per cent of revised capital base	4.6	6.2	6.7		17.5
Revised profit	5.6	6.1	4.4		16.1
Value added	1.0	(0.1)	(2.3)		(1.4)

Notes:

[a]Allocated on the same basis as previous goodwill write-offs (10.3/40.7) to Division B and 30.4/40.7 to Division C.

[b]Apportioned on the basis of divisional turnover. Ideally head office costs should be allocated to divisions on the basis of the benefits received by the divisions.

[c]Allocated on the basis of profits before interest and tax less head office allocated costs plus interest received less interest paid. The outcome of this calculation is £5.7m for Division A, £4.6m for Division B and £3.7m for Division C and tax is allocated pro-rata to these figures.

[d]Arbitrary allocation on the basis of sales revenue adopting the same allocation base as that used for head office expenses.

The above analysis suggests that value is being 'destroyed' in Division C and to a minor extent in Division B. Division A is adding value. This is not apparent from the initial presentation which indicates a ROCE of 25 per cent (£5.6m/£23.2m) for Division C. The limitations of the analysis include:

(i) The use of arbitrary apportionments to allocate head office expenses, the tax liability and head office net assets to the business.

(ii) The assumption that the same cost of capital is applicable to all divisions.

(iii) The use of historical asset values rather than economic values.

(iv) The failure to distinguish between managerial and economic divisional performance. The analysis focuses on the economic performance of the divisions.

(c) See 'return on investment' and the discussion of the survey evidence within the section entitled 'residual income' in Chapter 19 for the answer to this question. For a discussion of how the problems of short-termism might be overcome see 'addressing the dysfunctional consequences of short-term financial measures' in Chapter 19.

Transfer pricing in divisionalized companies

Solutions to Chapter 20 questions

Question 20.1

(a) The effects on each division and the company as a whole of selling the motor unit at each possible selling price are presented in the following schedules:

(i) *EM division*

Output level (units)	Total revenues (£)	Variable costs (£)	Total contribution (£)
1 000	16 000	6 000	10 000
2 000	32 000	12 000	20 000
3 000	48 000	18 000	30 000
4 000	64 000	24 000	40 000
6 000	96 000	36 000	60 000
8 000	128 000	48 000	80 000

(ii) *IP division*

Output level (units)	Total revenues (£)	Variable costs (£)	Total cost of transfers (£)	Total contribution (£)
1 000	50 000	4 000	16 000	30 000
2 000	80 000	8 000	32 000	40 000
3 000	105 000	12 000	48 000	45 000
4 000	120 000	16 000	64 000	40 000
6 000	150 000	24 000	96 000	30 000
8 000	160 000	32 000	128 000	nil

(iii) *Enormous Engineering plc*

Output level (units)	Total revenues (£)	Variable costs (EMD) (£)	Variable costs (IPD) (£)	Total contribution (£)
1 000	50 000	6 000	4 000	40 000
2 000	80 000	12 000	8 000	60 000
3 000	105 000	18 000	12 000	75 000
4 000	120 000	24 000	16 000	80 000
6 000	150 000	36 000	24 000	90 000
8 000	160 000	48 000	32 000	80 000

The above schedules indicate that EM division maximizes profits at an output of 8000 units, whereas IP division maximizes profits at an output level of 3000 units. Profits are maximized for the company as a whole at an output level of 6000 units.

(b) (i) Based on the tabulation in (a), IPD should select a selling price of £35 per unit. This selling price produces a maximum divisional contribution of £45 000.

(ii) The company as a whole should select a selling price of £25 per unit. This selling price produces a maximum company contribution of £90 000.

(iii) If IPD selected a selling price of £25 per unit instead of £35 per unit, its overall marginal revenue would increase by £45 000 but its marginal cost would increase by £60 000.

Consequently it is not in IPD's interest to lower the price from £35 to £25 when the transfer price of the intermediate product is set at £16.

(c) (i) Presumably profit centres have been established so as to provide a profit incentive for each division and to enable divisional managers to exercise a high degree of divisional autonomy. The maintenance of divisional autonomy and the profitability incentive can lead to sub-optimal decisions. The costs of sub-optimization may be acceptable to a certain extent in order to preserve the motivational advantages which arise with divisional autonomy. Within the EE group, EMD has decision-making autonomy with respect to the setting of transfer prices. EMD sets transfer prices on a full cost-plus basis in order to earn a target profit. The resulting transfer price causes IPD to restrict output to 3000 units, which is less than the group optimum. The cost of this sub-optimal decision is £15 000 (£90 000 – £75 000). A solution to the problem is to set the transfer price at the variable cost per unit of the supplying division. This transfer price will result in IPD selecting the optimum output level, but will destroy the profit incentive for the EM division. Note that fixed costs will not be covered and there is no external market for the intermediate product.

Possible solutions to achieving the motivational and optimality objectives include:

(1) operating a dual transfer pricing system;

(2) lump sum payments.

See 'Proposals for resolving transfer pricing conflicts' in Chapter 20 for an explanation of the above items.

(ii) Where there is no market for the intermediate product and the supplying division has no capacity constraints, the correct transfer price is the marginal cost of the supplying division for that output at which marginal cost equals the receiving division's net marginal revenue from converting the intermediate product. When unit variable cost is constant and fixed costs remain unchanged, this rule will result in a transfer price which is equal to the supplying division's unit variable cost. Therefore the transfer price will be set at £6 per unit when the variable cost transfer pricing rule is applied. IPD will then be faced with the following marginal cost and net marginal revenue schedule:

Output level (units)	Marginal cost of transfers (£)	Net marginal revenue of IPD (£)
1 000		
2 000	6 000	26 000
3 000	6 000	21 000
4 000	6 000	11 000
6 000	12 000	22 000
8 000	12 000	2 000

IPD will select an output level of 6000 units and will not go beyond this because NMR < marginal cost. This is the optimal output for the group, but the profits from the sale of the motor unit will accrue entirely to the IP division, and the EM division will make a loss equal to the fixed costs.

Question 20.2

(a) The proposed transfer price of £15 is based on cost plus 25 per cent implying that the total cost is £12. This comprises £9 variable cost (75 per cent) and £3 fixed cost. The general transfer pricing guideline described in Chapter 20 can be applied to this question. That is the transfer price that should be set at marginal cost plus opportunity. It is assumed in the first situation that transferring internally will result in Helpco having a lost contribution of £6 (£15 external market price less £9 variable cost for the external market). The marginal cost of the transfer is £7.50 (£9 external variable cost less £1.50 packaging costs not required for internal sales). Adding the opportunity cost of £6 gives a transfer price of £13.50 per kg. This is equivalent to applying the market price rule where the transfer price is set at the external market price (£15) less selling costs avoided (£1.50) by transferring internally.

(b) For the 3000kg where no external market is available the opportunity cost will not apply and transfers should be at the variable cost of £7.50. The remaining output should be transferred at £13.50 as described above.

(c) The lost contribution for the 2000kg is £3 per kg (£6000/2000kg) giving a transfer price of £10.50 (£7.50 variable cost plus £3 opportunity cost). The remaining 1000kg for which there is no external market should be transferred at £7.50 variable cost and the balance for which there is an external market transferred at £13.50.

Question 20.3

(a) *Preliminary comments*

The answer to this question requires that we compare the relevant costs for each of the three alternatives. Relevant costs will include incremental costs plus any lost contribution where a division has no spare capacity. Only RR is working at full capacity. Therefore the relevant costs are as follows:

Work undertaken by RP, RS and RT: Relevant cost equals incremental cost for the group as a whole.

Work undertaken by RR: Relevant cost equals incremental cost plus lost contribution from the displaced work. (This is equivalent to the lost sales revenue.). Therefore the relevant cost is £33 000.

Relevant cost of company A quote	(£)
Relevant cost of company B quote	
Cost of quote	35 000
Less benefits to group of subcontract work[a]	2 420
Relevant cost	32 580

Note:

[a]It is assumed that the £13 000 RS charge to Company B includes 25 per cent on the cost of its own work but no additional margin is added to the £7500 market price for the parts purchased from RR. Therefore the price of £13 000 by RS to Company B is assumed to include £7500 in respect of RR work plus the balance of £5500 for RS work. The total cost of RS work is £4400 (the question indicates that RS expects to earn a profit of 25 per cent on its *own* work).

Therefore the group contribution from subcontract work is as follows:

	(£)	(£)
Selling price of special unit		13 000
Less incremental cost to group of RR's own work (70 per cent × £4400)	3 080	
Relevant cost of RR's work (market price)	7 500	10 580
Contribution to group		2 420
Relevant cost of RS quote		

The following diagram illustrates the inter-group transfers:

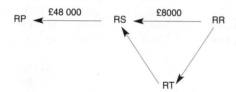

From the above information, it is necessary to ascertain the relevant cost of the *group* from producing the electronic control system. The relevant cost of RR work is the market price of £19 000 (£11 000 + £8000). The relevant cost of RS and RT work is the variable cost (excluding the cost of transfers within the group). The calculations are as follows:

	(£)
RS conversion cost:	
RS total cost	42 000
Less costs transferred from other members of the group (£30 000 + £8000)	38 000
Cost of RS conversion work	4 000
Variable cost of RS conversion work (70 per cent of £4000)	2 800

	(£)
RT conversion cost:	
Price charged by RT to RS	30 000
Less profit margin (20 per cent on total cost)	5 000
Total cost of RS work (including transfer from RR)	25 000
Less transfer price of parts purchased from RR	11 000
Total cost of work added by RT	14 000
Variable cost of work added by RT (65 per cent × £14 000)	9 100

Therefore the relevant cost to the group is as follows:

	(£)
Work undertaken by RR	19 000
Variable costs of conversion work by RT	9 100
Variable costs of conversion work by RS	2 800
Relevant cost	30 900

The order should be awarded to RS because this is the lowest relevant cost alternative.

(b) The following assumptions have been made in part (a):

(i) Incremental costs are represented by variable costs, and no additional fixed costs will be incurred for each alternative.

(ii) Variable costs are linear with respect to output changes.

(iii) RS and RT have sufficient spare capacity to accept the work. Hence no orders will be turned away and opportunity costs are assumed to be zero.

(iv) RP is not free to select its own source of supply. If RP has complete independence then it is likely to accept the quote that will minimize its costs (i.e. the Company A quote).

Question 20.4

(a) (i) Division O Budgeted profit for year ending 31 May 2015

Product	Painfree Branded	Painfree Unbranded	Digestisalve Branded	Digestisalve Unbranded	Awaysafe Branded	Total
Sales-packs (000s)	5 000	15 000	5 000	20 000	15 000	60 000
Selling price (£s)	2.40	1.20	4.80	3.60	8.00	
	£000s	£000s	£000s	£000s	£000s	£000s
Sales revenue	12 000	18 000	24 000	72 000	120 000	246 000
Cost of sales:						
Material/conv costs	4 250	12 750	9 250	37 000	42 000	105 250
Packaging costs	750	750	1 250	3 000	6 000	11 750
Total variable costs	5 000	13 500	10 500	40 000	48 000	117 000
Contribution	7 000	4 500	13 500	32 000	72 000	129 000
Fixed costs:						
Fixed overheads						81 558
Advertising and promotion costs						17 400
Net profit						30 042
Net profit						30 042
Required return (10 per cent)						12 000
Residual income (RI)						18 042
Invested capital (£000s)						120 000
Return on Investment (ROI)						25.04%

(ii) During the years ending 31 May 2015 and 2016 capacity is restricted to 65 million packs (780 million tablets/12). Expected demand in 2015 is 65 million packs but in 2016 it is expected to increase to 66 million packs resulting in demand exceeding capacity by 1 million packs. The failure to meet customer demand in 2016 may have an adverse impact on customer goodwill which may affect future sales. Attention should now be given to ways of increasing capacity in order to satisfy customer demand.

It is possible that customers may buy more than one different type of product from the company. In other words, product sales may be interrelated. In these circumstances it is important to ensure that a full product line is maintained. There is a danger that customers will migrate to competitors that offer a full product range if they are not offered a suitable range of products to choose from.

Competitor reactions should also be considered before altering the product mix by introducing new products or redesigning existing products.

(iii) See 'Residual income' in Chapter 19 for the answer to this question. In particular, the answer should point out how residual income can overcome some of the dysfunctional consequences of ROI, incorporate different cost of capital percentage rates to investments that have different levels of risk and provide a focus on utilizing capital efficiently in order to minimize the cost of capital charge.

(b) (i) The proposed transfer price is £5.60 (£8 less 30 per cent) but since the external purchase price is £5.50 the manager of Division L will choose to purchase externally. Quotation 1 is for 5 million packs and, assuming that Division O has no alternative use for its spare capacity of 5 million packs, the incremental cost of the order is £16 million (5 million × £3.20 variable cost). If the order is obtained externally the incremental purchase costs are £27.5 million (5 million × £5.50). Therefore the group will incur £11.5 million additional costs if the order is obtained from the external supplier.

Quotation 2 is for 9 million packs and Division O can only meet this demand by utilizing the spare capacity to produce 5 million packs and reducing sales volume of one of the existing products by 4 million packs. The sales volume of unbranded 'Painfree' should be reduced because it has the lowest unit contribution (£0.30 per pack). Therefore the incremental costs of supplying 9 million packs of 'Awaysafe' are £28.8 million variable costs but the company will lose a contribution of £1.2 million (4 million × £0.30) from reduced production of unbranded Painfree, giving a total incremental cost of £30 million. The external purchase cost is £49.5 million (9 million × £5.50). As indicated above the manager of Division L will choose to purchase externally resulting in the group incurring additional costs of £19.5 million.

(ii) In Chapter 20 it is pointed out that setting transfer prices at the marginal cost of the supplying division per unit transferred plus the opportunity cost per unit of the supplying division is a general rule that can be applied that should lead to optimum decisions for the company as a whole. For quotation 1 the demand can be met from existing capacity so opportunity cost is zero. Applying the general rule will result in a transfer price of £3.20 per pack or £16 million for 5000 packs. There is an opportunity cost of £1.2 million for quotation 2 in respect of the 4 million packs lost sales of unbranded 'Painfree'. The marginal costs of producing the 9000 packs are £28.8 million. Therefore applying the general rule the transfer price for the 9000 packs should be £30 million (£28.8 million + £1.2 million).

(iii) See 'Marginal cost plus opportunity cost' in Chapter 20 for the answer to this question. The answer should also point out that although applying the marginal cost plus opportunity cost rule meets one of the transfer pricing objectives of providing information for motivating optimal decisions, it fails to meet the transfer pricing objective of providing information for evaluating the managerial and economic performance of a division. For example, with quotation 1 applying the rule leads to the Division O obtaining zero contribution on the transfers and all of the contribution from the transferred packs being allocated to Division L.

(c) (i) If Division L buys externally from a local supplier the financial implications for the group are as follows:

	£m
Contribution obtained by Division O from the sales of 15 million packs of 'Painfree' at £0.30 per pack	4.5
Taxation (40 per cent)	1.8
After tax contribution	2.7
Division L purchases (9 million packs at £5.50)	49.50
Taxation savings (20 per cent)	(9.90)
After tax cost of purchases	39.60
Net cost to NAW group (£39.6 – £2.7)	36.90

If Division L buys internally from Divison O the financial implications are:

	£m
Division O sales	
Contribution from 11 million packs of Painfree at £0.30 per pack	3.3
Contribution from 9 million packs of 'Awaysafe' transferred to	
Division L at £2.40 per pack (£5.60 − £3.20)	21.6
	24.9
Less taxation at 40 per cent	(9.96)
After tax contribution	14.94
Division L purchases:	
Transfer costs on 9 million packs of 'Awaysafe' at £5.60 per pack	50.4
Taxation savings (20 per cent)	(10.08)
After tax cost of purchases	40.32
Net coast to NAW group (40.32 − 14.94)	25.38

NAW group will be £11.52 million (£36.90m − £25.38m) better off if Division L purchases product 'Awaysafe' from Division O compared with purchasing it from a local supplier.

(ii) See 'International transfer pricing' in Chapter 20 for the answer to this question.

(d) See 'Pricing policies' in Chapter 10 for the answer to this question.

Question 20.5

(a)

Analysis of sales

	Internal	External	Total
Number of components	50 000	150 000	200 000
	$000	$000	$000
Sales	768 000	3 072 000	3 840 000
Variable cost	384 000	1 152 000	1 536 000
Contribution	384 000	1 920 000	2 304 000

Note:

Internal sales = $768 000k (50 000 × $15 360) and the balance represents external sales. Unit variable cost $7680 ($1 536 000k/200 000).

(b) (i) Division Y is operating at 80 per cent capacity and producing 200 000 components so 250 000 units represents full capacity resulting in Division Y having 50 000 units spare capacity. An increase in division T's capacity by 25 per cent represents 12 500 units which will be sold at a unit selling price of $60 000.

Division Y therefore has sufficient capacity to supply the additional components to division T. Division T's variable cost per unit (including the transfer price) is $28 800 ($1 440 000k/50 000) giving a unit contribution of $31 200.

	$000
Present value ($31 200 × 12 500 units × 2.487)	969 930
Present value of residual value of equipment ($400m × 0.751)	300 400
	1 270 330
Investment cost	1 350 000
NPV	(79 670)

The manager of division T will not wish to undertake the investment.

(ii) It is apparent from part (a) that division Y's transfers are at variable cost + 100 per cent mark-up so the transfer price included in division T's cost is $15 360 full cost and $7 680 variable cost. The variable cost of the component to the group (TY) is $21 120 ($28 800 − $7 680) giving a revised unit contribution of $38 880. The revised present value of the total contribution is $1 208 682k ($38 880 × 12 500 units × 2.487) representing a contribution increase compared with that in (b) (i) of $238 752k. The revised positive NPV is $159 082k ($238 752k − $79 670k) so the investment is profitable for the company as a whole.

(c) The manager of division T would argue that division Y has spare capacity and is able to meet all of its external demand. Therefore variable cost is the opportunity cost to Division Y of the transfers since fixed costs would be incurred whether the internal sales take place or not. The manager of Division T will consider that the division is being overcharged with a current transfer price of variable cost plus 100 per cent.

The manager of division Y would argue that the full cost of internal sales is $17 430 per unit based on a unit fixed cost of $9750 ($1 950 000k/200 000) and a variable cost of $7680 and that the division would not be able to manufacture the components without incurring the fixed costs. Hence the current transfer price of $15 360 is below full cost. The manager of Division Y would also claim that the internal price is significantly below the market price that Division Y is charging on its external sales.

For the company as a whole the transfer price should have no impact unless it changes the decisions being made by the divisional managers so that they become sub-optimal for the group as a whole. This situation occurs in (b) above. Therefore the transfer price does not encourage optimal decisions and there are strong arguments for setting the transfer price at the unit variable cost of the supplying division plus a lump sum fixed fee (see chapter 20 for a description of this method).

Question 20.6

(a) Demand from the receiving division (R) is 20 000 components and capacity of the supplying division (S) is 35 000 components. For all of the alternatives specified in question S division will manufacture 35 000 components since internal and external demand will equal or exceed the available capacity. The question also states that R must buy from S and S must satisfy demand for R before making any external sales. Therefore internal sales will be 20 000 components and external sales will be 15 000 components for S for all alternatives given in the question. However, since transfers are at opportunity cost the opportunity cost to S will depend on whether internal transfers result in lost external sales.

For an external demand of 15 000 components there will be no lost external sales so opportunity cost will be zero and 20 000 components will be transferred at the variable cost of $105. When demand is 19 000 components meeting internal demand will result in lost external sales of 4000 components giving a transfer price of $200 ($105 variable cost plus $95 lost contribution) for 4000 components and a variable cost of $105 for the remaining transfers. When external demand is 35 000 components lost external sales will be 20 000 components and all transfers will be at $200 (the transfer price). The profits for each division will be as follows:

Division S

External demand (components)	15 000	19 000	35 000
	$000	$000	$000
Internal sales at variable cost of $105	2 100	1 680	
Internal sales at market price ($200)		800	4 000
External sales (15 000 at $200)	3 000	3 000	3 000
	5 100	5 480	7 000
Less production costs [Variable (3675) + Fixed (1375)]	5 050	5 050	5 050
Profit	50	430	1 950
Division R			
Sales	8 000	8 000	8 000
Internal purchases	2 100	2 480	4 000
Other variable costs	2 500	2 500	2 500
Fixed costs	900	900	900
Profit	2 500	2 120	600

(b) In part (a) external sales were 15 000 units for all demand levels. If R purchases externally S will increase its capacity for external sales from 15 000 to 35 000 components. If demand is 15 000 components S will not be able to sell any additional output, for a demand of 19 000 components it will be able to sell an additional 4000 components and if demand is 35 000 components it will be able to sell an additional 20 000 components. The total impact on the group will be as follows:

External demand for components	15 000	19 000	35 000
	$'000	$'000	$'000
Extra cost of external purchases 20 000 × (170 − 105)	1 300	1 300	1 300
Extra contribution by S external at $95 per component	0	380	1 900
Total impact	−1 300	−920	+600

(c) See 'International transfer pricing' in Chapter 20 for the answer to this question

Question 20.7

(a)

	Division C	Division D
	$000	$000
Internal transfers sales revenues[1]	2 400	
External sales[2]	2 600	10 000
	5 000	10 000
Internal transfers		2 400
Variable costs[3]	1 600	3 000
Fixed costs	2 400	1 750
Profit	1 000	2 850

Notes:

[1]Transfer price: $0.04 + ($2 400 000/$40 000 000) = $0.10 × 1.2 = $0.12

Internal transfers 20 000 000 cans at $0.12

[2]External sales by division C 20 000 000 cans at $0.13

External sales by division D 20 000 000 canned drinks at $0.50

[3]Division C variable cost 40 000 000 cans at $0.04; Division D variable cost 20 000 000 canned drinks at $0.15

(b)

	Division C	Division D
ROI	$1 000 000/$4 000 000 = 25%	$2 850 000/$12 650 000 = 23%
RI	$1 000 000 − ($4 000 000 × 7%) = $720 000	$2 850 000 – ($12 650 000 × 7%) = $1 964 500

(c)

	Division C	Division D
	$000	$000
Internal transfers sales revenues[1]	1 520	
External sales[2]	3 900	10 000
	5 420	10 000
Internal transfers		1 520
Variable costs[3]	2 000	3 000
Fixed costs	2 400	1 750
Profit	1 020	3 730

Notes:

[1] Capacity is now 50m can. External demand is 38m and internal demand is 20m so meeting the internal demand of 20m results in lost external sales of 8m. Transfers will be:

8 000 000 cans at $0.13 opportunity cost

12 000 000 cans at $0.04 variable cost

[2] External sales by division C 30 000 000 cans at $0.13

External sales by division D 20 000 000 canned drinks at $0.50

[3] Division C variable cost 50 000 000 cans at $0.04; Division D variable cost 20 000 000 canned drinks at $0.15

(d) Required profit = 25 per cent × $4.5m = $1.125m

Required contribution = required profit ($1.125m) + fixed costs ($2 400) = $3.525m

Contribution from external sales = 30m × ($0.13 − $0.04) = $2.7m

Contribution required from internal sales = ($3.525m − $2.7m) = $0.825m

Required contribution per can = $0.04125 ($0.825m/20m)

Required minimum transfer price = $0.04125 + variable cost ($0.04) = $0.08125

(e) • CD aims to build its brand based on the distinctive taste of its product. A key indicator of potential future success is the measure of consumer preference. A sample of consumers could be offered the CD soft drink along with that of a competitor and a measure of customers preferring CD soft drink could be reported.

• Percentage market shares and sales volumes analyzed by countries.

Question 20.8

(a) (i) If the selling price is $6000, demand will be zero and to increase demand by one unit the selling price must be reduced by $0.5 ($300/6000) so the maximum selling price for an output of x units is:

$SP = \$6000 − 0.5x$

The total revenue for an output of x units is $\$6000x − \$0.5x^2$

Therefore marginal revenue (MR) = $6000 − x$

Marginal cost (MC) = $1200

MR = MC where $6000 − x = 1200$

so $x = 4800$

Therefore SP at the optimal output level = $6000 − 0.5(4800) = \$3600$

Applying the above procedure to the body division:

$SP = 8000 − 1/3x$

Total revenue for an output of x units = $8000x − 1/3x^2$

MR = $8000 − 2/3x$

The MC in the body division for the complete camera is $5350 ($3600 + $1750)

The optimal output is where $8000 − 2/3x = 5350$

$x = 3975$

Therefore SP at the optimal output level = 8000 − 1/3(3975) = $6675

Total revenue from sales of the complete camera = 3975 × $6675 = $26 533 125

(ii) The optimum transfer price is the variable cost of the optics division ($1200) so the marginal cost for the complete camera is $2950 ($1200 + $1750).

Optimal output (MR = MC) is 8000 − 2/3x = 2950 so x = 7575

Optimal selling price = 8000 − 1/3 (7575) = $5475

Total revenue from sales of the complete camera = 7575 × $5475 = $41 473 125

(b) (i) Return required by PD = $288 000 ($2.4m × 12 per cent)

Required contribution = $2 688 000 ($2 400 000 + $288 000)

Let x = selling price per unit

(x − 1.40) 4 480 000 = $2 688 000

4 480 000x − 6 272 000 = 2 688 000

x = $2 so the minimum selling price per box is $2

(ii) Return required by SD = $720 000 ($6m × 12 per cent)

Required contribution = $6 720 000 ($6m + $720 000)

Let x = variable cost per unit

$13 500 000 − 500 000x = $6 720 000

x = $13.56

The maximum variable cost that would allow SD to earn a return of 12 per cent is $13.56. The variable costs from within SD are $12.00 so the maximum transfer price that it would be willing to pay for a box is $1.56.

(c) See 'marginal/variable cost plus opportunity cost transfer prices' in Chapter 20 for the answer to this question. In particular, the answer should point out that adopting this approach would result in the transfer price being set at the variable cost of $1.40 per box if PD had spare capacity but the division may be reluctant to trade at this price because it would not provide any reward. If PD is operating very close to capacity the opportunity cost would be the external sales that would be forgone and adopting the opportunity cost approach would result in the transfer price being set at the market price. This should be satisfactory to both divisions. However, if spare capacity exists rather than imposing a variable cost transfer price dual-rate transfer prices or marginal costs plus a fixed lump sum fee (see Chapter 20) should be considered.

Question 20.9

Schedule 1: Calculation of marginal cost, marginal revenue and net marginal revenue

Output of Alpha (units)	Alpha marginal cost (£000)	Alpha marginal revenues[a, b] (£000)	Beta net marginal revenue[a] (£000)
0–10	<28	65 (1)	57 (3)
10–20	<28	60 (2)	55 (4/5)
20–30	<28	55 (4/5)	53 (6)
30–40	<28	50 (8)	51 (7)
40–50	<28	45 (11/12)	49 (9)
50–60	<28	40	47 (10)
60–70	28	35	45 (11/12)
70–80	30	30	43 (13)
80–90	33	25	40
90–100	35	20	36
100–110	37	15	33
110–120	40	10	30
120–130	44	5	25

Notes:

[a] The numbers in parentheses represent the descending order of ranking of marginal revenue/net marginal revenue for Alpha and Beta.

[b] The question indicates that the marginal revenue function for Alpha decreases in increments of £5000 for each ten units increase in sales value of Alpha for output levels from 60 to 130 units. This implies that the total revenue and marginal revenue function of Alpha can be computed from this information on the basis of a £5000 decline in marginal revenue for each ten units of output.

The output of Alpha is allocated between the sale of the intermediate product on the external market and the transfer of the intermediate product for sale as a final product on the basis of the ranking indicated in the parentheses in Schedule 1. The allocation is presented in the following schedule:

Schedule 2: Allocation of output of Alpha

(1) Output of Alpha (units)	(2) Alpha marginal cost (£000)	(3) Allocation per ranking in Schedule 1[a]	(4) Marginal revenue or NMR[b]
0–10	<28	Alpha	65
10–20	<28	Alpha	60
20–30	<28	Beta	57
30–40	<28	Beta	55
40–50	<28	Alpha	55
50–60	<28	Beta	53
60–70	28	Beta	51
70–80	30	Alpha	50
80–90	33	Beta	49
90–100	35	Beta	47
100–110	37	Beta	45
110–120	40	Alpha	45
120–130	44	no allocation (MR/NMR < MC)	43

Notes:

[a]Alpha refers to sale of Alpha as an intermediate product. Beta refers to the transfer of Alpha internally for conversion to Beta and sale in the final product market.

[b]Appropriate MR/NMR per ranking in Schedule 1.

Conclusions

The optimal output level is 120 units. Below this output level MR > MC, but beyond 120 units MC > MR. To induce the output of 120 units, the transfer price should be set at £44 so as to prevent the receiving division from requesting a further 10 units, which will yield an NMR of £43. Examination of Schedule 2 indicates that 70 units should be transferred internally for sale as a final product and 50 units of the intermediate product sold externally. A transfer price of £44 will result in both divisions arriving at this production plan independently. Therefore, the optimal transfer price is the marginal cost of the supplying division for that output at which marginal cost equals the sum of the receiving division's net marginal revenue from using the intermediate product and the marginal revenue from the sale of the intermediate product – in other words, where column 2 equals column 4 in Schedule 2.

Cost management

Solutions to Chapter 21 questions

Question 21.1

(a) QW is presently using a form of JIT production system because each item that is produced is specific to the order placed by the customer resulting in QW not holding an inventory of finished items. The company does not use a JIT purchasing system because of the risk of being unable to fulfil customer orders due to lack of materials but raw material inventory levels are kept to a minimum thus resembling a JIT philosophy. The current system also encourages efficiency amongst the workforce because any delays may result in lost orders.

The production system required for the metal ornaments is different. It is based on constant rates of production and fluctuating levels of finished goods inventory to meet fluctuating sales throughout the year. This may result in high inventory holding costs so it is important that inventory levels are carefully monitored. For a more detailed answer to this question you should refer to 'Rearrangement of the production process' in Chapter 21.

(b) With a JIT system a defective part can stop the entire demand pull production flow line. Defective parts cannot be tolerated in a production environment that operates without stocks. Therefore total quality management with a never-ending quest of zero defects is an essential part of a JIT production system. In contrast, with a traditional batch production system WIP stocks are available at each production stage to meet the demands of succeeding operations so defective units are unlikely to halt the production process. Compared with a JIT system there is less need to eliminate defective output and therefore the same emphasis may not be placed on total quality management.

Question 21.2

(a) The answer to this question should point out that production will be organized based on a batch production functional layout (see Chapter 21) and materials scheduled using a material resources planning system (see Learning Note 24.1). There will be a need for a detailed product costing system that tracks work in progress movements throughout the factory and ensures that it can be valued at various stages at frequent intervals. Standard costing is likely to be extensively used to control costs.

(b) The answer to this question should describe a just-in-time production system and just-in-time purchasing (see Chapter 21).

(c) For the answer to this question you should refer to 'JIT and management accounting' (Chapter 21), 'The future role of standard costing' in Learning Note 18.5 on the open access website and 'Backflush costing' (Chapter 4). In addition, the answer should stress the need to place greater emphasis on non-financial measures (see balanced scorecard internal business perspective in Chapter 22), activity-based cost management and various other approaches to cost management described in Chapter 21.

Question 21.3

(a) See 'Benchmarking' in Chapter 21 for an explanation of the aims and operation. External benchmarking involves a comparison of performing activities with external organizations that are recognized as industry leaders, whereas internal benchmarking involves a comparison of performing similar activities in different units within the same organization.

Activity-based-costing information can be used to compare the cost of similar activities undertaken in different business units. The information would enable apparently high cost activities that may be inefficient if targeted for benchmarking. Alternatively, a unit may have established a reputation for being a leader for performing a particular activity. This may provide the stimulus for benchmarking the activity against other similar activities performed elsewhere in the organization. External benchmarking differs in that it is more difficult to obtain access to the industry leader and may be impossible where the leader is a competitor.

A major difficulty with benchmarking is identifying a relevant benchmark and ensuring that the activities being compared are similar in terms of their objectives and the constraints that apply. If internal benchmarking is used there is no guarantee that the targeted unit for comparison represents excellent practice. Hence there will be a danger that inefficiencies will be incorporated into the new methods of undertaking the activity. A further problem is that historical data may be used to compare activity costs, inputs and outputs. Such data may be distorted by changes in technology and methods of working.

(b) Possible reasons for similar standard costs in plants with differing technology include:

(i) The investments may have been made to reduce long-term cost savings and these savings may not have been reflected in cost reductions.

(ii) Cost reduction may not have been a primary objective for investing in new technology. Improved quality, delivery and flexibility to provide product variations and obtain the benefits of economies of scope may have been the objectives of the investment. The benefits will be reflected in an increase in customer satisfaction and future sales revenues rather than cost reductions.

(iii) The new technologies may be subject to the learning curve effect that has not been incorporated into the standard costs.

(iv) Standard cost may have been computed using a traditional costing system that has failed to capture the cost benefits of the new technology. Also if the plants with the new technology are initially operating partly with the old and the new technology they will initially be under-utilized. If short-term capacity, rather than practical capacity, is used as the denominator level to set the overhead rates the new technology will be over-costed. For an explanation of this point you should refer to the sections relating to denominator levels in Chapters 7 and Learning Note 11.1 on the dedicated website.

(v) The new technology plants may have had implementation problems and the extra costs arising from such problems may have been initially incorporated into the standard costs.

(vi) Standard costs may be inappropriate benchmarks if significant variances occur. In these circumstances actual costs would be a more appropriate benchmark.

A reduction in unit costs may not have been the primary objective for investing in new technology. Therefore the focus should be on a comparison between plants of physical measures such as defect rates, cycle times, set-up times, machine efficiencies, stock levels and customer response times.

Question 21.4

See 'Business process re-engineering' in Chapter 21 for the answer to this question.

Question 21.5

See 'Kaizen Costing' in Chapter 21 for a description of how this approach to cost management focuses on continuous improvement. In contrast, standard costs tend to be set annually and tend not to be updated during the year. Performance is measured against these standard costs and significant adverse variances form the basis for remedial action. Generally if the standard has been achieved no further action is taken.

In contrast, kaizen costing focuses on continual improvement. Therefore Kaizen cost goals are often updated frequently to reflect the improvement that has already been achieved and to challenge workers to improve still further. Rather than being a target to be achieved and then simply maintained, kaizen costing provides a constantly moving target.

Question 21.6

See 'Target Costing' and 'Kaizen Costing' in Chapter 21 for the answer to this question.

Question 21.7

Cost of Quality Report for the year ending 31 May

	Quantity	Rate $	Total costs $000
Prevention costs:			
Design engineering	66 000	75	4 950
Training			150
Total prevention costs			5 100
Appraisal costs:			
Inspection (manufacturing)	216 000	40	8 640
Product testing			49
Total appraisal costs			8 689

Internal failure costs:			
Rework (manufacturing)	1 500	3 000	4 500
Total internal failure costs			4 500
External failure costs:			
Customer support (marketing)	1 800	210	360
Transportation costs (distribution)	1 800	240	432
Warranty repair	1 800	3 200	5 760
Total external failure costs			6 552
Total costs			24 841
Opportunity costs	1 400	6 000	8 400
Total quality costs			33 241

Question 21.8

(a)

Statement of estimated quality costs

	$
Prevention costs	500 000
Appraisal costs	30 000
External failure costs (note 1)	286 880
Internal failure costs (note 2)	332 045
Total	1 148 925

Note 1

Customer demand is 24 000 units but 13 per cent of the units delivered are rejected by customers so 27 586 units (24 000/0.87) will be despatched to customers. Therefore 3586 units have to be replaced. The variable cost of producing these units is $75 per unit and the redelivery cost is $5 per unit so the total variable cost is $286 880 (3586 × $80).

Note 2

10 per cent of the items manufactured are discovered to be faulty before they are despatched so an initial production of 30 651 units (27 586/0.9) is required. Therefore 3065 units are produced and rejected at a variable production cost $229 875 (3065 × $75 per unit).

The cost of the components included in the units produced is $919 530 (30 651 units × $30). 10 per cent of the components bought are damaged prior to their use so the cost of these damaged components is $102 170 ($919 530 × 100/90).

Total Internal Failure Cost = $332 045 ($229 875 + $102 170)

(b) On the basis of a short-term financial analysis the company should not accept the proposal because there is an increase of $163 040 ($1 148 925 – $985 885) in quality costs. However, other qualitative factors must be taken into account such as the enhanced reputation of the company arising from improved quality that may result in increased future sales. The company should accept the proposal if it considers that the long-term qualitative benefits exceed $163 040.

Question 21.9

(a) Total quality management (TQM) is a term that is used to describe a situation where all business functions are involved in a process of continuous quality improvement. The critical success factors for the implementation of TQM are:

(i) The focus should be on customer needs. This should not just represent the final customer. All sections within a company should be seen as a potential customer of a supplying section and a potential supplier of services to other sections.

(ii) Everyone within the organization should be involved in TQM. Senior management should provide the commitment that creates the culture needed to support TQM.

(iii) The focus should be on continuous improvement. Continuous improvement seeks to eliminate non-value activities, produce products and provide services with zero defects and simplify business processes. All employees, rather than just management, should be involved in the process since employees involved in the processes are often the source of the best ideas.

(iv) The aim should be to design quality into the product and the production process. This requires a close working relationship between sales, production, distribution and research.

(v) Senior management should promote the required culture change by promoting a climate for continuous improvement rather than imposing blame for a failure to achieve static targets.

(vi) An effective performance measurement system that measures continuous improvement from the customer's perspective should be introduced. Simple non-financial measures involving real time reporting should be seen as a vital component of the performance measurement system.

(vii) Existing rewards and performance measurements should be reviewed to ensure that they encourage, rather than discourage, quality improvements.

(viii) Appropriate training and education should be given so that everyone is aware of the aims of TQM.

(b) For the answer to this question you should refer to 'cost of quality' in Chapter 21. In particular the answer should describe the different categories of cost that are included in a Cost of Quality Report and indicate how the report can be used to draw management's attention to the possibility of reducing total quality costs by a wiser allocation of costs between the different categories.

Question 21.10

(a) Prevention and appraisal costs are sometimes referred to as the costs of quality conformance or compliance and internal and external failure costs are also known as the costs of non-conformance or non-compliance. Costs of compliance are incurred with the intention of eliminating the costs of failure. They are discretionary in the sense that they do not have to be incurred, whereas costs of non-compliance are the result of production imperfections and can only be reduced by increasing compliance expenditure. The different cost categories are related to the extent that the more that is spent on conformance costs the lower should be the level of quality failures and therefore the lower the non-conformance costs. Organizations must decide on the quality/cost trade off but many organizations are now seeking to implement a zero-defect policy. The question suggests that CAL has positioned itself in the middle of the range of possible quality/cost trade offs because some of its competitors supply lower quality products whereas others supply high quality products.

(b) (i) Since customer demand is 20 000 good items and 2 per cent of the items supplied are faulty the total number of items to be supplied is 20 408 (20 000 × 100/98) so that 408 are returned for free replacement. The cost of these 408 units that are replaced free of charge is $18 360 (408 × $45). If failures can be eliminated the market share would increase to 25 per cent and this would result in an additional contribution of $75 000 (5000 × $15). Therefore the cost of non-conformance is $93 360.

(ii) The inspection process will not avoid internal failures but the lost sales and the delivery cost will be avoided. Thus the cost of internal failure could potentially be reduced to $16 320 (408 units × $40) giving a saving of $77 040 ($93 360 − $16 320). The introduction of the inspection process should also provide speedy feedback on internal failures which should result in action taken to reduce future failures.

Question 21.11

(a) See 'Pricing non-customized products/services using target costing' in Chapter 10 and 'Target Costing' in Chapter 21 for the answer to this question.

(b) The following four characteristics (see Chapter 22) distinguish services from manufacturing:

- Services are perishable and cannot be stored for future use.
- Services are intangible so unlike manufactured goods they cannot be physically touched.
- The production and consumption of many services are inseparable so that the service is consumed at exactly the same time that it is made available.
- Service outputs vary from day to day because services tend to be provided by different individuals whose performance is subject to variability that significantly affects the service quality that the customer receives. Standardization is difficult to maintain.

(c) (i) The pre-set tariff that is paid by the trust for each service is the appropriate target price for the 'payment by results' scheme. This is widely publicized and since the trust is a not-for profit organization there is not need to deduct a target profit margin from the target price to establish the target cost.

(ii) If possible the tasks that are required for undertaking the procedures should be determined and target prices applied. However, unlike manufacturing activities it is unlikely that tasks can be standardized so pre-set targets are more difficult to establish. Another alternative is to examine past data and set the target cost on the basis of the minimum cost that the procedures have been incurred in the past subject to meeting quality requirements.

(d) The difficulties that Sickham UHS Trust might find in using target costing in service provision are:

- The problem with using the pre-set tariff costs as the target cost is that the Trust has found that some services are provided at less and some at more than the target cost/price. Therefore some of the target costs will be difficult to achieve and thus be de-motivational whereas others will be easily achievable and thus will not provide an incentive to minimize costs.

- The provision of each service is subject to variability so it is difficult to establish future target costs based on standardized procedures. In the private sector target costs are established for new products/services based on predicted input/output relationships but it is difficult to apply this approach to hospital services where no past data is available for new services.
- The costing system at Sickham UHS Trust is poor so useful data is unlikely to exist to enable costs to be analyzed for setting target costs. Also a large proportion of the costs are overhead costs and it is unlikely that cause-and-effect allocations have been established so that inaccurate costs are likely to be generated. For target costing to be used to manage costs effectively service costs should be based on cause-and-effect allocations or direct assignments.

Question 21.12

(a) (i) See Figure Q21.12 for the answer to this question.

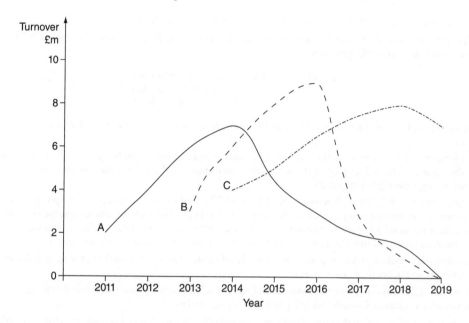

Figure Q21.12

(ii) Product life cycles consist of introductory, growth, maturity and decline stages. Products A and B have similar curves. Instead of an introductory stage they have a period of steady growth, a very short maturity stage followed by a period of rapid decline, but the decline phase is more rapid in B than A. Product A has a life cycle of eight years compared to six years for B. Product C has more of an introductory phase and a slower rate of growth than products A and B. It also appears to have a less rapid decline stage.

(iii) *Profit and loss analysis*

	2016				2017			
	A (£m)	B (£m)	C (£m)	Total (£m)	A (£m)	B (£m)	C (£m)	Total (£m)
Sales revenue	3.00	9.00	6.50		2.00	3.00	7.50	
Variable costs	0.90	2.25	2.60		0.60	0.75	3.00	
Contribution	2.10	6.75	3.90		1.40	2.25	4.50	
Product specific fixed costs	2.00	4.00	2.80		1.10	1.80	3.00	
Product profits	0.10	2.75	1.10	3.95	0.30	0.45	1.50	2.25
Company fixed costs				2.50				2.50
Net profit/(loss)				1.45				(0.25)

(iv) The forecasted total profit is £1.45m for 2016 and a loss of £0.25m for 2017. The total sales revenue for 2016 is £18.5m, which is close to the 100 per cent capacity level of £20m. In 2017 there has been a rapid decline in the sales revenue of product B resulting in total sales of £12.5m which represents only approximately 60 per cent of total productive capacity. There is a need to introduce new products or increase the sales of existing products. All of the products make a positive contribution to company fixed costs.

(b) (i)

NPV calculation for product D

	2017 (£m)	2018 (£m)	2019 (£m)
Contribution at 60 per cent	3.6	4.2	3.6
Less fixed costs	2.5	2.2	1.8
Net cash flows	1.1	2.0	1.8
Discount factor	0.909	0.826	0.751
Present value	0.9999	1.652	1.3518

NPV = Total present value (4.0037) − investment outlay (£4.5m) = − £0.4963m

(ii) For product D to be viable the increase in contribution sales ratio must be sufficient to cover the negative NPV of £0.4963m. Let x = the change in the contribution sales ratio.

$$6x(0.909) + 7x(0.826) + 6x(0.751) = 0.4963$$
$$15.742x = 0.4963$$
$$x = 0.0315$$

Therefore the required contribution/sales ratio would have to increase from 60 per cent to above 63.15 per cent for the NPV to be positive.

(iii) The target variable cost for the new product exceeds the estimated cost and ways must be found to drive the estimated cost to below the target cost. For a discussion of the actions that can be taken to drive the actual cost down to the target cost, you should refer to target costing in Chapter 21.

(c) The forecasted sales for 2017–2019 are respectively £18.5m, £17.5m and £13m. The company has approximately 10 per cent unutilized capacity for the first two years and 35 per cent in the final year. Although there is some scope for seeking methods of utilizing the spare capacity in the first two years, it is the final year where a considerable effort is required. It is important that steps are taken now to address the serious problem in the final year. Potential strategies include:

(1) In the short-term make a major effort to extend the sales of products A and B. Consider product redesign to improve its marketability and developing new markets.

(2) Seek to extend the maturity phase of product C and increase sales by seeking new markets and making more efforts to retain existing customers. Consider adopting new advertising strategies.

(3) Investigate ways of increasing the sales of product D by extending the market and considering alternative pricing and advertising strategies.

(4) Introduce a cost management programme that aims to reduce existing costs. This is particularly applicable in the first two years where only a small amount of unutilized capacity exists.

(5) Take steps now to ensure that new products and markets are developed for beyond 2019.

For all of the above strategies cost/benefit principles should be applied to ensure that additional benefits exceed the additional costs.

Question 21.13

(a) (i) *Total production units (pre-inspection)*

	Existing situation		Revised situation
Total sales requirements	5 000		5 000
Specification losses (5 per cent)	250	(2.5%)	125
	5 250		5 125
Downgrading at inspection (12.5/87.5 × 5 250)	750	(7.5/92.5 × 5 125)	416
Total units before inspection (100/87.5 × 5 250)	6 000	(100/92.5 × 5 125)	5 541

(ii) *Purchase of material X* (m^2)

	Existing situation		Revised situation
Materials required to meet pre-inspection production requirements $(6 000 × 8m^2)$	48 000	$(5 541 × 8m^2)$	44 328
Processing losses (4/96 × 48 000)	2 000		1 137

Input to the process (100/96 × 48 000)	50 000	(2.5/97.5 × 44 328)	45 465
Scrapped materials (5/95 × 50 000)	2 632	(3/97 × 45 465)	1 406
Total purchases (100/95 × 50 000)	52 632	(100/97 × 45 465)	46 871

(iii) *Gross machine hours*

Initial requirements (6 000 × 0.6)	3 600	(5 541 × 0.5 hours)	2 771
Rectification units (80% × 250 × 0.2 hours)	40	(80% × 125 × 0.2 hours)	20
	3 640		2 791
Idle time (20/80 × 3 640)	910	(12.5/87.5 × 2 791)	399
Gross machine hours (100/80 × 3 640)	4 550	(100/87.5 × 2 791)	3 190

(b) *Profit and loss accounts*

	Existing situation (£)		Revised situation (£)
Sales revenue:			
First quality 5 000 × £100	500 000	5 000 × £100	500 000
Second quality 750 × £70	52 500	416 × £70	29 120
Third quality 200 × £50	10 000	100 × £50	5 000
Scrap sales 50 × £5	250	25 × £5	125
	562 750		534 245

Costs			
Material × (52 632 × £4)	210 528	46 871 × £4	187 484
Insp/storage costs (52 632 × £0.10)	5 263	46 871 × £0.10	4 687
Machine costs (4 550 × £40)	182 000	3 190 × £40	127 600
Delivery of replacements (250 × £8)	2 000	125 × £8	1 000
Inspection and other costs	25 000	60% × £25 000	15 000
Product liability (3% × £500 000)	15 000	1% × 500 000	5 000
Sundry fixed costs	60 000	90% × £60 000	54 000
Prevention programme costs	20 000		60 000
	519 791		454 771
Net profit	42 959		79 474

(c) A cost of quality report is a major feature of a quality control programme. The report should indicate the total cost to the organization of producing products that do not conform to quality requirements. The cost of quality report should analyze costs by prevention costs, appraisal costs, internal failure costs and external failure costs. You should refer to Chapter 21 for a description of each of these cost categories.

The cost of quality report can be used as an attention-directing device to make top management aware of how much is being spent on quality-related costs. The report can be used to draw management's attention to the possibility of reducing total quality costs by a wiser allocation of costs among the four quality categories. For example, by spending more on prevention costs, the amount of spending in the internal and external failure categories can be substantially reduced, and therefore total spending can be lowered.

Examples of each of the four cost categories for Calton Ltd are as follows:

Internal failure costs:	Incoming materials scrapped due to poor receipt and storage organization, and downgrading products at the final inspection stage.
External failure costs:	Free replacement of goods, product liability claims, loss of customer goodwill.
Appraisal costs:	Inspection checks of incoming materials and completed output.
Prevention costs:	Training costs in quality prevention and preventative maintenance.

Strategic performance management
Solutions to Chapter 22 questions

Question 22.1

(i) The percentage of occupancy on flights to new destinations should provide feedback on how successful this policy is in terms of meeting the growth objective.

(ii) Measures of baggage loading/unloading times, aircraft cleaning times and fuel loading times can be used to implement a policy of continuous improvement and thus contribute to the achievement of the internal capabilities objective.

Question 22.2

(a) See 'The balanced scorecard' in Chapter 22 for the answer to this question. In particular, the answer should describe the four different perspectives of the balanced scorecard, the assumed cause-and-effect relationships and also provide illustrations of performance measures applicable to CM Ltd.

(b) See 'Benchmarking' in Chapter 21 for the answer to this question. The answer should stress the need to identify important activities or processes that may be common to other organizations (e.g. dispatching, invoicing or ordering activities) and to compare these activities with an organization that is considered to be a world leader in undertaking these activities.

Question 22.3

For the answer to this question you should refer to 'Benefits and limitations of the balanced scorecard approach' in Chapter 22. In addition to the points included in this section, the answer should also include the following items:

(1) It integrates financial and non-financial measures of performance and identifies key performance measures that link the measurements to strategy.

(2) It gives top management a fast and comprehensive view of the business unit.

(3) Each performance measure is part of a cause-and-effect relationship involving a linkage from strategy formulation to financial outcomes.

(4) It distinguishes and links both lagging and lead measures.

See the sub-sections that relate to the four different perspectives in Chapter 22 for specific examples of quantitative measures for each aspect of the balanced scorecard.

Question 22.4

Customer

Objective: To provide speedy results to enable patients' potential diseases to be diagnosed at their earliest possible stages.

Performance measure: Reporting times for each type of test

Comment: Specific tests have specific treatment periods so speedy feedback information from the tests is important for the doctors.

Internal processes

Objective: To provide accurate results for all tests

Performance measure: Percentage of spoiled/inaccurate tests

Comment: There is a need to ensure accuracy and avoid contamination (note the results should be compared against external quality benchmark figures).

Learning and growth

Objective: To have highly qualified staff trained in the latest techniques

Performance measure: Number of staff training days

Comment: There is a need to monitor continual professional development.

Question 22.5

(a) See 'The balanced scorecard' in Chapter 22 for the answer to this question.

(b) Within the customer perspective, the company could use measures such as the number of lost bags reported or the number of complaints received. These measures provide an indication of customer satisfaction. Internal operating efficiency measures include on-time performance and the aircraft capacity loadings. Learning and growth measures include the number of new routes operated by the airline thus indicating its ability to develop new services for its customers.

Question 22.6

(a)

	Original budget based on 120 000 gross hours	Standard hours based on actual gross hours	Actual hours	Variance (hours)	Variance (£) at £75 per hour
Gross hours	120 000	132 000	132 000		
Contract negotiation	4 800 (4%)	5 280 (4%)	9 240 (7%)	3 960A	297 000A
Remedial advice	2 400 (2%)	2 640 (2%)	7 920 (6%)	5 280A	396 000A
Other non-chargeable	12 000 (10%)	13 200 (10%)	22 440 (17%)	9 240A	693 000A
Chargeable hours	100 800 (84%)	110 880 (84%)	92 400 (70%)	18 480A	1 386 000A

There was a capacity gain over budget of 10 080 (110 880 − 100 800) hours at a client value of £756 000 (10 080 hours at £75) but because all of this was not converted into actual chargeable hours there was a net fall in chargeable hours compared with the original budget of 8400 (100 800 − 92 400) hours at a client value of £630 000.

(b) *Financial performance*

Profit statement and financial ratios for year ending

	30 April	
	Budget (£000)	Actual (£1 000)
Revenue from client contracts (chargeable hours × £75)	7 560	6 930
Costs:		
Consultant salaries	1 800	1 980
Sundry operating costs	3 500	4 100
	5 300	6 080
Net profit	2 260	850
Capital employed	6 500	6 500
Financial ratios:		
Net profit: Turnover	29.9%	12.3%
Turnover: Capital employed	1.16 times	1.07 times
Net profit: Capital employed	34.8%	13.1%

The above figures indicate a poor financial performance for the year. The statement in (a) indicates an increase in gross hours from 120 000 to 132 000 hours providing the potential for 110 880 chargeable hours compared with the budget of 100 800 hours. This should have increased fee income by £756 000 (10 080 × £75). However, of the potential 110 880 hours there were only 92 400 chargeable hours resulting in a shortfall of 18 480 hours at a lost fee income of £1 386 000. The difference between these two monetary figures of £630 000 represents the difference between budgeted and actual revenues.

Competitiveness

Competitiveness should be measured in terms of market share and sales growth. Sales are less than budget but the offer of free remedial advice to clients presumably represents the allocation of staff time to improve longer term competitiveness even though this has had an adverse impact on short-term profit.

Competitiveness may also be measured in terms of the relative success/failure in obtaining business from clients. The data shows that the budgeted uptake from clients is 40 per cent for new systems and 75 per cent for existing systems compared with actuals of 35 per cent and 80 per cent respectively. For new systems worked on there is a 16.7 per cent increase compared with the budget whereas for existing systems advice actual is 4 per cent less than budget.

The data indicate that client complaints were four times the budgeted level and that the number of clients requiring remedial advice was 75 compared with a budgeted level of 48. These items should be investigated.

Flexibility

Flexibility relates to the responsiveness to customer enquiries. For BS Ltd this relates to its ability to cope with changes in volume, delivery speed and the employment of staff who are able to meet changing customer demands. The company has retained 60 consultants in order to increase its flexibility in meeting demand. The data given show a change in the mix of consultancy specialists that may reflect an attempt to respond to changes in the marketing mix. The ratio of new systems to existing systems advice has changed and this may indicate a flexible response to market demands.

Resource utilization

The budget was based on chargeable hours of 84 per cent of gross hours but the actual percentage was 70 per cent (see part (a)). There was an increased level of remedial advice (6 per cent of gross hours compared with 2 per cent in the budget) and this may represent an investment with the aim of stimulating future demand.

Innovation

Innovation relates to the ability of the organization to provide new and better quality services. The company has established an innovative feature by allowing free remedial advice after completion of a contract. In the short term this is adversely affecting financial performance but it may have a beneficial long-term impact. The answer to part (a) indicates that remedial advice exceeded the adjusted budget by 5280 hours. This should be investigated to establish whether or not this was a deliberate policy decision.

Other points

Only budgeted data were given in the question. Ideally, external benchmarks ought to be established and the trend monitored over several periods rather than focusing only on a single period.

Question 22.7

(a) (i) *Profit and loss statements*

| | **Compuaid Ltd** | | | | **Competitors** | |
	Budget **(£)**		**Actual** **(£)**		**A** **(£)**	**B** **(£)**
Revenues						
Home visits	440 000	(22 000 × £20)	464 000	(23 200 × £20)	87 500	810 000
All other advisors	1 168 000	(58 400 × £20)	1 442 000	(72 100 × £20)	756 180	126 600
Annual fee customers	584 000	(5 840 × £100)	765 000	(76 50 × £100)	495 000[a]	1 000 000
	2 192 000		2 671 000		1 338 680	3 076 000
Cost of sales						
Service wages	832 000	(104 000 × £8)	998 400	(124 800 × £8)	720 000	1 099 000
Sundry operating costs	950 000	0	1 000 00		650 000	1 250 000
Total	1 782 000		1 998 400		1 370 000	2 349 000
Profit/(loss)	410 000		672 600		(31 320)	727 000
Profit/Revenues	18.7%		25.2%		−2.3%	23.6%

Notes:

[a]Company A = 6600 agreements at £75, Company B = 10 000 agreements at £100.

(ii) The figures show an improvement in net profits and net profits/sales compared with budget. The results also compare favourably with the competitor companies. The main reasons for the improvement and a better performance than the competitors include:

- Annual fee customers, other advisors and home visits revenues were respectively 30 per cent, 23 per cent and 5 per cent greater than budget.
- Home visit customers were charged at a rate of £20 per hour. This is lower than the rate charged by competitors A (£87 500/3500 = £25) and B (£810 000/36 000 = £22.50).
- The rate billed for telephone and written email advice was the same as company B (£1 266 000/63 300) but higher than company A (£756 180/ 42 010 = £18).
- The wage rate was £8 per hour compared with £9 per hour for A (£720 000/80 000 hours) and £7 per hour for B (£1 099 000/157 000 hours).

- Operating costs were budgeted at 43 per cent of sales revenues but the actual percentage was 37 per cent. Companies A and B had, respectively, operating costs as a percentage of sales of 49 per cent and 41 per cent.
- The actual hours taken up by the annual fee customers for Compuaid is significantly less than the competitors:

Compuaid Ltd. = 2.0 hours (15 300/7650)

Competitor A   = 4.5 hours (29 700/6600)

Competitor C   = 3.5 hours (35 000/10 000)

Compuaid receives an annual fee of £100 per customer (the same as B but more than A) but significantly less time is required, resulting in this area of the business being far more profitable for Compuaid. This could be reflected in a lower level of customer satisfaction and future growth.

(b) (i) Competitiveness can be measured by market share or sales growth. In terms of sales growth, the annual fee customers, other advisors and home visits revenues were respectively 30 per cent, 23 per cent and 5 per cent greater than budget for Compuaid. Competitiveness can also be measured by the success of the uptake of home visit enquiries received. For Compuaid the budgeted level was 67 per cent and the actual level was 50 per cent compared with 70 per cent and 62 per cent for A and B. However, competitor A had only a small number of visits so competitor B represents a more valid comparison.

(ii) Quality can be measured by remedial work and customer complaints. The budgeted home visits remedial work for Compuaid was 3 per cent but the actual level was 15 per cent. Nevertheless, the actual percentage was significantly less than A (400/1400 = 28%) and B (3400/15 000 = 23%). Customer complaints as a percentage of home visits were 1 per cent for the budget and 2 per cent for actual for Compuaid, compared with 5 per cent for A and 1.5 per cent for B.

(iii) Resource utilization can be measured by the relationship between output to input hours and the percentage of home visit hours that are chargeable and non-chargeable. The budgeted ratio of output hours to input hours is 91.3 per cent [(14 600 + 58 400 + 22 000)/104 000] and the actual ratio is 88.6 per cent. The corresponding figures are 94 per cent for A and 85.5 per cent for B. For home visits the data can be analyzed as follows:

	Compuaid (budget) %	Compuaid (actual) %	Company A %	Company B %
Travel	9.3	14.7	5.4	8.7
Re-work	1.8	6.1	8.2	10.1
Idle time	7.4	8.0	38.4	11.6
Chargeable hours	81.5	71.2	48.0	69.6
	100.0	100.0	100.0	100.0

Note:
Home visit hours = 2500 + 2000 + 500 + 22 000 = 27 000

The above analysis shows that the percentage of chargeable hours has declined from 81.5 per cent to 71.2 per cent of total home visit hours and there has been a marginal increase in all three categories of non-chargeable hours. However, the actual percentage of chargeable hours is greater than both competitors.

Question 22.8

(a) (i) *Analysis of the total costs of the millennium proposal*

	2016 (£m)		2017 (£m)	2018 (£m)
Target cost: variable	6.000	(40% × £15m)	7.200	8.000
Fixed	2.000		2.000	2.500
Internal failure cost	1.600	(20% × £8m)	0.920	0.525
External failure cost	2.000	(25% × £8m)	1.104	0.525
Appraisal costs	0.500		0.500	0.500
Prevention costs	2.000		1.000	0.500
Total cost	14.100		12.724	12.550

(ii) Target costs of £8m, £7.2m and £8m in each year are significantly below the expected costs of £14.1m, £12.724m and £12.55m. The target cost represents the cost that will enable the required return on the project to be obtained. The above table shows the analysis of the gap between the target cost and the estimated cost by different categories – internal and external failure costs, appraisal costs and prevention costs. For an explanation and examples of these categories see 'Cost of quality' in Chapter 21. The answer should also point out that there appears to be a step increase in fixed costs in 2018 and a significant decline in internal and external failure costs. This may have arisen because of the large investment in prevention costs in 2016. There has also been a large decline in prevention costs over the three years, possibly due to an investment in training costs in 2016 that has diminished over the years.

(b) (i) Corporate vision seeks to define the basis on which the company will compete. The company has indicated that it will seek to identify the key competitors and compete by focusing on close cooperation with its customers by providing products to meet their specific design and quality standards. The aim is to achieve the corporate vision through focusing on internal efficiency and providing an effective after-sales service.

(ii) Appropriate marketing measures indicate a projected increase in sales revenues of 20 per cent in 2017 and 11 per cent in 2018. The market share percentages are 12.5 per cent (£15m/£120m) in 2016, 14.4 per cent in 2017 and 15.4 per cent in 2018. Net profits are expected to increase each year from £0.9m in 2016 (£15m–£14.1m) to £5.28m in 2017 and £7.45m in 2018. Net profits as a percentage of sales are respectively 6 per cent, 29.3 per cent and 37.25 per cent. This may be partly due to the projected fall in quality costs.

(iii) There are several measures in the schedule given in the question that contribute to customer satisfaction. The percentage of production achieving design quality standards improves over the three years from 95 per cent to 98 per cent. Returns from customers also declines from 3 per cent to 0.5 per cent and the cost of after-sales service is predicted to decline from £1.5m to £1m. Sales meeting planned delivery dates increases from 90 per cent to 95 per cent in 2017 and a 99 per cent level is achieved in 2018. The cycle time from customer enquiry to delivery also declines over the three years. Therefore all of the measures support the potential for increased customer satisfaction.

(iv) Decreases in cycle times and levels of waste should contribute to the long-term financial success of the proposal. The average cycle time from customer enquiry to delivery also declines over the three years being six weeks in 2016, five-and-a-half weeks in 2017 and five weeks in 2018. Waste, as measured by idle machine capacity, declines from 10 per cent in 2016 to 2 per cent in 2018 and the percentage of components scrapped in production is also expected to fall from 7.5 per cent in 2016 to 2.5 per cent in 2018. The latter may be attributable to the investment in prevention costs. Overall the measures support improved productivity that contribute to the improvement in financial performance.

(v) Measures in (b) (iv) relate to the internal business processes of the balanced scorecard that appear to contribute to improved measures of customer satisfaction shown in (b) (iii), which in turn are assumed to contribute to improved financial performance. The answer should seek to highlight the cause-and-effect relationships that are assumed to occur from adopting a balanced scorecard approach and also show how the performance measures are linked to the mission and strategy of the organization.

Cost estimation and cost behaviour

Solutions to Chapter 23 questions

Question 23.1

Low	650 patients	$17 125
High	1 260 patients	18 650
Difference	610 patients	1 525

Variable cost per patient = $1525/610 = $2.50

Total fixed cost using 650 patients = total cost ($17 125) − variable cost (650 × $2.50) = $15 500

Estimated cost for 850 patients = variable costs (850 × $2.50) + $15 500 = $17 625

Answer = C

Question 23.2

It is assumed that advertising generates sales. Therefore advertising is the independent variable and sales revenue the dependent variable. Applying formula 23.2 (see Chapter 23) which was provided in the examination paper:

$$b = \frac{(6 \times 447\,250\,000) - (13\,500 \times 192\,000)}{(6 \times 32\,150\,000) - (13\,500)^2} = 8.714$$

Answer = C

Question 23.3

(a) Advertising expenditure is the independent variable (x) and sales revenue the dependent variable (y).

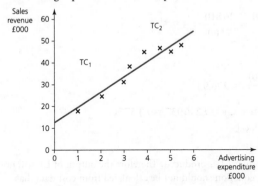

(b) Formulae 23.1 and 23.2 (see Chapter 23) were given in the examination for this question. Applying formula 23.2:

$$b = \frac{(8 \times 1055.875) - (26.35 \times 289.5)}{(8 \times 101.2625) - (26.35)^2}$$

$$= 818.675/115.7775 = 7.07$$

Applying formula 23.1 a = (289.5/8) − (7.07 × 26.35)/8 = 12.9

Therefore the regression line is $y = 12.9 + 7.07x$ where x and y are expressed in £000s. The line of best fit is shown in the graph in (a).

Question 23.4

(a) The first stage is to convert all costs to a 2017 basis. The calculations are as follows:

	2013 (£000)	2014 (£000)	2015 (£000)	2016 (£000)
Raw materials				
Skilled labour	$242(1.2)^4$	$344(1.2)^3$	$461(1.2)^2$	$477(1.2)$
Unskilled labour				
Factory overheads	$168(1.15)^3(1.2)$	$206(1.15)^2(1.2)$	$246(1.15)(1.2)$	$265(1.2)$
Power	$25(1.1)(1.25)^3$	$33(1.25)^3$	$47(1.25)^2$	$44(1.25)$
Raw materials				
Skilled labour	500.94	595.12	663.84	572.4
Unskilled labour				
Factory overheads	306.432	326.304	339.48	318
Power	53.625	64.35	73.32	55
Total (2016 prices)	861 000	986 000	1 077 000	945 000
Output (units)	160 000	190 000	220 000	180 000

The equation $r = a + bx$ is calculated from the above schedule of total production costs (2017 prices) and output. The calculations are as follows:

Output in units (000) x	Total cost (£000) y	x^2	xy
160	861	25 600	137 760
190	986	36 100	187 340
220	1 077	48 400	236 940
180	945	32 400	170 100
$\Sigma x = 750$	$\Sigma y = 3 869$	$\Sigma x^2 = 142 500$	$\Sigma xy = 732 140$

Applying formula 23.2 shown in the text:

$$b = \frac{4\,(732\,140) - 750\,(3\,869)}{4\,(142\,500) - (750)^2} = \frac{26\,810}{7\,500} = 3.575$$

Applying formula 23.1:

$$a = \frac{3\,869}{4} - \frac{3.575\,(750)}{4} = 296.937$$

The relationship between total production costs and volume in 2016 is: $y = £296\,937 = £3.575x$
where y = total production costs (at 2016 price) and x = output level.

(b) See Chapter 23 for the answer to this question.

(c) General company overheads will still continue whether or not product LT is produced. Therefore the output of LT will not affect general production overheads. Consequently, the regression equation should not be calculated from cost data that includes general company overheads. General company overheads will not increase with increments in output of product LT. Hence short-term decisions and cost control should focus on those costs that are relevant to production of LTs. Common and unavoidable general fixed costs are not relevant to the production of LT, and should not be included in the regression equation.

Question 23.5

(a) The dependent variable (y) is the maintenance cost (in £000) and the independent variable is production units (in 000).

$$\Sigma y = (265 + 302 + 222 + 240 + 362 + 295 + 404 + 400) = 2\,490$$
$$\Sigma x = (20 + 24 + 16 + 18 + 26 + 22 + 32 + 30) = 188$$
$$n = 8$$

Using formulae provided in Chapter 23 and also provided in the examination paper:

$b = [(8 \times 61\,250) - (188 \times 2490)]/[(8 \times 4640) - (188 \times 188)] = 12.32$

$a = (2490/8) - (12.32 \times 188)/8) = 21.73$

Therefore the linear equation is:

$y = 21.73 + 12.32x$ where x and y are in 000s. This can be interpreted as fixed costs being equal to £21 730 and the variable cost per unit of production is £12.32.

(b) Predicted maintenance cost at 44 000 units = $21.730 + (12.320 \times 44) = 563.81$ or £563 810.

The major reservation about this prediction is that 44 000 units of production is well outside the relevant range of data (16 000 to 32 000 units) that has been used to establish the linear regression equation. For example a step increase in fixed cost may apply outside the relevant range of output.

Question 23.6

(i) Cumulative average time for 64 units $(y = ax^b) = 225 \times 64^{-0.152} = 119.58$ hours

Total time for 64 units = 119.58 hours $\times 64 = 7653.12$ hours

The target profit is $75 000 is obtained at 7653.12 hours resulting in an hourly rate of $9.80 per hour.

Therefore the hourly rate can rise by $9.80 before the profit ceases to occur. This represent an increase of 24.5 per cent ($9.80/$40.00)

(ii) Total labour cost of 64 units = 7653.12 $\times$ $40 = $306 124.80

The labour cost can increase to $306 124.80 + $75 000 = $381 124.80 before no profit is obtained, giving a total of 9528.12 hours ($381 124.8/$40) and a cumulative average time of 148.88 hours per unit (9 528.12 hours/64 units).

The time for the first unit was 225 hours.

The cumulative average time per unit for the first 64 units as a percentage of the time for the first unit is 66.17 per cent. (148.88/225)

64 units is 6 doublings of output (2, 4, 8, 16, 32, 64) so 66.17 per cent is the sixth root of the learning rate.

Therefore the expected learning rate is 93.34 per cent ($\sqrt[6]{0.6617} = 0.93349$) giving a sensitivity of 3.72 per cent (3.35/90)

Question 23.7

(a) (i) Cumulative average time for 64 batches $15 \times 64^{-0.074} = 11.03$ hours

Total time for 64 batches = $64 \times 11.03 = 705.92$ hours

Cumulative average time for 63 batches $15 \times 63^{-0.074} = 11.04$ hours

Total time for 63 batches = $63 \times 11.04 = 695.52$ hours

Time for batch 64 = $705.92 - 695.52 = 10.40$ hours

(ii)

	$
Labour (10.4 hours $\times$ $25)	260
Materials ($52 $\times$ 10 units per batch)	520
Variable overhead (10.4 hours $\times$ $5)	52
Total variable cost	832

(b) The following conditions should exist for the learning curve effect to be realized:

- The production process must be labour intensive for the learning curve effect to apply;
- The production process should be complex in order to obtain the benefits of learning and efficiency improvements, and
- There should be a low labour turnover of production employees engaged on the production process that is subject to the learning effect. The steady state production time per unit once all production staff have sufficient experience

Question 23.8

(a) The average time for 64 hatches (i.e. 6400 units) is:

$$Y = ax^b = 1500 \times 64^{-0.2345} = 565.64 \text{ hours}$$

(b) The total time for 64 batches is 64×565.64 hours, which is a total of 36 200.96 hours

The average time for 63 batches is:

$$Y = ax^b = 1\,500 \times 63^{-0.2345} = 567.735 \text{ hours, which is a total of } 35\,767.31 \text{ hours}$$

Thus the time for the 64th and subsequent batches is 433.65 hours

(c)

	$
Revenue from 9000 units (9000 units @ $124)	1 116 000
Costs of 10 000 units:	
Variable costs:	
Non-labour (10 000 units @ $38)	380 000
Direct labour(see below)	621 748
	1 001 748
Fixed costs	80 000	1 081 748
Profit		34 252
Profit target		100 000
Revenue required from final 1000 units		65 748

Direct labour cost

The total time for 64 batches calculated in part (b) is 36 200.96 hours and the time per batch for the remaining 36 is 433.65 hours giving a total of 15 611.4 hours (36 batches × 433.65 hours). Therefore the total time for 100 batches is 51 812.36 hours so the total labour cost at $12 per hour is $621 748.32. The 1000 units that are to be sold in the decline stage need to be sold at an average selling price of $65.75 ($65 748/1000) in order to meet the profit target of $100 000.

Question 23.9

(a)
$$Y_{1000} = 18 \times 10\,000^{-0.1520}$$
$$Y_{1000} = 18 \times 0.3499$$
$$Y_{1000} = 6.2990 \text{ minutes}$$

The cumulative average time taken to produce 1000 units is 6.2990 minutes and the time taken to produce a total of 1000 units will therefore be 629.9 minutes (i.e. 104.98 hours).

	(£)
Standard cost of 1000 units:	
Materials (£28/0.95 × 1000)	29 474
Processing cost (104.98 hours at £25)	2 625
	32 099

(b)
$$Y_{5000} = 18 \times 50\,000^{-0.1520}$$
$$Y_{5000} = 18 \times 0.274$$
$$Y_{5000} = 4.93\,21 \text{ minutes}$$

Therefore the estimated time taken to produce 5000 units is 24 660 minutes (5000 × 4.9321 minutes)

$$Y_{6000} = 18 \times 60\,00^{-1520}$$
$$Y_{6000} = 18 \times 0.26\,65$$
$$Y_{6000} = 4.79\,73 \text{ minutes}$$

Therefore the estimated time taken to produce 6000 units is 28 784 minutes (6000 × 4.7973 minutes) so the 1000 units has taken an additional 68.73 hours (28 784 minutes − 24 660 minutes) giving a standard variable processing cost of £1718 (68.73 hours × £25). Adding the direct material cost of £29 474 gives a total standard variable cost of £31 192.

(c) Revised learning curve effect:

$$Y_{1000} = 18 \times 1\,000^{-0.320}$$
$$Y_{1000} = 18 \times 0.1096$$
$$Y_{1000} = 1.9737 \text{ minutes}$$

The estimated total time to produce 1000 units in April is 32.89 hours (1973.7 minutes/60) giving a total standard variable processing cost of £822 (32.89 hours × £25). The standard direct material cost will remain unchanged at £29 474 giving a total standard cost of £30 296.

Original budgeted profit (£)

Sales	60 000
Variable costs	32 099
Contribution	27 901
Fixed costs	20 001
Profit	7 901

Actual profit

	(£)	(£)
Sales (900 × £62)		55 800
Production costs: Direct materials	31 870	
Variable processing	1 070	
Fixed costs	24 840	
	57 780	
Closing stock (100 units at revised standard cost of £30.296 per unit)	3 030	54 750
		1 050

Variance calculations

Processing usage/efficiency variance (original standard of £2 625 − revised standard of £822)	£1 803F
Selling price variance (£62 actual price − £60 budgeted price) × 900 units	£1 800F
Sales volume (900 actual volume − 1000 budgeted volume) × revised stand. contrib. margin[a]	£2 970A
Direct material cost (standard cost of 1000 × £29.474 − Actual cost of £31 870)	£2 396A
Variable processing expenditure (Flexed budget of 2 425 minutes × £25/60 − actual cost)	£60A
Variable processing efficiency (1.9737 minutes revised standard × 1000 units − actual time of 2425 minutes) × stand. rate (£25 per hour)	£188A
Fixed cost expenditure (Budgeted cost of £20 000 − Actual cost of £24 840)	£4 840A
Total variances	£6 851A

Notes:

[a]revised standard contribution margin = £60 selling price − revised variable cost

$$(£29.474 + £822/1000) = £29.704$$

Reconciliation statement

Original budgeted profit	£7 901
Less net variances as shown above	£6 851A
Actual profit	£1 050

(d) If budgets and standards are set without considering the learning effect, meaningless standards are likely to be set that are easy to attain. Therefore favourable variances would be reported that are not due to operational efficiency. Where learning effects are expected, management should create an environment where improvements are expected.

Quantitative models for the planning and control of inventories

Solutions to Chapter 24 questions

Question 24.1

(i)
$$\text{Re-order level} = \text{Maximum usage} \times \text{Maximum lead time}$$
$$= 95 \times 18 = 1710$$

Answer = C

(ii)   Maximum stock = Re-order level + Re-order quantity − Minimum usage during minimum lead time
$$= 1710 + 1750 - (50 \times 12)$$
$$= 2860$$

Answer = B

Question 24.2

Re-order level = Maximum usage (750) × Maximum lead time (15 days) = 11 250 units
Minimum stock reduction before an order is received = 11 250 − (450 × 8days) = 7650 units
Maximum order size = 15 000 − 7650 = 7350 units
Answer = 7350 units

Question 24.3

The question indicates that the *annual* holding cost is 6 per cent and *annual* demand is 80 000 (4 × 20 000).

$$EOQ = \sqrt{\frac{2 \times 80\,000 \times 20}{(0.06 \times 25)}}$$
$$= 1461$$

Answer = C

Question 24.4

(a)

$$EOQ = \sqrt{\frac{2 \times 160 \times 26\,000}{1.40}} = 2438 \text{ units}$$

Answer = A

(b)

Number of orders = 26 000/2600 = 10 per year
Ordering costs = 10 × $160 = $1600
Holding costs = 2600 × 0.5 × $1.40 = $1820
Total ordering and holding costs = $3420
Answer = D

Question 24.5

(a)

Month	Demand Std hours	Basic production Std hours	Inc/(Dec) in inventory Std hours	Closing inventory Std hours	Average inventory Std hours	Inventory cost $
1	3 100	3 780	680	680	340	2 040
2	3 700	3 780	80	760	720	4 320
3	4 000	3 780	(220)	540	650	3 900
4	3 300	3 780	480	1 020	780	4 680
5	3 600	3 780	180	1 200	1 110	6 660
6	4 980	3 780	(1 200)	0	600	3 600
Total						25 200

Note that because production occurs evenly throughout the month average inventory standard hours are equal to opening inventory plus closing inventory divided by two.

With the JIT system of not maintaining inventories, demand in months 3 and 6 will require overtime working since there is a shortfall in output of 220 standard hours in month 3 and 1200 hours in month 6. The calculation of the overtime cost is as follows:

$$\text{Month 3} = 220 \text{ std hours}/0.96 = 229.17$$
$$\text{labour hours} \times \$15 = \qquad 3437.55$$
$$\text{Month 6} = 1200 \text{ std hours}/0.96 = 1250.00$$
$$\text{labour hours} \times \$15 = \qquad \underline{18750.00}$$
$$\underline{22187.55}$$

The net saving for the six-month period with the JIT system is $3012.45.

(b) The following factors should be considered:

- The need for a commitment to quality since substandard output cannot be replaced from inventories that are maintained as a safety net to guard against inferior production.
- The need to ensure that staff are trained in multi-tasking in order to respond immediately with any problems that occur in the production process since JIT production is dependent on a constant production flow.

Question 24.6

(a) TNG has a current order size of 50 000 units

Average number of orders per year = demand/order size = 255 380/50 000 = 5.11 orders
Annual ordering cost = 5.11 × £25 = £127.75
Safety stock held = 255 380 × 28/365 = 19 591 units
Average stock held = 19 591 + (50 000/^{2}) = 44 951 units
Annual holding cost = 44 591 × 0.1 = £4459.10
Annual cost of current ordering policy = 4459.10 + 127.75 = £4587

(b) EOQ = $\sqrt{(2 \times 255 380 \times 25)/0.1}$ = 11 300 units

Average number or orders per year = 255 380/11 300 = 22.6 orders
Annual ordering cost = 22.6 × £25 = £565.00
Average stock held = 19 591 + (11 300/2) = 25 241 units
Annual holding cost = 25 241 × 0.1 = £2524.10
Annual cost of EOQ ordering policy = 2524.10 + 565.00 = £3089
Saving compared to current policy = 4587 − 3089 = £1498

(c) Annual credit purchases = 255 380 × £11 = £2 809 180
Current creditors = £2 809 180 × 60/365 = £461 783
Creditors if discount is taken = £2 809 180 × 20/365 = £153 928
Reduction in creditors = £461 783 − £153 928 = £307 855

Finance cost increase = £307855 × 0.08 = £24628
Discount gained = 2809180 × 0.01 = £28091
Net benefit of taking discount = £28091 − £24628 = £3463

The discount is therefore financially acceptable.

(d) The EOQ model assumes that demand, holding and ordering costs can be predicted with certainty and are constant for the period under consideration. In practice, demand throughout the period is likely to be uncertain and not constant. Costs are also unlikely to remain constant. The EOQ model also ignores the cost of running out of stock but the model can still be applied by ensuring that safety stocks are maintained. See 'Other factors influencing the choice of order quantity' in Chapter 24 for an explanation of how these factors might cause a firm to depart from the EOQ. Nevertheless, the EOQ model may still be useful because the model may not be significantly affected if the underlying assumptions are violated or there are variations in cost predictions. See 'Assumptions of the EOQ formula' in Chapter 24 for a more detailed discussion of these issues.

(e) See 'Just-in-time systems' in Chapter 21 for the answer to this question. In particular, the answer should discuss the elimination of waste, reduced inventories, quicker customer response times, improved longer-term relationships with suppliers and the resulting cost savings associated with these factors.

Disadvantages include greater dependence on the reliability of suppliers for adhering to quality and delivery requirements. Delay in delivery or the delivery of poor quality materials can have a dramatic detrimental impact on JIT systems in terms of production stoppages and delays in customer deliveries.

Question 24.7

(a) *EOQ*

$$EOQ = \sqrt{(2DO/H)}$$

Where D = demand for period (43200 units)

O = ordering cost per unit (£900 + £750)

H = holding cost per unit (15% × £30 + 2 × £3.25) = £11

Note that, assuming constant demand, the average stock level is one-half of the EOQ. In this question the holding costs applicable to storage space will depend upon maximum (rather than average) stock levels. It is therefore necessary to double the holding cost per unit given in the question.

$$EOQ = \sqrt{[(2 × 43200 × £1650)/£11]} = 3600 \text{ units}$$

The EOQ is equivalent to one month's sales. Safety stocks equivalent to one month's sales are maintained. Consequently, stock levels will vary between 3600 and 7200 units.

Cash payments to trade creditors

The budgeted stock level of 21600 units could be reduced to 7200 units. This represents stock reduction of 14400 units, which is equivalent to four months' stocks. In other words, for the next four months, sales demand can be met from stocks. From month 5, purchases would be 3600 units per month.

$$\text{Budgeted monthly cost of sales} = £108000 \ (1296/12)$$

Trade creditors are therefore equivalent to two months' cost of sales. The schedule of payments to trade creditors would be as follows:

July and August 2015	£108000 per month
September to December 2015	No payments made
January and February 2016	£108000 per month

(b) (i) *Cash operating cycle at 30 June 2015*

	Months
Stockholding period (£21600/3600)	6
Debtors average credit period [198/(2376/12)]	1
Creditors average payment period (per (a))	(2)
	5

(ii) *Cash operating cycle at 30 June 2016*

	Months
Stockholding period (7200 units)	2
Debtors (no change)	1
Creditors (no change)	(1)
	1

(c) The answer should include a discussion of the EOQ assumptions and the extent which these may be appropriate in a practical situation. The following points should be included in the answer:

    (i) The formula assumes that demand can be accurately estimated and that usage is constant throughout the period. In practice, demand may be uncertain and subject to seasonal variations. Most firms hold safety stocks as a protection against variations in demand.

    (ii) The ordering costs are assumed to be constant per order placed. In practice, most of the ordering costs are fixed or subject to step functions. It is therefore difficult to estimate the incremental cost per order.

    (iii) Holding costs per unit are assumed to be constant. The financing charge for the investment in stocks is based on the average investment multiplied by the cost of capital. This will result in a reasonable estimate, provided that demand can be accurately estimated and that usage and the purchase price are constant throughout the period. Many holding costs are fixed throughout the period and are not relevant to the model, but other costs (e.g. storekeepers' salaries) are step fixed costs. Opportunity costs of the warehouse space and labour are other relevant holding costs that are included in the model. However, identifying lost opportunities from holding stocks is difficult to determine. Consequently, it is extremely difficult to accurately predict the holding cost for a unit in stock for one year.

    (iv) Purchasing cost per unit is assumed to be constant for all purchase quantities. In practice, quantity discounts can result in purchasing economies of scale.

    (v) Despite the fact that much of the data in the model represent rough approximations, the EOQ formula is likely to provide a reasonable guide of the EOQ because it is very insensitive to errors in predictions (see 'Effect of approximations' in Chapter 24). The EOQ model can also be adapted to incorporate quantity discounts. For a discussion of other issues relevant to this answer see 'Assumptions of the EOQ formula' in Chapter 24.

(d) The advantages of adopting a JIT approach include:

    (i) substantial savings in stockholding costs;

    (ii) elimination of waste;

    (iii) savings in factory and warehouse space, which can be used for other profitable activities;

    (iv) reduction in obsolete stocks;

    (v) considerable reduction in paperwork arising from a reduction in purchasing, stock and accounting transactions.

The disadvantages include:

    (i) additional investment costs in new machinery, changes in plant layout and goods inwards facilities;

    (ii) difficulty in predicting daily or weekly demand, which is a key feature of the JIT philosophy;

    (iii) increased risk due to the greater probability of stockout costs arising from strikes, or other unforeseen circumstances, that restrict production or supplies.

Question 24.8

(a) Order costs consist of variable purchasing costs (£300) plus transportation costs (£750 or £650). Note that the timing of the payments for 4200 units will be the same irrespective of the order size. Consequently, the cost of capital is omitted from the stockholding costs because it will be the same for all order quantities.

$$\text{EOQ with transportation costs of £750} = \sqrt{\left(\frac{2 \times 1050 \times 4200}{4}\right)}$$
$$= 1485 \text{ units}$$

At this level the company qualifies for the lower transport costs. Therefore the EOQ should be based on ordering costs of £950:

$$\text{EOQ} = \sqrt{\left(\frac{2 \times 950 \times 4200}{4}\right)} = 1412 \text{ units}$$

The company should therefore place orders for 1412 units.

Improvement in profit

		(£)
Gross profit (unchanged)		64 000
Purchasing department costs:		
Variable (4200/1412) × £300	(892)	
Fixed	(8 400)	(9 292)
Transportation costs:		
(4200/1412) × £650		(1 933)
Insurance costs on average stockholding:		
[200 safety stock + (1412/2)] × £4		(3 624)
Warehouse fixed costs		(43 000)
Revised profit		6 151
Original profit		3 250
Improvement		2 901

(b) The re-order level should be based on the expected usage during the period plus a safety stock to provide a cushion in the event of demand being in excess of the expected usage.

$$\text{Expected usage} = (500 \times 0.15) + (600 \times 0.20) + (700 \times 0.30) + (800 \times 0.20)$$
$$+ (900 \times 0.15) = 700$$

Thus it is necessary to consider safety stocks of 0, 100 or 200 units.

Expected usage (units)	Safety stock (units)	Re-order point (units)	Stockout (units)	Annual stockout cost £18 per[a] (£)	Probability	Expected annual stockout cost (£)	Holding cost[b] (£)	Total expected cost (£)
700	0	700	200	21 600	0.15	3 240		
			100	10 800	0.20	2 160		
						5 400	0	5 400
700	100	800	100	10 800	0.15	1 620	1 800	3 420
700	200	900	0	0		0	3 600	3 600

Notes:

[a]Expected costs are calculated on an *annual* basis by multiplying 200 units × £18 × 6 (that is, six two-monthly periods).

[b]In the answer to part (a) the interest on the value of the stock was not included, because the timing of the payments for stocks was not affected by the order quantity. Consequently, the interest charge was not relevant in calculating the EOQ. The holding cost in the above calculation consists of £14 interest cost (20 per cent of £70 purchase cost) plus £4 insurance cost. It is assumed that the safety stock represents an investment over and above the annual order quantity of 4200 units. In other words, safety stocks represent an incremental investment, and interest on safety stocks is therefore relevant to the safety stock decision.

Recommendation

Expected costs are minimized at a re-order point of 800 units (this includes a safety stock of 100 units).

(c) The answer to this question should include a discussion of the assumptions of the EOQ model (see 'Assumptions of the EOQ formula' in Chapter 24). The answer should stress that because demand is uncertain and not uniform and lead time is not constant, it is necessary to adjust the EOQ model to take account of these facts. The safety stock model applied in (b) is subject to a number of practical difficulties – for example, the difficulty of producing probability distributions for demand and lead time. In addition, stockout costs are extremely difficult to determine in practice. A further problem is that discrete distributions as estimated in (b) are unlikely to be a representation of reality because they are based on a limited number of outcomes. The answer produced represents the *expected value* of the stockholding costs, and as such represents a long-run average outcome. An alternative is to use continuous distributions, but this requires that the distribution conform to one that can easily be described mathematically (e.g. a normal distribution).

In practice, it is likely that stockout costs will be the most significant cost, and the problem is one of determining the minimum level of stock that is consistent with always satisfying demand. Most small companies are likely to concentrate on frequently reviewing stock levels and use their previous experience to subjectively determine order levels.

contribution line is extended outwards to determine the last comer point within the feasible region. This is point D where the lines S = 12 000 and 0.5P + 0.75S = 12 000 intersect.

$$\text{Substituting } S = 12\,000 \text{ in equation (2)}$$
$$0.5P + (0.75 \times 12\,000) = 12\,000$$
$$0.5P + 9\,000 = 12\,000$$
$$0.5P = 12\,000 - 9\,000$$
$$0.5P = 3\,000$$
$$P = 6\,000$$

Therefore the maximum contribution is earned when 6000 pool cues and 12 000 snooker cues are made and sold in a three month period.

The contribution earned is

$$C = (20 \times 6\,000) + (40 \times 12\,000)$$
$$C = 120\,000 + 480\,000$$
$$C = \$600\,000$$

Linear programming graphical solution for HC

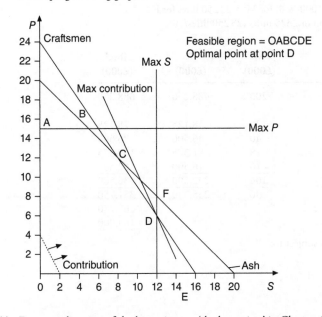

(c) For an explanation of shadow prices see 'shadow prices' in Chapter 25. There are unused resources of ash at the optimal output level. Given that the resource is not scarce the shadow price is zero. To determine the shadow price of labour we examine the impact of an additional labour hour so that:

$$0.5P + 0.75S = 12\,001$$
$$\text{Substituting } S = 12\,000$$
$$0.5P + 0.75(12\,000) = 12\,001$$
$$0.5P + 9\,000 = 12\,001$$
$$0.5P = 3\,001$$
$$P = 6\,002$$

This would result in an extra $40 contribution (2 × $20) so the shadow price is $40 per extra hour of craftsmen time.

(d) The company would be better off accepting the offer since the rate of pay is less than the shadow price but before accepting the company should try and negotiate a lower rate. Buying more craftsmen hours will extend the line outwards until it reaches point F, so that materials will become the binding constraint and there would be no point buying additional labour hours. At point F:

$$0.27P + 0.27S = 5\,400$$
$$S = 12\,000$$
$$\text{Substituting } S = 12\,000 \text{ in the above equation}$$
$$0.27P + 0.27(12\,000) = 5\,400$$

$$0.27P + 3240 = 5400$$
$$0.27P = 2160$$
$$P = 8000$$

Point F falls where S = 12 000 and P = 8000 so the craftsmen hours needed at this point are $(0.5 \times 8000) + (0.75 \times 12\,000) = 13\,000$ hours. Therefore Higgins should only buy 1000 hours (13 000 – 12 000).

Question 25.3

(a)

	M	F
Contribution per unit	£96	£110
Litres of material P required	8	10
Contribution per litre of material P	£12	£11
Ranking	1	2
Production/sales (units)	1 000	2 325[a]

Note:

[a]31 250 litres of P less (1000 × 8) for M = 23 250 litres for F giving a total production of 2325 units (23 250 litres/10)

(b)

	M (£000)	F (£000)	Total (£000)
Sales	200	488.250	688.250
Variable costs:			
Material P	20	58.125	78.125
Material Q	40	46.500	86.500
Direct labour	28	81.375	109.375
Overhead	16	46.500	62.500
	104	232.500	336.500
Contribution	96	255.750	351.750
Fixed costs (£150 000 + £57 750)			207.750
Profit			144.000

(c) Maximize Z = 96M + 110F (product contributions) subject to:

8M + 10F ⩽ 31 250 (material P constraint)

10M + 5F ⩽ 20 000 (material Q constraint)

2M + 2.5F ⩽ 8750 (direct labour constraint)

M ⩽ 1000 (maximum demand for M)

F ⩽ 3000 (maximum demand for F)

The above constraints are plotted on the graph shown in Figure Q25.3 as follows:

Material P; Line from M = 3906.25, F = 0 to F = 3125, M = 0

Material Q; Line from M = 2000, F = 0 to F = 4000, M = 0

Direct labour; Line from M = 4375, F = 0 to F = 3500, M = 0

Sales demand of M; Line from M = 1000

Sales demand of F; Line from F = 3000

The optimal solution occurs where the lines in Figure 25.3 intersect for material P and Q constraints. The point can be determined from the graph or mathematically as follows:

$$8M + 10F = 31\,250 \text{ (material P constraint)}$$
$$10M + 5F = 20\,000 \text{ (material Q constraint)}$$

multiplying the first equation by 1 and the second equation by 2:

$$8M + 10F = 31\,250$$
$$20M + 10F = 40\,000$$
$$\text{subtracting} - 12M = - 8750$$
$$M = 729.166$$

Substituting for M in the first equation:

$$8(729.166) + 10F = 31\,250$$
$$F = 2541.667$$

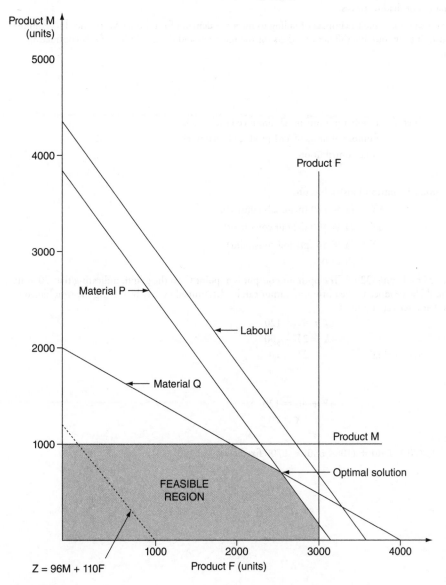

Figure Q25.3

(d)

		(£)
Contribution:	(729 units of M at £96)	69 984
	(2 542 units of F at £110)	279 620
		349 604
Less fixed costs		207 750
Profit		141 854

Moving from the solution in (c) where the lines intersect as a result of obtaining an additional litre of material Q gives the following revised equations:

$$8M + 10F = 31\,250 \text{ (material P constraint)}$$
$$10M + 5F = 20\,001 \text{ (material Q constraint)}$$

The values of M and F when the above equations are solved are 729.333 and 2541.533. Therefore, M is increased by 0.167 units and F is reduced by 0.134 units giving an additional total contribution of £1.292 [0.167 × £96) − (0.134 × £110)] per additional litre of Q. Therefore the shadow price of Q is £1.292 per litre.

(e) See Chapter 25 for an explanation of shadow prices.

(f) Other factors to be taken into account include the impact of failing to meet the demand for product M, the need to examine methods of removing the constraints by sourcing different markets for the materials and the possibility of sub-contracting to meet the unfulfilled demand.

Question 25.4

(a)

Let X = number of units of XL produced each week
Y = number of units of YM produced each week
Z = total contribution

The linear programming model is:

Maximize $Z = 40X + 30Y$ (product contributions) subject to

$$4X + 4Y \leqslant 120 \text{ (materials constraint)}$$
$$4X + 2Y \leqslant 100 \text{ (labour constraint)}$$
$$X + 2Y \leqslant 50 \text{ (plating constraint)}$$
$$X, Y \geqslant 0$$

The above constraints are plotted on Figure Q25.4. The optimum output is at point C on the graph, indicating that 20 units of XL and 10 units of YM should be produced. The optimum output can be determined exactly by solving the simultaneous equations for the constraints that intersect at point C:

$$4X + 4Y = 120$$
$$4X + 2Y = 100$$

Subtracting
$$2Y = 20$$
$$Y = 10$$

Substituting for Y:

$$4X + 40 = 120$$
$$X = 20$$

The maximum weekly profit is:

$$(20 \times £40) + (10 \times £30) - £700 \text{ fixed costs} = £400$$

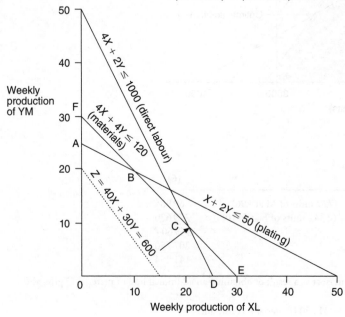

Figure Q25.4

(b) The present objective function is 40X + 30Y and the gradient of this line is −40/30. If the selling price of YM were increased, the contribution of YM would increase and the gradient of the line (−40/30) would decrease. The current optimal point is C because the gradient of the objective function line is greater than the gradient of the line for the constraint of materials (the line on which the optimal point C falls). If the gradient of the objective function line were equal to the gradient of the line for the materials constraint, the optimal solution would be any point on FC. The gradient for the materials constraint line is −1. If the gradient for the objective function line were less than −1, the optimal solution would change from point C to point B. The gradient of the line for the current objective function of 40X + 30Y will be greater than −1 as long as the contribution from YM is less than £40. If the contribution from YM is £40 or more, the optimum solution will change. Therefore the maximum selling price for YM is £190 (£150 variable cost + £40 contribution).

(c) If plating time can be sold for £16 per hour then any hour devoted to XLs and YMs loses £16 sales revenue. The relevant cost per plating hour is now £16 opportunity cost. The contributions used in the objective function should be changed to reflect this opportunity cost. The contribution should be reduced by £4 (1 hour at £16 − £12) for XL and by £8 (2 hours at £16 − £12) for YL. The revised objective function is:

$$Z = 36X + 22Y$$

(d) The scarce resources are materials and labour. This is because these two constraints intersect at the optimal point C. Plating is not a scarce resource, and the shadow price is zero.

If we obtain an additional unit of materials the revised constraints will be:

$$4X + 4Y = 121 \text{ (materials)}$$
$$4X + 2Y = 100 \text{ (labour)}$$

The values of X and Y when the above equations are solved at 10.5 for Y and 19.75 for X. Therefore YM is increased by 0.5 units and XL is reduced by 0.25 units and the change in contribution will be as follows:

	(£)
Increase in contribution of YM (0.5 × £30)	15
Decrease in contribution of XL (0.25 × £40)	10
Increase in contribution (shadow price)	5

If we obtain one additional labour hour, the revised constraints will be:

$$4X + 4Y = 120 \text{ (materials)}$$
$$4X + 2Y = 101 \text{ (labour)}$$

The values of X and Y when the above equations are solved are 9.5 for Y and 20.5 for X. Therefore XL is increased by 0.5 units and YM is reduced by 0.5 units, and the change in contribution will be as follows:

	(£)
Increase in contribution from XL (0.5 × £40)	20
Decrease in contribution from YM (0.5 × £30)	15
Increase in contribution (shadow price)	5

The relevant cost of resources used in producing ZN consists of the acquisition cost plus the shadow price (opportunity cost). The relevant cost calculation is:

	(£)
Material A [5kg at (£10 + £5)]	75
Labour [five hours at (£8 + £5)]	65
Plating (one hour at £12)	12
Other variable costs	90
	242

The selling price is less than the relevant cost. Therefore product ZN is not a profitable addition to the product range.

(e) The shadow price of labour is £5 per hour. Therefore the company should be prepared to pay up to £5 in excess of the current rate of £8 in order to remove the constraint. An overtime payment involves an extra £4 per hour, and therefore overtime working is worthwhile.

Increasing direct labour hours will result in the labour constraint shifting to the right. However, when the labour constraint line reaches point E, further increases in labour will not enable output to be expanded (this is because other constraints will be binding). The new optimal product mix will be at point E, with an output of 30 units of XL and zero of YM. This product mix requires 120 hours (30 × 4 hours). Therefore 120 labour hours will be worked each week. Note that profit will increase by £20 [20 × (£5 − £4)].

(f) The limitations are as follows:

(i) It is assumed that the objective function and the constraints are linear functions of the two variables. In practice, stepped fixed costs might exist or resources might not be used at a constant rate throughout the entire output range. Selling prices might have to be reduced to increase sales volume.

(ii) Constraints are unlikely to be completely fixed and as precise as implied in the mathematical model. Some constraints can be removed at an additional cost.

(iii) The output of the model is dependent on the accuracy of the estimates used. In practice, it is difficult to segregate costs accurately into their fixed and variable elements.

(iv) Divisibility of output is not realistic in practice (fractions of products cannot be produced). This problem can be overcome by the use of integer programming.

(v) The graphical approach requires that only two variables (products) be considered. If several products compete for scarce resources, it will be necessary to use the Simplex method.

(vi) Qualitative factors are not considered. For example, if overtime is paid, the optimum solution is to produce zero of product YM. This will result in the demand from regular customers for YM (who might also buy XM) not being met. This harmful effect on customer goodwill is not reflected in the model.

Question 25.5

Advanced:

(a) The optimal production mix can be found by solving the two equations given for F and T.

$$7W + 5L = 3\,500$$
$$2W + 2L = 1\,200$$

Multiplying the second equation by 2.5 produces:

$$7W + 5L = 3\,500$$
$$5W + 5L = 3\,000$$
$$2W = 500$$
$$W = 250$$

Substituting $W = 250$ in the fabric equation produces:

$$2 \times 250 + 2L = 1\,200$$
$$2L = 700$$
$$L = 350$$

The optimal production is 250 work suits and 350 lounge suits. The optimum contribution is $26\,000$ [(48×250) + (40×350).

(b) The shadow prices can be found by adding one unit to each constraint:

Shadow price of T

$$7W + 5L = 3\,501$$
$$2W + 2L = 1\,200$$

Multiplying the second equation by 2.5 produces:

$$7W + 5L = 3\,501$$
$$5W + 5L = 3\,000$$
$$2W = 501$$
$$W = 250.5$$

Substituting $W = 250.5$ in the fabric equation produces:

$$(2 \times 250.5) + 2L = 1\,200$$
$$2L = 1\,200 - 501$$
$$L = 349.5$$

Contribution = $(48 \times 250.5) + (40 \times 349.5) = 26\,004$ giving an increase of $4 so the shadow price of T is $4 per hour.

Shadow price of F

$$7W + 5L = 3\,500$$
$$2W + 2L = 1\,201$$

Multiplying the second equation by 2.5 produces:

$$7W + 5L = 3\,500.0$$
$$5W + 5L = 3\,002.5$$
$$2W = 497.5$$
$$W = 248.75$$

Substituting W = 248.75 in the fabric equation produces:

$$(2 \times 248.75) + 2L = 1\,201$$
$$2L = 1\,201 - 497.5$$
$$L = 351.75$$

Contribution = $(48 \times 248.75) + (40 \times 351.75) = \$26\,010$ resulting in an increase of \$10 so the shadow price is \$10 per metre.

(c) The shadow price is equal to the increased contribution that can be gained from obtaining one extra unit of the scarce resource. Therefore it represents the maximum premium above the normal rate a business should be willing to pay for more unit of the scarce resource. The shadow price of labour here is \$4 per hour and the tailors have offered to work for \$4.50 (a premium of \$3.00 per hour) so the offer appears to be acceptable provided that there is no decline in quality.

(d) If maximum demand for W falls to 200 units, the constraint for W will move left to 200 on the x axis of the graph. The new optimum point will then be at the intersection of:

$$W = 200 \text{ and}$$
$$2W + 2L = 1\,200$$
$$\text{If } W = 200, \text{ then } (2 \times 200) + 2L = 1\,200 \text{ so } L = 400.$$

The new production plan will be to make 400 of L and 200 of W.

Question 25.6

(a) The calculation of the contributions for each product is:

	X1 (£)	X2 (£)	X3 (£)
Selling price	83	81	81
Materials[a]	(51)	(45)	(54)
Manufacturing costs[b]	(11)	(11)	(11)
Contribution	21	25	16

Notes:

[a] The material cost per tonne for each product is:

$X1 = (0.1 \times £150) + (0.1 \times £60) + (0.2 \times £120) + (0.6 \times £10) = £51$
$X2 = (0.1 \times £150) + (0.2 \times £60) + (0.1 \times £120) + (0 \times 6 \cdot £10) = £45$
$X3 = (0.2 \times £150) + (0.1 \times £60) + (0.1 \times £120) + (0.6 \times £10) = £54$

[b] It is assumed that manufacturing costs do not include any fixed costs.

The initial linear programming model is as follows:

$$\text{Maximize } Z = 21X1 + 25X2 + 16X3$$
$$\text{subject to } 0.1X1 + 0.1X2 + 0.2X3 \leqslant 1\,200 \text{ (nitrate)}$$
$$0.1X1 + 0.2X2 + 0.1X3 \leqslant 2\,000 \text{ (phosphate)}$$
$$0.2X1 + 0.1X2 + 0.1X3 \leqslant 2\,200 \text{ (potash)}$$
$$X1, X2, X3 \geqslant 0$$

(b) The slack variables are introduced to represent the amount of each of the scarce resources unused at the point of optimality. This enables the constraints to be expressed in equalities. The initial Simplex tableau is:

	X1	X2	X3
X4 (nitrate) = 1 200	−0.1	−0.1	−0.2
X5 (phosphate) = 2 000	−0.1	−0.2	−0.1
X6 (potash) = 2 200	−0.2	−0.1	−0.1
Z (contribution) = 0	21	25	16

(c) The starting point for the first iteration is to select the product with the highest contribution (that is, X2), but production of X2 is limited because of the input constraints. Nitrate (X4) limits us to a maximum production of 12 000 tonnes (1200/0.1), X5 to a maximum production of 10 000 tonnes (2000/0.2) and X6 to a maximum production of 22 000 tonnes (2200/0.1). We are therefore restricted to a maximum production of 10 000 tonnes of product X2 because of the X5 constraint.

The procedure which we should follow is to rearrange the equation that results in the constraint (that is, $X5$) in terms of the product we have chosen to make (that is, $X2$). Therefore the $X5$ equation is re-expressed in terms of $X2$, and $X5$ will be replaced in the second iteration by $X2$. (Refer to Learning Note 25.1 for an explanation of this procedure.) Thus $X2$ is the entering variable and $X5$ is the leaving variable.

(d) Following the procedure outlined in Chapter 25, the final tableau given in the question can be reproduced as follow:

	Quantity	X3	X4	X5
$X1$	4 000	−3	−20	+10
$X2$	8 000	+1	+10	−10
$X6$	600	+0.4	+3	− 1
Z	284 000	−22	−170	−40

In Chapter 25 the approach adopted was to formulate the first tableau with positive contribution signs and negative signs for the slack variable equations. The optimal solution occurs when the signs in the contribution row are all negative. The opposite procedure has been applied with the tableau presented in the question. Therefore the signs have been reversed in the above tableau to ensure it is in the same format as that presented in Chapter 25. Note that when an entry of 1 is shown in a row or column for a particular product or slack variable then the entry does not appear in the above tableau. For example, $X1$ has an entry of 1 for the $X1$ row and $X1$ column. These cancel out and the entry is not made in the above tableau. Similarly, an entry of 1 is omitted in respect of $X2$ and $X6$.

The optimum solution is to produce 4000 tonnes of $X1$, 8000 tonnes of $X2$ and zero $X3$ each month. This gives a monthly contribution of £284 000, uses all the nitrate ($X4$) and phosphate ($X5$), but leaves 600 tonnes of potash ($X6$) unused. The opportunity costs of the scarce resources are:

Nitrate ($X4$)   £170 per tonne
Phosphate ($X5$)   £40 per tonne

If we can obtain an additional tonne of nitrate then output of $X1$ should be increased by 20 tonnes and output of $X2$ should be reduced by 10 tonnes.

Note that we reverse the signs when additional resources are obtained. The effect of this substitution process on each of the resources and contribution is as follows:

	Nitrate (X4) (tonnes)	Phosphate (X5) (tonnes)	Potash (X6) (tonnes)	Contribution (£)
Increase $X1$ by 20 tonnes	−2(20 × 0.1)	−2	−4	−420
Reduce $X2$ by 10 tonnes	+1(10 × 0.1)	+2	+1	−250
Net effect	−1	0	−3	+170

The net effect agrees with the $X4$ column in the final tableau. That is, the substitution process will use up exactly the one additional tonne of nitrate, 3 tonnes of unused resources of potash and increase contribution by £170.

To sell one unit of $X3$, we obtain the resources by reducing the output of $X1$ by 3 tonnes and increasing the output of $X2$ by 1 tonne. (Note the signs are not reversed, because we are not obtaining additional scarce resources.) The effect of this substitution process is to reduce contribution by £22 for each tonne of $X3$ produced. The calculation is as follows:

$$\text{Increase } X3 \text{ by 1 tonne} = +£16 \text{ contribution}$$
$$\text{Increase } X2 \text{ by 1 tonne} = +£25 \text{ contribution}$$
$$\text{Reduce } X1 \text{ by 3 tonnes} = \underline{−£63}$$
$$\text{Loss of contribution} = \underline{−£22}$$

(e)

(i) Using the substitution process outlined in (d), the new values if 100 extra tonnes of nitrate are obtained will be:

$$X1\,4000 + (20 \times 100) = 6000$$
$$X2\,8000 − (10 \times 100) = 7000$$
$$X6\,600 − (3 \times 100) = 300$$
$$\text{Contribution } 284\,000 + (£\,170 \times 100) = £\,301\,000$$

Hence the new optimal solution is to make 6000 tonnes of $X1$ and 7000 tonnes of $X2$ per month, and this output will yield a contribution of £301 000.

(ii) Using the substitution process outlined in (d), the new values if 200 tonnes per month of $X3$ are supplied will be:

$$X1\ 4\,000 - (3 \times 200) = 3\,400$$
$$X2\ 8\,000 + (1 \times 200) = 8\,200$$
$$X6\ 600 + (0.4 \times 200) = 680$$
$$X3\ 0 + (1 \times 200) = 200$$
$$\text{Contribution } \pounds284\,000 - (\pounds22 \times 200) = 279\,600$$

Hence the new optimal solution is to produce 3400 tonnes of $X1$, 8200 tonnes of $X2$ and 200 tonnes of $X3$, and this output will yield a contribution of £279 600. (Note that the signs in the final tableau are only reversed when additional scarce resources are obtained.)

Question 25.7

(a)

	Product 1	Product 2	Product 3	Total
Maximum sales value (£)	57 500	96 000	125 000	
Unit selling price (£)	23	32	25	
Maximum demand (units)	2 500	3 000	5 000	
Hours required on type A machine	2 500 (2 500 × 1)	6 000 (3 000 × 2)	15 000 (5 000 × 3)	23 500
Hours required on type B machine	3 750 (2 500 × 1½)	9 000 (3 000 × 3)	5 000 (5 000 × 1)	17 750

We now compare the machine capacity available with the machine hours required to meet the maximum sales so as to determine whether or not production is a limiting factor.

	Machine type A	Machine type B
Hours required (see above)	23 500	17 750
Hours available	9 800	21 000

Because hours required are in excess of hours available for machine type A, but not for machine type B, it follows that machine type A is the limiting factor. Following the approach illustrated in Example 9.3 in Chapter 9, we calculate the contribution per limiting factor. The calculations are as follows:

	Product 1	Product 2	Product 3
Unit contribution (£)	5	7	8
Contribution per hour of type A machine time (£)	5 (5/1)	3.50 (7/2)	2.67 (8/3)
Ranking	1	2	3

The optimal allocation of type A machine hours based on the above ranking is as follows:

Production	Machine hours used	Balance of machine hours available
2500 units of product 1	2 500	7 300 (9 800 − 2 500)
3000 units of product 2	6 000	1 300 (7 300 − 6 000)
433 units of product 3	1 300	—

The 433 units of product 3 are obtained by dividing the 1300 unused machine hours by the 3 machine hours required for each unit of product 3. The proposed production programme results in the following calculation of total profit:

	(£)
2500 units of product 1 at £5 per unit contribution	12 500
3000 units of product 2 at £7 per unit contribution	21 000
433 units of product 3 at £8 per unit contribution	3 464
Total contribution	36 964
Less fixed overheads	21 000
Profit	15 964

(b) There are several ways of formulating the tableau for a linear programming model. The tableau from the computer package can be reproduced as follows:

	Quantity	S1	S4	S5
S2	1 150	−0.5	0.143	0.429
X2	1 850	0.5	0.143	0.429
S3	3 800		0.429	0.286
X3	1 200		−0.429	0.286
X1	2 500	−1	0	0
C	35 050	−1.5	−2.429	−0.714

In Chapter 25 the approach adopted was to formulate the first tableau with positive contribution signs and negative signs for the slack variable equations. The optimal solution occurs when the signs in the contribution row are all negative. The opposite procedure has been applied with the tableau presented in the question. Therefore the signs have been reversed in the above tableau to ensure that it is in the same format as that presented in Chapter 25. Note that an entry of 1 in the tableau presented in the question signifies the product or slack variable that is to be entered in each row of the above tableau.

The total contribution is £35 050, consisting of:

2500 units of product 1 at a contribution of £5 per unit, 1850 units of product 2 at a contribution of £7 per unit, 1200 units of product 3 at a contribution of £8 per unit.

The revised fixed overheads are £18 000, resulting in a total profit of £17 050. This is higher than the profit before the fire (£15 964) because the fixed overheads saved by the fire exceed the lost contribution.

The shadow prices (or opportunity costs) for S4 indicate that if an additional type A machine hour can be acquired then profits will increase by £2.429 by increasing production of product 3 by 0.429 units and reducing production of product 2 by 0.143 units. Similarly, if an additional Type B machine hour can be acquired, then profits will increase by £0.714 by increasing production of product 2 by 0.429 units and reducing production of product 3 by 0.286 units. An extra unit of demand for product 1 will yield a contribution of £5, but, in order to obtain the resources, it is necessary to sacrifice half a unit of product 2. This will result in a loss of contribution of £3.50 (½ × £7). Therefore the net gain is £1.50.

The shadow prices indicate the premium over and above the present acquisition costs that the company should be willing to pay in order to obtain extra hours of machine time. The shadow price for product 1 indicates the upper limit to advertising or promotional expenses that should be incurred in order to stimulate demand by one further unit.

(c) In part A there was only one limiting factor. In Chapter 25 we noted that the optimal solution can be derived by using the contribution per key factor approach whenever there is only one production constraint. Where more than one limiting factor exists then it is necessary to use linear programming to determine the optimal production programme.